The Complete Guide for New Elementary Teachers

What do new elementary educators need to find success and joy in the classroom? National Board Certified teacher Steve Reifman presents a comprehensive, whole-child approach to help you think through all the key elements of your first classroom—including the learning environment, academic mission, character development, social-emotional learning, relationship building, student user experience, mindsets for success, and an intellectual framework that contains guiding principles of classroom life and effectively addresses issues of motivation and purpose.

This reader-friendly, accessible handbook offers strategies, activity ideas, implementation suggestions, printable pages, photographs, and diagrams. You will also find a plethora of tools such as classroom visuals, parent resources, rubrics, feedback methods, student work samples, goal-setting and self-evaluation sheets, checklists, charts, and more. Reifman enhances these clear, actionable tools and takeaways with numerous classroom anecdotes and examples and personal experiences. Whether you are reading in order or jumping to sections that most apply to your classroom, you are sure to benefit from his wisdom gained from a career spent helping children reach their amazing potential.

Becoming a new teacher takes a lot of preparation, and this book gives you everything you need at your fingertips so you can become a passionate, successful educator—while empowering your students to become passionate, successful learners.

Steve Reifman has been an elementary school teacher for the past 31 years. During that time, he has earned National Board Certification, travelled to Japan as a Fulbright Memorial Fund scholar, and completed two master's degrees. He has experience working with students in all the elementary grade levels, and he has taught in both public and private schools. He is the author of several books for educators, such as *107 Awesome Elementary Teaching Ideas You Can Implement Tomorrow*.

Also Available from Routledge
Eye on Education
www.routledge.com/k-12

107 Awesome Elementary Teaching Ideas You Can Implement Tomorrow
Steve Reifman

Classroom Management from the Ground Up:
Todd Whitaker, Katherine Whitaker, Madeline Whitaker Good

**Everything New Teachers Need to Know But Are Afraid to Ask:
An Honest Guide to the Nuts and Bolts of Your First Job**
Amber Chandler

**Teacher's Survival Guide, Gifted Education:
A First-Year Teacher's Introduction to Gifted Learners**
Julia Link Roberts, Julia Roberts Boggess

**Passionate Learners:
How to Engage and Empower Your Students**
Pernille Ripp

**What Great Teachers Do Differently:
Nineteen Things That Matter Most**
Todd Whitaker

The Complete Guide for New Elementary Teachers

Discover Joy and Success with a Whole-Child Approach

Steve Reifman

Routledge
Taylor & Francis Group
NEW YORK AND LONDON

Designed cover Getty Images

First published 2026
by Routledge
605 Third Avenue, New York, NY 10158

and by Routledge
4 Park Square, Milton Park, Abingdon, Oxon, OX14 4RN

Routledge is an imprint of the Taylor & Francis Group, an informa business

© 2026 Steve Reifman

The right of Steve Reifman to be identified as author of this work has been asserted in accordance with sections 77 and 78 of the Copyright, Designs and Patents Act 1988.

All rights reserved. No part of this book may be reprinted or reproduced or utilised in any form or by any electronic, mechanical, or other means, now known or hereafter invented, including photocopying and recording, or in any information storage or retrieval system, without permission in writing from the publishers.

Trademark notice: Product or corporate names may be trademarks or registered trademarks, and are used only for identification and explanation without intent to infringe.

ISBN: 978-1-041-11432-1 (hbk)
ISBN: 978-1-041-11431-4 (pbk)
ISBN: 978-1-003-65995-2 (ebk)

DOI: 10.4324/9781003659952

Typeset in Palatino
by Apex CoVantage, LLC

Access the Support Material: Routledge.com/9781041114314

Dedication

To Mom and Dad

Contents

Support Material xiii
List of Figures xiv
Acknowledgments xvii
Meet the Author xviii

Introduction 1

About This Book 5

1 Teach the Whole Child 6
Reference List 9

2 Culture 10
How Can Teachers Build Culture in the Classroom? 12
    Step 1: Determine the Kind of Culture We Want 12
    Step 2: Modeling 15
    Step 3: Teach Habits and Traits Explicitly 17
        Norms for Discussion 18
        Passion Survey 19
        Human Health Hunt 22
        Play-Doh Activity 22
        Picture Book Read-Alouds 24
        Compliments 25
        Habits of Character and Habits of Mind 26
    Step 4: Create Visual Reference Points 35
    Step 5: Follow Up in Both the Short Term and the Long Term 37
Reference List 42

3 Connection 43
Building Connections in the Classroom 44
Beginning-of-the-Year Activities 46
    High Fives 46
    Play-Doh Activity (Part 2) 47
    Passion Survey (Part 2) 47
    Cooperative Handshake 48
    Meet Me in the Middle 49

Roller Coaster	49
Special Object Sharing	50
Appointment Clocks	50
Resource Board	53
Yearlong Rituals	56
The Morning Check-In	56
Statements of Recognition	57
Updates	58
Morning Greeter	58
Five-Minute Chats	59
Friday Circle	60
Bonding With Challenging Students	62
Other Important Connections	63
Why Is Parent Involvement Such a High Priority?	64
Guiding Principles for Home–School Communication	65
Thinking Long-Term	65
Communicating Frequently	66
Creating a Sense of Inclusion	66
Listening With Understanding and Empathy	66
Encouraging Cooperative Problem-Solving	67
Showing Appreciation	67
Conveying a Sense of Optimism	67
Being Proactive	67
Building Goodwill	68
How to Build Parent Connections Right From the Start	69
Kickoff Gesture	69
First-Day Letter	70
Weekly Newsletters	72
Back-to-School Night	74
Parent Conferences	75
Additional Resources	77
Closing	78
Reference List	78
4 Purpose	**79**
The Overall Aim	82
Class Mission Statement	84
Writing the Class Mission Statement	85
Day 1	85
Days 2 and 3	86
Day 4	88
Analyzing a Class Mission Statement: A Deeper Dive	95
Creating Your Mission Statement: Fun With Formats	100

Class Mission Statement "Companion Visual"	104
The 7 Life Roles	106
The Tower of Opportunity	107
Lesson Lead-Ins	111
Closing	112
Reference List	114

5 Quality   115

Applying Deming's Approach to Education	116
Defining Quality	118
Defining Quality Across the Curriculum	122
Math Problem-Solving	122
Paragraph Writing	125
Reflections	128
Measuring Quality	130
General Scoring Rubric: A Useful Template	131
Writing Workshop Examples: Rubrics for Ideas and Conventions	132
Math Problem-Solving Rubric	135
Bringing Quality to Life With Models and Anchors	138
Fostering a Quality Mindset With Our Students	141
Use Quotes to Inspire Children to Pursue Quality	142
Use Visuals to Inspire Children to Pursue Quality	143
"Making the Choice" Visual	143
"Tug-o'-War" Visual	144
"Work Like a Champion Today" Sign	146
The Challenge Bear	147
D-Fence Sign	147
You and Future You	149
Closing	149
Reference List	149

6 Motivation   151

Classroom Parallels	154
The Problems With Rewards	155
Rewards Punish	155
Rewards Rupture Relationships	156
Rewards Ignore Reasons	157
Rewards Discourage Risk-Taking	158
Rewards Decrease Interest	158
Coming to Grips With These Findings	161
A Different Approach	163
The Nurturing Forces of Intrinsic Motivation	167

Purpose	167
Contribution	168
Interest	169
Challenge	170
Success	170
Inspiration	171
Cooperation	173
Trust	173
Feedback	173
Recognition	176
Statements of Recognition	176
"Way to Go" Notes	176
Recognition Day	177
Intrinsic Motivation: A Summary	178
Introducing the Concept of Intrinsic Motivation to Children	179
Fostering an "Intrinsic" Mindset With Our Students	181
"Finding a Flow" Chart	181
The Drive for 5	182
Closing	184
Notes	186
Reference List	186

7 Expectation — 187

The Importance of Thorough Training	188
Launching a Classroom "Training Camp"	190
Additional Points About Training	200
Setting High Personal Expectations	205
Individual Case Studies	208
Sarah	208
Riley	208
Jessica	210
A Final Thought: Understanding Student Vulnerability	211
Reference List	212

8 Empowerment — 213

10 Teacher Moves to Create an Empowering Learning Environment	215
Don't Do Things for Children That They Can Do for Themselves	215
Ask, Don't Tell	217
Embrace Moments of Productive Struggle	219
Incentivize Empowerment and Choice With More Empowerment and Choice	219
Structure Student Choice Thoughtfully	221

Capitalize on Potential Empowering Moments	226
Be a Consistent Model	232
Share Inspirational Stories	233
Recognize Noteworthy Student Efforts	234
Shine a Spotlight on Empowerment	236
Note	245
Reference List	245

9 Improvement — 246

Introducing Children to Continuous Improvement	247
Continuous Improvement: Key Principles	252
Cultivate a Growth Mindset	252
Foster a Realistic View of Improvement	253
Encourage Personal Bests	256
Facilitate Peer-Inspired Improvement	257
Appreciate the Harmony Between the Individual and the Group	258
"Coach 'Em Up"	259
Continuous Improvement: Key Practices	260
Retakes	260
Analyze One Round of Assessment Results to Improve the Next	263
Engage Your Students in Group Brainstorming	265
Use "Before and After" Samples to Point Out Improvement	269
Incorporate Storytelling to Improve Student Behavior	270
Deliver a Good Old-Fashioned "Pep Talk"	272
Continuous Improvement: Effective Tools	274
End-of-day Flowcharts	276
Check Sheets (Version 1)	278
Check Sheets (Version 2)	278
Math Cover Sheets	280
My Day in a Nutshell	282
Group Work Evaluation Sheet	282
How Was My DRIVE-ing Today?	283
Reading Goals	283
Informal Reflection and Self-Evaluation Options	285
Our Development as Professional Educators	286
Reference List	287

10 Personalization — 289

Student Leader Tributes	290
Give All Your Students Their Own "Thing"	291
Who I Am as a Learner	295

Personal Mission Statements	298
Student-Led Conferences	304
Personalized Motivational Visuals	312
Classroom Display Case	314
Keys to Victory	315
POPP Time	316
Personalized Academic Projects	322
Conclusion	323
Reference List	324
Resource A: Habits of Mind List and Information	325
Resource B: Beginning-of-the-Year Activities	329
Resource C: Parent Involvement Information	330
Resource D: The 7 Life Roles	334
Resource E: Sample Biography from 2-Minute Biographies for Kids	336

Support Material

To help you implement the book's ideas, printable versions of the following resources can be found on the Routledge website:

Figure 2.2 Human health hunt.
Figure 2.3 "Respect" sign (along with a full Habits of Character and signs for each).
Figure 2.4 Habits of Character and Habits of Mind rubric.
Figure 4.4 Tower of Opportunity template.
Figure 5.4 Math problem-solving template.
Figure 5.6 Writing Workshop reflection sheet.
Figure 5.7 General scoring rubric.
Figure 5.8 Ideas rubric.
Figure 5.9 Conventions rubric.
Figure 5.10 Math problem-solving rubric.
Box 7.1 List of Training Resources
Figure 8.2 Self-evaluation sheet for student goals.
Figure 9.1 "Baseball Diamond" math facts progress sheet.
Math problem-solving menus, organizer, and answer keys (mentioned in Chapter 9)
Figure 9.8 Math cover sheet.
Figure 9.9 Math cover sheet self-assessment scale.
Figure 9.10 "My Day in a Nutshell" self-assessment sheet.
Figure 9.11 Group Work Evaluation Sheet.
Figure 9.12 "Drive for 5" self-assessment sheet.
Figure 10.1 Strengths and Challenges sheet.
Figure 10.4 "What Should Be in My Portfolio?" sheet.
Figure 10.5 Student-Led Conference Outline.
Figure 10.8 POPP Time project sheet.
Figure 10.9 POPP Time action plan.

Access the Support Material: Routledge.com/9781041114314

Figures

Chapter 1

Figure 1.1	Focusing on the whole person.	8

Chapter 2

Figure 2.1	Passion Survey chart.	21
Figure 2.2	Human health hunt.	23
Figure 2.3	"Respect" sign (along with a full Habits of Character and signs for each).	30
Figure 2.4	Habits of Character and Habits of Mind rubric.	32
Figure 2.5	"Are You Being Good to Your Brain?" visual.	37

Chapter 3

Figure 3.1	Sample first-day letter.	71
Figure 3.2	Sample class newsletter.	73

Chapter 4

Figure 4.1	Class mission statement with "front wall" theme.	101
Figure 4.2	Class mission statement companion visual.	105
Figure 4.3	Two sides of the Tower of Opportunity.	108
Figure 4.4	Tower of Opportunity template.	109
Figure 4.5	Front wall of my classroom.	113

Chapter 5

Figure 5.1	Deming chain reaction.	116
Figure 5.2	Education chain reaction.	117
Figure 5.3	Quality work rubric.	120
Figure 5.4	Math problem-solving template.	124

Figure 5.5	Paragraph "Hamburger" visual.	126
Figure 5.6	Writing Workshop reflection sheet	129
Figure 5.7	General scoring rubric.	132
Figure 5.8	Ideas rubric.	134
Figure 5.9	Conventions rubric.	136
Figure 5.10	Math problem-solving rubric.	137
Figure 5.11	"Making the Choice" visual.	144
Figure 5.12	"Tug-O'-War" visual.	145
Figure 5.13	QR code—Notre Dame's "Play Like a Champion Today" sign.	146
Figure 5.14	"Work Like a Champion Today" sign.	146
Figure 5.15	"D-Fence" sign.	148

Chapter 8

Figure 8.1	QR code—United Nations Sustainable Development Goals.	222
Figure 8.2	Self-evaluation sheet for student goals.	231

Chapter 9

Figure 9.1	"Baseball Diamond" math facts progress sheet.	250
Figure 9.2	Linear and non-linear improvement.	255
Figure 9.3	Pareto chart.	265
Figure 9.4	Enthusiasm Survey display.	267
Figure 9.5	Freddie's end-of-day flowchart.	277
Figure 9.6	Serena's check sheet.	279
Figure 9.7	Sample check sheet (version 2).	279
Figure 9.8	Math cover sheet.	281
Figure 9.9	Math cover sheet self-assessment scale.	282
Figure 9.10	"My Day in a Nutshell" self-assessment sheet.	283
Figure 9.11	Group Work Evaluation Sheet.	284
Figure 9.12	"Drive for 5" self-assessment sheet.	284

Chapter 10

Figure 10.1	Strengths and Challenges sheet (front and back).	296
Figure 10.2	Personal timelines.	301
Figure 10.3	Sample sides from personal mission boxes.	303

Figure 10.4	"What Should Be in My Portfolio?" sheet.	307
Figure 10.5	Student-Led Conference Outline.	308
Figure 10.6	Personalized motivational visual.	313
Figure 10.7	Sample "key to victory."	316
Figure 10.8	POPP Time project sheet.	320
Figure 10.9	POPP Time action plan.	321

Acknowledgments

To Lauren Davis, Hannah Sroka, and the rest of the team at Taylor & Francis who contributed to the production of this book. It was a pleasure collaborating with you.

To my EPEW peeps, for making our summer workshop experience the best week of the year, every year.

To my friends at Roosevelt School—teachers, staff, students, administrators, and parents—whose kindness, support, and encouragement have meant a great deal to me and have made our campus feel like home.

To W. Edwards Deming, Stephen Covey, Theodore Sizer, William Glasser, Lee Jenkins, and the many other experts cited in this book, for inspiring me to be the best teacher I can be.

To Paul Kingston, my professor at the University of Virginia, who taught the "Sociology of Education" course during my final semester that sparked my interest in becoming a teacher.

Every effort was made to find the creators of all the ideas and activities cited in this book. We apologize for any oversights.

Meet the Author

Steve Reifman is an elementary teacher, author, and speaker in Santa Monica, CA. During his career, he has earned National Board certification, traveled to Japan as a Fulbright Memorial Fund scholar, and completed two master's degrees. Steve has experience working with students in all the elementary grade levels and has taught in both public and private schools. Steve has written several resource books for educators and parents, including 107 Awesome Elementary Teaching Ideas You Can Implement Tomorrow; Eight Essentials for Empowered Teaching and Learning, K-8; Rock It!; and Changing Kids' Lives One Quote at a Time. He is also the creator of the award-winning Chase Manning Mystery Series for children 8–12 years of age. When Steve is not teaching his awesome students, you can find him spending time with family and friends, working out at the gym, playing pickleball, listening to music, or cheering on his hometown Los Angeles Dodgers.

Books by Steve Reifman

The Chase Manning Mystery Series
Chase Against Time (Chase Manning Mystery #1)
Chase for Home (Chase Manning Mystery #2)

Chase Under Pressure (Chase Manning Mystery #3)
Chase to the Finish (Chase Manning Mystery #4)
Chase on the Edge (Chase Manning Mystery #5)

Resource Books for Teachers and Parents

107 Awesome Elementary Teaching Ideas You Can Implement Tomorrow
Changing Kids' Lives One Quote at a Time
2-Minute Biographies for Kids
22 Habits That Empower Students
10 Steps to Empowering Classroom Management
15 1/2 Ways to Personalize Learning
Rock It!: Transform Classroom Learning with Movement, Songs, and Stories
Eight Essentials for Empowered Teaching and Learning, K-8
The First 10 Minutes: A Classroom Morning Routine that Reaches and Teaches the Whole Child
The First Month of School: Start Your School Year with 4 Priorities in Mind
Build a Partnership with Parents
Math Problem Solving Menus
The Ultimate Mystery Writing Guide for Kids

Introduction

During my graduate training program at UCLA, I had the cool opportunity to complete my second student teaching placement at the elementary school I attended as a child. It felt amazing to be "back home," walking the hallways that now seemed considerably smaller and working with kids who played in the same Little League I did, went down the slide at the same local park, and got their Slurpees from the same 7-Eleven. On my first day, I was thrilled to discover that my fourth and sixth grade teachers still taught at the school. Even though people like to say that nothing is impossible, calling Ms. Taniguchi and Mrs. Luchsinger by their first names challenged that notion.

A couple of weeks into my placement, I was tidying up the classroom after school when one of my fifth graders was still around. I asked if he would like to help out. To this day, nearly 30 years later, his answer remains firmly implanted in my mind: "What do you give me for it?" I'm not sure how loud of a thud my jaw made when it dropped to the floor, but I was later told that a few neighbors called the school to see if everything was okay.

Needless to say, that was not the answer I was expecting. I remember driving home that day feeling very uncomfortable with that brief interaction. I knew with every fiber of my being that I didn't want my relationships with future students to be governed by rewards. I wanted to lead a class in which kids worked hard, behaved well, and looked to help others because they were invested in the mission of the group, not because they were seeking prizes. I wanted everyone to know they were an important part of a strong, caring team, where all children felt valued and appreciated and where kids gave their best effort because they genuinely enjoyed learning and were committed to achieving at high levels. When I began my teaching career the following year, I knew I wanted this type of environment. I knew where I wanted to go. There was just one small problem: I had no idea how to get there.

Around this time, I remember classroom management being a consistent emphasis of my teacher education courses. Even though the teaching and learning of reading, writing, math, and other academic areas were my primary interests, I understood that effective classroom management was a necessary precondition for quality learning to occur. I knew that classroom management had to come first, and that my skills in that department would go a long way in determining how successful my students and I would be during our time together.

The day my field coordinator introduced the topic of classroom management to my cohort, he mentioned two main approaches, one rooted in the theory of behaviorism, the other based on routines, procedures, and clear expectations. Though the latter appealed to me far more, 99% of what we read in our textbooks and discussed in our courses focused on the former. From what I gathered, behaviorism could be reduced to the practice of issuing rewards and punishments. In my mind, my fellow students and I were learning nothing more than how to control and bribe kids. Behaviorism dominated our learning. It was all around us. Once my classmates and I began our school visitations and student teaching placements, every classroom I entered featured some form of extrinsic rewards and/or punishments—table points, marble jars, prize boxes. It seemed as if no other legitimate options existed when it came to the topic of how teachers could lead their classrooms.

When I completed my graduate program and landed my first teaching job, I was confused. I didn't want to implement someone else's extrinsic classroom management system; I wanted to create my own classroom culture. Still unsure how to proceed, I began my career as a first grade teacher making posters of rules, rewards, and consequences. I didn't know any other way. During my initial weeks in the classroom, I was extremely uncomfortable administering this system. It wasn't me, and it didn't feel right. The results absolutely bore this out. Perhaps, I thought, everything was going fine, and my worries were all in my head. That was when three parents asked if they could meet with me after school. When we gathered around the table, the spokesperson (the mom in the middle) looked at me and said, "Steve, we're concerned about the management of this class." My response: "So am I."

That conversation marked a turning point for me, and I renewed my search for a culture-building approach consistent with my goals and priorities. There was a more effective alternative out there somewhere, and I was determined to find it. My resolve strengthened even more when my principal arranged for me to visit another school to observe a lesson taught by a teacher he had recently met. I remember looking forward to my visit and hoping I could learn some new management techniques not based on behaviorism. When I arrived a few mornings later, the teacher had just launched the lesson and was standing by the center of the board in the front of the room. The student desks were arranged in rows. At first, the children paid close attention to the lesson and seemed engaged. A couple of minutes later, though, student attention waned and several kids began playing around with their neighbors. Their teacher noticed. I was curious to see how he would respond. The teacher paused the lesson and, slowly and dramatically, moved to the side of the board that displayed each table's points and announced that he was on the lookout for students who were doing a great job. Instantly, the kids began sitting up tall in their chairs and paying better attention. The teacher added a point to each table's total and resumed the lesson. Shortly thereafter, the students started playing around again. I didn't learn any new methods or strategies that morning. Instead, I received a powerful reminder of just how prevalent and deeply ingrained extrinsic motivation is in our classrooms. When things got difficult, rewards were what held the class together. I needed something more.

Fortunately, I was enrolled at that time in a weekly after-school continuing education course organized by a local university. At one session, a principal from my school district ended his presentation with a few book recommendations, the first one being *The Quality School* by William Glasser. Reading Glasser's work initiated a chain reaction that introduced me to a group of author-educators who profoundly impacted my teaching philosophy and altered the trajectory of my career. Without that book recommendation that arrived one minute before the end of class that evening while I was packing up my supplies, I don't know how the rest of my first year would have played out. That lucky break led me to W. Edwards Deming, Theodore Sizer, Alfie Kohn, Lee Jenkins, and Dale Parnell. Eventually, I would discover more authors from the field of education as well as a variety of other areas, including business management, athletic coaching, and personal growth. Learning of these works changed everything for me and started me down the path I had been seeking.

Little by little, I began incorporating new ideas into my classroom teaching—focusing on quality, helping students understand the purposes of their learning and find meaning in their work, developing within the group a set of valuable habits, and nurturing children's intrinsic motivation to learn and grow, without the use of rewards and punishments, a practice that I learned was both ineffective and destructive to many of the ideals I wanted to promote. Without realizing it, I had started developing the whole-child approach that would become my life's work.

Now, nearly three decades later, I am delighted to share with you the results of the quest I began back in graduate school to create a classroom environment consistent with my beliefs—a whole-child approach that empowers students and emphasizes academic excellence, lasting Habits of Mind and Habits of Character, valuable work habits and social skills, and health and wellness. This book features guiding principles, activity ideas, research, anecdotes, experiences, ups and downs, and perhaps a bit of wisdom. It is my sincere hope that you find the information useful and that it helps you create a classroom culture that works for you, one in which students work hard, work together, and work with purpose, display habits that will serve them well now and later, demonstrate perseverance and grit, manage themselves and look out for others, show uncommon respect and kindness, take pride in who they are, display impressive levels of enthusiasm and motivation, set goals and work to achieve them, and become the primary driving forces in their own learning. This whole-child approach aims high and encourages children to do the same so they can fulfill the amazing potential they all possess.

In the chapters that follow, I present an integrated set of ideas designed to address two primary aims: (1) empowering children to become joyful, successful learners, and (2) empowering us to become joyful, successful educators. Put differently, just as we commit ourselves to teaching the whole child, we must also prioritize the needs of the "whole educator" so that we can enjoy long careers in a field that sadly loses too many of our colleagues after just a few years.

In *The Quality School* William Glasser (1990) identifies five needs that he asserts all human beings are constantly attempting to satisfy—survival, belonging, power, freedom, and fun. One of the wonderful aspects of classroom teaching is that it provides the daily opportunity for us to satisfy all five. The salaries we earn enable us to afford housing, food, clothing, and other survival needs. The connections we build with students, colleagues, and parents can give us a tremendous sense of belonging that, in many cases, can last a lifetime. The ability to make a profound contribution to the lives of our students and their families demonstrates our power. We have the freedom to use our judgment, creativity, talents, and problem-solving skills to lead our classrooms in the ways we believe to be most efficient and effective. Finally, working with children is a blast and can keep us young and fill our hearts and souls with a satisfaction that no other profession can match.

Reference List

Glasser, W. (1990). *The Quality School*. New York: Harper & Row.

About This Book

This book draws and includes sections from *8 Essentials for Empowered Teaching & Learning, K-8* (Corwin Press, 2008); *107 Awesome Elementary Teaching Ideas You Can Implement Tomorrow* (Routledge, 2020); and other books, e-books, and blog posts I have written. Most of the ideas contained in this resource are appearing in print for the first time. With this project, my goal is to present a comprehensive "whole-child" framework you can use to guide your teaching. In all likelihood, there are way too many ideas to implement in a single school year. As you read, I recommend that you identify the highest-priority ideas you wish to implement in the coming school year, as well as others you may wish to keep "in the parking lot" for future use. There's no rush; these strategies and suggestions age well.

1

Teach the Whole Child

This whole-child approach is founded on the idea that all children are unique and special and possess unlimited potential. As their teachers, we serve an essential societal purpose and occupy a position of trust and privilege. We have a solemn responsibility to treat all individuals with dignity, act in ways that promote their long-term best interests, and do everything in our power to provide a positive learning experience for everyone. We honor the differences in our group, assume good intentions, and value the knowledge, feelings, and histories that children bring with them into the classroom. In addition, we keep a close eye on their physical and social-emotional well-being. We strive to bring out the best in every child.

The pursuit of academic excellence is, of course, a top priority. We want students to learn as much as they can about math and science, reading and writing, social studies and art. As the old adage goes, though, we don't teach content. We teach children. We meet them where they are, form trusting partnerships with them and their parents, and "coach 'em up" to accelerate progress and maximize student learning. Content standards and test scores are important, but what we do in the classroom is about so much more than that. We never want our classrooms to become places where we hustle students to their desks right after the morning bell, open our textbooks to page 67, and sprint through the schedule from one activity to the next to cram as much content as possible into our day. Instead, it is instructive to view the academic areas we teach not as ends in themselves but as beginnings—as springboards that teach children about life, expand their perspective, and facilitate other equally valuable types of learning. We aim to build character, develop work habits and social skills, and promote health and wellness.

The most effective way to accomplish these goals is to weave them together into a seamless whole. A central tenet of this humanistic approach is that academics, character, and health and wellness are not separate, mutually exclusive entities. Rather, they are mutually enriching. Children will learn more about character, for example, when opportunities to develop important traits are embedded in their daily academic instruction. Consider perseverance. Inviting a guest speaker to the auditorium to talk with students about character development can certainly motivate and inspire. Unfortunately, though, special assemblies are one-shot deals. Long-term character development is significantly more likely when we introduce the concept of perseverance, for example, before students begin a challenging math problem-solving activity, encourage everyone to keep going until they find a solution, and reflect on both the math and the problem-solving process at the end of the lesson and beyond. We can build character development, work habits, social skills, and health and wellness into the fabric of each day. It's like putting banana slices directly into the batter when making banana pancakes rather than placing them on top once the pancakes have been cooked.

Enthusiasm for learning is another major priority of teaching the whole child. Young children can have surprisingly strong feelings about the academic areas they study. Kids might enjoy some subjects tremendously, powerfully dislike others, and find the rest to be just okay. Our job is to promote meaningful engagement with curricular content and encourage everyone to take an interest in and discover joy in their learning. Dr. W. Edwards Deming, a statistician trained in mathematics, physics, and engineering who helped Japan rebuild its industrial base after World War II, is one of the authors I was fortunate to discover at the start of my career. Even though his books on leadership and quality were intended for an audience of business executives, I felt as if he was talking directly to me. (The purpose of highlighting text while reading is to make certain words stand out. That rule went out the window with Deming.) In *Improving Student Learning* Lee Jenkins (1997) writes that in 1992, Deming suggested that the overall aim for education be: "Increase the positives and decrease the negatives so that all students keep their yearning for learning." He believed that if educators preserved students' love of learning by removing the practices that decrease enthusiasm and spread those that foster it, more students would succeed in school. Furthermore, Deming once said that a successful teacher is one whose students are more interested in learning about a subject at the end of the year than they were at the beginning. Teachers who accomplish this feat perform an incredible service because curious, joyful students are likely to become lifelong learners.

When teachers focus on the whole child, we begin analyzing a student's school experience with a wider lens (see Figure 1.1). Academically, we closely monitor reading levels, math assessment scores, writing pieces, and other indicators of student progress. In terms of children's physical health, we pay attention to what they are eating for their morning snack, whether they are participating fully in physical education class and, perhaps, pursuing athletic endeavors outside of school, and if they are drinking enough water throughout the day to remain hydrated. Children's social-emotional development is also critical. We promote kindness and empathy, notice if students have a friend to sit with at lunchtime, and help them learn strategies to manage stress and solve the problems that inevitably arise in our classrooms and on our playgrounds. We try to build self-esteem and confidence and nurture the intrinsic motivation to learn and grow that all children possess. We encourage everyone to feel comfortable being themselves in class, freely admit mistakes, and ask for assistance or share concerns when necessary. Teaching the whole child means looking out for the whole child.

The thread that ties this whole-child approach together is the quest to help children develop lifelong habits. In the next chapter, I describe an indispensable part of my classroom morning routine known as the Quote of the Day. One of the most impactful sayings we discuss each year comes from Aristotle: "We are what we repeatedly do. Excellence, then, is not an act, but a habit." The central point is that to be successful in school and elsewhere, we can't

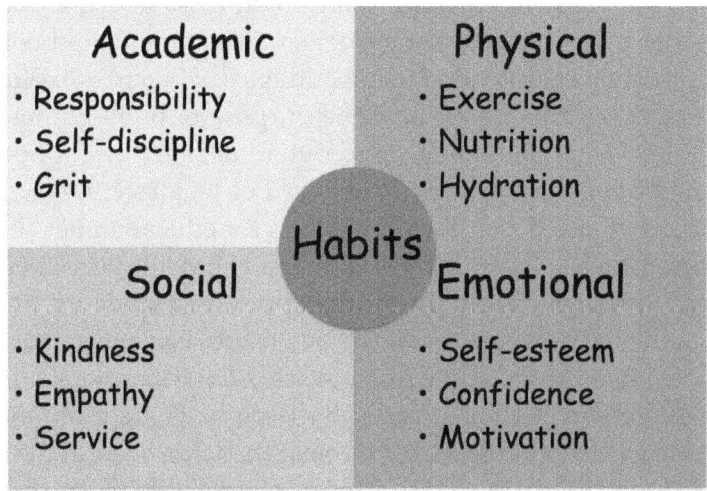

Figure 1.1 Focusing on the whole person.

give our best effort once in a while. Quality isn't a sometimes thing; it's an everyday thing. We empower students by helping everyone develop habits that enable them to soar academically, remain healthy and strong, maintain positive relationships with others, and face daily challenges with a genuine belief in themselves.

According to well-known educator and author Theodore Sizer, the purpose of schooling goes far beyond helping children acquire knowledge and master skills. Instead, it involves the broader goal of helping students learn to use their minds well and develop enduring intellectual habits. In *Horace's Hope*, Sizer (1996) reinforces the importance of habits when he says, "Knowing stuff is nice. Being able to use that stuff makes sense. Being disposed to use it always, as a matter of habit, is the brass ring, the ultimate standard." Sizer's quote connects directly to what he calls "Habits of Mind," a set of dispositions, such as judgment and thoughtfulness, that help children become better thinkers and better students. In Chapter 2, I describe how we can help our students develop these and other types of habits. Children who develop a solid foundation of "whole-child habits" will learn the knowledge, skills, and attitudes needed to venture confidently into the world and become wildly successful in their chosen endeavors, positively affect those around them, and make their communities better places.

Reference List

Jenkins, L. (1997). *Improving Student Learning: Applying Deming's Quality Principles in Classrooms*. Milwaukee: ASQC Quality Press.

Sizer, T. (1996). *Horace's Hope*. New York: Houghton Mifflin Company.

2
Culture

As an educator, I have many rituals, of which one of my favorites is heading to Staples the week before school begins and spending the morning filling my shopping cart with writing notebooks, pencil boxes, and the many other classroom supplies my students and I will need for the coming months. In my mind the new school year doesn't officially kick off until I make this annual excursion. I know I can save time buying everything online, but I genuinely enjoy browsing the aisles, hunting for bargains, and checking items off my list. I think my fondness for this activity started when I was a kid. I cherished my summer vacations and never wanted them to end. But I loved buying school supplies, especially the clear plastic pencil pouch that sat front and center in my three-ring binder. My enthusiasm for school supply shopping isn't a secret. I occasionally mention it in class and joke that this task was actually the reason I became a teacher in the first place. The working-with-kids part? That's pretty good. But buying school supplies? Pure joy.

However fun and satisfying it may be, though, to add colorful border to our bulletin boards and replenish countertops and cabinets with new supplies, the most important classroom assets cannot be purchased. Sitting right atop that list is our culture. Classroom culture involves the feeling tone of our environment and describes "how we do things around here." Culture expresses our identity as a unique group of people, demonstrates our priorities, and influences how we work, how we take responsibility for ourselves and our learning, how we treat one another, how we communicate, how we solve problems, how we handle setbacks, and how we view ourselves and our classmates and teachers. Though intangible, an organization's culture is unmistakable and undeniable. Upon entering a classroom, visitors can usually sense its culture immediately. A cooperative, productive culture cannot be imported; it must be home-grown, created from the ground up.

Culture is a living entity. Building culture is an ongoing process. Our words and actions contribute to this effort every hour of every day, especially at the start of a new school year, when culture is still taking shape. (A quick aside: In recent years, I've stopped using the term *classroom management* and instead describe this aspect of my teaching as *creating a championship culture*, since the latter more accurately conveys my intentions.) Culture-building is a top priority that requires daily attention. Like a flower, it needs consistent "watering" and nurturing.

Stephen Covey (1989, 2001), whose *7 Habits of Highly Effective People* and *First Things First* have greatly impacted my professional practice, is another author I was fortunate to discover early in my career. He once remarked that after every interaction we have with someone, whether it be a student, friend, or family member, we leave something behind. That notion still resonates with me. As a teacher, I take it to mean that with each conversation I have with a child, no matter how short (the interaction, not the child), I can make that individual feel better about themself or worse, strengthen our bond or weaken it, add sunshine to their day or clouds. It's important to share this idea with students to raise their awareness of the profound daily impact, positive or negative, team members can have on one another. We can encourage everyone to feel a sense of responsibility to the group and take full advantage of the incredible opportunity we have to make our classmates feel like superstars and create a tremendously caring, productive learning environment in which all of us can thrive. We invite students to be our partners in this endeavor and ask them to take this role seriously. The sum total of our words and deeds ultimately determines our culture. Together, we build a strong foundation during our initial weeks of school and then seek to fortify it with daily contributions from everyone. We can never go on autopilot, assume the job is finished, or take anything for granted.

From time to time, we hear stories in the news about the significance of culture in professional sports, the corporate world, and other aspects of society. These types of stories are especially popular when an NFL football team, for example, experiences a dramatic turnaround with a new leader after parting ways with its former coach after one or more poor seasons. Players often credit the team's success to a fresh, new energy, increased accountability, and better communication—all hallmarks of an improved culture. Similarly, we read about how employees of a private sector company become more productive and experience greater joy, satisfaction, and fulfillment after a leadership change. A positive culture is no less important for elementary school children. The common thread that runs through all these examples is that the environment in which we spend a large share of our waking hours exerts a massive effect on our motivation, effort, performance, and happiness. And though we may never be able to put a finger on exactly what makes a given culture special, when we find ourselves operating within one, everybody feels it.

How Can Teachers Build Culture in the Classroom?

Though culture will always be an intangible entity, there are concrete steps we can take to create a healthy, positive, and inspiring learning environment at the start of each school year. In the "Introduction," I mention the five human needs William Glasser identifies and share that we, as educators, have the power to make a profound contribution to the lives of students and the freedom to use our judgment, creativity, talents, and problem-solving skills to lead our classrooms in the ways we believe to be the most efficient and effective. This annual endeavor offers a great opportunity for us to satisfy both these needs and make an impact that can last well beyond students' elementary school years. Committing to this enterprise, and embracing it as a top priority, requires us to invest our hearts and minds. The result: a culture in which children will invest *their* hearts and minds.

Step 1: Determine the Kind of Culture We Want

No matter what instructional materials, curriculum calendars, and assessment protocols our school sites and districts may mandate, teachers create classroom culture. I have long believed that one of the most exciting, appealing, and satisfying aspects of our job is that we are the leaders of this process. If we think big and focus on what is best for children, the possibilities are amazing. Launching this endeavor poses tremendous challenges yet offers even larger potential payoffs.

The first step is determining the kind of culture we want. This exercise is a form of backward planning known as "beginning with the end in mind," one of Stephen Covey's seven habits of highly effective people. The idea is that when beginning any process, it is best to first determine the results or goal we are seeking. Then, we can focus on the steps that will lead us there.

We can begin this brainstorming process a few different ways. The most basic is to list individual traits, habits, and/or elements we want the culture to feature. Though it may be tempting to jot down dozens of traits,

I recommend picking a small number of high-priority ideas to serve as the foundation of your culture. You can always grow your list over time. Our lists may include such ideas as self-discipline, quality, kindness, responsibility, respect, enthusiasm, accountability, cooperation, empathy, creativity, and grit. Whichever specific priorities you mention, I will describe later in the chapter how we can build them into the fabric of our classrooms.

A second brainstorming option takes the form of a vision statement, either a phrase or full sentence, that conveys the core of our desired culture. Such a brief statement will not be, and cannot be, as comprehensive as a list, and that's fine. A vision statement is designed to be a short, powerful expression of what priority or priorities we hold most dear. A vision statement is meant to be a landmark or guidepost to which we turn to help us stay on course, keeping us focused on what we most value. In what follows you will find some examples.

- Enthusiastic students who work hard, work together, and work with purpose
- A determined group of children who display character and integrity
- Self-motivated learners who demonstrate uncommon kindness and respect
- A warm, enthusiastic environment where everyone feels valued and special
- Learners and leaders who take responsibility for themselves and look out for others
- Children developing important habits for today and tomorrow

A final brainstorming method allows us to add depth and detail to this process. To begin, identify a specific, hypothetical situation in which you and your students may find yourselves, and describe the ideal way you would want everyone to conduct themselves in that situation. You can also choose a situation from your teacher training or previous experiences as a student. If you opt for a situation that really happened, it can be a positive one you wish to repeat or a negative one you wish had turned out differently. Sometimes the most powerful "shaping" moments teachers experience are those in which we were put on the spot, criticized, or embarrassed as children and that we vow never to repeat in our classrooms. Possible scenarios could involve a lesson you are leading, a problem the kids must solve on the playground, a cooperative learning task in which students are working in pairs or small groups, or an activity occurring outside of the classroom.

Consider the following sample situation. It happened about 10 years ago, during our school's annual Picture Day. Traditionally, each class begins its turn by lining up in the auditorium to take individual snapshots and then heads outside to the risers for the group photo. Usually, I line up first for the individual pictures so I can be available to lead the transition outside to the risers and minimize any behavior that arises due to the fact that early finishers need to wait a while for the rest of their classmates. I forgot to do that this year, and I ended up ninth in line. After I took my individual photo, I noticed that the kids who preceded me were not in the auditorium, and I was a bit worried they had made their way outside unsupervised and were fooling around.

When I walked outside, I was pleasantly surprised by what I saw. Six kids were already in line in order from tallest to shortest, ready for the group photo. Two others had decided to take charge. Each time a new student exited the auditorium, these volunteers helped that person find their place in line. It turns out that I wasn't the first adult who noticed this. A parent whose child was in my class the previous year and who was assisting on Picture Day approached the pair and asked what they were doing. Samantha replied that a part of our class mission statement talked about leadership, and they decided to show leadership when their teacher wasn't there.

More information about mission statements, how to create them with your students, and how to use them for guidance throughout the year will be coming in Chapter 4. We had written ours during the first full week of school and had reviewed it every Friday as part of our morning routine. To see these kids internalize and act on the ideas we had included in the mission statement was incredible. When we returned to class after taking our class picture, I shared this story with the whole group so the students who were not there to witness it could understand how powerful it is when we take an abstract idea from our mission statement and apply it without being asked or prompted.

The scenarios we write enable us to "tease out" and identify specific traits, habits, and priorities we wish to build into the fabric of our culture. From the preceding scenario, I focus on the fact that two children felt empowered to lead and took charge of the situation to make a positive impact on their classmates, who, in turn, demonstrated cooperation by accepting their place in line without any arguing or other shenanigans.

Feel free to choose any of the three brainstorming methods in this section and perhaps use more than one. As long as you end up with a clear sense of what you want your classroom culture to look and feel like, you've made a great choice. No method is superior to the others, and there's no "right" answer. I once heard someone say that, in life, there are no answers, only options. I believe that idea fits this situation perfectly.

Step 2: Modeling

During my graduate training at UCLA, an instructor once remarked to our class that no matter what subject any of us went on to teach, we would all impact our students most powerfully with the examples we set. He cautioned us not to lose sight of the fact that though we may teach science or English, more than anything else, we are teaching *ourselves*; we are teaching who and what we are. Years later, when students look back on the time spent in our rooms, they might not remember all the content. But they will remember us.

As classroom teachers, we need to pay careful attention to the example we set for our students. This doesn't mean we need to be perfect or hold ourselves to some unrealistic standard. It does, however, mean that we make every effort to model for our students the qualities and behaviors we promote. When leaders walk our talk, we accomplish a great deal more than we do with words alone.

Leading by example is by far the most powerful way to help children develop the skills, traits, and habits we want to build into our classroom cultures. Encouraging reflective thinking and incorporating self-evaluation and goal setting into our practice also play an important role in our effort to help children internalize these ways of thinking and acting, but nothing matches the power of modeling. Of course, there will be many times when students don't seem to be paying attention to what we're saying and doing, but they are. And they will remember the example we set.

Consider the habit of honesty for a moment. In the beginning of every school year, one of my main objectives is to create an environment of trust in my classroom, and that can only happen when everyone acts in an honest manner. What is the most effective way for me to promote honesty? Is it to establish a rule that everybody must be honest? No. It is to *be* honest. I must make and keep promises to my students so their trust in me grows. I show them how to be honest by modeling honesty every chance I get and acting as a living embodiment of this trait. A walking billboard. Talking at my students will not achieve the same results.

Kindness is another huge emphasis of my initial culture-building efforts. We can encourage the spread of kindness by using a pleasant tone of voice, saying *please* and *thank you*, and looking out for the well-being of others. In addition, we can share compliments freely, display a super positive demeanor (even in the face of challenging student behavior), and basically become human dopamine dispensers to help everyone feel good about themselves.

A final trait I'd like to discuss in this section is enthusiasm. In my initial interactions with students and communications with their families, I strive to convey a sense of excitement, possibility, and optimism about the months ahead. While I believe this benefits all children, it is especially powerful for those students who haven't yet had positive experiences in school or committed themselves fully to academic pursuits. Our attitude can show them that maybe this year will be different. Maybe this will be the year we achieve greater academic success and view school as a "need-satisfying" place where we want to spend our days. In the classroom, we, as teachers, determine the weather. We control the environmental thermostat. Our energy, mood, and will are the most influential factors in creating culture, and our enthusiasm sets the tone. We remain consistently upbeat, even when it might be difficult to do so.

In the early weeks of the school year, I share with my students that there are basically two types of people in the world: battery chargers and battery drainers. Battery chargers fill the room with positivity, possess infectious energy, and make the classroom a better place simply by walking through the door. Battery chargers are people we want to be around. They make us feel good about ourselves. In contrast, battery drainers tend to complain, focus on the downside of things, and suck the energy from the room. The battery charger concept resonates with children and has a significant effect on behavior and attitude. Teachers need to be the ultimate battery chargers—bringing out and reflecting our students' best qualities, trying to make everyone feel special, articulating a glowing and unconditional view of their potential, and recognizing children's strengths as we begin the challenging work of identifying growth areas, communicating honestly about them, and working to address them.

Our modeling efforts can permeate any and all aspects of our teaching. Once we embrace the opportunity to lead by example, it's fun to explore different ways we can promote our highest priorities. With regard to enthusiasm, one of the best times to model this trait comes during instructional lessons. We convey enthusiasm through our words, body language, and facial expressions. When introducing new content, we emphasize that participating in the lesson and learning new information or a new skill is something we *get* to do, not a task we *have* to do. Learning is always an opportunity and a privilege, never a chore. New content provides us with a chance to learn, grow, and challenge ourselves. We wouldn't want to launch a lesson by speaking negatively of the content, saying that we found it really boring when we were in school, or expressing the need to just get through it or that we are learning it simply because the school or district requires us to do so. Those words sap enthusiasm. Instead, we articulate why we're learning this information, point out how learning it can help us now and later, and encourage everyone to do their best to find joy and interest in the material.

In recent years, the idea that we are a "want-to class, not a have-to class" has become a mantra with my students, and I have worked hard to "bake" it into our culture. This expression reminds me of an episode of the *Big Bang Theory* in which Leonard attempts to convince his roommate and fellow scientist Sheldon that the two need to take advantage of an opportunity that recently surfaced. Sheldon responds that they don't *need* to, because anything beyond basic biological functions—like breathing, eating, and expelling waste—is optional.

Whenever one of my students asks me if they *have to* complete a specific question on a worksheet or segment of an activity, my response typically paraphrases Sheldon's, minus the part about expelling waste. The list of what we have to do is small; the rest is up to us. It all depends on our attitude, commitment, and motivation.

There's a saying in team sports that players will take on the personality of their coach. When coaches lead with character and integrity and consistently try to model positive habits and traits, their actions can initiate a ripple effect—a chain reaction that impacts their players, who, in turn, impact those at home and in their communities. I believe the role of a teacher is also that of a coach. Both teachers and coaches bring together a diverse group of individuals, foster a sense of unity and common purpose, and strive to maximize the potential of each team member and the group as a whole.

Committing ourselves to serving as a consistent model of enthusiasm and other traits we hold dear feels good and allows us to satisfy many of the needs Glasser identifies. We present lessons with a positive attitude because, as teachers, we have more fun that way, and we understand that our attitude can become our students' attitude. If we are positive, they will be more likely to view their learning positively too. The same principle holds true when we spread kindness and conduct ourselves with character and integrity. Embracing our responsibility as a role model empowers us to be our best selves and helps bring out the best in our students. It can create within classrooms a productive, cooperative culture in which children can flourish. And it can create deep within us a sense of pride, satisfaction, and joy.

Step 3: Teach Habits and Traits Explicitly

Setting a consistent example for students with our words, deeds, and attitude will go a long way toward establishing the type of culture we envisioned in step 1 of this process. We can extend our culture-building efforts by teaching specific traits and habits explicitly. That means we introduce ideas such as responsibility and kindness the same way we would introduce academic concepts, such as addition and subtraction. We multiply the power of this instruction by pairing it with an engaging activity that shines a spotlight on the trait or habit we have selected. The accompanying activity provides children with an opportunity to think about, practice, and/or deepen their understanding of that idea.

This section includes several activities you may wish to use in class during the first few weeks of the school year. Looking at a blank lesson plan book can be daunting, and many times we seek to fill our initial days with as many engaging icebreakers, team builders, and games as possible. Though there's nothing wrong with that, I believe it's beneficial to be more intentional and purposeful with what we ask students to do and schedule activities that promote the traits and habits we want to build into our culture. Fortunately, those happen to be fun too.

Norms for Discussion

The effort to teach habits and traits explicitly begins on our first day together. I feel it's important to begin with an emphasis on respect and call students' attention to this idea 10 minutes into the school year. Once I have given the kids a chance to put away their belongings and settle in, I welcome everyone and ask each child to sit in a circle so we can introduce ourselves to the group. Next, we move into rows to give everyone a clear view of the board. The first item I display is our "Norms for Discussion" poster (Box 2.1). This is when I explicitly begin teaching the concept of respect. I promise that I will try always to treat them the way I want to be treated and ask them to treat their classmates and me the same way. I mention the golden rule as well. We are all human, and of course, we will mistakes this year. None of us is perfect. We will occasionally say the wrong thing and hurt someone's feelings, but we always try to treat others with respect.

We then turn our focus to the ideas on the poster. I invite a few student volunteers to read aloud one of the norms. I define the five norms, and we practice them for a couple of minutes. I share that these norms are expectations that we agree to follow anytime we gather for a class conversation. Our introduction to the Norms for Discussion concludes when I choose a *brave* volunteer to join me at the front of the room for a conversation about their summer vacation. I announce in advance that, as this child and I speak, I will violate one norm at a time (hopefully for the only time that year!) and challenge the group to identify my mistakes (by holding up the number of fingers that corresponds to the norm's placement on the list.) As the conversation proceeds, I will violate every norm, first in order (to build class confidence) and then randomly. The kids are very excited to catch their teacher staring at the ceiling, yawning, cutting off a classmate mid-sentence, and declaring that the volunteer's choice of favorite color is simply wrong. After a sincere apology to the volunteer for my behavior, I inform the class that we will be reviewing our norms throughout the day and during the first few weeks of the year until they become second nature. Adhering to these norms will demonstrate our daily commitment to being a respectful participant in class discussions.

> **Box 2.1 Norms for Discussion**
>
> *Norms for Discussion*
> 1. We listen intently as others speak.
> 2. We listen without interrupting.
> 3. We let each other finish speaking before raising our hands.
> 4. We make eye contact with the speaker.
> 5. We may politely disagree, but we do not criticize other people's comments.

Passion Survey

The Passion Survey is another first-day staple of my teaching. Earlier, I mentioned the importance of enthusiasm in a whole-child classroom and described my efforts to model it for my students. The highest form of enthusiasm is passion. While I am enthusiastic about many topics, I am truly passionate about a select few. Passion is enthusiasm with a full charge. When we spend time on a personal passion, we bring to it maximum motivation and boundless energy. We enter a "flow state," in which we experience total immersion, lose awareness of the passage of time, and fire on all cylinders. Though I am the first to admit that it is probably unrealistic to expect elementary students to bring this level of passion to all their schoolwork every day, I do believe that setting the bar high and encouraging this level of motivation, excitement, and effort needs to be a significant aspect of my classroom culture. I would rather aim too high and not quite get there than aim too low and miss valuable opportunities or sell my students short. We begin this endeavor by helping children identify their passions.

The Passion Survey is my initial move to encourage children to be excited about their learning and develop this element of our culture. When I first administered the Passion Survey several years ago, I knew right away I would use this activity every fall during the first week of school. It was educational love at first sight. The survey is simply a piece of paper on which students list their four favorite hobbies and activities and then draw themselves pursuing these passions.

At the top of the sheet, I include the following introduction. On the paper you distribute, feel free to include a similar opening that reflects your passions.

> I absolutely love football. I could watch it and talk about it all day long and then look forward to doing it all over again the next day. I also love music, working out, reading, and writing. These are some of my passions. *Passions* are hobbies and activities that we love. They are our favorite things to do, talk about, and think about. Passions are what we would do all day long if we could, and we would never get bored or tired of them. Passions are what we like spending time doing when nobody is asking us to do something else.

Once everyone finishes, I take the papers home to create a chart displaying the results (Figure 2.1). If the class, as a whole, names more passions than the top of the chart can accommodate, I combine topics or create larger categories and then use letter codes to identify each child's specific passions. For example, in the "Art" section of the accompanying chart, *D* stands for "drawing," *P* for "painting," and *A* for overall "art." After sharing and discussing the chart with the children, I display it prominently on one of the closet doors for the rest of the year.

The Passion Survey is perfect for the first week of school because it's simple and engaging and because its results are powerful. Specifically, this activity produces three wonderful outcomes. First, when students have the opportunity to make curricular choices, the passions provide a concrete starting point. For example, if I am stuck trying to find a topic for my information book during Writing Workshop, I can think about my passions and choose one to spark an idea. Since I love the Los Angeles Dodgers, I can write my book about the team. Motivation, interest, and productivity increase substantially when I am able to choose my topic, and they skyrocket when I pick one about which I am passionate. Originally, this was the main reason I decided to give the survey—as an aid that would help students personalize the choices they make about their academic learning.

In addition, the fact that, as a class, we are thinking and talking and writing about our passions sends the message that being passionate about things can greatly enhance our lives. Students who may not yet have found their passions will become more encouraged to look, especially when they see their classmates excited by their own passions. Furthermore, people tend to be happiest when they are pursuing their favorite interests, and if your students have regular opportunities to incorporate their passions into their schoolwork, your classroom will naturally become a happier, more

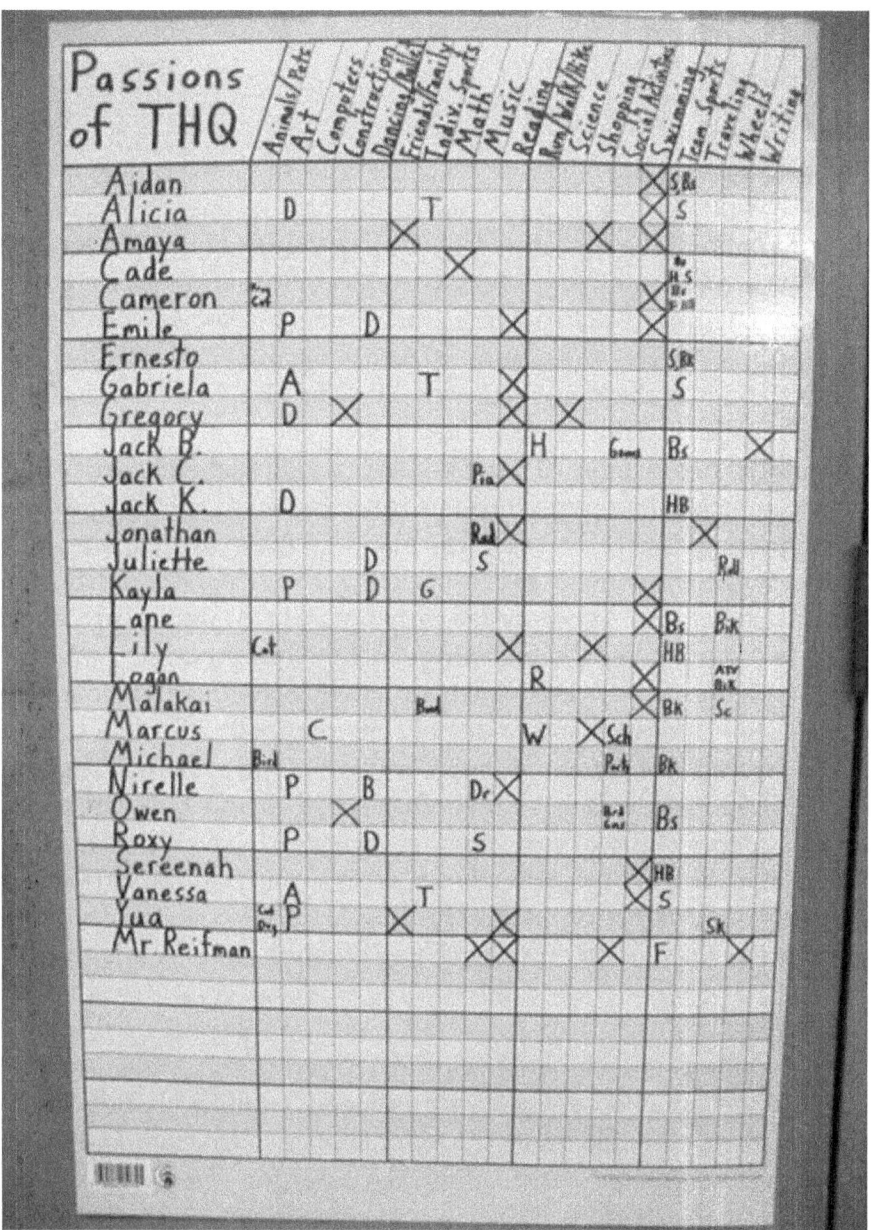

Figure 2.1 Passion Survey chart.

productive, more need-satisfying place. Over the years, I have also noticed a significant "carryover" effect. Our focus on passions boosts children's overall enthusiasm for learning, and their focus and motivation typically remain high even when they aren't working on an activity related to one of their primary interests.

I will describe a third and final benefit of the Passion Survey in the next chapter.

Human Health Hunt

Health and wellness are other important aspects of a whole-child classroom culture. My initial effort to introduce health and wellness concepts comes on the afternoon of the first day. The Human Health Hunt is a variation of the well-known "People Hunt" activity found in Jeanne Gibbs's (2001) book *Tribes* and contains a list of sentences that connect to specific healthy habits and behaviors. (You can find a sample Human Health Hunt in Figure 2.2 and a printable copy on the Routledge website.) The object of the activity is for students to walk around the room and collect the signatures of classmates who exemplify one or more of these behaviors. I stipulate that each child can sign a given paper only once, thus ensuring that everyone mingles with as many people as possible. The kids can also sign their own papers one time. While it is not necessary to fill every line, many children make it their mission in life to reach that goal. (I encourage early finishers to "double up" by trying to obtain two signatures for each item, even if that means asking some people a second time once every classmate has already signed.) The Human Health Hunt raises awareness of important health concepts while also promoting positive social interactions, building teamwork, and creating situations in which children need to help one another. I like to end the activity with a whole-class debrief so that everyone has a chance to share the items which they were able to sign. Reviewing the sheet gives me a natural opportunity to reinforce the importance of making healthy food choices, staying hydrated, living an active lifestyle, and taking charge of other aspects of our health.

Play-Doh Activity

Creativity is an aspect of classroom culture I haven't yet discussed, and it may definitely be one we choose to embrace as one of our highest priorities. In the summer of 2013, I attended a teaching conference in Chicago and learned a terrific idea from educator and author Dave Burgess. He suggested giving each child a small can of Play-Doh and asking everyone to create something that represents themselves in some way. Since then, when my students enter the room on the first day of school, they see a can of Play-Doh, a plate, and a paper towel on every desk. Immediate smiles. After I introduce the Norms for Discussion, we transition to the Play-Doh Activity. I provide very brief instructions (mostly about keeping their Play-Doh works of art on the plate and their area clean) and encourage the kids to be as creative as possible. Then the students each choose a desk, usually based on Play-Doh color, and empty the contents of the can onto their plates to get started.

Name_____

Human Health Hunt

1. _____ doesn't add salt to food.
2. _____ exercises daily or almost daily to stay in shape.
3. _____ regularly eats a healthy breakfast.
4. _____ fastens seat belt whenever in a car.
5. _____ is careful not to eat too much sugar.
6. _____ loves being a student.
7. _____ wears sunscreen to protect their skin.
8. _____ will always be a non-smoker.
9. _____ drinks plenty of water.
10. _____ likes wheat bread more than white bread.
11. _____ enjoys a good, hard workout.
12. _____ flosses every day.
13. _____ owns or has owned a furry pet.
14. _____ tries to avoid fried and fatty foods.
15. _____ has looked forward to the start of school.
16. _____ is an enthusiastic swimmer.
17. _____ has given up an unhealthy habit.
18. _____ is careful not to drink too many soft drinks.
19. _____ likes at least two vegetables.
20. _____ tries to think positively at all times.

Figure 2.2 Human health hunt.

The benefits of the Play-Doh Activity are numerous. First, working with Play-Doh is relaxing. Children are often anxious the first day, and having the opportunity to participate in this task can calm their nerves and help them adjust to their new surroundings and bond with their neighbors. In addition, because the kids are engrossed in their creations, behavior is usually not an issue. As a result, I am able to accomplish multiple objectives simultaneously. I can visit with every child to learn their name, spend a little time chatting with them, and take an interest in what they are making. I am also on high alert for imaginative uses of the Play-Doh and out-of-the-box thinking. I notice, for example, when two kids give each other half their stash to gain use of a second color, stand their Play-Doh up to go 3D, or ask to use the edge of a paper clip to carve details into their basketballs, cars, and pets' faces. I call attention to these moves while trying not to be obvious about it. Instead of addressing the whole group, I'll face the child and share (fairly loudly) my observations about what I see them doing. Since the room is pretty quiet, everyone will hear me and often incorporate that strategy into their process. After approximately 15–20 minutes, we conduct a whole-class share in which each child has a chance to stand and describe what they made. That gives the kids an opportunity to learn everyone's name, gain a little insight into their classmates, and enjoy a moment in the spotlight while affording me an opportunity to celebrate the creativity in the room and encourage that type of thinking in their daily work. I also like to snap a picture on my phone of each child holding up their artwork.

Picture Book Read-Alouds

Elementary students of all ages love picture books. Older kids might act like they are too cool to participate in this type of read-aloud, but upper-grade students enjoy hearing these stories and looking at the pictures as much as anyone. Don't let them tell you any different. Because the stories, characters, images, and messages resonate with children on such a deep level, picture books offer us a tremendous opportunity to introduce important traits and habits in a natural way.

I read a different picture book to my third and fourth graders each day for the first couple of weeks of school before switching to longer chapter books. My favorite picture book to read during this time is Robert Kraus' (1999) *Leo the Late Bloomer*, the story of a young lion who experiences difficulty performing the tasks young lions are expected to master—reading, writing, drawing, eating, and speaking. Leo's father becomes worried while his mother urges patience. In time, Leo blooms. He learns how to do these tasks and feels proud of himself.

After I finish the read-aloud, I make a big deal out of the fact that this new school year will give all of us an amazing chance to bloom, just like Leo did. I mentioned earlier in this chapter that in my initial interactions with students and communications with their families, I strive to convey a sense of excitement, possibility, and optimism about the months ahead. The class discussion that follows the *Leo the Late Bloomer* read-aloud is the first time I address this idea with the kids. I want to send the message that we have no limits. If we have experienced difficulty in school in the past, this year can be different. If reading has been a challenge in earlier grades, this can be the year we can make a huge jump. Many children believe that if they currently struggle in a given area, they will always struggle in that area. I want to counter that notion strongly. Massive improvement is possible—this year, in this class, with this teacher and these classmates. Let's get fired up, dream big, and believe we can accomplish hard things. I repeat this message to parents at Back-to-School Night and seek their investment and involvement in this endeavor.

Once I have communicated my message, I ask everyone to think of the most important way in which they would like to bloom this year. That goal can involve an academic area or skill, making new friends, a work habit or social skill, becoming more active, or anything else a child might find personally meaningful. Typically, every child raises their hand to participate, and I call on everybody, even though it takes a few minutes. It's time well spent because it gives each child a chance to publicly share a goal and signal their commitment to "blooming." Hearing students mention their desire to improve in reading, math, writing, printing, and other areas is heartwarming and affirms my deeply held belief that all children genuinely do want to learn and grow. It's wonderful to see how seriously kids take this activity.

There are, of course, tons of picture books whose themes can greatly contribute to our initial culture-building efforts. Other favorites include *Don't Laugh at Me*, which focuses on treating people with kindness and respect, and *Mindful Monkey, Happy Panda*, which introduces mindfulness. With these books and others, planning some type of follow-up discussion that invites the children to share ideas, demonstrate their commitment, offer comments, and reflect on key points is critical. If you would like to set an intention, pose a question, or call students' attention to a key aspect of the book before starting the read-aloud, that can often be an effective move as well.

Compliments

One way to create a culture of kindness is to encourage children to compliment their classmates for outstanding academic work, excellent effort, and noteworthy deeds. Both giving and receiving a compliment feel good, and we want our classrooms to be places where these kind words flow freely. Encouraging compliments conveys the message that we value cooperation, not competition, and want children to view classmates as friends and assets, not rivals. In this type of environment, we care about one another, cheer on our classmates, and are genuinely happy for their successes. This activity is especially useful for those kids who would love to share positive messages but may not yet possess the vocabulary to do so.

In this activity, students brainstorm a list of compliments to use throughout the year. During this process, we are helping students build the type of spirit we wish to promote in our classrooms. The following four steps can also serve as a useful template for any type of group brainstorming you may wish to do in the future.

> Step 1: Students fold a piece of blank drawing paper into 16 squares. Independently, the kids think of all the different "compliment words" and "compliment expressions" they know and write them on their papers, one word or expression per square. The children can use the back or fold the paper to create more squares, if necessary. Many kids get very excited to do this.
>
> Step 2: Everyone circulates throughout the room and participates in a "give 1, get 1" activity, where, in pairs, each child shares one idea with a partner and receives one idea from that partner before moving on to a different person. Students write these new ideas in blank squares on their papers. This exchange of ideas is a variation of an activity Ron Nash (2013) presents in *The Active Classroom*.
>
> Step 3: The kids return to their seats for a whole-class share. As volunteers say their ideas, the teacher or student recorder lists everything on a chart for future reference while everyone else adds ideas to their papers.
>
> Step 4: Each student circles their three favorite compliments, memorizes them, and commits to using them in the coming months. Follow up with these compliments as opportunities arise.

Habits of Character and Habits of Mind

The next effort I describe is not so much a one-time activity, like many of the previous examples, as it is the launch of a multi-week process. Its purpose is to introduce Habits of Character and Habits of Mind, two sets of ideas that empower children to become better students, better thinkers, and better people. Taken together, these habits form a foundational piece of my whole-child teaching philosophy. Let's begin with the Habits of Character.

Habits of Character focus on student behavior, work habits, and social and moral development. These habits involve the valuable intrapersonal and interpersonal skills and traits we seek to integrate with academic instruction and build into our classroom culture. I regard character learning to be as significant as academic learning, if not more so. While our students may not all go on to become world-class scholars, they can all become world-class people. They can learn to work hard, get along well with others, and act with honor and integrity.

I believe character learning to be especially relevant these days because we are living in a time of great economic change and uncertainty. The global economy has rendered previously marketable "skill sets" useless, and many of our students' jobs have yet to be invented. Our goal as teachers is to prepare children for the future, but we simply can't know what that future will look like. Where we can establish a foothold, though, and where we can build capacity, is by focusing on strengthening children's character. Developing effective intrapersonal and interpersonal habits will empower students to succeed no matter what looms over the economic horizon.

In Chapter 1, I argue that the most effective way to accomplish our most important goals is to weave them together into a seamless whole. Character development, then, is best achieved when we are able to incorporate meaningful Habits of Character into the curriculum on a daily basis. Cooperation, for example, is a great habit to address as the kids are learning to work in groups. My students and I discuss responsibility the first time they receive homework that is due the following day. Perseverance is a terrific topic to explore the first time students engage in a truly rigorous, challenging activity, during which they are likely to encounter frustration and perhaps be tempted to quit. Soon, we reach the point where literally every academic activity has embedded within it at least one lesson about character. A multiplication game played in pairs, of course, is designed to improve everyone's multiplication skills, but its purpose is also to help us become kinder and more cooperative. Once we, as educators, start analyzing our daily teaching for ways to incorporate lessons about character, it will be almost impossible to operate any other way. Over time, these lessons will greatly impact student behavior both inside and outside the classroom.

Character education is not an add-on, nor should it be viewed as a topic that will take time away from the long list of standards we are already being asked to teach. Rather, infusing our curriculum with Habits of Character will result in a mutually beneficial situation. Children will learn academic material better than they would have without the emphasis on character, and students will learn more about developing character than they would have had we approached it as a separate entity.

For approximately the past 25 years, I have used the same list of 13 Habits of Character with my third and fourth graders, with only minor modifications. The habits, along with their definitions, are listed in a later paragraph. Proceed with caution as you decide which of these to use with your students. More is not necessarily better. Consider which ones are age-appropriate for your kids, and be careful not to overwhelm your students with too many at once. I recommend starting with a small number. As you gain skill and confidence incorporating these habits into your curriculum, you can always add more at a later time.

Habits of Character

1. Cooperation
   - Working well with others
2. Courage
   - Asking for help when I need it
   - Being willing to take risks
3. Fairness
   - Sharing equally
   - Taking turns
   - Raising my hand before speaking (not calling out)
4. Honesty
   - Telling the whole truth
5. Kindness
   - Thinking about the needs of others
   - Being polite
6. Patience
   - Staying calm and relaxed when I have to wait in line or in class
7. Perseverance
   - Trying my best and never giving up
8. Positive Attitude
   - Being pleasant to be around
   - Looking at the bright side of things
   - Trying to enjoy the work I do
9. Pride
   - Being driven by intrinsic motivation
   - Caring deeply about my work
   - Continuously trying to improve
10. Respect
    - Treating others how I want to be treated
    - Listening attentively (sitting flat, making eye contact, not interrupting, listening carefully)

11. Responsibility
    - Owning my actions
    - Turning in complete homework on time
    - Taking my bag of books home and bringing it back to school each day
    - Using restroom, water bottles, and drinking fountain at proper times
    - Keeping the room clean and keeping my papers and supplies neat and organized
12. Self-Discipline
    - Working quietly at my seat
    - Lining up on time
    - Entering the room quietly
    - Following signal and directions the first time
    - Having quick and quiet transitions
13. Service
    - Trying to be helpful to other kids and adults
    - Giving support without giving answers

There are advantages and disadvantages to using one list over time versus creating a new list from scratch each year. In a nutshell, keeping the same list from year to year saves time and allows me to begin the year with a tool that has proven to be effective in the past. In contrast, starting from scratch can give each group a stronger sense of ownership. Because I have never found the ownership issue to be a problem, and because I use the list over the summer for planning purposes, I have kept the list consistent from year to year. This is a professional decision you will need to make for yourself.

I begin teaching the Habits of Character and their definitions on the second day of school. I recommend starting with *respect* because it is one of my highest "class culture" priorities and nicely follows the Norms for Discussion introduction from the day before. To help students learn these terms and definitions, I have created a set of signs for our front classroom wall and a set of digital slides I can project onto our interactive whiteboard. The sign for *respect* is shown in Figure 2.3. (You can find a printable copy of the Habits of Character list, with definitions, and a complete set of signs on the Routledge website.)

Specifically, I point to the location on the front wall of the classroom that displays the Habits of Character and explain what they are and how they can help us. I then announce that we will be learning one habit per day until we complete the set. Standing beside the respect sign, I read and model the indicators listed and turn everyone's attention to the blank "Looks Like/

Respect

Respect is a necessary ingredient for all positive relationships. When we respect others, we treat them the way that we would like them to treat us. An important part of showing respect to people involves being an attentive listener. It is respectful to look people in the eye when they speak and listen closely to what they have to say.

Indicators:
- Treating others how I want to be treated
- Listening Attentively
  (Sitting flat, making ete contact,
  not interrupting, listening carefully)

Figure 2.3 "Respect" sign (along with a full Habits of Character and signs for each).

Sounds Like" chart I have posted next to it. I ask, "What does respect look like to you? What does it sound like?" We don't fill in the chart at this point; rather, we launch an inquiry that lasts until just before recess. As we engage in our morning activities, I am on the lookout, and I ask the kids to be on the lookout for examples of respect they observe in the room. A few minutes prior to recess, we return to the rug and add ideas to the chart. (A sample chart is shown in Table 2.1.) We review the chart again before lunch and prior to dismissal and write any new ideas we may discover. As my students and I proceed through the remaining Habits of Character over the next few weeks, we will use the Looks Like/Sounds Like chart on some days, but not every day. If we employ the same learning tool too often, we run the risk of diminishing its value and minimizing its impact. I suggest using the chart with habits such as kindness and positive attitude because what we say and how we say it are such vital parts of these traits. (Children displaying patience and self-discipline tend not to do much talking!) By observing and discussing what it would look like and sound like in the classroom when a given habit is in evidence, we paint a more complete picture of how we can bring the habits to life on a daily basis.

The following day, we focus on fairness. (The indicators are shown in what follows.) Pairing respect with fairness is a strategic choice I make because the two habits each have indicators that strongly impact the quality of instructional lessons and class discussions that take place with the kids

Table 2.1 Looks Like/Sounds Like Chart for "Respect"

Respect	
Looks like...	**Sounds like...**
She made eye contact with me. *He heard me out.* *Let me go first because that's how they would want to be treated.*	*She used a polite tone of voice.* *Even when I messed up on a math problem, he didn't get mad at me.* *It may sound weird, but it sounded quiet because my partner didn't interrupt me. (That happened a lot last year.)* *Calm voices.*

sitting on the rug in the front of the room. Many children experience difficulty raising their hand before speaking and maintaining a strong posture for learning. They tend to slouch or sit in other positions that make eye contact an anatomical unlikelihood. Calling out an answer without first being recognized by the teacher is a particularly problematic tendency. Calling out disrupts the flow of instruction or conversation and can discourage the participation of quieter classmates. By addressing these issues proactively, we set the stage for smooth lessons and discussions in which everyone feels an equal part.

Fairness

- Sharing equally
- Taking turns
- Raising my hand before speaking (not calling out)

On the day we focus on *fairness*, I also unveil the rubric shown in Figure 2.4. By linking the Habits of Character to the rubric early in this process, I convey the message that our goal isn't merely to learn the definition of each habit; it is to focus on how we can improve in these areas throughout the year. Continuous improvement is a foundational idea that I try to build into the fabric of our classroom, and the most valuable type of improvement I attempt to foster involves our performance with these habits. Improvement will be the focus of Chapter 9.

The rubric features a 4-point scale (4 = exceeds expectations, 3 = meets expectations, 2 = below expectations, 1 = significantly below expectations) that we also use for our academic work in the different disciplines. This continuity helps the kids internalize the meaning of each level. While the rubric is applicable to both sets of habits, my students and I use it mainly for the Habits of Character, especially during the first part of the school year.

Habits of Character & Habits of Mind Rubric

We will use this rubric whenever we self-evaluate our performance in any of the habits of character or habits of mind. The scores will always be based on the definitions that we have for each habit. For example, if we were doing a self-evaluation for the habit of Fairness, we would base our self-evaluation on the definition of fairness: share equally, take turns, raise hand before speaking (not calling out). Our goal is for everyone to be at least a 3 in every habit of character by June. In other words, the goal is to become more automatic with the habits.

4 = Exceeds Expectations "Going Above and Beyond"
- I am a role model in this habit that others can look to for guidance.
- I never need reminders from an adult or a classmate about this habit.
- My performance in this habit is completely automatic.

---

3 = Meets Expectations "Consistently Solid"
- I do what the definition says almost all the time.
- I usually don't need reminders from an adult or classmate about this habit.
- My performance in this habit is usually automatic.

---

2 = Below Expectations "Close, but not Quite There"
- I do what the definition says some of the time, but not most of the time.
- I tend to need frequent reminders from an adult or a classmate about this habit.
- My performance in this habit is not yet automatic.
- My performance in this habit may interfere with my learning or the learning of others.

1 = Significantly Below Expectations "Still Much to Be Done"
- I do very little of what the definition of this habit says.
- I need reminders from an adult all throughout the day about this habit. Talking to me about my behavior takes up a large amount of my teacher's time.
- My performance in this habit strongly interferes with my learning or the learning of others.

Figure 2.4 Habits of Character and Habits of Mind rubric.

Of course, it isn't possible to assess a student's character as we would a Writing Workshop essay or science project. Character is too complex and too deeply personal to reduce to a single number. What we can do, however, is break down the larger concept of character into smaller components (habits) and begin defining these components in ways that kids will understand (specific indicators of each habit). The rubric provides a structure that makes meaningful assessment possible.

Improvement cannot be forced. Children aren't going to become more honest or more responsible simply because their parents or teachers want them to be. The desire to improve has to come from within. Adults can encourage and nurture, but the kids need to be the primary driving force in the improvement process. The good news is that all students want to learn and improve. Deep down inside, they all want to do better. This desire may be difficult to notice sometimes, but it's there, and we can help children bring it to the surface. Specifically, we can facilitate this progress through storytelling, reflection, self-evaluation, and goal setting.

The storytelling begins on the day I introduce the rubric. Just before I present the rubric and its 4-point scale, I share with my students a brief anecdote about a conversation I had at a party that occurred several years ago. Upon discovering that I was an elementary school teacher, a gentleman said, "Boy, isn't it difficult to control that many kids?" My response was that I have never viewed my job in that way. I have never tried to control kids before, and I couldn't do it even if I did try.

The fact is that no teacher can control a child's behavior. We can only attempt to control ourselves, and that's difficult enough to do. I then tell the class that this year we're going to become really good at controlling ourselves and improving our behavior, and I am about to show them a tool that will help us do that. I then unveil the rubric and the scoring system on which it is based. I inform everyone that we will all be in charge of controlling our own behavior and trying to improve it because I know that is something we all want to do.

The levels of the rubric and the specific indicators they contain are important in this effort because they provide a structure. They enable us to see how well we are currently doing, while also showing us what it will take to move to a higher level. (Typically, the athletes and video gamers in the class become especially interested in the rubric because it gives them a way to keep score.) The purpose of my presentation is to shift ownership of behavior from me to my students because many children enter school with the belief that the adults on campus control their behavior.

Once the kids know they are the ones in charge of controlling their own behavior and trying to improve it, I provide frequent opportunities for everyone to self-evaluate. There are times, of course, when I will be assessing everyone's progress, but I make the point that the students' assessment of their performance with the Habits of Character is far more important and meaningful than mine. After all, nobody knows our behavior better than ourselves. With Honesty, for example, only I know if I am telling the whole truth about a given situation, and if someone claimed to understand the honesty of my actions better than I did, I would be pretty mad. So, as teachers, we can offer opinions, suggestions, and support, but we need to understand that the students are in the best position to make these determinations.

In short, self-evaluation is the most effective way to help students improve their performance with the Habits of Character. Self-evaluation encourages reflection. When students reflect on how well they are doing, they are thinking deeply about what they do well and what they may not yet do well. Frequent opportunities for self-evaluation empower students to take ownership of their behavior and internalize the habits and attitudes we are trying to promote in our classrooms. In addition, providing these opportunities shows kids that we trust them to make these decisions independently. With self-evaluation, no parent or teacher is attempting to control student behavior. Nobody is holding out the promise of an extrinsic reward for excellent conduct or threatening punishment for poor conduct. Nobody is trying to force children to behave in certain ways. Such strict adult control only robs students of opportunities to develop self-control. An approach rooted in reflection and self-evaluation acknowledges that the students are in charge of their own behavior and that they will only achieve genuine improvement when they care enough to think about that behavior and make a commitment to improve it.

I mentioned previously that at the very beginning of the year, I introduce a new Habit of Character each day. Later that morning, and again in the afternoon, I follow up to reinforce the indicators of our new habit. As part of this review, I ask all the children to evaluate their performance with the day's new habit using the rubric.

Before the kids carry out their self-evaluation, I model the process myself. Specifically, I match my behavior to the indicators on the rubric to select the most appropriate score. Let's return to our focus on fairness. If I took turns during playground games, shared materials equally in class, and raised my hand before speaking for most of the day, my score would be a 3, which is our class goal. If I interfered with the learning of my neighbor and needed reminders from the teacher a few times, my score would be a 2. I would continue to talk through the indicators of the other levels so everyone could clearly see how to arrive at the most accurate judgment.

I need to honor the fact that these assessments are personal and private, so when it comes time to share our self-evaluations, I ask the children to display their scores by closing their eyes and holding up the appropriate number of fingers. (Note: Some children are uncomfortable closing their eyes and prefer to cover them with their hand or look down. Both are reasonable alternatives.) Afterward, I ask for volunteers who are willing to share their scores aloud and explain the rationale for them. I never require anyone to share a score aloud. Typically, though, many kids will raise their hand. As the children share, my objective is to hold everyone accountable by making sure their scores match up to the rationales they are providing. For example, children should not be giving themselves a score of 4 if they needed teacher reminders throughout the day. Initially, several kids are too easy themselves; others, too hard. This sharing exercise helps students come to a better understanding of the rubric's different levels of achievement. For many children, this is the first time they have engaged in this type of self-assessment, and it may take a while before they assess themselves accurately. Because the ability to self-assess is such a critical skill in and out of school, this time is worth taking.

After approximately the first three weeks of school, the kids have received an introduction to each habit, and I can then refer to these ideas during our academic day. I don't begin presenting the Habits of Mind until I have concluded my introduction to the Habits of Character. Usually, I will wait several weeks. I don't want to overwhelm my students with too many habits at once. Introduce Habits of Mind when you feel your class is ready for them, and remember to start small and begin with the ones you feel are the most appropriate for the age you teach. I believe the Habits of Character have to come first because they feature behaviors that are so integral to building a cooperative, productive work environment, and creating this type of environment has to be done right away. You can find a Habits of Mind list, with indicators, along with implementation information, in Resource A.

Obviously, helping children develop these habits requires a tremendous amount of time and effort, but I believe it is the most satisfying work we can do, and it is the aspect of students' lives to which we can add the greatest value. There is something special about interacting with kids who have developed the habit of saying *please* and *thank you*, who work hard and never think of quitting, who treat one another with uncommon respect, and who generally conduct themselves in a manner that should make themselves and their families extremely proud.

Step 4: Create Visual Reference Points

After investing the time and effort to introduce, model, and practice foundational elements of our culture, we want them to remain "living ideas" in our students' hearts and minds.

To support this goal, we can create a visual reference point for each of our highest culture-building priorities. A visual reference point is simply a sign or poster we can place in the classroom that reminds the kids of one or more important ideas and gives us a resource we can use anytime we wish to call students' attention to those ideas. We all know the expression: "Out of sight, out of mind." Adding visuals to our physical environment is the opposite of that. By keeping these elements within eyeshot, we can help keep them in mind.

Take the Passion Survey, for example. If students filled out the sheets with their favorite hobbies and interests and then left for the day, the excitement and enthusiasm we generated during this activity would likely be lost. Creating the chart identifying everyone's passions, however, and placing it on a closet door provides a sense of permanence. After all, the kids will see this chart every day, and I can display it at the front of the room whenever it's time to make a project choice.

The good news is that if you choose to incorporate activities such as the Passion Survey, Norms for Discussion introduction, Compliments brainstorming session, and Habits of Character rollout into your initial weeks, many reference points will already be complete and not require additional work. Your Passion Survey chart, Norms for Discussion poster, Compliments list, Habits of Character signs, and Looks Like/Sounds Like charts will be ready to place around the room once you have introduced them to the group.

Creating visual reference points for the Human Health Hunt, Picture Book Read-Alouds, and Play-Doh Activity may require some additional effort. For the Human Health Hunt, I like to post the "Are You Being Good to Your Brain?" visual in Figure 2.4 to show how many items on the sheet we used connect to important aspects of our physical and mental health. Displaying cover images of the picture books we read aloud is a terrific way to remind students of the traits and messages those stories feature. Finally, for the Play-Doh Activity, consider filling a bulletin board with the pictures you took as the students shared their works of art. If creating physical reference points is too difficult, time-consuming, or expensive, digital representations you can display on an interactive whiteboard or document camera also work well, if that's an option for you. Instead of attaching Habits of Character signs to a wall, for example, show slides on your interactive whiteboard. Have fun with this endeavor, and seek creative ways to make visual reference points for your highest-priority concepts and ideas. In a previous section, I introduced class mission statements. I consider these documents to be the ultimate reference points and, as I mentioned, will describe them and their use in detail in Chapter 4.

Are You Being Good to Your Brain?

Excercising daily?	Embracing challenges?
Eating well?	Sleeping enough?
Staying hydrated?	Staying positive?
Managing stress?	Good relationships?

Figure 2.5 "Are You Being Good to Your Brain?" visual.

Another benefit of posting visual reference points is that it enables us to fill our classroom wall space organically, collaboratively, and gradually with items that the children will find meaningful. It may be tempting to cover each section of wall space prior to the first day of school with colorful purchased items, but I caution against doing this. Students will be more invested in the class, take greater ownership of their learning, and find the classroom environment more engaging when they feel a part of the room design process. In addition, kids will produce better work, put forth more effort, and become more excited about their learning. It's as if the kids themselves and the classroom wall space are "growing together." If the kids enter class on the first day and see the walls already covered, we take away the opportunity for that pride and ownership to develop.

Step 5: Follow Up in Both the Short Term and the Long Term

Visual reference points allow for easy follow-up anytime we wish to call students' attention to important aspects of our culture. These visuals offer us a sense of reassurance—we can take comfort in knowing we won't be introducing critical concepts and letting them escape into the ether. Instead, we will be introducing important concepts and using these visual reminders to come back to them again and again in the months ahead. This follow-up begins immediately as we seek to reinforce critical habits and traits and "bake" them into our learning environment. Revisiting foundational ideas is necessary because one exposure, experience, contact, or "touch" is never sufficient for students to learn any concept or skill thoroughly, whether it be an academic standard, such as subtraction with regrouping, or a behavioral trait, such as responsibility. Experience has taught me that even when activities like the Norms for Discussion introduction go extremely well and students appear to quickly "get" the points we are trying to make, we can't ever stop there. Though there will likely be times when additional follow-up may not appear to be necessary, it always is.

The need for follow-up becomes clearer and more urgent when we step back and consider the totality of influences in children's lives these days. With social media, online ads, television commercials, and corporate marketing efforts sending kids a dizzying number of messages every day, there is a very real competition occurring for children's attention, hearts, and minds. It may not be pleasant to think about, but teachers are part of this competition. We need to send consistent messages of our own—about kindness, enthusiasm for learning, character development, and other high-priority cultural elements. In some respects, of course, it may not appear to be a fair fight, taking into account the glitz, GIFs, memes, and other enticing images children constantly encounter. That said, I believe an important aspect of our job involves helping students learn, remember, and value the high priorities we promote in our classrooms. Working in our favor is that we, as teachers, have the best message of all to offer children, one saying that if you commit yourselves to being the best person and the best student you can be, you will experience a joy and a satisfaction that no product, app, or online content can match. Along the way, you will get to spend your days with a group of battery chargers who love learning, treat you with kindness and respect, and bring out the best in you. For teachers to achieve this result, however, we need to follow up with children about the priorities we hold dear. A lot. Reviewing important concepts regularly enables these traits to become part of our "functioning selves."

Short-term follow-up can begin anytime after we introduce a new element of our culture. One effective way to achieve short-term follow-up is simply to encourage students to employ a newly learned skill or habit as they begin an academic activity. That requires no additional time yet produces noticeable benefits. For example, before you send pairs off to play a math game, remind everyone to use one or more of the compliments they recently selected. At the end of the period, when you review the math content, ask volunteers to share a compliment they gave or received from their partner. Every time we encourage a behavior in this manner, we increase the likelihood that students will adopt and repeat this behavior.

A second type of short-term follow-up involves recognizing positive traits and habits when we see them and calling students' attention to it afterward. By being on the lookout for examples of kindness, respect, and other awesome behavior, we create situations in which the conduct comes from the kids. In this manner, positive examples "percolate up" from the kids rather than come from the "top down." Even though elementary students value the words and deeds of their teachers, that same behavior tends to resonate more deeply when it is displayed by a peer and publicly recognized.

One of my favorite instances of recognizing noteworthy student behavior occurred approximately ten years ago, after the kids had completed their second Enthusiasm Survey of the year. (I will present more information about Enthusiasm Surveys in Chapter 9.) Once I had tabulated the results, I asked everyone to choose a clear, interesting way to display them. Many children opted for graphs, others selected charts, while still others invented their own methods. As I concluded my project instructions, I emphasized the importance of producing quality displays that were neat, organized, and carefully done. Not five minutes after I gave this encouragement, a student we'll call Nadia raised her hand and brought me her paper. While she headed over to my chair, I admit that I jumped to a conclusion. I assumed Nadia was about to tell me she was finished, and I was about to tell her that a quality job simply isn't possible in such a short amount of time. Had she not heard my inspirational words about producing careful work? A moment later, she said, "Mr. Reifman, I'm not happy with how I started my display. May I start over?" Never in my career had I been prouder of a student's commitment to quality while simultaneously feeling like such a fool.

I gladly allowed her to begin again and made a huge deal out of her decision right before recess when we stopped for the day. With the kids gathered on the rug, you better believe I pounced on this opportunity to relay what she had done. I shared how wonderful it was to see a student care so much about her work that she was willing to start over, even though that meant she would need additional time. She didn't care about finishing quickly or being done; instead, she wanted to design something that met her high personal standards and would make her proud. Nadia was excited to experience a turn in the spotlight for her dedication. Her decision to start again just might have inspired one or more of her classmates to make a similar choice in the future.

Encouraging specific behaviors at the outset of an academic activity and recognizing them afterward are both examples of capitalizing on "learnable moments." We are probably all familiar with the expression *teachable moments*. Several years ago, physical educator extraordinaire and friend Wendy Jones coined the phrase *learnable moments* to emphasize the fact it's not about what teachers are teaching; what matters is what children are learning. Capitalizing on learnable moments means that we, as teachers, take advantage of the opportunities that present themselves in the classroom to reinforce what we are all about. In some cases, we can be proactive and plan these opportunities, such as when we encourage students to employ their newly minted compliments prior to a cooperative learning activity. At other times, we keep a close eye on our students and respond to what we observe.

Of course, some of the behavior we see in children will be positive, often exemplary. Other conduct will not be so positive. We need to be on the lookout for both. When we observe kids demonstrating kindness, respect, enthusiasm, and other critical traits, we call attention to those words and actions and celebrate them! With negative behavior, our focus is different. During those times when students are not acting in ways that exemplify the type of culture we are striving to build, we call attention to it and hold the group accountable. Holding children accountable for their actions isn't fun and, in all likelihood, not an aspect of the job that drew us into teaching. It is, however, indispensable. Children need to know what is acceptable and what isn't. It is during these moments when significant culture building occurs. One of the reasons the first few weeks of a new school year tend to be so draining is that we always need to be alert and ready to establish and reinforce boundaries. The more consistent we are in our follow-up, the better our students will perform. The time we invest in the initial weeks of school will pay enormous dividends later in the year. Though we will likely be following up throughout the school year with messages regarding our culture, this review and reinforcement will be far smoother and easier once a strong foundation is built.

I conclude this chapter by describing the Quote of the Day, an aspect of my morning routine I mentioned in the previous chapter and one of the two most effective forms (along with our weekly class mission statement discussions) of long-term follow-up we have available to us in the classroom.

For over 25 years, discussing the Quote of the Day has been one of the most enjoyable and fulfilling parts of my job. Even though it's called the Quote of the Day, my students and I typically hold these talks two to three times a week. The exercise starts when I present the day's quote on the board. These sayings come from a variety of sources and relate to and reinforce important aspects of our culture, such as our Habits of Character, quality, achievement, and health and wellness.

After a volunteer reads the quote aloud, I give everyone a few moments of "quiet think time" to consider its meaning and relevance. Next, we do a pair-share to maximize participation in the activity, and then I call on several students to share their thoughts with the group. Sometimes I select volunteers; other times, to ensure that we are hearing from a wide variety of voices, I choose a popsicle stick from the cup I keep in the front of the room. Each child's name is printed on a different stick. I conclude the activity by offering my own thoughts.

In these whole-class discussions, students may choose to identify the habit or larger idea the quote addresses, give their interpretations of the quote's meaning, or share examples demonstrating how the quote applies to their daily lives. It is important to emphasize that there are no right or wrong answers.

Though the conversations take only a few minutes, the exercise is a valuable one because it provides me with natural opportunities to review critical aspects of our culture, encourages kids to think deeply, reinforces the important purposes we are serving by attending school, features an uplifting tone that appeals to the best in people, and enables the group to start the day on a positive note. Further payoffs to consistent use of this activity include better student behavior, stronger work habits and social skills, improved attitudes towards school, greater enthusiasm for and increased dedication to learning, more connections made between school and students' present and future lives, and enhanced vocabulary development.

One aspect of these discussions that I have come to appreciate more and more over the years is what an incredible chance this exercise affords me to share inspirational stories and examples that resonate with the kids and make a deep impact on them. Some of these anecdotes come from my own life experience, while others feature people they may know and admire.

Perhaps my favorite quote to discuss comes from Harry F. Banks. It reads: "For success, attitude is equally as important as ability." After the kids share their ideas during our whole-class conversation, I love to tell the story of a middle schooler named Mike who tried out for a baseball team I coached many years ago. Eighteen kids participated in the tryouts, but my assistant and I could keep only 14 due to the capacity of the bus we drove to away games. During the tryout, the kids displayed their hitting, throwing, and other baseball skills, but it was something else that earned the star of my story his place on the team.

In batting practice, Mike was playing left field as all the kids took their turn to hit. After one play, the ball accidentally got past the first baseman and headed down the right field line. The right fielder should have been the one to reach the ball first and toss it back to the pitcher, but he wasn't. Instead, I saw a blur sprinting from his spot in left field across the diamond to retrieve the ball. It was Mike. I draw a picture of the field on the board as I tell this story and make a big deal about the impression Mike made on the coaching staff with his effort.

The player who was farthest from the ball was the first one to make the play—not because of speed or ability, but out of pure desire and hustle. Based on current skill level alone, Mike likely would not have made the team that year. It was his determination and "want to" that made the difference, and Mike ended up being an important contributor to the group.

Kids love stories like these. Not only do they humanize us, but also they convey important life lessons that children find relevant and interesting. The world around us is full of wonderful examples of inspiration, and when we make a consistent effort to find and share them, we add tremendous value to our students' lives. With our busy academic schedules, time to share inspirational stories can be difficult to find. "Quote of the Day" discussions offer the perfect forum for this endeavor, one that we can build into our morning routine two to three times a week.

My belief in the effectiveness of this activity to bring out the best in children, develop lasting habits, and help establish an enthusiastic, productive, team-oriented classroom culture led me to write the book *Changing Kids' Lives One Quote at a Time* so that teachers everywhere could enjoy these same benefits. This resource features 121 inspirational sayings that relate to the same ideas mentioned previously—character, quality, success, and health and wellness. From beginning to end, the quotes spiral through these topics to empower children with multiple opportunities to think about and discuss each one. Each page of the book contains an inspirational quote and a corresponding set of "talking points" that teachers and parents can choose to use for reference when discussing the quotes with children.

Summary of Culture-Building Steps

Step 1: Determine the Kind of Culture We Want
Step 2: Modeling
Step 3: Teach Habits and Traits Explicitly
Step 4: Create Visual Reference Points
Step 5: Follow Up in Both the Short Term and the Long Term

Reference List

Covey, S. (1989). *The Seven Habits of Highly Effective People*. New York: Fireside.
Covey, S. (1994). *First Things First*. New York: Fireside.
Gibbs, J. (2001). *Tribes: A New Way of Learning and Being Together*. Cloverdale, CA: Center Source Systems.
Kraus, R. (1999). *Leo the Late Bloomer*. New York: HarperCollins.
Nash, R. (2013). *The Active Classroom*. Thousand Oaks, CA: Corwin Press.
Reifman, S. (2008). *Eight Essentials for Empowered Teaching & Learning, K-8*. Thousand Oaks, CA: Corwin Press.
Reifman, S. (2011). *Changing Kids' Lives One Quote at a Time*. Author.
Reifman, S. (2016). *15 1/2 Ways to Personalize Learning*. Author.

3
Connection

After my first year of teaching, two colleagues invited me to join them in San Luis Obispo, California (about three hours from where I live), for a week-long physical education conference. At that time, PE was one of the curricular areas I was expected to teach. Because I had grown up as an athlete, I initially thought teaching PE would be a piece of cake. Boy, was I wrong! Each day of my rookie year offered a powerful reminder of how utterly unprepared I was to provide quality PE instruction to my first graders. I recognized the sizable void in my curriculum and enthusiastically accepted their offer. I returned to SLO the following summer and the summer after that. Even when I switched schools and my teaching responsibilities no longer included physical education, I kept going back. In the summer of 2023, the Elementary Physical Education Workshop (EPEW) celebrated its 50th anniversary, its second year in our new home at Cal Poly Pomona. I attended for the 29th consecutive year and will continue to return for the rest of my life.

Attending EPEW has been, by far, the most valuable professional development experience of my career. At first glance, the conference may simply appear to be a work function. In reality, it is so much more than that. EPEW is about making connections. All types of connections. To the fellow participants, to the presenters, to the committee, to the volunteers, to the content, to our profession, and to our best selves. This book focuses on reaching and teaching the whole child. EPEW reaches and teaches the whole educator. It is easy to read the workshop slogan, "Come to Learn, Leave as Family," and think it's merely a clever phrase someone in the group created, but it's not. It is true. Each year, it seems to become truer.

At EPEW, connections come first. The connections begin as soon as you walk in the door to register. Everyone claps and cheers and celebrates your arrival as if you're a rock star. Participants build more connections during the sessions when we partner up for group activities, play together, and learn together. We stay in the same dorms, eat together, and spend our free time together. One of the most powerful expressions of EPEW's culture of connections occurs at mealtimes, when veteran workshoppers look out for first-timers traveling solo and invite them to sit at their tables or ride in their cars to nearby restaurants and ice cream pilgrimages that now seem to be happening on a nightly basis. This amazing inclusiveness leads to lasting friendships. I feel blessed to have met some of my closest friends at this workshop.

Building Connections in the Classroom

As teachers, we want a similar feeling of "connectedness" and inclusion to permeate our classrooms. Relationship building is an integral part of culture building and another high priority at the beginning of each school year. We need to be intentional in our efforts during this time to establish caring, trusting relationships with our students and encourage them to form strong connections with one another. I strive to build these connections right away. When I introduce myself on the opening morning of the school year, I tell the group how long I have been teaching, share how excited I am to begin what I know will be an incredible year, and then make two promises.

One relates to the fact that I am likely the first male teacher the children have had, and I happen to be pretty tall. As a result, many kids are a bit nervous. To put everyone at ease, I promise I will not raise my voice to them all year. Interestingly, several kids go home and relay that message to their parents, who later inform me how much they and their children appreciated those words. I have kept that promise for nearly 30 years—with one lone, intentional exception that I will describe in a later chapter.

I then let my students know that as soon as they walk through the classroom door, they immediately become 30 (or whatever our class size is that year) of the most important people in my life. Because their happiness and success mean so much to me, I promise to do everything in my power to support them, help everyone "level up" (as kids these days like to say), and make the most of their amazing potential. Sometimes, I explain, that means offering encouragement and opening their eyes to new goals and possibilities; other times, it may mean having difficult conversations and sharing my belief that they need to try harder, expect more from themselves, or take their learning more seriously. No matter what, though, I will always look out for their best interests and have their back. I share this same message at Back-to-School Night with their parents.

There's a well-known saying in the education world that students don't care how much their teachers know until they know how much their teachers care. In other words, kids need to feel connected to their teachers before they will feel comfortable learning from us and with us. They need to view us as caring, competent, and credible. (In Chapter 6, I describe how credibility becomes an especially significant leadership asset when we commit to supervising our classrooms without using extrinsic rewards.) In short, the connections have to come first. The good news is that our efforts to build and strengthen relationships with each of our students at the beginning of the school year will demonstrate how much we care and, in turn, gain our students' trust.

A huge part of forming bonds with children involves humanizing ourselves. To build caring connections in the classroom, we want to know our students well, we want them to know one another well, and we want them to know *us* well. Sometimes children don't see teachers as real people. They may not realize that we have hopes and fears, hobbies and interests, and strengths and weaknesses, just like everyone else does. For example, I live a few blocks from my school and often run into students and their families at the supermarket. Many kids are shocked to see me there. Their expressions seem to say, "Wait a minute? You eat food? You don't live at the school? No way!" To enable children to view us as human beings, we can share personal stories and experiences, show pictures of our families and pets, and bring in interesting artifacts from our lives, such as medals from a local running event or our pickleball paddles.

The best stories tend to be ones that connect to important aspects of our class culture or other ideals we hold dear. If, for example, we ran our first marathon the previous weekend, felt serious pain, and needed to summon all our grit to make it to the finish line, that's an incredible story for the kids to hear. What a special opportunity for students to get to know us on a deep, human level while also receiving reinforcement about a crucial trait. If you choose to have a weekly student leader (see Chapter 10) and have the kids bring pictures and certificates from home, take a turn in this role as well. One additional note: Over the years, I have seen teachers refer to themselves in the third person when speaking with children. I strongly caution against doing that. It serves to objectify us, not personalize us. We need to speak about ourselves in the first person.

The time and effort we invest in relationship building with our students will pay big dividends both during the months we are together in the classroom and in the years, perhaps even decades, that follow. In fact, many of the most fulfilling and satisfying moments of my career have come when I had the opportunity to reconnect with former students once they reached higher levels of schooling or graduated into adulthood. Bumping into former students at restaurants, the gym, or on a walk and seeing how well they are doing brings a special joy. When these individuals thank us for the role we played in their development and tell us that we somehow look even younger than we did back in the day, it greatly enhances these moments. I remember 6-year-old Chris, a student from my very first class who claimed to have magical powers, finding me on Twitter years later, sharing the news that he was about to begin law school, and thanking me for inspiring him. More recently, I was standing outside a Japanese restaurant, waiting for a table, and heard the host call out a name that I sensed belonged to a former student. Sure enough, it was her. That third grader who didn't seem to enjoy science was now a 25-year-old engineer. Finally, our district began a tradition a few years back in which high school seniors return to their elementary campuses in cap and gown the week of their graduation and march through the halls to the cheers of all the children. I always invite my former students inside to meet my current ones, announce their plans for the following year, and share a favorite memory or two from the class. These occasions are unique to the teaching profession, and they are moments to be cherished.

Beginning-of-the-Year Activities

This section contains several activities we can use during the first two weeks of school to foster the development of strong, caring classroom connections. Please note that many of the culture-building activities in the previous chapter also offer relationship-building benefits (e.g., Human Health Hunt), while the ones in this section powerfully affect culture. The two entities are very much intertwined. To make it easier for you to implement the ideas presented in Chapters 2 and 3, I provide a complete list of beginning-of-the-year activities in the Resources section.

High Fives

The first step in any relationship involves learning another person's name and pronouncing it correctly. Saying a person's name correctly doesn't just facilitate friendly communication; it's a major respect issue. The "High Fives" activity offers a quick, simple way for students to learn one another's names and build a spirit of friendship and positivity at the same time, especially if you play upbeat music in the background. I schedule this activity a couple of times, with the first round occurring on the opening day of school. Once the music begins, the children walk through the room, "high-fiving" their classmates. Each time the students give a high five, they smile, look the other person in the eye, and tell the other person their name. The goal is to high-five every other person in the room, teachers included. The energy and volume level tend to rise with all this high-fiving, and I try to be strategic with the timing of this activity. I like to schedule it right before recess or lunch, so that I don't need to settle the group back down and transition directly into another activity. I recommend doing a second round the following day or two when most of the kids have likely learned most of their classmates' names. This time around, while high fiving a classmates, the children say *the other person's* name. In the event of an interaction in which one or both kids don't know the other's name, each child should say their own name. Feel free to repeat this activity whenever you find yourself with a few spare minutes, want to make the atmosphere more festive, or wish to provide more opportunities for the children to learn names.

Play-Doh Activity (Part 2)
Another excellent opportunity to help students learn their classmates' names can be built into the Play-Doh activity described in the previous chapter. I mentioned that after everyone has completed their creations, I walk around to ask each child to describe what they made and snap a photo. Every time I visit five or so desks, I return to the first child, stand behind their chair, and hold my hand above their head (like a halo). The rest of the class says the child's name in unison and does the same for each child I move behind. We repeat this routine for every group of five. This additional practice adds only a couple of minutes to the activity and especially benefits those students who haven't yet learned many names. Because we are saying each name in unison, nobody feels as if they are being put on the spot. There's safety in numbers. If you are feeling bold, conclude the activity by returning to the first sharer and go all the way around the room. Challenge the kids to see how many names they can remember.

Passion Survey (Part 2)
A second culture-building activity from the previous chapter that also facilitates connection-building is the Passion Survey. As I described, having the kids complete the survey and then charting the results helps everyone make curricular choices and incorporate their favorite interests and hobbies into their schoolwork. An additional benefit arrives once we post the chart showing everyone's selections in a visible spot in the room. Children love looking at these results and noticing their classmates' passions. It produces a tremendous amount of group bonding and team building. Perhaps the best part is that many friendships form or strengthen because of the shared interests that children identify. Sometimes kids have been in the same class for many years and are only now learning about their shared love of certain topics or activities. After looking at the chart, many children have even scheduled after-school playdates to pursue their common passions. This type of bonding is

particularly valuable for children who are new to the school or who, in the past, have had difficulty forming friendships. Taken together, the benefits of the Passion Survey have a tremendous effect on the culture and the connections I try to foster at the beginning of each school year. Thinking about the topics we love the most, making new friends, and demonstrating enthusiasm and excitement about our learning brings out the best in everyone and helps us get our year off to a great start.

Cooperative Handshake
When I arrived at my first EPEW conference in the summer of 1995, I expected to learn more about the sports and playground games I grew up with. I quickly discovered, however, that the workshop's philosophy de-emphasizes large group competitive games in which kids are gradually eliminated or that create situations in which a small number of students are moving while everyone else stands around and watches. Instead, and much to my delight, the presenters shared activities that invite all children to participate meaningfully, emphasize cooperation, and encourage personal bests. Many sessions focused on traditional sports, yet the offerings also included rainy day activities, team building ideas, health and wellness sessions, and a variety of other topics that enabled me to learn a ton of useful information I could incorporate into my classroom. That's why my principals still encouraged me to attend the conference after my job responsibilities no longer called for me to teach PE.

Because they have such a powerful effect on classroom culture and connections, I find the team-building activities particularly valuable. The following two examples provide students with supercool bonding opportunities during the initial weeks of school. According to PE teacher Melanie Champion, the "Cooperative Handshake" activity builds listening skills, challenges short-term memory, and improves cooperation. The kids begin by finding a partner and starting on opposite sides of any indoor or outdoor space. I find that a distance of approximately 20 ft works best. Kids love it when their teachers take activities outside, but supervision can be a bit of a challenge, and it's often difficult for the kids to hear us. Just something to keep in mind. If you have an odd number of students (which, I have learned, is different from having a number of odd students), form a trio.

Begin by calling out the first command, such as a left-handed fist bump. The partners walk toward each other and perform the task before returning to their starting positions. We then announce the second command, such as a right-handed fist bump. The partners again walk toward each other, perform the left-handed fist bump, and then add the right-handed fist bump. For the remaining commands, I suggest proceeding with a series of "left, then right" moves. It's easier for the kids (and us) to remember the sequence that way.

(I also keep an index card listing the sequence in my pocket in case I forget.) In an eight-move sequence, for example, we might want to try "left fist bump, right fist bump, touch left elbows, touch right elbows, touch left toes, touch right toes, touch left shoulder, touch right shoulder." Add moves to the sequence until you reach a number that is appropriate for your students. Other potential moves include "high tens" and "low tens." Regardless of age, though, I recommend having the kids determine the last two moves. That's where creativity and bonding soar. So for the preceding eight-part sequence, prior to the ninth and tenth move, I would call out, "You choose!" Once you proceed through each move individually, challenge the pairs to go through the sequence on their own one or more times. Please note that this activity allows each child to bond with one other child. If you conduct a second round or come back another day, be sure to switch partners so the kids have a chance to experience this level of bonding with new people.

Meet Me in the Middle

A second EPEW-inspired team builder that produces substantial bonding and numerous smiles is known as "Meet Me in the Middle." Either indoors or out, the kids form a large circle with us in the middle. Begin by calling out a preference or "favorite" that will likely be true for some but not all your students. Examples include: "Meet me in the middle if your favorite color is orange," "Meet me in the middle if you play basketball," or "Meet me in the middle if your favorite ice cream flavor is chocolate." Each time you announce an idea, the students who "fit" that idea walk to the middle of the circle and high-five one another before returning to their spots. Try to include a wide variety of ideas so that every student has a chance to visit the middle multiple times. Be mindful, though, about whether an idea you say may have the unintended consequence of making one or more kids feel excluded. For example, we wouldn't want to say, "Meet me in the middle if you are wearing an Apple Watch" or "Meet me in the middle if you have traveled to a different continent," due to the high cost of those purchases. At the end, it's fun to change things up and call out an idea that is true for everyone, such as "Meet me in the middle if you breathe air." The kids get a kick out of that.

Roller Coaster

Some of the most memorable bonding moments occur when children have the chance to interact on a one-on-one basis to complete an engaging task, such as when they are partners in the "Cooperative Handshake" activity. Meaningful bonding also happens when students participate in a shared experience in a whole-class setting. Read-alouds offer some of the best examples of this phenomenon. *Roller Coaster* by Marla Frazee (2003) affords students the opportunity to take read-aloud to the next level. The story transports children to a day at the amusement park, where they see a group of people wait in line for their turn, board the roller coaster, experience a thrilling ride, and react to the trip in a variety of ways.

At the end of the first day of school, I inform the children that they did such a great job, I have a special treat for them. That's when I unveil this book and read the story aloud. "But wait," I announce, "there's more! We're not just going to read about a roller coaster; we'll be going on a class roller-coaster ride too!" Immediately, many kids look at me skeptically. (By the way, it won't be the last time that happens.) Perhaps they react that way because it's 2:57, and school ends at 3 p.m. I then ask everyone to stand to prepare for our ride. First, we insert our invisible seat belts into the invisible buckles. Next, we lean back to simulate the ascent to the top, accompanying our progress with that mechanical clicking noise roller coasters are known for. At the highest point, we pause dramatically before raising our arms in the air and yelling, "Whee!" on the descent. We'll repeat that sequence a couple more times before catching our breath at the conclusion of the journey. Later that night, when parents ask their children what they did on the first day of school, the kids can reply, "Oh, nothing much. We just went on a roller-coaster ride."

Special Object Sharing

I send home a note on the first day of school asking the children to bring a special object to share with the class the next day. The object needs to be small, nonliving, and placed in a bag with the child's name on the outside. No pets or Emmy Awards allowed. (I have had students bring both. I do teach in the Los Angeles area, after all.) Children of all elementary ages love this activity. On the afternoon of the second day, the kids sit in a circle with all the bags clustered in the center. That way, nobody is tempted to play with their object when other children are sharing theirs. As we go around the circle, each child has a minute or so to present the object, tell us what it is, and explain why they brought it. I bring an object too. We all learn a great deal about one another. Like the Passion Survey, Special Object Sharing offers a terrific way for children to discover common interests. There is also a multicultural dimension to this activity, because many times kids will bring objects related to their family or cultural background. About a month into the school year, I launch our weekly student leader role, giving each child another chance to share—this time, pictures they bring from home of family, friends, and events. (Pets and Emmy Awards are allowed in the pictures.) I mention another aspect of the student leader role later in this chapter and provide a complete description in Chapter 11.

Appointment Clocks

Several years back, during the first couple of weeks of the new year, the mother of one of my fourth graders shared with me that her daughter experienced significant difficulty making friends and didn't have a close companion at school. The mom hoped the situation would change in our class. As soon as I heard this, I remembered that the kids would soon be filling out their "Appointment Clocks," and I was confident that this classroom feature would help the child meet the friends she was seeking because it lays the groundwork for multiple, substantial, ongoing opportunities for children to work together and get to know one another on a deeper level.

An Appointment Clock is an organizational tool we can use in situations in which students will be working in pairs. Appointment Clocks save valuable class time, empower kids to make meaningful choices, ensure that students have the opportunity to collaborate with a variety of classmates, and facilitate smooth transitions.

Here's how Appointment Clocks work: Imagine you are planning a class activity and want the kids to work in pairs. Once you have finished explaining the directions and are ready for the kids to begin the activity, you ask everyone to find a partner and get started. Though this request may seem simple enough, many students will struggle. Some may not feel comfortable approaching a classmate, others may not be able to decide how to choose one friend over another, and still others may select the same friend every time you schedule cooperative learning. The potential exists for wasted time, stress, hurt feelings, a loss of focus from the task at hand, and, perhaps, total chaos.

We can avoid these problems by employing Appointment Clocks. This tool is simply a piece of paper with an analog clock printed on it and lines extending out from each hour. Though there are 12 hours on the clock, I have my students use only six at the start of the year (from 1:00 to 6:00).

Before asking the kids to fill out their clocks, I explain that everyone should use these sheets to record the names of six different people they would like to have as partners in the coming months. I emphasize the importance of choosing people with whom they will get along and be able to focus. It's perfectly fine, I add, if your best friend is not on your clock if the two of you believe you will be too distracted to concentrate. I have found that having six partners on the clock works well for middle- and upper-grade students because it ensures variety while still providing the opportunity to work with close friends frequently. If you teach a primary grade, I would suggest having a smaller number of partners and introducing Appointment Clocks more slowly and gradually.

It usually takes about 15–20 minutes for the children to walk around and find their six partners. The kids take this seriously, and many share that they feel like adults since they have a chance to schedule appointments the way grown-ups do. Once almost all the kids have completed this task, I call everyone back together to check for accuracy. When I say "1:00," all the kids stand shoulder-to-shoulder with their 1:00 partners. If some kids accidentally wrote a name in the wrong space or if a few do not yet have a 1:00 partner, we can make the required adjustments at this time. I proceed through all six hours of the clock until everything is accurately recorded. If necessary, some students may work with the same classmate for more than 1 hour on the clock, and if your class has an odd number of students, each hour of the clock will contain a trio.

With our clocks complete, organizing cooperative learning is much easier. I attach a 1–6 spinner to the top of the whiteboard. For our first pair activity I point the spinner to the 1 and have the kids join forces with their 1:00 partners. Next time around, I move the spinner to the 2 and ask everyone to work with their 2:00 partners. The spinner enables me to keep track of where we are in the sequence so that students work with all their partners the same number of times. It also keeps me from having to remember our spot in the sequence. Students will quickly memorize their six partners. Until they do, I have them write their "clock partners" on a small sheet they then tape to the top right corner of their desks for easy reference.

Now, for example, whenever I want students to work in pairs, I simply say, "You will participate in this activity with your 4:00 partner." Our transition into the activity is a smooth one, and the kids are happy because they have the chance to partner with someone that they, themselves, chose. I have found that there's a certain psychological comfort in this fact. Children are more invested in the task because they were the ones who chose their six partners. Later in the year, I often have students complete the remaining hours on the clock so they have the opportunity to work with an even wider variety of classmates. With these six new spaces, I'll allow them to repeat one or two of their original six partners.

Children love collaborating with their partners, and over the years, many have entered the classroom in the morning asking if we were going to use our Appointment Clocks that day. Typically, my students will work in pairs once or twice per day. Sometimes I will have them team up with their desk partners, but more frequently, they will join their clock partners, giving everyone regular opportunities to build meaningful connections. Well-known author Howard Gardner (1993) notes that cooperation has been "shown to have a positive effect on students' social and psychological well-being, which eventually leads to higher academic achievement." Because cooperative learning satisfies our need for belonging, usually makes activities more enjoyable, and increases the likelihood of success (two heads are better than one), William Glasser, in *The Quality School*, argues that cooperative learning should be the default mode of learning in our classrooms and that children should work alone only when the need arises. With many children experiencing considerable loneliness inside and outside of school, the time they spend with their partners is particularly valuable because it might be the only meaningful chance they have to experience a positive connection with another person and, in some cases, be the best part of their day. For the student I mentioned earlier in this section, Appointment Clocks enabled her to form six new positive connections and make a couple new friends.

Resource Board

In Chapter 2, I describe how, as part of my initial culture-building efforts, I attempt to raise student awareness of the profound daily impact team members can have on one another and encourage everyone to join me in creating a caring, positive environment in which we make those around us feel like superstars. I introduce this topic by pointing out how the physical layout of our classroom facilitates this kind of mutual impact.

Many adults, I say, perform their jobs in something called a cubicle or sit in some other type of private, independent workspace, either in an office or at home. They may, of course, attend meetings and interact with other adults for parts of the day, but a majority of their time is spent alone. In a classroom, however, our experience is completely different. We typically sit in close proximity to multiple classmates and interact with a lot of people throughout the day. While becoming increasingly more independent as a learner is an important goal, our environment also enables us to become more interdependent.

Sometimes, I continue, the effect we have on our classmates will come from our kindness. Complimenting our partner during a pair activity, sharing our eraser with a neighbor, or allowing someone to stand in front of us in line are just some of the gestures that will make a classmate's day brighter. In fact, these kind deeds may well be the first thing a child shares later that evening when a family member asks how school was that day.

My favorite example of this battery-charging behavior occurred a week into my teaching career in a first-grade classroom. It's important to note at this point that when I walked into the room a few days earlier, I hadn't been in a first-grade classroom since I was in first grade! I had done my student teaching in third- and fifth-grade classrooms. At that time, I thought I might want to become a principal one day and reasoned that having experience in multiple elementary grade levels would be beneficial. (By the way, that desire set sail a long time ago and hasn't turned back toward the harbor.)

On the morning in question, the first student to arrive was Kevin. I had placed a phonics worksheet on the kids' desks and was trying to establish the routine of having everyone put their belongings in the closet right when they enter the room, head directly to their desks, and begin whatever activity was waiting for them. Kevin led the way ably, and over the next couple of minutes, more students followed. I was very much into savoring small victories at this time and was feeling pretty good about myself. Soon, almost every child who had entered the room performed the routine beautifully and was busy circling pictures whose initial sound matched the large letter on the sheet. The one exception—Kevin.

How could the first child in the room now be the only one out of his seat? I wondered. And probably more importantly, where did he go? A moment later, I saw Kevin by the front door. He was holding it open for another student named Michelle, who had cerebral palsy and walked with some difficulty. The next thing I knew, Kevin took Michelle by the hand, walked her to the closet to hang up her backpack, led her to her desk, pushed in her chair, and went back to his table to finish his phonics sheet. To this day, it remains the greatest thing I have ever seen in a classroom. I share this story with every new group of students I have.

In addition to brightening our classmates' day with kindness, we can also powerfully impact their academic learning with our knowledge, skills, and strategies. To promote this type of information sharing, I tell the class at the beginning of each year that the most important things they learn in school will probably not come from me or a book or a website. Rather, they will come from a classmate. And while we all have much to learn, we also possess vast amounts of knowledge that we can contribute to the group. We are all resources. Valuable resources. These words come as a surprise to many children, who think they will learn most of their information directly from the teacher. After I make this declaration, I need to support it with action.

The most effective way to encourage children to value the knowledge, skills, and strategies that they and their classmates bring with them to school is to set aside a section of wall space for a Resource Board. This board simply lists subjects, topics, and skills and shows which children believe they possess strength in those areas. Begin by displaying a small number of categories, either subject areas, such as reading and writing, or specific skill sets within those categories, such as decoding and editing. Then, one category at a time, ask the kids to raise their hands if they feel confident about their current capabilities with those skills and would be willing to help others.

Once you have "staffed" these areas, repeat this process with additional categories that the children themselves suggest. Seeking student input increases their ownership and buy-in. It also opens the door to tons of interesting possibilities, especially ones related to the Passion Survey that the kids can employ in class. Examples might include coding, drawing, and helping others solve problems.

It's important to ensure that each child is represented at least once on the Resource Board. When seeking volunteers for each category, we want to celebrate, loudly and enthusiastically, the fact that everyone in the room absolutely has skills that can benefit everyone else. Some kids may be hesitant to add their names to the board and may need some private encouragement after this activity in order to feel comfortable offering their skills. If it makes these children feel better, we can always give them a chance to add their name at a later date, though we will be offering further encouragement in the meantime. Other kids will not hesitate for a second and raise their hands for every category. Because we don't want to squelch their enthusiasm or self-esteem, we may choose to announce beforehand a three-category maximum for each person, or another number you consider reasonable. If new category ideas arise organically weeks or months later, we can always include them on the board.

Once complete, the Resource Board becomes an important classroom reference point. Any child who experiences difficulty or has a question during independent work time or a cooperative learning activity can check the board, find an "expert" in that subject or skill area, and approach that person for assistance. It's the ultimate win–win scenario. The child seeking support receives the help they need, while the consultant receives a major self-esteem and confidence boost and experiences the satisfaction that comes from knowing they made a difference in another student's learning.

Sometimes a single student can save the group's collective bacon. During a class coding project about five years, practically every child in the room became stuck at the same point. I would have loved to step in, but there was one problem. I didn't know very much about coding. Fortunately, Boyan had an international following on Scratch, a popular free coding site, and patiently showed everyone what to do, demonstrating a willingness to give up some of his own coding time for the greater good. Even better, a few kids he assisted quickly grasped how to resolve this issue and, in turn, walked around the room, helping others. It was beautiful.

I think it is healthy for teachers to acknowledge that in some areas there will be kids who know more than we do, especially when technology is involved. Rather than attempt to hide this fact, we should celebrate it. Doing so reinforces the notion that we are all teachers and all learners. We are all in this together, and we can serve as resources for one another, view one another as resources, and positively impact everyone's classroom experience. Freely and eagerly seeking and offering support to anybody who needs it creates and strengthens connections among our students.

Another way to promote and reinforce the idea that all of us are important classroom resources is to employ the well-known "ask 3 before me" strategy. During independent work time, any child needing support must ask three nearby classmates for help before approaching the teacher. This practice enables us to feed two birds from the same feeder. (From now on, let's use this expression with children so they never hear about killing birds with stones.) First, the kids become increasingly comfortable seeking and offering assistance and viewing one another as resources. Second, in a class with a large number of students, getting around to every child who requires support can be difficult, often unrealistic. By encouraging students to be regular helpers, the "ask 3 before me" strategy enables us to lighten our load a bit and focus our attention on the children who need it the most.

Yearlong Rituals

In the previous chapter, I described how we want to follow up on our initial culture-building efforts throughout the year to keep important priorities alive and well in the hearts and minds of our students. I recommend a similar process as we seek to build connections with the kids and encourage them to connect with one another. Once we have planted the seeds for caring relationships to blossom, we can nurture these connections and promote the growth of new ones with consistent rituals that children very much enjoy. Because these rituals tend to be brief and occur at regularly scheduled times, we probably won't need to do additional planning to guarantee their inclusion in our classrooms.

The Morning Check-In

Once my students enter the room and store their belongings, we begin our morning routine with a variation of a team-building activity described by Jeanne Gibbs (2001) in her wonderful book *Tribes*. I was fortunate to discover the *Tribes* program prior to my first year of teaching, and I have started every day of my career with the following exercise. Even if we are heading to an off-campus field trip or school assembly that requires us to leave the room practically right after we come inside, we will always do this check-in first.

Using a 1–10 scale, each child checks in with the group by stating a number expressing how they are doing that day. A *10* means life couldn't be better. I'm happy, energetic, and ready to have a great day. On the other hand, a *1* means that a serious issue may be occurring. Perhaps I am sick, upset, or troubled by something at home. From their assigned circle spots on our class rug, the kids can pick any number between 1 and 10, fractions and decimals included, to share with the group. I ask everyone to sit in a circle so all the kids can make eye contact with one another. Students who do not wish to participate have the choice to pass. When I introduce this activity on the first day of school, I emphasize the importance of being honest with our numbers. Otherwise, kids will occasionally say a low number to seek attention or match their number to the one their best friend just said in order to have a bonding moment.

Going around the circle takes only a minute or two because the kids are just saying numbers; they aren't revealing the reasons behind their numbers, thus preserving everyone's right to privacy. I'm always on the lookout for low numbers so that, as the day unfolds, I can offer these students comfort and cheer to boost their spirits. I encourage the children to do the same. This activity builds a sense of inclusion and mutual caring; it also strengthens the bonds among team members.

As time permits, I recommend trying to find a minute or two before dismissal for a second trip around the circle. That way, we can determine whether there have been any changes from earlier in the day. Several years ago, Drew announced in the morning that she was a 2. At the end of the day, she proudly declared that she was a 10! Because low numbers tend to be uncommon, the others remembered her morning number and reacted with smiles to her 10. I asked if she would mind sharing the reason for the big jump. Drew said that a friend of hers across the rug noticed her earlier low number and made an effort to spend time with her during the day and cheer her up. I relay this anecdote annually on the first day when I introduce this ritual. Kids love filling this important "battery charger" role and appreciate working in a learning environment where others look after their well-being.

Statements of Recognition

Whenever you have a few free moments before the end of a class period, ask your students to sit in a circle and point out the special efforts of their classmates. The acknowledgments can focus on academic achievements, positive behavior, or gestures of friendship. Make sure the children mention both who they are recognizing and why they are recognizing that person. For instance, it is not enough for Alexis to say, "Henry." She would need to offer a more specific statement, such as, "I recognize Henry for working really hard on his math lately." The kids can even employ some of the compliment words and expressions they brainstormed. Also, encourage everyone to acknowledge as many different people as possible. That way, each child experiences the pride that comes from being recognized. If you notice that certain children do not receive recognition from classmates, make it a point to acknowledge them yourself. Every child must feel valued. On the other hand, if participants all seem to be recognizing the same child (it happens), establish that each student needs to receive one shoutout before anyone receives a second. (It's the classroom equivalent of the "Thanksgiving buffet" rule my family instituted.)

It's wonderful to see how kids light up when receiving a thoughtful recognition. We're really cooking with gas when those kind words come from a classmate a child recently met or doesn't yet know well. The expression on the recipient's face seems to say, "Wow! Really? I didn't think he even knew my name, and he said *that* to me. Awesome!" In no time at all, two children can go from being strangers to friends simply because of one positive statement. That recognition will likely be the first thing the child relays to their family later that evening.

Updates

During my teacher training program at UCLA, I enjoyed learning several engaging "sponge" activities that students could complete at their desks as they entered the room either first thing in the morning or after a break. "Updates" is currently my favorite sponge activity, but it's not something children do independently at their seats. Rather, updates are brief, whole-class conversations that occur right after lunch, when we are gathering on the rug to begin our next lesson, or after students pack up to go home at the end of the day, before read-aloud. When giving an update, kids may share anything meaningful that's happening in their lives outside of class. Popular topics include pets, athletic events, family visits, movies, and trips. I share updates as well. It's another excellent chance for us to humanize ourselves.

Providing team members with this opportunity is a wonderful way for all of us to learn more about one another and bond. At the beginning of the year, I caution everyone to avoid sharing information about private family business, parties, or outings to which everyone in the class may not have been invited, or anything else that may lead to hurt feelings or come across as bragging, such as getting expensive new shoes. We don't want anyone feeling left out. Because kids love giving and hearing updates, they tend to carry out their transitions and come to the rug quickly, affording us more time for the activity that follows. If you want to be even cooler in the eyes of your students, refer to this activity as "S'updates," so the kids can tell everyone what's up.

Morning Greeter

Earlier in this chapter, I mentioned how one child per week has the opportunity to serve as student leader. As part of the job, this individual carries out the responsibility of being our morning greeter. Once the bell rings to start our day and the kids head to class, the student leader stands outside the door and welcomes their classmates as they come inside. Specifically, the student leader looks everyone in the eye, smiles, and greets each person by name. Many children want to high-five each classmate, but I discourage this practice to reduce the spread of germs and, depending on which children you speak with, "cooties." Air high fives or thumbs-ups work just as well.

Learning how to look another person in the eye and offer a friendly greeting is an important life skill, and connecting with classmates in this manner, each morning for a full week, offers special bonding moments.

Five-Minute Chats

Each school day is so packed with activity there rarely seems time to stop and talk with students about the issues, challenges, and other happenings that inevitably arise. Basketball coaches are fortunate in this regard. They can rely on having several timeouts and a halftime break to interact with their players. As teachers, we must create these opportunities ourselves. Because all of us really need our recess and lunchtime to socialize, run around, and take a well-deserved break, I recommend protecting this time and carving out opportunities to talk with the kids when we are in class. Sometimes, we need to speak with the kids in a whole-group setting; other times, one-on-one. The next two ideas, Five-Minute Chats and the Friday Circle, are effective tools we can employ to create the regular communication opportunities we need to keep everyone moving in the right direction and stay connected.

A Five-Minute Chat is a one-on-one conversation we schedule during independent work time. I conduct my chats during silent reading. Ideally, the child and I will be able to focus our full attention on the matter at hand without interruptions, but that can never be guaranteed. Every team member has the ability to initiate a Five-Minute Chat. When I have something to talk about with a child, I call them over to my chair. Should a student wish to discuss a matter with me, they sign up for a chat on a sheet of paper I place in front of the room. (I try to avoid writing the names of students on the board, for any reason, to preserve privacy.) The children know that I may not be able to meet with them right away but usually don't have to wait long for an appointment.

Conduct a Five-Minute Chat to discuss the following:

- ◆ Academic progress
- ◆ Habits of Character or Habits of Mind
- ◆ Learning or behavioral strategies
- ◆ Individual pieces of student work
- ◆ Challenging academic content or interpersonal difficulties
- ◆ Assessment results
- ◆ Long-term projects
- ◆ Recent successes or accomplishments
- ◆ Any other private issue

Finding the time to communicate in this manner recognizes the intrinsic worth of each child and sends the message that we care about everyone and that our door is always open. Five-Minute Chats offer a private setting where the kids are able to speak freely, without worrying about what their classmates are going to say or think, and where we are able to get to know our students on a deeper level. Trust grows, bonds strengthen, and performance improves as a result of these chats.

Friday Circle
The Friday Circle is a weekly class meeting, conducted during the last hour of the school week, that facilitates consistent, positive communication. During this time, the kids and I sit in a circle so we can all see and hear one another easily. I like to hold these gatherings on Friday afternoons, for three reasons. First, concluding the week with a class meeting allows my students and me to review the previous week and look ahead to the next. Second, Friday afternoon is a strategic time for these meetings because the last hour of the day before the weekend is generally when kids have the greatest difficulty focusing on academic work. Third, ending with a team-building activity gives me the opportunity to wrap up the week in a positive fashion and send everyone home happy.

A full Friday Circle agenda consists of nine items. Proceeding through every item usually takes between 30 and 45 minutes. When our schedule doesn't allow us this much time, and usually it doesn't, we do what we can. Typically, my students and I will have approximately 15 minutes at the end of the day on Fridays, and we can complete three or four items. I try to do "Recognitions" and "Accomplishments" every week and rotate through the other items over time. Agenda items can also be completed individually on other days of the week as time allows. Each agenda item is listed in what follows along with a brief description. Taken together, these sections enable us to openly discuss class issues, solve problems, build confidence in the group, minimize drama, and reinforce the traits and habits we want to build into our culture.

> Recognitions: This section offers regular opportunities for the kids to share the Statements of Recognition described earlier in the chapter. These comments help the kids feel appreciated and valued and positively affect their intrinsic motivation and sense of connection to the group.
>
> Accomplishments: A time for everyone to share their most significant accomplishment of the week, with regard to their academic learning, Habits of Mind or Character, or any other whole-child priority. Celebrating achievements builds confidence, boosts motivation, and makes us feel more successful.
>
> Contributions: Students describe what they or a classmate did during the week to make the class a better place, such as donate supplies, help

clean the room, or assist a friend. Such a discussion highlights the importance of service.

Next Week: In this part of the meeting, the kids express what they hope to accomplish and/or contribute during the week ahead. Looking to the immediate future in this manner whets their appetite for what's to come and strengthens their commitment and ability to plan ahead.

Learning Connections: Students discuss something they learned during the week and explain how it relates to their everyday lives or how it may relate to their future lives. For example, Aline may say, "This week I learned about the human body, and that helps me because I want to be a doctor when I grow up." Thinking about these connections reinforces the purposes of classroom learning.

Numbers: As we do each morning, the kids go around the circle and say a number from 1 to 10 or pass. Building this activity into the Friday Circle agenda ensures that even if there isn't time to compare our morning and afternoon numbers any other day that week, there will be a chance to do so on Fridays.

Solutions: We openly and honestly discuss any problems we may be having and try to solve them together in a positive way. This part of the meeting enables us to continue the dialogue we began during our beginning-of-the-year training period. (More about this in Chapter 7.) We use this time to practice problem-solving strategies, share those that have proven to be successful, and talk about how to prevent similar problems from occurring in the future. The constructive tone that underlies these conversations helps me reinforce the point that the proper response to problems is not anger and blame but thoughtful action. By naming this item *Solutions* rather than *Problems*, we keep the focus on achieving a mutually satisfying outcome, not on blaming or complaining about things we don't like.

Suggestions: An opportunity for team members to suggest any ideas they believe will improve the performance, appearance, or morale of the class. Every individual has valuable ideas and should have the chance to express them to a teacher who's willing to listen. Implement as many suggestions as possible so the kids know you take their proposals seriously. Keep and post a running list of all the suggestions your kids offer so they take pride in the contributions they are making to the class.

Sharing: Once your students have participated in the Special Object Sharing activity on the second day of school, each child will have another chance to share items from home during their turn as student leader. Should you wish to provide additional sharing opportunities, make this time a Friday Circle agenda item.

Bonding With Challenging Students

Our efforts to create a friendly classroom culture and build meaningful connections with children at the beginning of each school year will usually enable us to bond fairly quickly with a vast majority of our students. There will be times, though, when we find ourselves experiencing difficulty bonding with some kids. When this happens, it's important not to take it personally, feel as if we have done something wrong, or put pressure on ourselves to force the issue. These situations require patience. One of the beauties of teaching is that there's always tomorrow. We can play the long game and aim to develop a connection gradually over time. Baby steps. The more time a given child spends in our care and the more they see that we consistently act in their best interests, the more they will come to trust and relate positively with us.

I recommend trying two strategies to increase the likelihood that strong teacher–student bonding will occur. First, make an effort to find something the two of you share in common. Sometimes, the Passion Survey will identify these commonalities for us. I once taught a child who was extremely quiet and shy. His face typically didn't show emotion, and I was having a difficult time connecting with him. When I found out he loved pro football, it was game on. I asked about his favorite players and teams, and those conversations helped us build rapport. Interestingly, what we share in common with another person doesn't have to be something we both like. I recently read that when two people discover something they both hate, that can lead to bonding too. It can be a food, song, radio ad—you name it. Keep an eye out for a time the child expresses a dislike, and perhaps you two will share that in common!

Second, try to find opportunities when you can spend additional one-on-one time with that child. The occasion doesn't have to be lengthy to bear fruit. If we see the child before school, we can ask them if they would like to come inside to sharpen pencils. If we are walking students to the cafeteria at lunchtime, we can stand next to the child along the way. If we are sitting at a school assembly in the auditorium, we can have the child next to us. We can initiate a conversation by telling a joke, sharing an observation, or asking a question. All these opportunities provide potential bonding moments. There's no way to know how we may ultimately connect with a child, so we keep making the effort in a variety of ways, no matter how long that effort takes.

Creating strong teacher–student connections takes on even greater importance when we consider the many conversations we will have throughout the year with children who experience significant behavioral difficulties. No matter how hard we try to remain positive and encouraging during these talks, some of them will be difficult. Hard conversations require a caring, trusting connection between the two participants if the interaction has any chance of producing a positive outcome. Without a strong relationship undergirding these conversations, children will be unlikely to truly listen to and value what we are saying. Consequently, their behavioral challenges will likely continue. Children will take our messages more seriously when they trust, respect, and feel a solid connection with the messenger and know that the messenger trusts, respects, and feels connected to them.

Other Important Connections

The primary focus of this chapter involves building caring, trusting connections with our students. There are, of course, many other members of our school community with whom it is important to build strong relationships. First and foremost, we have our fellow teachers. Connecting with our colleagues satisfies our need for belonging and friendship and makes coming to work more fun. The bonds we form with colleagues can last a lifetime. Be mindful of the first impression you make. We want to come across as professional—dedicated, humble, willing to learn, and focused on the best interests of children. We need to avoid gossiping, complaining, and giving off the impression that we already know everything there is to know about teaching and about children. (I may have learned that last lesson the hard way.) I encourage you to ask your colleagues questions, learn from their experiences, discuss challenging issues you might be encountering, and use them as sounding boards when planning projects or trying something new. Your school may assign you a mentor. If not, seek out your own. These educators don't need to teach at your grade level. At faculty meetings and professional development sessions, be on the lookout for those who may share your philosophy or whose practices you may want to emulate. Many new teachers report feeling lonely and isolated in the classroom. Investing the time and effort to approach and befriend your colleagues will prevent loneliness from occurring and add tremendous joy, satisfaction, and fulfillment to your teaching experience.

It is also important to form caring, trusting connections with our site administrators. Because our administrators supervise and evaluate our performance, however, the bonds we form with them will likely differ from those we form with our teaching colleagues. More professional, less personal. As busy as we are in the classroom, our site administrators are typically even busier, and we want to respect their time. If we request a time to speak with them, it should be about something truly important. We want to pick our spots and approach administrators when they are the only people who can help us. If a colleague or a member of the office staff can assist us with an issue, we should seek them out first.

In addition, I strongly recommend making the effort to build connections with the members of your school's staff. This group includes the office staff, librarians, nurses, cafeteria workers, custodians, instructional aides, and other personnel. If you teach in a large school, this roster may be quite large, and you may not see many of these people that often. Just do the best you can. When you pass these individuals in the hallway, smile and say hello, try to learn their names, treat them with respect, and ask about their role. Members of our school staff comprise another source of potential friendships that can bring joy and greatly enhance our daily experience at school.

The final group I would like to mention in this section is our students' parents. Interestingly, even though they are not present at school on a daily basis, I believe these adults exert the most powerful impact on our work in the classroom. Parents have tremendous influence over their children's overall performance and directly affect the quality of our day-to-day experience. We need to invest the time and effort to work closely with parents throughout the year to keep them informed and involved. Consistent parent involvement dramatically increases the likelihood that quality learning and positive behavior will occur. Parents play such a crucial role in their children's academic, physical, social, and moral development that we, as teachers, make a huge mistake if we view them as anything other than indispensable collaborators. It's not enough to keep parents pleased, appeased, or out of our hair. If we're committed to bringing the best out of our students, we need to build and maintain long-term relationships of loyalty, trust, and respect with their parents. When teachers build a true three-way partnership with parents and students, kids thrive.

Why Is Parent Involvement Such a High Priority?

The following points provide a strong rationale as to why teachers should make parent involvement a top priority:

1. Parents are their children's first and most important teachers. Although not all teachers are parents, all parents are teachers. As such, they have the greatest impact on a student's motivation to learn. Parents are usually eager to play a significant role in their children's education, but they often don't know how. By establishing caring relationships with parents, we can help them help their children.
2. Consistent communication between the home and the school enables parents to reinforce the skills, knowledge, and habits that we emphasize in class.

3. It's important that teachers are aware of students' strengths and weaknesses, likes and dislikes, areas of special sensitivity, and any factors at home that are affecting school performance. Parents are in the best position to provide this information.
4. Students act, behave, and perform differently when they know their parents and teachers communicate frequently.
5. Frequent communication earns parents' confidence, trust, and respect. With open lines of communication, it's unlikely that feelings of uncertainty, mistrust, and alienation will ever arise. The favorable impression we create makes problems easier to solve when they occur.
6. When teachers and parents communicate in a respectful manner, we model positive adult interactions for the kids. These occasions serve a prosocial function because many children, unfortunately, don't often have the opportunity to observe this type of relationship.
7. Parents can become our biggest supporters and most loyal allies. Should a colleague or supervisor ever doubt our methods or question our approach to teaching, these allies will be there to come to our defense.
8. Parents are often valuable classroom resources. The better we know parents, the more we will be aware of the various ways in which they can assist the class.
9. Forming trusting relationships with parents can reduce the feelings of isolation that so many teachers, especially newer ones, often experience.

Guiding Principles for Home–School Communication

The principles that follow set the tone for all communications with parents. Together, they constitute a comprehensive framework designed to make our interactions as positive and productive as possible.

Thinking Long-Term

Forming trusting relationships occurs over time; it is not a one-shot deal. Don't be discouraged if your early efforts to contact parents don't bring an immediate response. During my first year of teaching, I didn't meet a certain parent until February. After months of one-sided communication, I could easily have given up on him, but I didn't. Finally, he found me one afternoon on the playground and introduced himself. Because of his busy work schedule, he was unable to stop by sooner. He informed me that he had read everything I had been sending home and promised to become more involved. Leaving the door open allows parents to come in when they are ready.

Communicating Frequently

The more frequently we communicate with parents, the better. Parent communications come in two forms, standardized and individualized. "Standardized" means that every parent receives the same message. At a minimum, I send home one standardized communication, such as a newsletter, per week. Doing so establishes consistency and keeps parents informed about important class business. Individualized communications, on the other hand, are unique to each student and usually relate to issues of academic progress and behavior. Phone calls are one example of this form. While I hold myself to a set routine with standardized communications, I allow myself greater flexibility with individualized ones. I generally strive for one or two per month, depending on the time available and the needs of each child. You must decide how much time you are willing and able to devote to this aspect of your teaching. As a rule of thumb, start small and build from there. It's much better, for example, to begin the year sending newsletters home every month and then increasing the frequency later in the year than it is to begin with weekly bulletins and then lose steam. Any type of "backtracking" can diminish our credibility.

Creating a Sense of Inclusion

In my communications with parents, both written and oral, I try to create the feeling that we're all in this together. I welcome each family's participation by encouraging every parent to take an active role in class. I extend this invitation, though, fully understanding that many parents will be unable to devote time because of heavy work or family commitments. It's important, therefore, not to alienate parents by putting too much pressure on them to get involved.

Listening With Understanding and Empathy

Listening is one of the most important life skills a person can develop. Because of its significance, teachers spend a tremendous amount of time trying to help students improve in this area. With listening, we need to practice with parents what we preach to the kids. Listening, though, isn't easy. It takes patience, caring, and a genuine desire to understand what the other person says and means. When we are talking one-on-one with parents, listening is all the more difficult because the conversations generally take place right before school, when we have a great deal on our minds, or right after school, when we've often just about lost our minds. When parents take time out of their day to speak with us, however, it's usually for an important reason. We must do our best to listen intently and understand matters from their perspective so that we can effectively address their concerns.

Encouraging Cooperative Problem-Solving

When a problem arises, I work with parents to solve it. Working together as a team allows us to create solutions that benefit all parties involved. In his book *The Seven Habits of Highly Effective People*, author Stephen Covey calls this approach "win–win thinking." The emphasis is on producing mutually beneficial results, not on winning an argument or finding fault with one another. Placing blame serves no useful purpose. Fix the problem, not the blame.

Showing Appreciation

Parents work hard to raise their children. The sacrifices they make to feed, clothe, assist, and support their kids remain largely hidden from the view of teachers, but they are very real. Many parents spend so much time satisfying their children's needs that they rarely take time for themselves. Because of all the time and energy parents spend on behalf of their kids, make a concerted effort to thank them for any service they provide to the class. Express appreciation for contributions large and small.

Conveying a Sense of Optimism

Because each school year is full of possibility, use your communications to convey a sense of excitement and optimism. Tell parents, for example, how happy you are to have their child in your class and how much you are looking forward to a wonderful year together. Making this effort is especially valuable for students who have never before had successful school experiences. When their teachers communicate in an enthusiastic, upbeat tone, these kids will sense that this year may be different. They will know that they are in a new place with a new attitude, and they will feed off this optimism.

Being Proactive

Being proactive has two major benefits. First, it gives you the opportunity to package your ideas and articulate them in the best possible light. Acting first, you shape the conversation, saying your ideas in the way you want to say them, not in the way someone else has already characterized them before ever having the chance to hear from you. Being proactive increases your credibility, strengthens your voice, and reaffirms your position of leadership.

Second, being proactive is the best approach to problem prevention. Consider the following example. Imagine that a brand new shipment of expensive, state-of-the-art math manipulatives has just arrived at school. Because the school could only afford one set, the staff decided that each class would get the manipulatives for three weeks. When our turn comes, I lengthen the daily math period from 45 minutes to 2 hours so we can try all the hands-on activities shown in the accompanying teacher guidebook. To compensate for the extra time that we spend on math, I don't give any math homework for the next three weeks.

Immediately, parents become concerned. "Where's my child's math homework?" they ask. "Why did you stop assigning math homework?" they wonder. "Don't you know that my child will fall behind without math practice every night?" they insist.

Now, I have to react. The parents have already made up their minds. Based on the information they have received from their kids, they have concluded that I have stopped assigning math homework, and they don't understand why. I have dug myself a hole, out of which I must climb.

All this trouble could have been avoided had I been proactive. Before the first day of our three-week manipulative exploration, I could have sent home a newsletter explaining the situation. Then, the parents would have known in advance of the unique, short-term opportunity that we had to use these manipulatives and understood the value of these types of experiences. I could have told them that to take full advantage of this opportunity, I would be lengthening our daily math period, and that because of the extra time the kids spent on math in class, I would be decreasing the time they spend on math at home. I could have emphasized that this hiatus from math homework would last only three weeks and that the kids would not be at all disadvantaged because they were gaining valuable practice in class. Informing parents beforehand would have enabled me to accentuate the positive.

Experience has taught me that teachers' greatest difficulties with parents often arise from a lack of proactivity. When parents are not informed in advance about rules, units, grading policies, and the like, they have every reason to come back after the fact and say, "I didn't know." Once that happens, teachers are forced into a reactive, often defensive, position. The trouble is, no matter how effectively we later explain ourselves, the damage has already been done. Furthermore, by the time we have responded to one problem situation, the next crisis has occurred and needs to be addressed. A pattern soon begins. We find ourselves spending a tremendous amount of time putting out fires instead of using it to communicate proactively.

Building Goodwill

In his book *The Seven Habits of Highly Effective People*, Stephen Covey introduces the concept of an emotional bank account, a metaphor that can help teachers build and maintain strong relationships with parents. Unlike a traditional bank account, where people keep money, an emotional bank account is where we store feelings of trust and goodwill. Covey makes the point that each individual has an emotional bank account with every other person with whom they come into contact. With these friends and acquaintances, there are times when we add positive feelings to our accounts (deposits) and times when we take away some of these feelings (withdrawals).

There are several ways to make deposits in another person's emotional bank account. These include the following: giving compliments, sharing, doing favors, taking the time to talk, and being polite. Similarly, there are numerous ways of making withdrawals: arguing, blaming, lying, and showing disrespect. When a relationship between two people is strong and their emotional bank accounts contain a large reservoir of goodwill, then an occasional withdrawal won't cause a great deal of harm. When a relationship is weak, however, a single withdrawal may have a severe negative effect. Therefore, when dealing with parents, commit yourself to making frequent deposits so that your relationships are strong and the trust level is high.

How to Build Parent Connections Right From the Start

Kickoff Gesture

Prior to my second year, I came across an idea I just had to try. First, I obtained a class list of my first graders' names and phone numbers. With permission from my administrator, I called every family, introducing myself to the parents and telling them I was tentatively scheduled to be their child's teacher that year. I used the word "tentatively" to cover myself and the school in case any last-minute enrollment changes were made. Since I knew I'd be setting up the classroom during the week before school started, I invited each family to stop by to meet me in person. About 10 of my 32 students accepted this offer. With these 10, I was able to learn their names, talk with them briefly, and get a sense of who they were. I greatly enjoyed and appreciated this one-on-one time.

I then found the previous year's kindergarten class pictures in the yearbook. By matching the names on my list to the faces in the yearbook, I learned the names of the rest of my returning students. In addition, I was expecting only two new students, one boy and one girl. So I quickly learned their names. On the night before school started, I made a simple name tag for each student and arranged the tags on a table by the front door of the classroom.

That next morning, I was ready. I stood at the door eager to welcome my new students. While I was praying that none of them had gotten haircuts over the summer, they began to arrive. I greeted each one by name, handed them a name tag, and invited them to sit down on the rug. Standing outside on the yard, a number of parents watched the whole thing, wondering how

I could possibly know the names of people I had never met. I felt fantastic. Before the school year was barely 3 minutes old, I had created a favorable first impression and made a major deposit in the emotional bank accounts of my students and parents. This proactive gesture had set the tone I wanted.

Begin the year with some sort of powerful, dramatic initiative or "kickoff gesture." If you are unable to obtain a class list before the start of the year or do not receive permission to contact families before the school year begins, do something the first day. Write a short, personalized note to each student, call each parent after school expressing how much you are looking forward to the year ahead, or send a postcard through the mail. Just do something. The more novel, the better. Families will remember your thoughtful gesture, and your efforts to build strong parent connections will be off to a flying start!

First-Day Letter
Making a proactive gesture to introduce yourself and build goodwill will capture parents' attention. Capitalize on this momentum before it disappears. Send home a detailed letter discussing the upcoming year. Although I refer to it as the First-Day Letter, it's a good idea to wait a few days before sending it home. On the first day of school, parents are so inundated with paperwork from the school office that a letter from us may get lost in the shuffle. Earlier in this chapter, I mentioned that I send a brief note home on the first day of school. On this sheet I introduce myself, share a small number of business items (such as the invitation for each child to bring a special object to school the following day), and alert parents to watch out for a more detailed letter that I will be sending home in a few days.

The First-Day Letter is the educational equivalent of a movie trailer. It offers a sneak preview of the year ahead, whetting parents' appetite for what's to come. The First-Day Letter is a sincere articulation of who we are, what we value, and what we hope to accomplish. Our words paint a picture for parents of what the upcoming months will look like and create a sense of possibility, optimism, and excitement by charting the direction in which we want to take the class. Writing a First-Day Letter provides us with our first and best opportunity to establish our leadership of the class, saying what we want to say in the way we want to say it.

The following list contains *ingredients* you may want to include in your First-Day Letter:

- Biographical information about yourself
- Your educational philosophy
- Your personal goals for the year
- Introduction to any content standards or other academic expectations with which parents may not be familiar

- Major curricular emphases
- The type of classroom culture you want to create
- Highlights of the year
- How you will communicate with parents and how they can reach you
- A blank page at the end of the letter for parents to use to inform you about any concerns, abilities, interests, or areas of sensitivity their children may have

The First-Day Letter that I send home is shown in Figure 3.1. I used the concept of "quality education" to structure my thoughts. By organizing the letter around a central theme, I was able to present my beliefs, ideas, and expectations in a coherent, integrated fashion. Without a broad theme, First-Day Letters can too easily become long laundry lists of topics, unconnected to one another or to any larger idea.

Dear Families,

This is the letter I promised you last Wednesday. As I mentioned in my earlier note, my name is Steve Reifman, and I am delighted to welcome you to what I know will be an outstanding year. I consider myself very fortunate to be at such a special place as Roosevelt School. The quality of our staff, the dedication of our volunteers, and the supportiveness of our families and neighboring community are truly precious assets. In this letter I would like to share with you a little bit about who I am and what I hope to accomplish this year.

I am strongly committed to providing your child with the highest quality of education possible. To me, quality education means several things. First, quality education begins with the recognition and appreciation of the fact that each child is unique and special. I believe that all children should be valued for who they are and encouraged to discover their full potential. Each child has something to offer, and each child is a potentially valuable resource to their community. I strive to bring out the best in every child. I want all children to take pride in who they are, have a healthy self-esteem, and become independent, self-directed learners.

I place particular emphasis on the importance of character. My top priority is that my students become good people. We will talk about principles such as honesty, kindness, self-discipline, and perseverance. I want to develop students who try their best, never give up, and conduct themselves in a courteous manner. I will try my very best to lead by example.

Second, quality education involves taking each individual student and bringing everyone together to form a cohesive, supportive team. Just as I try to develop a sense of identity and self-esteem in each child, I also try to develop a sense of group identity and group esteem. I want students to be proud of being members of our classroom. As a community of learners, we will spend a great deal of time discussing ideas such as respect, cooperation, responsibility, service, and fairness. We will work together, help one another, and make meaningful decisions together. I will do whatever I can to create an emotionally safe, nurturing environment where students feel comfortable taking risks, sharing information, and being themselves. The whole can be greater than the sum of the parts.

Third, quality education focuses directly on the habits of mind and habits of character that students will need in order to make a contribution to society and lead quality lives. I will attempt to connect classroom learning to these higher purposes. Specifically, I hope to show the kids how what they learn in school will help them become lifelong learners, productive workers, active citizens, intelligent consumers, and caring individuals. I seek to empower my students so that they will be able to perform these roles successfully now and in the future. When students understand the purposes of their learning and when they are encouraged to find meaning in it, motivation increases and greater learning gains result.

Figure 3.1 Sample first-day letter.

Fourth, quality education demands high expectations for everyone. All students are capable of achieving excellence. My job involves getting the students to expect great things from themselves. Once children believe in themselves and are motivated to put forth consistent effort, wonderful things start happening. It is my goal to build the students' confidence and nourish the intrinsic motivation that lies inside of them so they experience the joys of learning. I will demand a great deal of responsibility from everyone, but I will be there to support them every step of the way. I will set them up for success any way I can.

Fifth, quality education requires the active involvement and support of parents. It is crucial for us to remain in close contact throughout the year. Every Monday you will receive a newsletter containing important information about our class. It is absolutely essential that you read this newsletter every week and discuss it with your child. I will also contact you by phone, via e-mail, or with a note whenever the need arises. Please feel free to do the same. I am always happy to discuss school matters with you.

Parental involvement and support also means that you closely monitor your child's performance at home and at school. Every time you ask your child about a homework activity, every time you take an interest in one of his or her projects, and every time you make sure your child has a designated time and place for homework, you are showing you value education and think school work is worthy of the time and effort your child puts forth. This is a message your child needs to hear constantly.

I actively encourage parents to volunteer in the classroom. I hope to have parent volunteers in the classroom on a daily basis. The assistance that parents provide is invaluable. For those of you who are interested, I will be distributing a volunteer sheet in the near future. If you are unable to volunteer in the classroom but would like to help out in other ways, such as with photocopying or by providing supplies, that would be fantastic as well. Any help that you could give us this year would be greatly appreciated.

There are many more things I would like to share with you about the upcoming year, but I feel it is best if I stop here. In this letter I hope I have made it clear bow important it is for all of us to work together in the coming months. When parents, students, and teachers form trusting relationships and work together, then we give the kids their greatest chance for success in the classroom. I hope this letter finds you in good spirits, and !look forward to speaking with you soon.

Sincerely,

Steve Reifman

Figure 3.1 (Continued)

Weekly Newsletters

Once you have sent home the First-Day Letter, don't stop there. Continue to inform parents on a regular basis about important classroom matters. The best vehicle for maintaining this type of communication is the Weekly Newsletter. Use the Weekly Newsletter to do the following:

- ◆ Summarize the previous week.
- ◆ Offer a sneak preview of the week ahead.
- ◆ Describe various features of the classroom.
- ◆ Highlight pieces of student work.
- ◆ Promote upcoming events.
- ◆ Ask for special favors.
- ◆ Introduce units and policies.
- ◆ Give "State of the Class" updates.
- ◆ Suggest tips that parents can use to help their children at home more effectively.

- Remind parents of important dates (e.g., assessments, due dates, field trips).
- Continue discussing ideas and themes you introduced in the First-Day Letter.
- Recognize class improvements and successes.
- Thank those who have helped the class in important ways.

You can find a sample newsletter in Figure 3.2. (It describes Student-Led Conferences, a variation of the traditional Parent Conference that I will discuss in

Volume 11, November 20th

What's Going On In Room 27?

A Weekly Newsletter

Student-led Conferences

This week we conclude our first round of parent conferences. These meetings provide us with a chance to discuss in depth your child's progress in the various academic areas as well as in our habits of character. Though the ovembcr conferences are the only official ones that Roosevelt schedules for the year, I am planning a second set a few months from now. I have not set an exact date yet, but the conferences will probably occur in late February or early March.

This time around, however, the meetings will take the form of a Student-led Conference. In a Student-led Conference each child is entrusted with the responsibility of conducting the meeting. I will be present in the room during these conferences, but l will not have an active role in them. The conferences will be private meetings between you, your child, and any other family members you would like to invite.

During the conference your child will share with you the contents of his or her portfolio. The portfolio will include work samples from the various academic areas along with a few other special items. Some of the items in the portfolio items will be chosen by the kids, others by me.

I believe that allowing students to have the opportunity to lead their own conferences is an important step in helping them build responsibility and take charge of their own learning. The students will decide how they will organize their conferences and how they will explain their portfolio contents to you.

We are very excited to begin the process of planning these conferences. In the future I will send home a sign-up shect for time slots that are convenient for you. Please remember that I am always happy to meet with you to discuss your child's progress. Student-led Conferences are designed to supplement my ongoing efforts to keep you informed and involved, not replace them.

Figure 3.2 Sample class newsletter.

Chapter 10.) Begin creating your own version by choosing a title and making a template so your newsletter has a distinctive look that parents will recognize immediately. Reproducing these bulletins on a different color paper will further distinguish them from other school correspondence. I write my newsletter every Thursday and send it home the following Monday. When you have a consistent routine, parents know to watch out for the newsletter on the same day every week. If all the parents have email access, you might choose to send your newsletters electronically.

Initially, writing weekly newsletters may require a significant amount of time. But the good news is that the time commitment decreases each year because you will be able to reuse many of the newsletters, sometimes in their entirety, and because you will become more comfortable with this style of writing. Remember, start small and build from there. If you're comfortable with monthly newsletters, then try sending them home every two weeks.

Invite students to contribute articles or entries to the newsletter. This will also decrease your workload, but that's not why you do it. Including their submissions represents another way of sharing ownership and building teamwork with the kids. You may also want to consider creating your newsletters together, as a shared writing activity. This collaborative venture enables you to simultaneously produce a meaningful correspondence and practice important writing skills. Your willingness to incorporate student writing into the newsletter shows that you value the contributions of everyone and that you are committed to making this truly a *class* newsletter.

Back-to-School Night

Elementary schools typically schedule a Back-to-School Night event during the first few weeks of the school year so we can speak with parents about the year ahead. A Back-to-School Night presentation is like the State of the Union Address the President delivers to the nation. It is a chance to speak with a sense of optimism and articulate a compelling vision of the upcoming year. Because your presentation provides such a strong introduction to the school year, it is important to have as many parents there as possible to hear it. Do whatever you can to maximize turnout. I recommend having students create personalized invitations to the parents and highlighting the event in your Weekly Newsletter.

Use the evening to emphasize the major ideas you introduced in your First-Day Letter. Describe your most important goals, and explain how they drive what you do in the classroom. Help parents understand what you expect of their children and how you will assess them. Also, discuss the major emphases of the curriculum, your approach to culture building, home–school communication system, homework policy, and any other issues of special interest or importance to you. Be sure to leave time for questions, because many of these ideas may be new to parents and require further clarification.

(Questions shared in this whole-group setting need to be general in nature and not focus on a specific child.) Ensuring that your presentation is well organized and speaking to the group with positivity and enthusiasm will make a strong impression on the parents, especially those whom you are meeting for the first time.

Here are some other tips for getting the most out of this evening.

- Prepare for the parents a folder of handouts that includes copies of all the information you share that evening. These handouts will make it easier for everyone to follow along with your presentation. Also, by putting the students' names on the folders, you can take attendance for the evening by seeing which folders remain at the end. (You will want to have a sign-in sheet as well.)
- Post a parent volunteer sign-up sheet on the wall so you can recruit parents who are available to help out in class during the school day.
- Be careful about offering specific information about individual students to any parents. With so many people around, this isn't the time for in-depth, one-on-one conversations, and you don't want to say something you might later regret. If parents ask you about their child before or after your presentation, offer to schedule a private meeting so you can have the opportunity to talk in a less congested atmosphere.
- Have student-created name tags waiting for the parents as they enter the room. Placing the name tags on the kids' desks enables parents to see where their children sit each day.
- Simulate an actual school day as much as possible so that parents can appreciate what it feels like to be a student in your class. For example, if music is playing each morning as the students arrive in class, play music as the parents arrive. Little touches matter.
- Consider starting off the evening with an ice-breaking activity to build camaraderie among the parents.
- Attach a sentence to the bottom of your next newsletter thanking the parents for attending.

Parent Conferences

The most productive Parent Conferences include teachers, parents, *and* students. For a number of reasons, the students' presence at these meetings is highly desirable. First, involving the kids provides another of those rare opportunities when I can focus my attention on only one child. One-on-one time with each student allows me to strengthen relationships and discuss sensitive issues away from the other kids. Second, I learn a great deal by observing how the children interact with their parents. Specifically, I discover more about the inner workings of each family and develop a greater understanding of each child's home life. Possessing this knowledge helps me do my job better.

Third, because the students are the subjects of these meetings, they need to hear what their parents and I are saying about them, and they have a right to express their thoughts and feelings about their own learning. Fourth, with all of us there together, I know that parents and students are hearing the same message from me. When the students aren't there, they hear secondhand what I said about them. As a result, the message they receive from their parents may not be the one I intended to send. Fifth, I occasionally like to assess students at these conferences. These assessments couldn't occur without the children present. Finally, when students attend the conference with their parents, they get a feel for what these meetings are like. Consequently, when Student-Led Conferences roll around a few months later, the kids will be more prepared and less anxious about leading them.

Above all, however, inviting the students to attend Parent Conferences is a matter of respect. Because I truly value my students, I believe they deserve to be present when I discuss their progress with their parents. In the event that I need to discuss a piece of sensitive information with only a parent, I simply ask the child to wait outside the room for a moment.

As you plan for the conferences, create an agenda containing all the topics you intend to discuss. Following this agenda during the meetings keeps everyone's attention focused on the business at hand. Give parents a copy of this sheet at the start of the conference so they can take notes throughout the meeting. Each item on your agenda should connect directly to an important "whole-child" priority, from academics and behavior to other relevant topics, such as the kids' friendships, snack choices, and types of exercise they prefer.

With assessment and anecdotal data by your side, explain to parents how their child is progressing toward each goal. As you move through your agenda, invite the students to offer their own opinions and self-assessments as often as you can. Asking the kids to discuss their strengths and weaknesses encourages them to take ownership of their learning. The most important agenda item is the goal setting that occurs near the end of the conference. Together, set three goals that will guide the child's efforts over the next few months. (In Chapters 7 and 9, I will describe this goal-setting process in more detail.) Leave time at the end of the conferences for parents to ask questions and share concerns, and remind them that you are always available should they ever want to meet with you again in the future.

When sharing assessment data with parents, make a special effort to ensure that they understand your rubrics, scoring methods, and terminology. Nontraditional scoring systems can cause quite a bit of confusion. For example, one year many parents viewed the 6-point writing rubric we used at that time as identical to the traditional letter grades they encountered in school. As a result, they interpreted a 6 to be an A, a 5 to be a B, a 4 to be a C, and so on. This correlation, however, was inaccurate. No connection whatsoever existed between any number and any letter grade; the two systems were completely unrelated. Number 4 was the standard. Our goal was for all students to earn at least that score. Two parents whose child earned a 2 were shocked at what they perceived to be failing scores. Once they realized, however, that the goal was 4, not 6, and understood the requirements and criteria on which the rubric was based, they had a better grasp of how our assessments worked. Taking the time to discuss this matter with parents prevents them from misinterpreting the data and from viewing either their children's abilities or ours unfavorably. Strive to educate and clarify during these meetings.

Here are some other suggestions to improve your Parent Conferences.

- Provide a private, comfortable setting. Place some chairs outside the room in case the next parents arrive early.
- Welcome each parent. Smile and make eye contact.
- Express appreciation for their presence, and establish rapport by talking informally for a few moments at the outset.
- Have data and work samples to support your opinions.
- Discuss ways for parents to help their children at home.
- Ask parents for their questions, comments, and suggestions.
- Remind parents of the procedure for reaching you at school.
- End on a positive note, and thank the parents again for coming.
- In the following week's newsletter, thank the parents once more for coming and explain how beneficial you believe the conferences were and how important it is for all of you to continue communicating on a regular basis.
- Follow up on your meetings by informing parents the first time their child shows improvement in one of the areas you discussed.

Additional Resources

Parent involvement has long been an important emphasis of my teaching. Over the years, I have written a few resources focused on this topic, and I would like to provide you with additional information, tips, and strategies to help you develop this aspect of your professional practice. In Resource C, you will find ideas related to the following: ways to promote working together, helping parents help their children, and open house. I created my most recent resource, the "Parent Conference Starter Kit," for the TeachersPayTeachers website. This user-friendly item contains effective tips and strategies that guide you from the beginning of the preparation process, through the conferences themselves, to important follow-up steps. You will learn how these meetings can set the stage for student growth and improvement and serve as precious opportunities to exchange information with parents, share perspectives, convey a clear sense of children's current performance, problem-solve, plan for the future, and suggest concrete ways parents can assist their children's learning at home. The "Handouts" section includes a variety of visuals and "takeaways" you can use at the conference and give to families to improve student learning and enhance overall classroom performance.

Closing

Investing the time and effort to join forces with our students to build a cooperative, productive culture and develop friendly, caring relationships will get our school year off to a tremendous start. Kids who feel connected to their classmates, their teacher, and their learning environment will be ready to thrive academically, socially, and behaviorally. They will be enthusiastic and motivated. For children to become wildly successful in their academic learning and maximize their potential, though, they need more than that. Students must possess a deep understanding of why they come to school. Before they will dedicate themselves fully to academic pursuits, they must be aware of and value the important purposes they are serving in their role as student. They need to know how working hard in school each day and learning as much as they can will improve their lives, both now and in the years ahead. We explore the topic of purpose in the next chapter.

Reference List

Frazee, M. (2003). *Roller Coaster*. New York and San Diego: Harcourt.
Gardner, H. (1993). *Multiple Intelligences: The Theory in Practice*. Alexandria, VA: BasicBooks.
Gibbs, J. (2001). *Tribes: A New Way of Learning and Being Together*. Cloverdale, CA: Center Source Systems.
Reifman, S. (2008). *Eight Essentials for Empowered Teaching & Learning, K-8*. Thousand Oaks, CA: Corwin Press.
Reifman, S. (2020). 107 *Awesome Elementary Teaching Ideas You Can Implement Tomorrow*. New York: Routledge.

4

Purpose

My father took me to my first Major League Baseball game when I was 6 years old. It was Opening Day at Dodger Stadium. I was too young to understand what was happening on the field, and my older brother had to explain everything to me when I got home. But I remember the beautifully manicured natural grass field, the majestic "birthday cake" colors of the stadium's multiple levels, and those classic Dodger blue-and-white uniforms. From that point on, I have been a loyal Dodger fan—a hardcore, passionate, my-morning-mood-partially-depends-on-whether-the-team-won-or-lost-the-day-before type of fan.

The boys in blue have been the most successful franchise in MLB over the past ten years, qualifying for the playoffs in each of those seasons, compiling more regular season victories than any other team, and winning the World Series in 2020 and 2024. Many of my non-Dodger-fan friends attribute the club's success exclusively to its large payroll. Granted, the team does spend a lot of money on its players. A lot of money. In fact, just two days before I began drafting this chapter (December 9, 2023), the Dodgers signed pitching and hitting superstar Shohei Ohtani to the largest contract in North American team sports history, a 10-year deal worth $700 million. (You read that correctly.)

But a deeper dive reveals another, and perhaps more important, reason the Dodgers have become such a juggernaut—the team's commitment to building a strong Minor League system that develops homegrown talent year after year. A recent article by Jack Harris (2023) in the *Los Angeles Times* sports section (my required morning reading) details this player development process. The Dodgers organizational philosophy is widely known throughout baseball to place a huge emphasis on creating a positive culture, building connections among the team's various departments to ensure productive communication, and a clear sense of purpose.

According to pitcher Emmet Sheehan, who made his Major League debut in 2023:

> From when you show up, they tell you, basically, "If you come up to us and ask us why we are doing something, and we can't tell you how it translates on the field, you don't have to do it." They teach us the reason behind everything we do. And everything is personalized to the player.

Upon arriving at the team's Camelback Ranch facility in Glendale, Arizona, players immediately begin working on their skills, especially their weaknesses, participate in strength training, and attend classroom sessions led by their coaches.

A clear, powerful sense of purpose brings out the best in all of us. Whether we are young baseball prospects chasing our Big League dreams or individuals pursuing other career, family, social, service-oriented, or personal aspirations, the same basic principle holds true. When we can identify and understand the reasons we are participating in a task and those reasons resonate with us on a deep, personal level, it's game on. Launching our chosen endeavor from a foundation of purpose harnesses our energies, fires our souls, and engages our hearts and minds. A beautiful chain reaction ensues. Our effort intensifies, motivation skyrockets, enthusiasm soars, and overall performance and happiness increase. When this happens with a hobby, that interest becomes a passion. When it happens in our careers, our job feels less like work and more like a mission or a calling. If we look back on our proudest achievements, it's likely they were fueled by a strong sense of purpose. My decision to pursue a career in teaching, for example, stemmed, in large part, from the fact that the job matters so much, fills me with a profound feeling of contribution, and provides unparalleled opportunities to make a difference in the lives of children and their families (and yes, purchase vast quantities of school supplies).

Our students deserve to feel and benefit from this same kind of energizing purpose. In my experience, however, purpose is one of the two most "under-discussed" topics in our schools, with motivation (i.e., intrinsic vs. extrinsic) being the other. As teachers, we have the responsibility to establish a sense of purpose in our classrooms so the kids know why it's important to come to school every day and so they understand how learning can benefit them now and in the future. Raising this issue helps children connect classroom learning to their own lives. When educators neglect to discuss the worthwhile purposes of attending school, working hard, and learning as much as possible, students frequently fail to see the meaning in their work and lack the motivation to persevere when challenged. There is no more important, no more fundamental question we can pose to children than "Why are we here?" We can't assume they already know.

With regard to purpose, school occupies a unique place among the organized activities in which children participate. Take Little League Baseball, for example. When I played for the Yankees (a difficult undertaking for a diehard Dodger fan), my teammates and I practiced one afternoon a week to prepare for the Saturday morning games. We spent our practice time working on the skills that would help us play better in the games. We ran around the bases, hit balls off the batting tee, and caught pop flies. Even though we were young, my teammates and I quickly grasped the purpose and importance of every practice activity. A clear connection existed between what we did in practice and what we would need to do in a game. The coach didn't have to take much time to explain these connections because we could figure them out for ourselves.

Similar clarity of purpose exists with other kids' activities. At band practice, for instance, musicians understand why they need to rehearse. They know that rehearsing is important because at a later date the group will perform its songs to a live audience. Again, the connection between today's preparation and tomorrow's performance is straightforward. Young actors in a drama club are also aware of this relationship.

School is different. Though it usually occupies more of a child's waking hours than all their other activities combined, the purposes of attending school each day tend to be less well understood by its young participants. For one thing, there's no big game, final performance, or end-of-session culmination that drives our daily efforts, making the connection between our hard work and its results, both tangible and intangible, more difficult to perceive. For another, the payoffs to our work in the classroom typically occur over a longer period of time. Unlike a Little League Baseball season, whose playoffs begin a few months after the first practice, the rewards of an education may not be fully realized for years, decades even. Finally, the purposes of education are much more varied and multifaceted and generally address a greater range of "whole-child" domains—academic, social, physical, and emotional.

What are the purposes of attending school? Most children answer that they come to school to learn. But when pressed further, they are often unable to articulate compelling reasons why learning is important. Some students mention the need to learn "to get a good job" or "to get into a good college." Rarely, though, does a child express that learning adds quality to our lives, that it enables us to contribute to the lives of others, that it maximizes our options later in life, or that the development of the mind is a joy and benefit in and of itself. The larger purposes of education are not as obvious as those of Little League, band, or drama club. As a result, children have greater difficulty discovering on their own what these purposes are.

Establishing a sense of purpose is a process that requires an investment of time and energy. The process must start during the first few days of a new school year, because what occurs in our classrooms at this time sets the tone for the months ahead. Taking the time to establish purpose promotes the creation of a productive work environment, a necessary precondition of quality learning. But students can only work with a sense of purpose when their teachers have established a sense of purpose.

The Overall Aim

The process of establishing purpose begins on a general level with the introduction of the classroom aim. The aim is the overall objective you and your students work to accomplish. The first brick in the foundation of a quality classroom, the aim begins to answer the question "Why are we here?" Once introduced, the aim pervades every aspect of class functioning, driving decisions and determining goals.

Following the 1994–95 school year, the Enterprise School District in Redding, California, became one of the first districts in the nation to adopt an aim. Many factors led to this decision. During the three years preceding adoption of the aim, Enterprise had conducted a yearly attitude survey in which students, K–8, expressed their feelings about each subject they studied. A happy face meant students liked a subject, a neutral face meant ambivalence, and a sad face meant the students disliked a subject.

The data that was collected enabled district staff to compare the percentage of happy faces by grade level for each year of the survey. In his terrific book *Improving Student Learning*, Lee Jenkins (1997), who was then the Enterprise superintendent, presents a graph that shows a slow, gradual loss of enthusiasm that begins when students are in kindergarten and continues every year thereafter. Jenkins comments that "the data clearly show that each grade level contributed to the loss of enthusiasm." To heighten awareness of this decline, Jenkins makes the point that if 30 kindergartners enter school together and a couple children per year lose their enthusiasm for learning, then only a handful would still be enthusiastic as they finish high school.

Jenkins believes that teachers are responsible for both learning and enthusiasm. He considers student enthusiasm to be an invaluable asset that educators must cherish. Students who have lost their enthusiasm for learning are less motivated to learn, less likely to put their learning to use in creative ways, and more likely to cause discipline problems. Jenkins contends that typical kindergartners have enough enthusiasm to last a lifetime, but they don't have all the knowledge. Educators, he stresses, must guard this enthusiasm, must protect it throughout a child's academic career. It is a school's most precious resource.

Dr. W. Edwards Deming's proposed aim for education also influenced the Enterprise School District's decision. As I mentioned in Chapter 1, Deming suggested that the overall aim for education be to "[i]ncrease the positives and decrease the negatives so that all students keep their yearning for learning." He believed that if educators preserved students' love of learning by removing the practices that decrease enthusiasm and spreading those that foster it, more students would succeed in school.

In response to both the survey data and Deming's proposal, the staff of the Enterprise School District wrote and adopted the aim: "Maintain enthusiasm while increasing learning." Jenkins remarks:

> [O]rchestrating classrooms so that all students progress in learning and maintain their enthusiasm for learning is an incredible challenge. It is, however, the responsibility of educators to maintain enthusiasm while increasing learning. We must not allow ourselves to stray from this path.

After learning of the pioneering work done by the Enterprise District at the beginning of my career, I decided to adopt a classroom aim for the 1997–1998 school year. Rather than adopt Enterprise's aim of "[m]aintain[ing] learning while increasing enthusiasm" verbatim, I chose to modify it. I felt the word "maintain" was ineffective for three reasons. First, once students lose enthusiasm for a subject, there is nothing left to maintain, and the term no longer applies. In this situation, restoring enthusiasm becomes the goal. Second, if students already enjoy a subject, there's no reason they can't enjoy it more. I wished to achieve more than maintenance. At the end of the year, I wanted students to like each subject more than they did at the beginning. Third, the pursuit of quality demands a commitment to continuous improvement. It is not enough simply to maintain *anything*. Successful teachers constantly look for ways to make every aspect of classroom life better. Nothing is already at such a high level that we can settle for maintenance. Because of these reasons, I needed a stronger, more aggressive word than *maintain*. I adopted this aim:

"Increasing learning while increasing enthusiasm." I have used this aim with my students ever since.

An aim provides focus and direction. It states what we consider to be our very highest priorities. In my case, the aim declares that learning and enthusiasm are inseparable entities and that our success as a classroom community depends on increasing both. Furthermore, our aim is brief, making it easy for children to memorize and, ultimately, internalize. Students will even become eager to contribute toward the realization of this aim because they will appreciate being in a class where the teacher truly wants them to enjoy the learning process. In addition, the aim helps students discover two reasons they attend school: (1) to learn and (2) to love learning. I also mentioned in Chapter 1 that Dr. W. Edwards Deming once said a successful teacher is one whose students are more interested in learning about a subject at the end of the year than they were at the beginning. With an aim in place to guide us, we create an opportunity for ourselves to meet this worthwhile challenge.

An aim doesn't have to focus exclusively on the concepts of learning and enthusiasm. You may find that your highest priorities include other emphases. For example, prior to the 1998–1999 school year, a group of teachers with whom I worked at Anderson School in Lawndale, California, decided to incorporate the idea of service into their aim to highlight the importance of helping others. They adopted the aim "Increasing learning while increasing enthusiasm and service." Whichever concepts you choose to include in your aim, limit yourself to the two or three with the broadest application and the greatest strength. You don't want your aim to be a laundry list that nobody can remember. Less is more.

Developing an aim is only the beginning of the journey to establish a sense of purpose with students. Jenkins describes the aim as the "bull's-eye of the organizational target." If the aim represents the center of the target, then the ring surrounding the bull's-eye is the class mission statement.

Class Mission Statement

After plenty of hype for class mission statements in previous chapters, we finally made it to this section! Before I begin describing these documents, though, I would like to offer more hype. A mission statement is the most effective "whole-child" teaching and learning tool ever devised. Writing a class mission statement with students and revisiting it regularly throughout the year for guidance, support, and inspiration is the single most powerful move teachers can make to establish purpose, build teamwork, set high expectations, boost confidence, and emphasize valuable character traits. If

I were allowed to share only one idea in this book, it would be the class mission statement. Hands down. I simply couldn't teach children without it.

A *mission statement* is an organization's formal statement of purpose. According to Stephen Covey (1989), author of *The 7 Habits of Highly Effective People* and *First Things First*, mission statements "capture what you want to be and what you want to do . . . and the principles upon which being and doing are based." Alan Blankstein, author of *Failure Is Not an Option*, adds, "The mission of an organization is essential to its success. A mission statement should be created and published as a means of giving those involved with the organization a clear understanding of its purpose for existence."

A class mission statement picks up where the aim leaves off, further developing your highest-priority ideas and supplementing them with others that identify yours as a unique group. The document enables students to see themselves not just as individuals but also as "contributing parts to a greater whole." Developing the mission statement provides individuals with an opportunity "to envision ways their combined talents and energies can make a difference."

Sadly, many teachers have not had the opportunity to use a mission statement to its full potential. Oftentimes, mission statements are "presented" to school staff by administrators or district personnel, and employees are asked to embrace the documents, even though they had no chance to offer any input during the creation process. With no input, there is no ownership, no emotional investment, and no buy-in. To make matters worse, after mission statements are introduced with great fanfare, they are frequently put in a drawer and forgotten. If you have experienced a situation similar to the one I have described, someone owes you an apology. Please keep an open mind as you read the rest of this section. When we are in our own classrooms, we can create these documents with everyone's involvement, refer to them throughout the year, and achieve maximum impact.

Writing the Class Mission Statement

I have found that a four-day process works well for creating a class mission statement. My students and I write ours during the first full week of the school year.

Day 1
Begin the process of creating your class mission statement by discussing the word *mission*. In my experience, kids more easily understand the term when I introduce it as part of the phrase "on a mission." I tell them that when people

are on a mission, they are determined to accomplish something important. I accompany my definition with examples of historical figures, athletes, and other well-known individuals who were determined to accomplish worthwhile goals, names such as Martin Luther King Jr., Susan B. Anthony, and Michael Jordan. Next, I ask students to share personal stories of when they have been on a mission. I then explain that when groups of people come together to work as a team, they frequently create something called a mission statement to describe the significant things they want to accomplish. Finally, I relate that, in my opinion, the project we are about to launch is the most important team activity we will do all year.

Next, working either alone or in pairs or small groups, students answer the questions listed in what follows:

1. Who are we?
2. Why is it important to come to school to learn?
3. What goals are we determined to reach together?
4. What kind of class do we want to be?
5. What actions and behaviors must we demonstrate each day to reach our goals?

Students will later draw on their responses to these questions when they create the first draft of the class mission statement. I also send these five questions home with the kids that night so they have an opportunity to discuss and expand on their ideas with family members. Sending the questions home with the kids accomplishes the following: (1) It gets parents and children talking about fundamental issues that too often go undiscussed, (2) it involves parents early in the school year in a meaningful project and shows them that we value their participation in the educational process, and (3) it greatly increases the likelihood that the kids will generate high-quality, thoughtful responses.

Days 2 and 3

Show the kids actual corporate and organizational mission statements to familiarize everyone with the format and substance of this type of writing. Mission statements are readily available in stores and restaurants, as well as online. (I have also included several samples in Resource D.) Try to use examples from companies with which children are familiar, such as Disney. Emphasize to your students that groups of people create these documents to describe who they are and what they want to become.

As you read through each example with your students, ask everyone to highlight the words and phrases they think would be appropriate for a class mission statement. After the kids have had some quiet time to complete their highlighting for a given mission statement, encourage volunteers to share aloud one to three of the words that resonated with them. Chart these words for easy future reference. Typically, most, if not all, of my students eagerly raise their hands to tell the group their highlighted words from *every* mission statement. For children who tend to be shy or reluctant to participate in class discussions, this activity offers a safe, enjoyable opportunity to raise their hands a lot (and build confidence) because each child is saying only a few words, the turns are brief, I compliment every choice they make, and there's no pressure to answer a question or share an insightful point, since the words are provided to them. I aim for four to six mission statements per day in the 30–35 minutes we devote to this activity.

Analyzing mission statements to locate suitable words teaches students the power of language. For example, let's take a look at the Noah's Bagels mission statement shown in Box 4.1. This was their mission statement at the time I did this activity with Team Total Quality, whom you'll read more about later. From this mission statement the kids will likely suggest that you chart words such as *fun, fair, honest, friendly,* and *supportive*. The words the children choose and the way they phrase ideas will determine the overall effectiveness of the class statement. Pay special attention to the final section. Notice that it doesn't say, "To be a pretty good bagel company." It reads, "To be the best bagel company in America!" The words used here convey high expectations. It is important for students to see that and carry the spirit of high expectations to their own mission statement.

Box 4.1 Noah's Bagels Mission Statement

Noah's Bagels Mission Statement

Noah's Bagels strives in
all words and actions:
To create a fun, supportive,
and fair work environment;
To provide friendly, personal
service to our customers;
To ensure the highest standards
of product quality;
To be fair, honest, and considerate
in our relationships with our suppliers;

> To be an active and
> positive force
> in the communities
> where we do business; and
> To be the best bagel
> company in America!

Day 4

Now it is time for the kids, working either alone or in pairs or small groups, to use the answers to the five questions from day 1 and the charted words from the samples on days 2 and 3 to begin drafting the mission statement. Many children also like to use the sheets with the responses they generated with their parents as part of their homework. I give students several choices as to how they wish to contribute to the drafting process. I believe it is appropriate to differentiate the process at this point due to variations in children's readiness and in their overall comfort level with this type of project.

Encourage your most ambitious students to try to write a complete class mission statement. These multi-paragraph efforts should address all five of the questions and include many of the words and phrases you charted. Kids who undertake this challenge should also feel free to add thoughts and ideas of their own. Nobody should feel bound or constrained by these other two sets of ideas. Sometimes, the sentences that best convey the mission of the class are those that students create all by themselves.

Children who may not feel confident or comfortable enough to create an entire mission statement can still make an equally valuable contribution to the project by choosing one of the other drafting alternatives. With these options, the students should still draw from their responses to the five questions, the charted words, and their own imaginations. One great option is for the kids to list individual words that they want to see in the final class statement; another gives children a chance to write individual phrases and sentences. The latter two options can also be combined, affording students the opportunity to write individual words and short phrases and sentences. A final possibility allows kids to begin by listing words and then follow up by connecting pairs of words to form short phrases. For example, if a child listed the words *achieve* and *quality*, she could then draw a line connecting them, thus creating the phrase "achieve quality."

Regardless of which option the kids choose, the students should feel no pressure—there is no right or wrong. This time is simply an opportunity for each child to offer input as to how the final statement will read. Motivation will be high as the kids work seriously to craft a class statement. Your students will appreciate the chance to do something they view as "adult."

The last step in the missioning process requires us, the teachers, to read the drafts and combine them into a formal class statement. You will notice from the students' papers that several major themes recur. In the final draft, include these commonly expressed ideas, as well as any outstanding words, phrases, or sentences that appear only once or twice. The highest priority during this stage is to ensure that you use at least one word or idea (and hopefully more) from each child's or group's paper. That is the only way to create a sense of ownership and buy-in from everyone in the class.

Creating the final draft is not an easy task. At first, you may find yourself with a mission statement that is 15 pages long because you didn't want to leave out any input, or you may not know where to start because you see so many fine ideas spread out in front of you. To simplify the task, I create a note-taking sheet with the five questions printed on it from top to bottom, with plenty of space between them. (A sample note-taking sheet is shown in Box 4.2.) As I read every student's paper, I take what I consider to be that child's best ideas and write each contribution under the question it addresses. I try to avoid repeating ideas so that everything is as streamlined as possible. This note-taking step produces five sets of related ideas that I then use to write the five paragraphs of the mission statement. The end result is that each paragraph serves as a detailed answer to one of the questions. The goal is to shape the ideas from the note-taking sheet into a cohesive, powerful mission statement.

Box 4.2 Sample Mission Statement Note-Taking Sheet

Mission Statement Note-Taking Sheet

Who are we?

- ★ Highest hopes for our future.
- ★ We are a community of enthusiastic, determined learners who believe in ourselves and our classmates.
- ★ We try our hardest in everything, all the time, every day. Together, we work like champions to get to higher levels and exceed expectations.
- ★ This class is where we feel at home.

Why is it important to come to school to learn?
- ★ Pursuing excellence in third grade matters for our future.
- ★ The quality of our work, effort, and behavior will make us amazingly successful.
- ★ We come to school to become smarter and happier, get spectacular grades, earn college degrees, get the jobs we want, and have more choices in life.
- ★ We are striving to become the great people we want to be.
- ★ Our talent, discipline, and integrity will be our contribution to a new and better world.

What are we determined to accomplish together?
- ★ We are 100% committed to becoming the highest-quality class we can be. We don't want to be just okay; we want to be (or settle for nothing less than) the best of the best.
- ★ Committed to work hard with a sense of urgency to achieve our goals and have high standards.
- ★ We love completing all levels of challenge, and to do so, we will either find a way or make one.

What kind of class do we want to be?
- ★ To learn as much as we can, encourage others, and become better people.
- ★ Supportive, friendly battery chargers who treat one another with uncommon kindness and respect, dignity, and compassion.
- ★ Every day we create an environment where everyone is friendly and fun, fair and honest, active and positive, considerate and cooperative, patient and proud.
- ★ Everyone is a winner.
- ★ Our class knows it is important to try our best, care about our work, and never give up.
- ★ Our leadership style inspires trust, teamwork, and continuous improvement

What actions and behaviors must we demonstrate each day to reach our goals?
- ★ We believe we must earn the right to dream.
- ★ Attentive listeners, independent decision-makers, organized/sparkling clean class.
- ★ We try to be on-task all the time and use our time well.
- ★ At all times our actions speak louder than our words. Time to learn!

We can also use the following criteria, offered by Covey, to guide us. Effective mission statements should:

1. Be clear and understandable to all team members
2. Be brief enough to keep in mind
3. Be focused yet flexible
4. Excite people into action
5. Focus on worthwhile purposes

Enlarge the class mission statement you create from your students' ideas so that it can occupy a prominent place on a classroom wall and/or the front door for the entire year. The first time you read it with the class, you will notice something special occur. Because you took the time to have the kids answer the same five questions, charted words from the same sample statements, provided the opportunity for the kids to incorporate these words into their own drafts, and included input from all the drafts, every single child will be able to look at some part of the final version and say, "I had that." Or "That word came from mine." Or "That sentence was from mine." This creates shared ownership. There is a realization that everyone contributed to the final draft. As Covey puts it, "the process changes us. It changes our relationships with others who are part of it." Covey also notes, "It bonds people together. It gives them a sense of unity and purpose that provides great strength in times of challenge."

The missioning process produces a powerful founding document. According to Covey (1994) in *First Things First*, the statement now "becomes the constitution, the criteria for decision making in the group." Its words will guide us throughout the school year, helping to keep everyone focused on what it is we are here to accomplish. It is our map that shows us the way in times of trouble and uncertainty. In *Failure Is Not an Option*, Blankstein (2004) refers to the mission as the group's "polestar," and writes, "[J]ust as a ship sails toward but never actually reaches its guiding star, we too strive toward but never actually fulfill our mission." Our mission statement establishes our identity as a unique group of people with a unique sense of purpose. It reminds us of the combined actions we need to take if we are to live up to the high expectations we set for ourselves. It is the ultimate reference point.

Once you have unveiled the entire statement and read it with your students, set aside time for a brief "signing ceremony," during which each child, one at a time, walks to the front of the room to add their name to the bottom of the poster. (The time right before recess, lunch, or dismissal works best.) Signing the mission statement is each child's way of declaring, "Count me in. I helped write this statement, and I officially commit to trying my best to bring these ideas to life." After all the kids have signed the mission statement (including any absent students), laminate the poster so it remains in good condition for the rest of the year. I cannot stress enough the importance of gathering student signatures before laminating the poster. (I forgot to do that one year!)

With the statement completed, signed, and laminated, devote time at least once a week to reviewing it as a class. As I mentioned previously, I incorporate these conversations into our morning circle time every Friday. The process takes only about five minutes, and the results are powerful. During this time, we never read the whole statement. Instead, I ask my students to focus on a specific word, phrase, sentence, or paragraph. Once I have identified our focus for that morning, I will ask the students to offer examples of how they have brought that idea to life that week, describe how we can improve in that area, or connect that idea to some aspect of our classroom environment.

Some weeks, instead of selecting a focus in advance, I ask the kids to share any part of a given paragraph that happens to jump out to them. During these "open forum" conversations, students can choose a word or phrase and explain why it stood out to them. In the first half of the year, I tend to do most of the choosing because I want to familiarize the kids with all the major ideas in the statement and go into depth with them. Later in the year, I like to have more "open forum" discussions.

A few final points before I wrap up this section.

- Keep in mind that a mission statement represents an ideal. Our classes will have to make a concerted, consistent effort to bring this ideal to life. None of our aspirations will happen automatically. Each student must do their part each day—quality is everyone's responsibility. The mission statement cannot just be words on a piece of paper. For a class to realize its mission, the ideas contained therein must live in the hearts and minds of all group members. As Covey notes, these lofty ideas must constantly be translated from the mission to the moment.
- The class mission statement provides children with something to say "yes" to:
  - "Yes, I want to reach my goals in life."
  - "Yes, I want to do well later in school."
  - "Yes, I will try my best and never give up."
  - "Yes, I will be a good role model for younger students."
  - "Yes, I want to learn so I can help others."

According to Austrian psychologist Victor Frankl, a survivor of the concentration camps of Nazi Germany, this future-oriented vision, this compelling, deep-burning "Yes!" was the primary force that kept many prisoners alive despite the unbearable conditions they encountered. "Empowering mission statements [that] focus on contribution, on worthwhile purposes . . . create [this] compelling, deep-burning 'Yes!'" This point is especially significant for children whom we are constantly telling to say no: no to drugs, no to alcohol, no to cigarettes, and no to sex. Telling them to say no is not enough. Children will only find it satisfying to say no to these temptations when they have a powerful, positive, future-oriented vision in their lives that provides them with something to say yes *to*.

- In addition to your weekly mission statement discussions, take advantage of learnable moments as they arise in the classroom. If your students are showing tremendous focus during math, for example, show them the mission statement at the end of the period and connect their positive behavior to the part of the document expressing the desire to be hard workers. This type of positive recognition will build the kids' confidence and self-esteem and reaffirm their commitment to bringing the mission statement's ideas to life. Conversely, if your students are not cooperating well during group work time, point out how their actions are not consistent with the part of the document expressing the desire to work together. Use this occasion as a problem-solving opportunity, and ask what the group can do differently or better next time. This is an excellent way to hold children accountable. The more frequently you are able to connect the kids' actions to the mission statement's words, the more of a presence the document will have.
- It is fine for the class mission statement to be quite long. Typically, our statements are five paragraphs, such as the sample I present later. We have our students for a whole year, and we have plenty of Fridays to revisit this document and get to know it very well. Businesses that post mission statements on their walls have only seconds to capture their customers' attention and need their statements to be short. We have the luxury of more time, and we have different intentions. I don't recommend exceeding one page, but filling up that page is perfectly acceptable. As classroom teachers, we have so many worthwhile goals and so many culture-building priorities to address that it makes sense that we would want to include a large number of ideas to use throughout the year as reference points.

- In a typical, daily classroom activity, each student will produce their own piece of work, such as a math sheet or a writing exercise. Sometimes, partners or small groups will collaborate on a project, but rarely does every child in the class have the opportunity to contribute energy and ideas to an important project that the team as a whole will use throughout the year. Writing a class mission statement offers this type of special opportunity.

A sample class mission statement can be found in Box 4.3.

Box 4.3 Class Mission Statement

TTQ Mission Statement

We are Team Total Quality. We are a community of smart, happy learners and strong leaders. We are committed to achieving the highest standard of excellence in education. You can count on us to be a serious, hardworking class and to make our school a better place. We are determined to accomplish everything.

We are in third grade now, but we are already looking ahead to the future. We come to school on time ready to learn so that we can be what we want to be. The work we do matters. It helps us get smarter and prepares us for when we grow up. We want to graduate from college, get spectacular jobs, earn money, reach our goals in life, and make a difference in the world. Learning makes us successful.

We do not want to be just okay. We want to be the best of the best. We always expect our class to try our hardest and never give up so that we can keep moving to higher levels. We use our time well, make intelligent decisions, and accomplish extraordinary things.

We are all great people, and together we make an amazing team. Our work, effort, and behavior get better every day. We strive to create a fun, supportive, and advanced atmosphere. We love working hard on difficult challenges. We try to be outstanding at listening and self-discipline. We want to be inspiring role models for younger students. We don't do the least; we do the most.

As a group of helpful, thoughtful battery chargers, we care about one another and treat everyone as a trusted friend. We care about being proud, honorable people who act with character and integrity. We are active and positive, friendly and kind, honest and respectful, fair and giving, organized and responsible.

Analyzing a Class Mission Statement: A Deeper Dive

In this section I examine in greater detail the mission statement shown earlier. A better understanding of its features, purposes, and intentions will help you when it comes time to write your own. The first item I would like to point out is the short phrase that precedes the actual mission statement. I have used this introductory phrase many times and love how it captures the twin goals of empowering ourselves and helping others. It is easy for young children to focus exclusively on their own wants and needs, and it is important to highlight the importance of service as often as possible.

Next, I would like to call attention to our class name, *Team Total Quality*. Many of the ideas that have formed the foundation of my teaching and inspired my previous books originate from the literature on quality control. Specifically, the ideas come from a body of work known as "total quality management." I love the phrase "total quality" because I believe it correctly conveys the idea that if an organization wants to achieve quality, then everyone in it shares the responsibility of ensuring that each aspect of the team's work is done at the highest possible level. In short, it takes a "total effort" to achieve the lofty goals a group creates for itself.

The name "Team Total Quality" captures this idea well. Frequently, I explain to my students that in order to produce quality work, many things need to happen. We have to work hard, listen well, follow directions, cooperate, take pride in what we are doing, ask for help when we need it, and maintain a high level of focus from the beginning of a project or activity to the end. It isn't enough to do just one or two of these things well. We need to do all of them. Thus, the team name itself becomes an important reference point to help students understand what it takes to achieve quality.

Two other notes on the team name. First, our class name is for "internal use" only. It's never mentioned to compare our class with others or serve as a reason for anyone to brag. Our name is aspirational—intended to help us become the best class we can be and maximize our collective potential. Second, I am always uncomfortable when adults on campus refer to our team as "Mr. Reifman's class." I know this is an innocent, common way to refer to classes and it's been around forever. Still, I much prefer a team name because it includes all of us—no one person more important than another, teachers included. Every chance I get, I refer to our group as TTQ and encourage the kids to do the same. On those occasions when we create a group poster to honor parent volunteers, design a class T-shirt, or communicate any other type of message on behalf of the class, we use our team name. My name appears only when every child's name does as well.

The remainder of this section offers a paragraph-by-paragraph analysis of the sample mission statement provided.

Paragraph 1

We are Team Total Quality. We are a community of smart, happy learners and strong leaders. We are committed to achieving the highest standard of excellence in education. You can count on us to be a serious, hardworking class and to make our school a better place. We are determined to accomplish everything.

The purpose of the first paragraph is to capture students' attention, establish a productive learning environment built on high expectations, and introduce important aspects of our culture. This paragraph lets everyone know that in order to achieve lofty goals, we need to think big. In particular, the third and fifth sentences of this paragraph set the bar high.

Words such as *determined*, *committed*, and *excellence* play a significant role in establishing this type of environment. Writing a mission statement offers some wonderful lessons about word choice. The words we choose matter greatly, and we need to emphasize the power of words to our students. Powerful words convey loftier goals, and loftier goals require greater effort and determination. So right off the bat, we are sharing with students the critical idea that in this class we want the best for ourselves, and we will work as hard as we can to achieve that standard.

Notice that the critical ideas of service, leadership, community, and hard work are also included in this initial paragraph, and they represent some of our highest priorities. Students' self-esteem gets a boost as well with the inclusion of the phrase "smart, happy learners." Seeing this phrase throughout the year can have a profound effect on those children who may not yet believe in themselves or believe they have what it takes to be successful.

Each individual has the potential to be successful, and the encouragement and inspiration provided by this phrase, and others, go a long way toward helping the kids develop a confident mindset. Every student is intelligent in many ways, and we need to do everything in our power to convince even the most skeptical child that this is the truth.

Paragraph 2

We are in third grade now, but we are already looking ahead to the future. We come to school on time ready to learn so that we can be what we want to be. The work we do matters. It helps us get smarter and prepares us for when we grow up. We want to graduate from college, get spectacular jobs, earn money, reach our goals in life, and make a difference in the world. Learning makes us successful.

One of the primary benefits of a class mission statement lies in its ability to help teachers connect daily learning activities to the bright futures we are committed to creating for ourselves. By making this connection, we can help students find greater meaning in their work and better understand why dedicating themselves to educational pursuits is so vital. Ever since I started creating mission statements with my students, I have used the second paragraph to focus on this present-to-future connection.

Though it may seem obvious to adults, the idea that working hard in school prepares us to be successful adults is new for many children, and the sentiments expressed in this paragraph seek to establish this idea. In addition, the goal of attending and graduating from college after we finish high school is new for many kids. The sentences in this paragraph can expand children's perspectives and open their eyes to new possibilities. The link between educational attainment and financial success is another significant idea that a mission statement can convey, as is the notion that an education can empower us to help others and contribute to society.

Another aspect of this paragraph that I like is its flexibility. Though the paragraph states we all want to get spectacular jobs and reach our goals in life, it does not specify what these goals or jobs should be. Thus, it subtly acknowledges the fact that we are all unique individuals with unique aspirations. This type of phrasing is an example of the "focused yet flexible" approach Covey recommends, and I try to keep his suggestion in mind when taking the ideas my students have written during the missioning process and turning them into a final class statement. When my students and I discuss various aspects of our mission statement on Friday mornings, this paragraph gives us many opportunities to engage in rich conversation.

Paragraph 3

We do not want to be just okay. We want to be the best of the best. We always expect our class to try our hardest and never give up so that we can keep moving to higher levels. We use our time well, make intelligent decisions, and accomplish extraordinary things.

This paragraph enables teachers to establish an expectation level—for our work, our effort, and our behavior. The words are powerful and will resonate with children. In class discussions, students frequently cited the first two sentences: "We do not want to be just okay" and "We want to be the best of the best." Over time, what may begin as my expectation or a parent expectation becomes a class expectation. Ideally, it becomes a *personal* expectation held by every member of our team.

One of my favorite parts of this paragraph is the word *expect* found in sentence 3. There is a big difference between *hoping* to achieve great things and *expecting* to achieve great things. When we expect maximum effort, for example, we are more likely to hold ourselves to higher standards and work with greater determination and urgency.

Finally, I would like to highlight the phrase "accomplish extraordinary things" that ends the paragraph. It is another "focused yet flexible" idea. Yes, we all want to achieve extraordinary things, but what that means is different for each of us. Some of us may strive to excel in sports, others in art, still others in science. The specific areas in which children choose to pursue excellence matter, of course, but what matters more is that, as teachers, we are creating a mindset in our students and creating a classroom environment that values the pursuit of excellence.

Paragraph 4

We are all great people, and together we make an amazing team. Our work, effort, and behavior get better every day. We strive to create a fun, supportive, and advanced atmosphere. We love working hard on difficult challenges. We try to be outstanding at listening and self-discipline. We want to be inspiring role models for younger students. We don't do the least; we do the most.

In the previous sections, I described two benefits of a class mission statement: (1) its ability to help teachers connect daily learning activities to important future purposes and (2) to enable teachers to establish an expectation level for student work, effort, and behavior. The fourth paragraph builds on these benefits and offers a third: A mission statement helps teachers build a confident mindset in our students.

Part of our "culture-creating" role involves building a sense of group identity. The words we use in our mission statement to develop this identity are critical because these are the words and phrases to which we will be referring over the coming months. The words we use should inspire our students, appeal to the best in them, boost self-esteem, and instill a sense of pride and responsibility.

I love the lead sentence of the fourth paragraph because it simultaneously builds individual self-esteem and creates a feeling of group esteem. In addition, phrases such as "love working hard on difficult challenges" and "we don't do the least, we do the most" help build a mindset that will serve students well when they encounter difficult work that tests their patience, perseverance, and self-discipline.

My favorite phrase in the paragraph is "advanced atmosphere," a focused yet flexible idea that presents exciting discussion opportunities. Choosing these words to serve as our Friday morning focus enables the children to share what this phrase means to them, recent times when they might have brought that term to life with their actions, or what visitors to our classroom are likely to see and hear when we are performing at our best.

Paragraph 5

As a group of helpful, thoughtful battery chargers, we care about one another and treat everyone as a trusted friend. We care about being proud, honorable people who act with character and integrity. We are active and positive, friendly and kind, honest and respectful, fair and giving, organized and responsible.

Teaching the whole child means that we don't focus solely on academic matters. We also promote valuable work habits, social skills, attitudes, and health and wellness. One way to ensure that our Habits of Character occupy a prominent position in class conversations throughout the year is to mention several of them in our mission statement, either explicitly or implicitly, along with the more general emphasis on acting with character and integrity. The fifth and final paragraph does that.

By including habits in the mission statement, we can refer to these ideas throughout the year, either on Friday mornings or when taking advantage of learnable moments that arise during the week. For example, imagine it is Friday, and we are having our weekly mission statement discussion. Yesterday, Natalie went out of her way to help Susan with her math homework. Natalie stayed after school to talk with Susan to help her solve a difficult problem. Now, as part of our Friday morning discussion, I can mention Natalie's act of service and connect it to the phrase in our mission statement "friendly and kind." By connecting specific student behaviors to the larger ideas the statement contains, we accomplish two important goals: (1) We increase the likelihood that such behavior will increase in the future, and (2) we help the mission statement carry greater weight in our students' eyes and fulfill its potential as an indispensable classroom reference point.

One final thought about the mission statement as a whole. With words such as "happy" (first paragraph) and "fun" (fourth paragraph) that connect to the idea of increasing enthusiasm and phrases such as "committed to achieving the highest standard of excellence" and "determined to accomplish everything" (first paragraph) that connect to the idea of increasing learning, we have maintained a tight connection with our aim. As I mentioned previously, the aim provides the main focus. The mission statement expands on the concepts contained in the aim and expresses other worthwhile ambitions.

Teachers cannot force learning and enthusiasm to happen. With our students, however, we can create the conditions where these entities will thrive. Learning and enthusiasm will flourish in an atmosphere of teamwork, kindness, honesty, and respect. Children contribute to this cause by being outstanding listeners, supportive teammates, and intelligent decision-makers. They further strengthen the learning environment by trying their best and never giving up, committing themselves to continuous improvement, and taking responsibility for their actions. Thoroughly discussing these crucial ideas and codifying them in a mission statement ensure that they will occupy a prominent position in classroom conversations throughout the year.

Creating Your Mission Statement: Fun With Formats

Many of the mission statements you come across online, as well as the examples you find in Resource D, possess interesting formats and features we can incorporate into our own designs. For many years I went with the straightforward approach (exemplified by the preceding sample), and simply including a title with one or more paragraphs works well. It is fun, though, to explore different options, spice things up, and evolve our designs over time. Engaging visual features can capture children's attention and help us highlight important points.

One year I stumbled upon an online image (unrelated to education) that inspired the layout shown in Figure 4.1. Rather than present our ideas as a series of paragraphs, I designed the document to look like the front wall of a classroom. The text was fit inside a whiteboard, two bulletin boards, a clock, a flag, and other "classroom-themed" shapes. As much as possible, the meaning of the text matched the object in which it was placed. For instance, inside the clock was a natural spot to mention our desire to use time well.

The Levi Strauss & Company mission statement (Box 4.4) offers another way to format our mission statements. The sample that follows is an abridged version of what their mission statement was at the time I first did this activity with my class. Over the years, this approach has become my favorite. Once I started employing this design, I never stopped. I believe that opening every paragraph with a brief heading followed by a slightly longer description is very effective and instantly enables readers to identify the focus of each section. In addition, I thought the sentence fragments, centered, at the end of the document presented interesting opportunities for us to be creative and conclude the statement with some oomph. Part of the Levi's mission statement inspired the classroom counterpart that follows in Box 4.5.

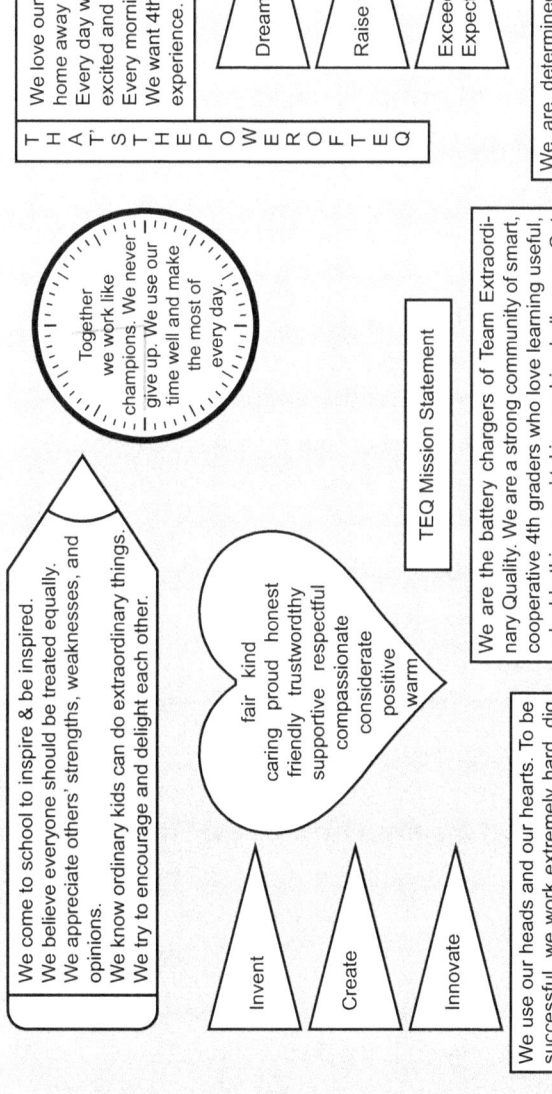

Figure 4.1 Class mission statement with "front wall" theme.

Box 4.4 Levi Strauss & Company Mission Statement

Levi Strauss & Company

Our values are as much a part of Levi Strauss & Co. as the people who live them, every day.

Empathy—Walking in other people's shoes

Empathy begins with paying close attention to the world around us. We listen and respond to the needs of our customers, employees and other stakeholders.

Originality—Being authentic and innovative

The pioneering spirit that started in 1873 with the very first pair of blue jeans still permeates all aspects of our business.

Integrity—Doing the right thing

Integrity means doing right by our employees, brands, company and society as a whole.

Courage—Standing up for what we believe

It takes courage to be great. Courage is the willingness to tell the truth and to challenge hierarchy, accepted practice and conventional wisdom.

We are the embodiment of the energy and events of our time, inspiring people from all walks of life with a pioneering spirit. . . . Reverent, irreverent—[our customers] took a stand.

Cut from the best cloth.

Crafted with expert care.

Designed for the long haul.

Box 4.5 Class Mission Statement Inspired by the Levi Strauss Format

TTQ Mission Statement

We are the go-getters of Team Total Quality. We are a class of friendly, determined battery chargers who want to accomplish extraordinary things. We commit ourselves to working for the highest quality of education possible and making this year one of the greatest experiences of our lives. We are active and strong in both mind and body. Our classroom is a garden of bloomers.

Our Work—A Total Commitment to Quality

We are passionate about learning new things and producing quality work. Every day we work like champions—we try our best, use our time well, and never even think of giving up. Difficult challenges are fun and help us become smarter and move to higher levels. Learning makes us powerful. The more we learn now, the more choices we will have in the future and the more goals we can reach. We take amazing pride in being responsible students, attentive listeners, and independent learners. We are serious, focused people who make every day count.

Our Character—Holding Ourselves to the Highest Standards

We strive to represent honor and integrity in everything we do. We are honest and respectful, cooperative and kind, fair and patient, confident and disciplined. Everyone on this team is equal and special, and we believe in our classmates. We are mindful of everyone's feelings and try to inspire one another. When it comes to character, our standards are uncompromising. We are courageous leaders and thoughtful problem-solvers who speak up for ourselves and stand up for what we believe. Our actions speak louder than our words.

Our Expectations—Determined to Raise the Bar

Each day is a new beginning, and we come to school every morning energetic and ready to learn. We push ourselves to the limit and aim to soar beyond the expectations of a typical fourth-grade classroom. We do not want to be just okay; we want to be the best of the best. It is important for us to improve continuously so we can achieve both personal excellence and team excellence. It's like we are each a chapter in a great book. We will stop at nothing in our efforts to be successful. We are driven to become the best students and best role models we can be.

Our Classroom Community—Encouraging One Another to Grow and Shine

We believe that when we work together with trust, we become unstoppable. Our classroom is warm, safe, and fun—free of bullying and full of empathy, enthusiasm, and outstanding behavior. At all times, we try to act with maturity, courtesy, and sportsmanship. We put smiles on everybody's faces. We do not criticize; we are 100% positive. We are dedicated to making the school community a better place and having a positive impact on others. We are all in this together and devote ourselves to creating a calm, happy atmosphere where we feel comfortable.

Born to dream, invent, and shine.
Filled with the highest of hopes.
Motivated to achieve greatness.
That's the power of TTQ.

Class Mission Statement "Companion Visual"

After reading Dan Roam's (2016) terrific book *Draw to Win* one summer, my students and I started creating a companion visual to represent the mission statement's main ideas. The rationale behind making the companion visual is that seeing the statement as an image may help students understand the ideas on a deeper level, and the ideas may resonate with the kids in a way they might not with text alone.

The kids all had the opportunity to contribute to the process of creating the visual, and one student made our final draft using Google Draw. (More on that later.) To keep these ideas in everyone's mind, we put the image on one of our classroom doors and on the front of our class T-shirt. Many class T-shirts display the teacher's name and perhaps the room number. There's certainly nothing wrong with that. The front of a shirt that the kids will wear multiple times during the year, however, is prime advertising space. I believe we should take full advantage of that space by having it represent something important about our team. Our visual, aim, or a few key words from the mission statement or about our culture would all be great choices. One year we used the letters of our team name to create an acrostic poem featuring many words at the core of our mission. Another year we spelled out our team name using each child's name (and mine) as the "building blocks" of each letter.

Though my students and I use the visual as a complement to our class mission statement, it can also, if necessary, serve as a stand-alone effort to establish purpose, set an expectation level, and describe the kind of environment you and your students would like to build. In fact, I recommend creating this type of image if you are a physical education specialist, music teacher, or other type of educator who works with different groups of children throughout the day and don't have the time to write a mission statement with each group. The visual also serves as an effective option if you are currently well into your school year and would like to try out this process with an eye toward writing a class mission statement at the start of the next school year.

To begin the process of creating a visual with your students, either start from scratch or use the one shown in Figure 4.2 as a starting point. The children may have a clearer idea of what you're asking them to design if they can see what another class has already done. If you have a completed class mission statement, read through it paragraph by paragraph and provide time after each one for the kids to represent the ideas pictorially. This may take a few sessions. If you have not yet written a mission statement, pose the same five questions I shared earlier in this chapter. Working alone, with partners, or in small groups, the kids will answer the questions using pictures. Next, create a draft of the image or have one or more kids take responsibility for the draft and then revise it as a class until you are satisfied with it.

Figure 4.2 Class mission statement companion visual.

Here is a description of the various parts of the first class visual my students and I created. Let's begin on the bottom left. The image of the sun rising reminds all of us that every day is a new opportunity to do some great learning. No matter what might have happened the day before, each day offers a fresh start.

In many ways, our school year can be viewed as a quest to improve continuously and level up. "Leveling up" is a concept we can apply to each academic area, our Habits of Mind and Habits of Character, even to our friendships and our health and wellness. Leveling up is the idea that the two kids moving up the stairs represent. It's important to note that they're not walking up the stairs; they are charging.

They're bringing energy, determination, and passion to their learning. That's what the lightning bolt on the left conveys.

As each of us commits to continuous improvement, we don't go at it alone. There's a strong sense of teamwork, kindness, and cooperation in the class. That's why the two kids are reaching for each other's hands. As we try to improve, individually, we are also trying to help others level up.

The battery near the top step relates to the impact we can all have on one another. I mentioned previously that a term we frequently use in class is "battery charger," a person whose sheer presence makes the classroom environment better and happier because of the positive spirit they consistently display.

Above the head of each child, you see light bulbs that show how we are all bright, talented people with amazing potential. One thing that's different about each child is their expression. On the left, the smiling face is designed to show that learning should feel good and that our classroom experiences should be joyful. Furthermore, the smile means that we're confident, enthusiastic students who are engaged and intrinsically motivated. On the right, the expression and beads of sweat show that sometimes things can be difficult, and doing our work can be a grind. When this happens, we don't shy away from it; we embrace challenges and demonstrate perseverance and grit.

Finally, the "HQ" in the top right corner connects to our expectations. Specifically, it expresses that we are always working for the highest quality and won't settle for less than our best.

The 7 Life Roles

With the classroom aim and mission statement firmly in place, it is now our responsibility to show children how the work they do each day contributes to the fulfillment of that mission. According to Dale Parnell (1995), author of *Why Do I Have to Learn This?*,

> the major task of the teacher [is] to broaden students' perceptions so that meaning becomes visible and the purpose of learning immediately understandable. It is not enough to help students see the specific objectives of a lesson or even an overall course. Instead, teachers must help students understand the larger meaning of a particular study—how it relates to real-life issues and actual life roles.

By "life roles" Parnell means those experiences and sets of responsibilities that individuals have in common. Parnell believes that "no matter what our specific interests, talents, or backgrounds," humans all perform the following seven life roles throughout their lives:

- Lifelong learner
- Citizen
- Consumer
- Producer (worker)
- Individual (self)
- Family member
- Leisure participant

Parnell makes the point that teachers should not view these roles as responsibilities that children will occupy later in life but as roles they already occupy today. It is necessary, therefore, for students to have a clear understanding of each one. See Resource E for priorities associated with each role. Because students will be able to relate to these human commonalities, Parnell believes that the life roles offer teachers a promising start in the quest to help kids find meaning in their work. The life roles, then, can serve as a bridge, helping children connect their daily learning to the higher purposes embedded in the aim and class mission statement.

Examples of how we can integrate the life roles into our curricula are limitless. At the most basic level, we can incorporate the life roles into individual lessons pertaining to any academic area. One simple example occurred in a first-grade classroom during our study of subtraction. I invited a student volunteer, David, to the front of the room to participate in a role-play situation. We imagined we were in a candy store. I was the clerk; David, the customer. He purchased a chocolate bar for $2, paying me with a $5 bill, which we represented with a stick of five unified cubes. I turned around, pretending to put the bill in the cash register, and I intentionally gave him only $1 in change. At the end of the activity, I explained to the class that if David didn't yet understand how to subtract, he could easily fall victim to a dishonest clerk. While observing the demonstration, a classmate, who was fond of money, spontaneously responded, "Wow, subtraction *is* important!" The ability to subtract would, thus, empower students to be effective shoppers. With that brief demonstration and the unexpected curricular validation that followed, I connected a math lesson on subtraction to the larger idea that we learn because it makes our lives better, a sentiment expressed in one form or another each year in our mission statement by highlighting the importance of being an intelligent consumer.

The Tower of Opportunity

However you choose to incorporate the life roles into your curriculum, a powerful visual metaphor called the Tower of Opportunity will greatly strengthen your implementation. An architect friend helped me design the Tower several years ago. The four-sided structure contains seven stories, one for each role. The role names occupy one side of the tower, while specific examples of each role occupy the other three. Figure 4.3 shows photographs of two of the sides. Figure 4.4 displays a template of the Tower, from which you can make copies for your students, fold the sides into a freestanding replica, or design a larger model for your classroom. (You can find a printable copy of the template on the Routledge website.)

Examples of each role are printed on doors that include tiny doorknobs. The design of the Tower allows us, as teachers, to convey the message that life is rich with opportunities, choices, and options, but that in order to take advantage of these opportunities, maximize our choices, and give ourselves the greatest number of options, we need an education. Put simply, education

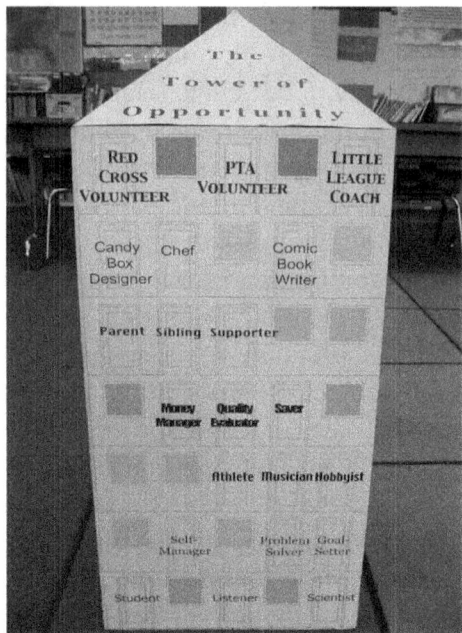

Figure 4.3 Two sides of the Tower of Opportunity.

is the key that opens doors. The harder we work in school and the more we learn, the more doors we can open for ourselves. Thus, the Tower provides a powerful visual metaphor that enables educators to take normally abstract notions about the future and make them more concrete and relevant.

An important aspect of the Tower's design relates to the sequence of roles from bottom to top. The arrangement isn't random; rather, it is an attempt to illustrate each role's potential for contributing to and impacting the larger society. While the potential certainly exists for people assuming any role to make a difference in the lives of others, the roles located on the bottom tend to focus primarily on individual needs, goals, and priorities, while those higher on the Tower tend to involve progressively larger numbers of people. I am the first to concede that this order is rough at best, yet I believe it benefits children to arrange the roles in this manner to highlight the idea of service. As long as we discuss the inexactness of the sequence with the kids so they don't view the order as being overly rigid, there shouldn't be any problem.

The Tower, like the class mission statement, becomes a significant reference point that children should revisit frequently. Each Wednesday, as part of our morning routine, my students and I focus on a specific aspect of the Tower and discuss how our classroom learning connects in some way to our current or future goals. In what follows, you will find a list of topics from which we choose to structure our "Tower Talks." In addition to these scheduled

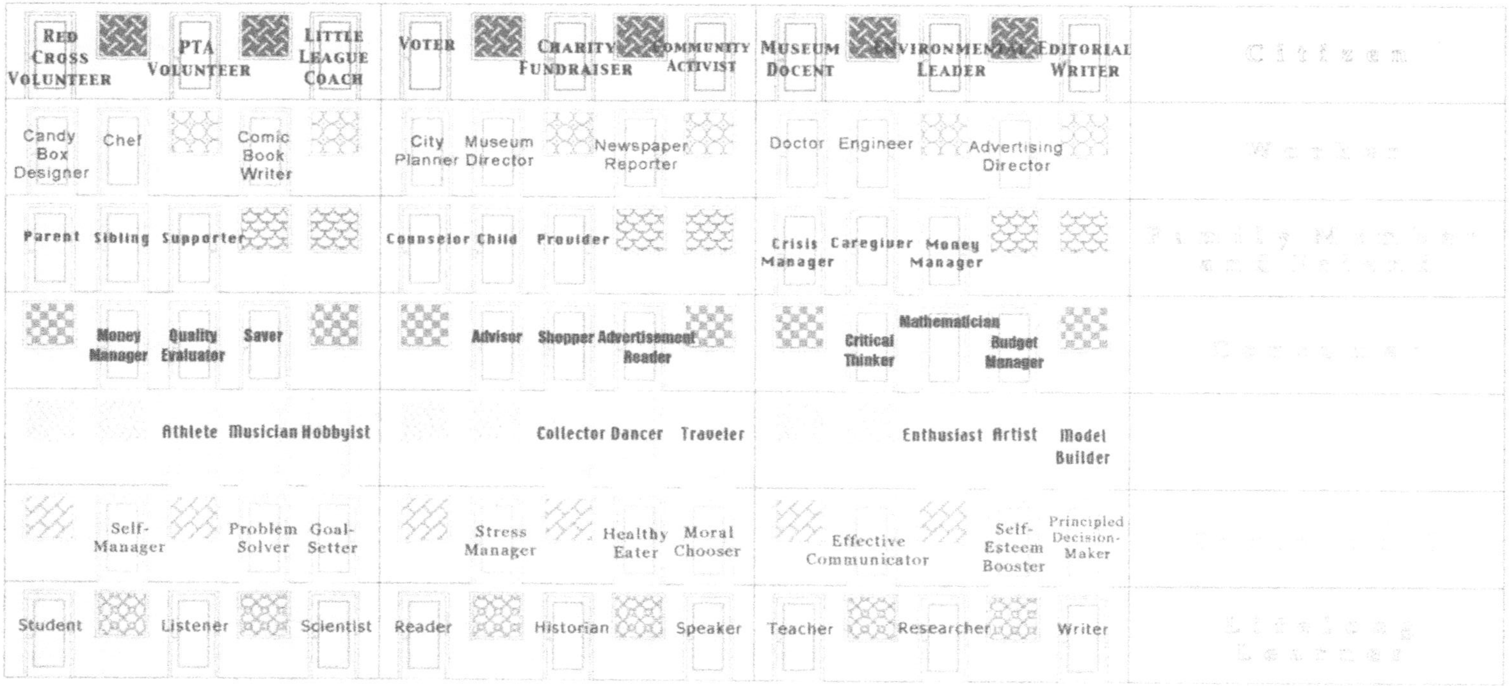

Purpose ◆ 109

Figure 4.4 Tower of Opportunity template.

discussions, we conduct others that occur spontaneously—at the start of a new unit or project, for example, or when we choose to talk about an item we heard on the news, share a personal story, or try to capitalize on a learnable moment. The goal is for the Tower to maintain a consistent presence in the classroom throughout the year. Every time we reference the Tower, I am able to remind students of the numerous ways in which their learning can be put to use and the many reasons learning matters so much. When teachers use the Tower with students, we expand their perspective and encourage them to think beyond their present reality. Furthermore, we provide a glimpse of what a productive, well-rounded life can look like.

"Tower Time" Topics

Tower introduction: I provide a brief introduction and overview of each role and focus on one role per week for our first seven "Tower Talks."

Arrangement of floors: I explain the bottom-to-top sequence of roles. As I mentioned previously, while the potential certainly exists for people assuming any role to make a difference in the lives of others, the roles located on the bottom tend to focus primarily on individual needs, goals, and priorities, while those higher on the tower tend to involve progressively larger numbers of people. During this talk, we also discuss the inexactness of the sequence so the kids don't view the order as being overly rigid.

"Zooming in": I focus on specific floors or doors that may hold special significance. During an election year, for example, conversations can center on the role of *citizen*. Specifically, teachers and students can discuss candidates, issues, voting procedures, and how education and the importance of an education connect to them. If we don't have time in our schedules for a full elections unit, we can use "Tower Time" for brief discussions, presentations, and sharing of information and opinions.

Learning connections: The students and I connect what we are currently learning in class to future goals or larger purposes.

Open forum: Periodically, I have the students pick a role or door and connect it to something currently happening at school or in their lives outside of school.

Upcoming events: When I mention upcoming local events (e.g., The *Los Angeles Times* Festival of Books) or institutions (e.g., museums, libraries), I can connect them to one or more roles on the Tower.

Articles: Information found in newspaper or magazine articles can tie in well with the emphases of the Tower. For example, every year I share an article describing a study that compares the cumulative earnings, life expectancies, and health outcomes of people who graduate from high school with those of individuals who don't. Very powerful.

Biographies: Sometimes I read short biographies or excerpts of biographies about well-known individuals and highlight the role that education played in helping these people achieve their successes.

"A Glimpse of the Future" discussions: Teachers select a role, and students share their goals or plans related to that role. For example, if I select the role of *lifelong learner*, students can share a college they hope to attend or an academic area they wish to pursue. If I select the role of *worker*, kids can share the types of jobs they want. If we are discussing the role of *family member and friend* or *citizen*, the children can talk about the contributions they want to make to their families and communities. I have always believed that the most important decision young people can make is the one to commit themselves to education and make becoming a successful student a top priority. Listening to students who have already made this commitment speak intelligently, thoughtfully, and sincerely about what they hope to accomplish as they get older is one of the great joys I experience in my job.

Lesson Lead-Ins

Once we have established a sense of purpose at the "macro-level" with our aim, mission statement, and life roles, we can then move to the "micro-level" and focus on the purpose of individual lessons. When students can see how "micro-level" lessons further their progress toward valued "macro-level" purposes, they are more engaged, more motivated, and more willing to commit themselves to academic pursuits. In our teacher training programs we learn how to craft a lesson plan based on a clear objective. While it is important to state the objective at the start of a lesson, we don't want to stop there. It is beneficial to couple that objective with a brief explanation of why we are learning it—why we are devoting valuable instructional time to this content. Our explanations can relate to a life role, a part of our mission statement, a larger academic goal, an aspect of our classroom culture, or any other "whole-child" priority. I refer to this pairing of objective and purpose as a lesson lead-in. We can view the lesson lead-in as a type of anticipatory set, a term popularized by well-known educator Madeline Hunter, that sets the stage for the learning that follows. (I consider myself extremely fortunate to have been a graduate student in the final class she taught at UCLA.)

My favorite lesson lead-in pertains to the topic of revising, an important part of the writing process that elementary students tend to rush through. In our Writing Workshop, we use a revising checklist that spells out the various tasks I ask everyone to complete when working with a partner. Once I demonstrate how to accomplish these tasks collaboratively, I explain how learning to revise makes us more capable writers and describe a variety of jobs and roles that require this skill set. I then turn my attention to two significant aspects of our class culture, kindness and service. I refer back to my "cubicle story" and share that the partner revising we are about to begin offers another wonderful opportunity to use our knowledge and skills to positively and powerfully impact someone else's day. By caring deeply about our partner's work and demonstrating a genuine desire to help improve it, we are being a strong partner and a good friend.

Make an effort to launch academic lessons with some type of lead-in. Whether you connect the learning to one of the life roles, a phrase from your mission statement, the development of your students' number sense or math reasoning skills, or a Habit of Mind or Habit of Character, you are providing a terrific service. You are helping children expand their perspective and see the bigger picture. And in the event that a child ever asks you why they are learning something, don't get upset! Many times educators view that as an impertinent or inappropriate question and marvel at the nerve a child is showing by daring to ask that! Instead, let's celebrate that question. Let's encourage this type of thinking. It means a student genuinely wants to better understand the purposes of their learning and find meaning and relevance in it. If we are able to provide a satisfying answer, it's a win–win for everyone. If not, if we can't explain the purpose, following the lead of the Dodgers Minor League coaches, perhaps we remove it from our curriculum.

Closing

Three rings of the organizational target are now complete. I will describe the fourth and final ring, personal mission statements, in Chapter 10. Starting from the aim and moving outward to personal mission statements, we proceed inside out from the general to the specific, from the group level to the individual level. Each successive ring advances our cause to establish a sense of purpose in our classrooms. Establishing purpose requires that we commit ourselves to making an ongoing effort to help students find meaning in their work. We achieve this objective by connecting daily classroom learning to higher, worthwhile purposes that kids value.

To keep these purposes fresh in students' minds, I devote one side of our front classroom wall to what I call our "Big Picture Diagram" (Figure 4.5). The

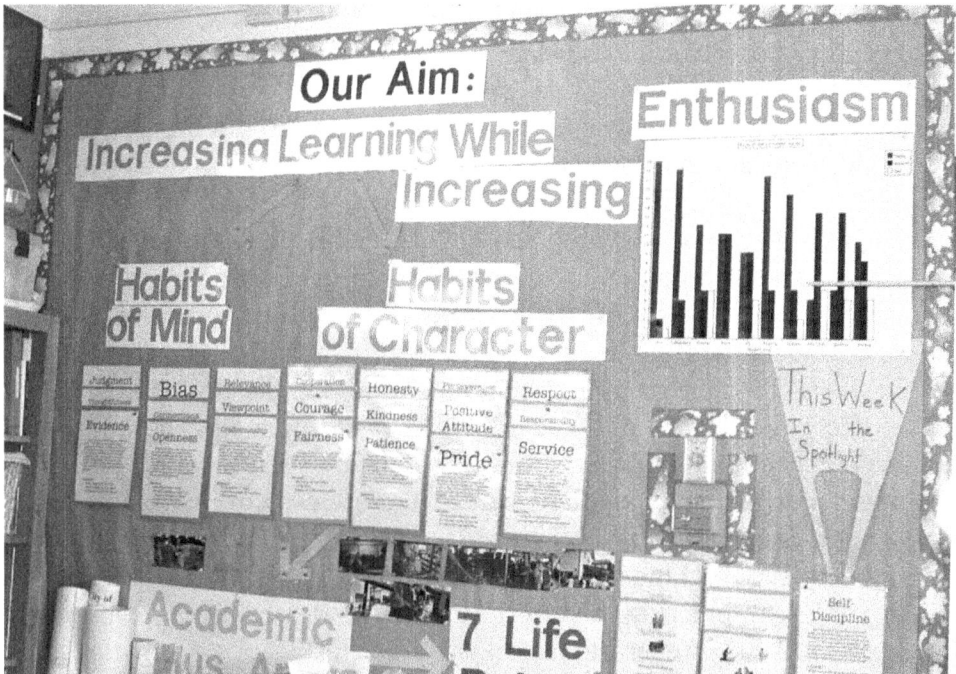

Figure 4.5 Front wall of my classroom.

display enables the children to understand how many of our highest-priority ideas fit together. A photograph of this wall can be found in what follows. In Chapter 2, I urged you to resist the temptation to cover your classroom walls before the start of the school year, so the kids can experience the joy of seeing this space fill over time. The one annual exception I make to that recommendation involves this display. With the mission statement visible on the door just to the left of this wall and the Tower of Opportunity on the floor to the right, I am able to use this area of the classroom as a consistent reference point for the entire school year. We discuss this diagram, in whole or in part, frequently.

Let's take a look at the diagram's parts. We start at the top with our biggest idea of all, our overall aim of "increasing learning while increasing enthusiasm." The aim establishes that our primary goal is to learn as much as we can and be as excited about our learning as possible. The graph on the right displays the results of our Fall Enthusiasm Survey (described in Chapter 9), a brief exercise inspired by the Enterprise School District's attitude survey mentioned earlier. The term *learning* from our aim is divided into two types, academic learning and "character" learning. With each type, the emphasis is on developing lifelong habits. Not shown in the diagram is the area below the two sets of habits, which contains our various academic disciplines. Placing the habits above the academic disciplines shows that we are always trying to enrich our work in the different subjects by incorporating the Habits of Mind and Habits of Character. On the right side of the academic disciplines section is an arrow pointing to the "7 Life Roles." Placing these two bottom sections side by side is a move designed to remind students that our academic learning is always meant to help them now and in the future with one or more of the roles. Finally, the small pictures beneath the Habits of Character signs show a Japanese cabinet-making factory I was fortunate to visit in 2003 while on a 3-week study tour with 200 American teachers. The company is known worldwide for its high-quality furniture, and I posted the photos to illustrate the concept of craftsmanship, that week's featured Habit of Mind.

Taken together, the diagram's components address critical issues that go far beyond passing tests and mastering standards: how students feel about the subjects they are studying, how they relate to one another, how they operate as thinkers, and how they manage themselves throughout the learning process. The diagram, then, illustrates a broader, more balanced view of learning and supports the notion that a successful classroom focuses on the whole child—empowering students to succeed academically while also helping them build strong character, learn valuable work habits and social skills, and take charge of their health and wellness.

Reference List

Blankstein, A. (2004). *Failure Is Not an Option*. Thousand Oaks, CA: Corwin Press.
Covey, S. (1989). *The Seven Habits of Highly Effective People*. New York: Fireside.
Covey, S. (1994). *First Things First*. New York: Fireside.
Harris, Jack. (23 July, 2023). "Inside the Dodgers' Juggernaut Farm System, the Lifeblood of the Club." *Los Angeles Times*.
Jenkins, L. (1997). *Improving Student Learning: Applying Deming's Quality Principles in Classrooms*. Milwaukee: ASQC Quality Press.
Parnell, D. (1995). *Why Do I Have to Learn This?* Waco, TX: CORD Communications.
Reifman, S. (2008). *Eight Essentials for Empowered Teaching & Learning, K-8*. Thousand Oaks, CA: Corwin Press.
Reifman, S. (2020). *107 Awesome Elementary Teaching Ideas You Can Implement Tomorrow*. New York: Routledge.
Roam, D. (2016). *Draw to Win*. New York: Penguin Random House.

5
Quality

Following the devastation of World War II, the people of Japan faced an uncertain economic future. The tiny island nation, already hampered by a lack of natural resources and an international reputation for producing second-rate goods, now had to overcome the destruction of its industrial base. Prospects for a strong recovery looked bleak: Survival was the immediate goal. In the years to come, however, the Japanese people would do more than just survive; they would achieve perhaps the greatest economic turnaround in modern history.

Ironically, the individual widely credited with initiating the Japanese postwar transformation was an American. Born in 1900, W. Edwards Deming was trained in mathematics, physics, and engineering, earning his PhD from Yale University in 1928. While working as a statistician for the US Census Bureau in the 1930s, he first received notoriety pioneering the use of sampling techniques in the gathering of data. Under Deming's leadership, the bureau won recognition for its ability to provide accurate information on a broad range of areas at a cost that no other organization, public or private, could match. Deming's successes earned him an invitation to Japan in the summer of 1950 to meet with top business leaders who were determined to revitalize their nation.

On arriving in Japan, Deming insisted that producing high-quality goods was the key to the nation's future. In her book *The World of W. Edwards Deming*, author Cecelia Kilian (1992) explains that improving quality, as the chain reaction in Figure 5.1 illustrates, leads to greater productivity due to

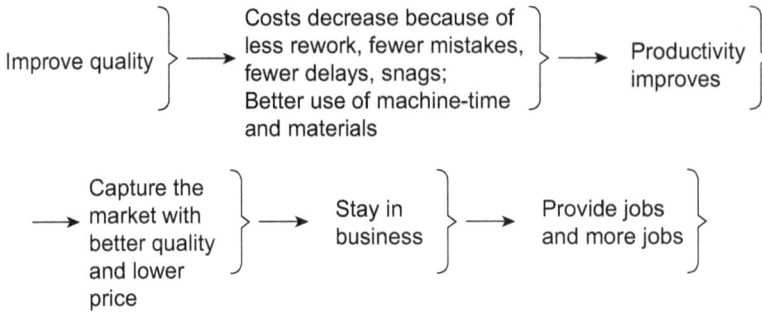

Reproduced from Deming's Out of the Crisis p.3

W. E. Deming (1986), Out of the Crisis, MIT Center for Advanced Engineering Study, Cambridge, MA, p. 3

Figure 5.1 Deming chain reaction.

a decrease in costs and a better use of machine time and materials. With the resulting higher-quality, lower-priced goods, companies capture the market, enabling them to stay in business and employ more people. As the chain reaction reverberates throughout society, the number of jobs grows and the entire standard of living rises. Citizens live more comfortably, and workers take more pride in their efforts. In this situation, according to Deming, everybody wins.

Deming contended that if business leaders followed his teachings, Japanese products would become the envy of the world. His declaration that Japanese industry could shed its poor manufacturing reputation and achieve economic prosperity within five years shocked his audiences. Although the leaders dared not to believe such rapid progress was possible, they were receptive to Deming's hopeful message. They listened intently, spending the next few years learning and implementing his theory. Ultimately, though, Deming's prediction proved to be inaccurate. According to Kilian, it didn't take five years for the Japanese to turn out top-quality goods. It took four.

Applying Deming's Approach to Education

Focusing on quality in our schools will set off a new chain reaction. The process, as Figure 5.2 indicates, begins with a focus on producing quality work. Enthusiastically pursuing quality provides abundant, natural opportunities for students to develop and internalize effective Habits of Mind and Habits of Character, patterns of behavior that are essential to success in school and

Focus on Quality} > Development and Internalization of Habits} > Success in School} > Success in 7 Life Roles} > Lead Quality Life} > Contribute to Society

Figure 5.2 Education chain reaction.

beyond. Children who commit to this cause will mature into adults who are able to care for themselves and those around them and who are able to look outward and make meaningful contributions to society. Focusing on quality during their school years will ultimately empower future generations with the knowledge, skills, and habits to lead fulfilling lives and help others. Again, everybody wins.

Even though Deming's primary focus was industry, not education, he has made a greater impact on my teaching philosophy than anyone. When he spoke of factory employees working together, experiencing joy and pride, and communicating openly and respectfully, he might as well have been writing about children functioning in the type of classroom I wanted to set foot into every day. And when he describes employees understanding the purpose of their efforts, taking ownership of the process, and embracing the pursuit of quality, he could have easily been referring to the approach I wanted children to adopt with regard to their schoolwork. Upon reading Deming, I knew deep down in my bones that the ideal type of manager–worker relationship he details was the type of teacher–student relationship I was determined to create. In both settings, after all, the goals are similar—to produce quality in a motivating, collaborative, need-satisfying environment. His teachings, though developed in a business environment, aren't *business* principles but *quality* principles that promise exciting possibilities to leaders of any organization. Whether its mission involves producing cars or educating children, focusing on quality is the rising tide that lifts all boats.

When writing about quality in education, it's nearly impossible for me to mention Deming without referencing William Glasser—first, because Deming influenced Glasser; second, because I learned about both individuals at the same point in my career. Glasser introduced me to a body of work known as quality theory. Sure, I knew what the word *quality* meant and that striving to produce quality work was an important goal, but I wasn't aware that a school of thought existed that described how to define *quality*, how to measure it, and how to create the conditions where quality was most likely to flourish. In *The Quality School*, Glasser presents a non-coercive approach to education featuring classrooms where teachers lead, not boss, and students work hard to improve, not to earn rewards or avoid punishments, but because producing quality work satisfies their most basic needs and feels good, especially when kids have frequent opportunities to participate in cooperative learning activities.

In the type of need-satisfying classrooms Glasser describes, children are happy because they are producing worthwhile work that engages their minds, and teachers are happy because students are putting out genuine effort and learning. Students behave well because they understand it is in their best interest to behave. Doing so will have the most powerful effect on their learning and the most positive impact on the group. There is a problem-solving orientation that characterizes Glasser's approach, one that promotes teamwork and shared decision-making. Under this approach, students are less likely to rock the boat because they helped build it, are co-owners, and have a stake in making sure it reaches its destination.

Defining Quality

The first step in launching a collective commitment to produce quality work involves defining the word *quality*. For the pursuit of quality to become the driving force in our classrooms, children need a clear understanding of what the term means. *Quality* can be a tricky word to define because it is subjective. If we asked 20 people to share their definition of the term, we could very well get 20 different answers.

What I consider to be a quality pickleball paddle, for example, you may not. Imagine for a moment that you and I pay a visit to our local pickleball superstore. Immediately, the latest 13 mm paddle catches your eye. For good reason. It offers maximum power and impressive spin, and its red-and-yellow design reminds you of your two favorite fruits. Plus, the rather small handle fits your hand perfectly. The paddle may not provide as much control, but that's not an issue for you since control has always been a staple of your game. Not me. I need a 16 mm paddle for greater stability and support, as well as an extra-long handle to accommodate my two-handed backhand. Furthermore, as a lifelong UCLA Bruin, I know anything red and yellow instinctively provokes an allergic reaction. Whereas you might pick up my paddle, inspect it, and put it right back down, I give the clerk my credit card with no hesitation. Because we are human and have our own tastes, preferences, and opinions, the subjective nature of quality will always exist.

If, however, quality is to become the driving force in our classrooms, we need to find a way to acknowledge the individual, subjective nature of quality while working toward a more objective definition we can all share. We need a shared definition to enable team members to speak the same language. Without a common definition, everyone will rely on their own personal notion of quality, making communication more difficult and progress less likely. Recognizing the subjective while seeking something objective in a manner that maintains the integrity of both may seem logically impossible, but it can be done.

In *The Quality School*, William Glasser (1990) introduces the concept of the "quality world" and, in so doing, demonstrates how it is possible to create a shared, objective definition of a term that will always be subjective and personal. According to Glasser, as I have mentioned previously, human beings are constantly attempting to satisfy five basic needs: survival, power, friendship, fun, and freedom. From birth, he claims, we learn and remember all the people, things, and situations that help us satisfy these needs. In fact, we store pictures and perceptions of all these need-satisfiers in a part of our memory that Glasser calls the quality world. Thus, when defining *quality*, Glasser focuses on the mental pictures that all of us have stored in our quality worlds, whether they include the homes in which we grew up that satisfied our need for survival, our favorite childhood board games that satisfied our need for fun, or 13 mm pickleball paddles that satisfy our need for power. Glasser's would be a shared, objective definition of *quality* because it is based on five needs we all try to meet. Because each of us stores different mental pictures in our quality worlds, however, this objective definition also recognizes the subjective nature of quality.

Although I originally found (and still find) the quality world construct fascinating, I realized I needed a more practical, user-friendly definition to employ in the classroom. I continued my definitional quest until I hit educational pay dirt with the work of quality expert Philip Crosby. In his book *Quality Without Tears*, Crosby (1984) asserts that the major problem with most definitions of *quality* relates to the fact that the word is usually defined in terms of "goodness." As a result, these definitions do nothing to advance a common understanding, because we all have different ideas of what goodness means; what's good to one person isn't to another. Or as Crosby puts it, when someone speaks of goodness, "nobody knows what that means except the speaker."

As an alternative, Crosby argues that quality must be defined as *conformance to requirements*. Imagine, for example, I was in the market for a new pair of running shoes. I need my shoes to be gray, provide extra toe support, consist of waterproof material, and cost less than $100. Under this definition, any shoes that conform to these requirements would be quality running shoes.

For several reasons, conformance to requirements is the most effective definition of *quality* to use with children. First, it best resolves the difficulties associated with acknowledging the subjective while requiring something objective. Assume, for example, your students are set to begin work on a poster project summarizing their recently completed independent science investigations. You explain that you expect everyone to produce a quality poster. Were your instructions to end there, without a common definition, the kids would simply try their best to create posters that satisfied their own ideas of goodness, and the results would vary widely. As author Mary Walton (1986), in her book *The Deming Management Method*, puts it, though, "[t]rying your best isn't enough. You have to know what to do, *then* do your best." So you brainstorm with your class a list of criteria that would constitute quality work for this project. Likely, students would suggest a write-up of the various stages of the scientific method, perhaps a photograph of the materials used or some other visual aid, and maybe a few nuts-and-bolts items, such as the title of the project and their names. You may choose to add other criteria, such as neatness, or some suggestions regarding organization. After further discussion, you and your students will have co-created a list containing a reasonable number of specific criteria that exemplify quality. The list will never be perfect, and although people will never completely agree on goodness, we can agree on requirements. Not everyone will get their way regarding every criterion, but you will reach agreement on a shared definition born from everyone's personal, subjective opinions.

The posters your students create using your quality criteria as a common reference point will be far better than those they would have created based solely on their individual notions of goodness, and any child's project that conforms to your class-generated requirements will deserve to be considered quality work. In addition, the brainstorming process itself, as with the class missioning process, builds teamwork, increases cohesiveness, and provides students with genuine opportunities to contribute to the group. Another advantage of using Crosby's definition lies in its flexibility. The idea of defining *quality* as conformance to requirements can be applied with equal effectiveness to any type of work or endeavor for which quality is the goal, from creative writing to science investigations to behavior at an assembly.

Another example of this definition's flexibility can be found in the generic quality work rubric shown in Figure 5.3. I created the rubric after reading Deming, Glasser, and Crosby, when I was first attempting to implement their

Quality Work Rubric
How Do I Give Myself the Best Chance to Produce Quality Work?

1) Care Deeply - "Quality = Caring." This simply means that in order to accomplish great things in any endeavor, individuals must care a great deal about the work they do.

2) Very Best Effort - Quality students give their very best effort, day in and day out.

3) Take Pride In It - When students produce quality work, you can see the pride in their faces and in the way they act.

4) Improvement - The idea of continuous improvement means that each piece of work represents, in some way, an improvement over the last one.

5) Intrinsic Motivation - For work to be considered quality, the effort, desire, and focus must come from within. Quality students do not need to be reminded to get started or stay on task.

6) Purpose - Quality work is important work; it serves a purpose. Students should understand how completing a given activity will benefit them, and perhaps others, now and in the future.

Figure 5.3 Quality work rubric.

teachings into my classroom practice. As the title implies, this rubric is not meant to relate to any specific subject or project but to the idea of quality in general so that students can better understand the relationship between the work itself and the attitudes and ingredients needed to produce it. When children satisfy these six criteria, they will be far more likely to achieve quality.

Students should learn to define *quality* as conformance to requirements early in the school year. Discussing either the quality work rubric or Glasser's quality world construct is a possible way of introducing Crosby's definition to your students. Another interesting approach involves choosing an object relevant to your students' lives and asking them what makes that object a *quality* object. Take a cupcake, for example. Begin the exercise by holding up a cupcake in front of your class and asking, "Do you think this is a quality cupcake?" Whether the kids answer yes or no doesn't matter; what matters are the reasons they give to support their opinions. Juan believes it is a quality cupcake because it has icing, while Emily argues that it isn't because it's partially burnt. As the kids offer their opinions, we list criteria on the board. At this point, we accept all contributions without judgment, a recommended practice when participating in any type of brainstorming. Later, we will comb through our list, combining overlapping ideas, filling gaps, and perhaps removing nonessential criteria. Thus far, we have two requirements: Quality cupcakes have icing and are thoroughly baked. (This is better than saying "aren't burnt." We always want to state matters positively and mention what the object has or is, not what it's missing or what it isn't.) In a short time, you will have a complete list of requirements. Again, not everyone will agree with each criterion, but the group will reach agreement on a *quality cupcake* definition that can be used as a reference point to evaluate future cupcakes.

Should you not wish to promote high-calorie desserts in your classroom, many other "object possibilities" exist for this exercise, including baseball cards, pencils, and backpacks, just to name a few. Any object will do. As part of my whole-child focus on health and wellness, I generally avoid mentioning sweets and, instead, sing the praises of fruits and vegetables. Discussing what makes a quality salad, soup, or sandwich works just as well. The crucial factor is that children receive valuable practice defining *quality* in terms of specific criteria. Once the kids can carry out this type of task comfortably, they will be ready to define *quality work* for the various academic areas, projects, and worthwhile endeavors that await them throughout the school year. One final note: Because the phrase *conformance to requirements* can be difficult for children, particularly younger ones, to remember or to say, you may prefer a more kid-friendly definition: *Quality means that something has what it is supposed to have.*

Defining Quality Across the Curriculum

Once we commit to defining *quality* as conformance to requirements, we can apply this practice to any academic area and choose criteria for any type of project, assessment, or performance. In both the science investigation and cupcake examples I shared previously, the children had the opportunity to help us brainstorm and determine criteria. Inviting student participation in this manner brings numerous benefits, such as a more thorough understanding of a given project, as well as greater buy-in and ownership of the process. That said, after we have introduced the kids to our class definition of *quality*, it is perfectly fine for us to establish quality criteria for specific endeavors on our own and present them to the class. One factor in this decision is simply time. If we plan to choose quality criteria for many projects across multiple subject areas throughout the school year, that requires precious instructional minutes that are already in short supply. If you feel the benefits of student participation warrant that investment of time, go for it. In addition, for activities that may be new to children, it may not be reasonable to expect them to brainstorm a comprehensive list of requirements. If we need to chime in and add one or two, that's not a big deal. If, however, we find ourselves doing too much of the talking during a brainstorming session, it could be a sign that we might have been better off doing it ourselves. One more thing to consider. When I find a list of quality criteria that proves effective, I like to reuse it in future years. In these cases, if I were to launch a brainstorming session, I might be tempted to steer the kids toward a predetermined outcome, which is something I always try to avoid. How often we involve students in selecting quality criteria is a professional decision each of us needs to make for ourselves.

Math Problem-Solving

Here are some examples of what quality criteria might look like for a few different types of learning activities. In each case we are striving for a reasonable number of requirements (say, three to five) that are clear and comprehensive. Let's begin with math problem-solving. Many years ago, I created a series of math problem-solving "menus" that each contain four engaging challenges for students to solve whenever they finished our main math activity early. The nine-menu set can be found on my TeachersPayTeachers page. Here's a sample problem:

The Lemonade Problem

It was so hot one day after school that Tikal went across the street to Pavilion's to buy some lemonade. He bought six six-packs of his favorite lemonade. On his way back to the classroom, he saw four of his friends, and he gave each of them one can of lemonade. Just then, his mom came and gave him eight more cans of the very same kind of lemonade. Imagine that! Then, he saw four more of his friends and decided to split all his cans equally among the group, including himself. How many cans did Tikal have at the end?

When a child solves this problem and turns it in, what would a piece of quality work look like? Would it contain just the answer? Would we expect the child to show their work? Would other items need to be included on the paper? Establishing quality criteria in advance answers these questions and offers much-needed clarity. Children thrive within a structure of clear expectations. A week or two into the school year, my students and I complete a sample problem together, and that's when I introduce our quality work requirements.

To achieve a quality solution to the Lemonade Problem, children need to:

1. Identify the question they are being asked to answer.
2. List the important facts and, if applicable, conditions (special rules) needed to generate a correct answer.
3. Declare their strategy.
4. Show all their work.
5. State a correct answer with the proper label.

To assist the kids during this process, I provide the Problem-Solving Organizer, shown in Figure 5.4, that includes space for the kids to satisfy each criterion. The organizer sheet is a template that offers a consistent structure, helps students gain comfort with these steps, and promotes a patient, methodical approach to their work. Children also receive practice with multiple Habits of Mind and Habits of Character as they proceed from the beginning of this sheet to the end.

This type of template demonstrates another huge advantage of identifying quality criteria for class activities and projects. Once everyone knows exactly what it takes to produce quality work, we can gather and/or create useful tools that greatly impact student learning and improve our ability to satisfy these requirements. Said differently, with criteria serving as our destination, we can employ tools that can help get us there. These support tools may take the form of templates, checklists, instructional visuals, or any other type of resource that sharpens our focus and directly contributes to successful completion of a given task. Locating a suitable tool online or creating one myself can be quite satisfying, even thrilling. As I share the next few examples,

Name_____ Date_____

Problem Solving Organizer for

The _____ Problem

Question: _____

_____?

Important Facts: (It may be easier to use key words and phrases than complete sentences.)

1) _____

2) _____

3) _____

4) _____

Conditions: (Conditions are special rules. Just write "N/A" if there aren't any conditions.)

1) _____

2) _____

3) _____

Choose a Strategy: (Tell which strategy you are using & show work in the space below.)

Name of my strategy: _____

Solution (labeled):

Is your solution reasonable? (Be sure to check your work carefully.)   Yes   No

Figure 5.4 Math problem-solving template.

I will point out other specific tools we can use that increase the likelihood that students will produce quality work. In addition, when teachers determine quality criteria for specific tasks, not only can we reuse those requirements year after year, but also we can reuse the support tools that accompany these requirements.

Paragraph Writing

Middle-grade children are commonly expected to learn how to write using paragraph structure. Whether the kids are asked to support an opinion, create a description, or examine a topic, the structural elements are similar. This type of endeavor is one of many in which we will not need to brainstorm quality criteria from scratch. Rather, we can gather them from the Common Core standards or any other set of learning expectations your school or district uses. Many times quality criteria are already listed individually in content standards, and we can simply piece them together to form a cohesive list.

To write a quality paragraph, children need to:

1. Begin with a topic sentence that clearly conveys the main idea.
2. Support that main idea with relevant reasons and examples.
3. Use transition words and phrases to signal movement from one reason or example to the next.
4. Provide a concluding sentence that restates the main idea from the topic sentence.
5. Ensure that each sentence is directly connected to the main idea.

As is the case with math problem-solving, clear quality criteria not only enable children to achieve success with this task but also inspire the creation of useful support tools. For my money, one of the all-time greatest learning tools is a visual relating the contents of a well-written paragraph to the parts of a hamburger. You can find numerous examples online or design your own. (See Figure 5.5.) When introducing this image to students, I first point out the bun. The fact that the top and bottom bread pieces are similar and "go together" enables children to forge that same type of connection between the topic and the concluding sentences. Next, we turn to the lettuce, cheese, patty, and other ingredients that give the hamburger its flavor, account for much of its size, and "support" the top bun, just as the details of a paragraph support the main idea. If you have students who are vegetarians or vegans, employing a sandwich visual with only non-meat ingredients, also available online

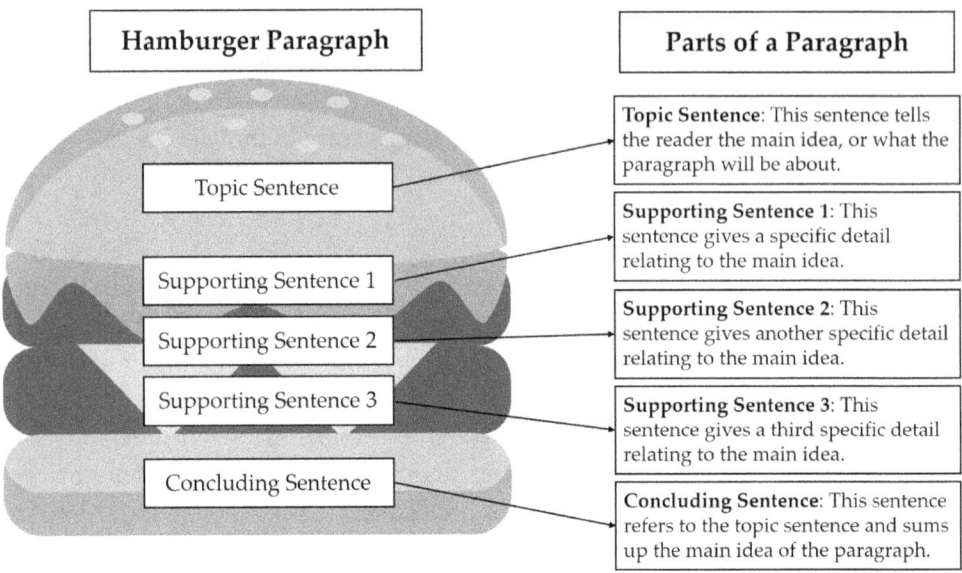

Figure 5.5 Paragraph "Hamburger" visual.

(with a bit more searching), works just as well. To add a clever twist, display your visual with a bite taken out of the top left corner to remind students to indent.

Another effective support tool that furthers our pursuit of quality with this and many other endeavors is the checklist. Once we establish quality criteria for a given task, creating a checklist is a simple, straightforward undertaking, and you will likely find yourself using this tool frequently. In its most basic form, a *checklist* contains each quality criterion, and the kids place a check next to each one after including that part. I recommend phrasing every item on the checklist as an "action step" so students feel a sense of pride and accomplishment after completing each one.

Here's what a checklist for paragraph writing might look like:

_____ I began with a topic sentence that clearly conveys the main idea.
_____ I included at least three to five details that support my main idea.
_____ I used transition words every time I moved to a new idea.
_____ I wrote a concluding sentence that restates the main idea from the topic sentence.
_____ I checked to make sure that each sentence is directly connected to the main idea.

Though checklists are typically created for individual student use during the writing process, these tools are also valuable for peer revising once an initial draft is complete. Reviewing one's work with a partner offers numerous benefits—encouraging the children to view one another as trusted resources, developing vital communication skills, providing a sense of friendship and belonging, and increasing the likelihood that quality learning will occur. As the old saying goes, two heads are better than one. Having a second set of eyes look at our work and gaining a perspective other than our own are extremely valuable. If we can help students appreciate the usefulness of peer feedback at a young age, that's a gift that will keep on giving as they get older.

Sometimes, we will be able to employ the exact same checklist during revising that we used during drafting. Other times we might choose to make minor adjustments, such as adding a second blank to the left of each item for the partner to initial after reviewing the paragraph or placing a line at the bottom of the sheet for the partner to sign as a way of saying, "You're good! Your paragraph has what it's supposed to have!" Feel free to put in an additional blank and line if you want each child to meet with two partners for extra thoroughness. Having partners sign at the bottom also offers a measure of accountability. Should I notice, for example, a missing requirement or two when reading Marcia's paragraph, I will definitely follow up with her about it; however, if the issue pertains to something that Jason had signed off on, I will speak with him as well. I want students to understand that serving as a classmate's revising partner is an important responsibility and that they should care as much about improving their partner's work as they do their own.

As part of our effort to teach the whole child and help kids develop social skills, we need to be mindful of a couple of things when introducing revising checklists to the class. Specifically, we want to focus not just on the procedural steps but on the emotions and feelings of the writer as well. Every classroom activity contains some type of emotional component, and when children hear that classmates will be reading their draft, many worry that their work will be criticized or judged. I emphasize to everyone that when we speak with others about their writing, it is important to approach our conversations with empathy, with positivity, and with encouragement. (Revising sessions are great opportunities to bust out our compliment words from the first week of school.) As we proceed through a checklist with our partner, we are not playing a game of "gotcha," in which we try to find mistakes and make the author feel bad; rather, it's "I got your back"—meaning we're in this together, and I'm trying to help you, partner. My job is to support, not judge, you as we strive to improve our paragraphs. If an item on the checklist deserves to be checked, that's awesome. Then we do it with a smile, and maybe even a thumbs-up or a compliment. If, however, it turns out that the writer checked an item, such as the one regarding transition words, when no transition words can be found in the paragraph, then we politely point that out and work on that part together with a spirit of unity and teamwork until both of us agree the item deserves a check.

Reflections

Our instructional schedules are typically quite crowded, and it can be difficult finding consistent time for many beneficial activities that can easily end up on the back burner. The Friday Circle class meetings mentioned in Chapter 3 are one example. Ideally, we would have time every week for a full agenda, but that's usually not realistic. So we do what we can with the time we have available to us. Reflection activities also fall into this category. Providing children with frequent opportunities to reflect on various aspects of their learning deeply enhances that learning and facilitates future learning. Reflecting on their work empowers students to get to know themselves better as learners, improves their metacognitive skills, heightens awareness of their strengths, and helps them identify areas of improvement.

My favorite time to ask students to reflect is at the conclusion of a multi-week writing project. During the final week of each unit, when the kids edit, publish, and celebrate their finished pieces, I have everyone complete a sheet with four to five reflection questions that require one to two sentence answers. "Baking" this activity into the final week puts me at ease and ensures that my students will receive regular opportunities to reflect on their writing. The sheet provides children with a chance to look back on the process they just completed, describe what they learned, share other aspects of their experience with that writing unit, and look ahead to the next project. A sample reflection sheet is shown in Figure 5.6. It is a generic form that can be used with any writing genre. I created an entire set of Writing Workshop reflection sheets for my TeachersPayTeachers page. (You can find a printable copy of this reflection sheet on the Routledge website.)

Beyond end-of-unit writing reflections, I also aim to schedule reflection activities after individual lessons and at certain points during the year, such as right before Parent Conferences or an extended school break. On these occasions, I like to give a single question or prompt and ask everyone to take 10–15 minutes to respond at length. With this option we can give the same prompt to every child or offer a small number of choices from which each students selects one.

Here are some sample reflection prompts:

1. What has been your biggest accomplishment in recent weeks? Explain why you chose this achievement.
2. What has been your greatest challenge in class recently, and how have you responded to it?
3. What is currently your most important school goal? Explain what specific steps you need to take to achieve it.
4. Over the past few weeks, what piece of work makes you the proudest? Explain why.

Name_____ Date_____

Writing Workshop Reflection Sheet

<u>Directions:</u> Answer the following questions as honestly and thoughtfully as you can. Be sure to write in complete sentences.

1) What was the most valuable lesson you learned about writing while working on this project?

_____

_____

_____

2) Which part of your project makes you the proudest? Explain why.

_____

_____

_____

3) Currently, what do you think is your greatest strength as a writer?

_____

_____

_____

4) What part of your writing are you most determined to improve in your next project?

_____

_____

_____

Figure 5.6 Writing Workshop reflection sheet.

5. What is the most important thing your teacher can do to help you reach the next level as a learner?
6. Which Habit of Character is currently your strongest? Explain why.
7. Which Habit of Character are you working on the most? Explain why, and describe the specific steps you will take to improve in that area.
8. Describe a problem you recently solved by yourself. Explain how you did it.
9. Describe a time recently when you showed great judgment.

Once the students finish their reflections, it is easy for them (and us) to wonder what constitutes a quality response. In other words, what are the requirements of a quality reflection? Unlike our experience with the paragraph writing example, coming up with these types of criteria is probably an endeavor we will need to do from scratch, either alone or with our grade level colleagues. To my knowledge, content standards do not offer this kind of guidance. Several years ago, after some brainstorming, I generated the list that follows. Once we take the time to produce a list of quality criteria such as these, it is important to test them out. If we read a batch of student reflections and it appears our list is thorough and comprehensive, we may choose to stop there. If, however, a reflection response meets these requirements yet doesn't seem to exemplify quality, perhaps we need to add another criterion or two. On the other hand, if several responses seem to represent quality work yet none of them meet a given criterion, maybe we need to remove that criterion, as it may not be necessary. When you feel comfortable with your list of quality criteria for a given endeavor, share these requirements with your students right before they engage in that activity. The work they produce will likely be far stronger now that they have a clearer understanding of what constitutes quality.

- Reflections show an honest and accurate awareness of strengths and growth areas.
- Reflections are completed thoughtfully and with detail.
- Reflections show deep engagement in learning.

Measuring Quality

In the previous section I shared the first step to helping students produce quality work on a consistent basis: defining quality as conformance to requirements. Forming a short yet comprehensive list of clear criteria for a given project or task yields two massive benefits—empowering children with a greater understanding of what quality work is supposed to have and inspiring the creation of templates, checklists, visuals, and other useful tools that support our pursuit of quality. Defining *quality* in this manner also leads to a third benefit, and that takes us right into our next step. Defining *quality* as conformance to requirements allows us to *measure* quality.

You may be wondering why we need an additional step if we already have a list of requirements for a given project or activity. Isn't a short list of clear requirements sufficient to measure quality? For certain basic tasks, such as writing a paragraph, yes, criteria, by themselves, may enable us to assess the quality of student work. For this type of task, we can use a checklist such as the one introduced earlier. If we read a child's paragraph, for example, and can place a check next to each required part, then we can conclude they wrote a quality paragraph. There are limits, though, to employing criteria alone to measure quality, and I will explain them shortly. Still, if you are seeking a quick, straightforward method to measuring the quality of student work for basic tasks, this approach can get the job done.

As tasks become more complex, however, the decisions will no longer be binary. We won't be able to answer with a simple yes or no when trying to determine whether a piece of work satisfies one or more quality criteria. Instead, we will be encountering a greater range of performance, more possible outcomes, and more nuance. Because quality is always subjective, these tasks will require more judgment on the teacher's part. As a result, there will be more "levels" of quality that the work can fall into. For these more sophisticated pieces of work, we will need to employ the most effective measurement tool we have at our disposal—the rubric.

General Scoring Rubric: A Useful Template

In Chapter 2, I introduced the Habits of Character and Habits of Mind rubric my students use to assess their progress with these traits. I created that rubric, as well as all the other subject- and project-specific rubrics we implement in class, using the general scoring rubric, shown in Figure 5.7, as a template. Each rubric is constructed on a 4-point scale, and the meaning of each level always remains the same. This continuity helps children internalize the meaning of each level and enables them to understand each new rubric fairly quickly. A *3* signifies that student work has what it is supposed to have and, thus, deserves to be considered quality work. This score always serves as our initial goal. Once kids consistently earn 3s, then 4 becomes the goal. A 4 expresses that the work somehow exceeds the criteria or contains something more. If a piece of work does not quite satisfy all the criteria and falls short of quality, the score would be a 2. A *1* indicates that the work is significantly below expectations.

Occasionally, you will see 3-point, 5-point, or even 6-point rubrics. Over the years, I have come to embrace four as the ideal number because once

General Scoring Rubric

All of our class rubrics will follow the structure of the rubric shown below. It uses a 4-point scale, in which "3" represents the standard. The goal will always be for everyone in the class to earn a score of at least a "3."

4 = Exceeds Expectations
- The work or performance meets class expectations and somehow surpasses them or contains something more.

---

3 = Meets Expectations
- **The work or performance has everything it is supposed to have.**

---

2 = Below Expectations
- The work or performance falls just short of having everything it is supposed to have.

1 = Significantly Below Expectations
- The work or performance falls well short of having everything it is supposed to have.

Figure 5.7 General scoring rubric.

we have "locked in" 3 as the standard of quality, we then have one level above for work that exceeds the standard and two levels below for work that doesn't yet meet the requirements, one level for work that comes close and another for work that is further from this goal. Having more than four levels, in my opinion, seems unnecessary and potentially confusing.

Writing Workshop Examples: Rubrics for Ideas and Conventions

Since the numbers and levels remain constant with every rubric, the only differences among the ones we use in class involve the quality criteria we "plug" into these levels and the wording we use to distinguish one level from another.

Defining *quality* as conformance to requirements, then, facilities the measuring of *quality* by providing the criteria we use to build our rubrics. Let's explore the process of rubric construction by analyzing two rubrics that I developed for our Writing Workshop.

Many years ago, my school embraced the Six Traits approach that aims to help children become better writers by focusing on the following areas: ideas, conventions, organization, voice, word choice, and sentence fluency. The Six

Traits resources our staff was provided included a rubric for each trait, and I modified them to adhere to my preferred 4-point structure. I began the *ideas* and *conventions* rubrics in Figures 5.8 and 5.9 with a brief explanation of the trait and then listed the quality criteria, labeled on these sheets as "Performance Indicators."

As a general rule, we can then insert the performance indicators directly into the "Meets Expectations" section because children who produce work will, by definition, meet these requirements. (This step is a huge time-saver anytime we want to create a new rubric.) Said differently, their writing will have what it's supposed to have. For a piece of writing to rise to the level of 4, it will go above and beyond a 3 somehow. With the *ideas* rubric, children will likely achieve that score because of the second, fourth, and fifth indicators. (It's difficult for writing to make "extra" sense or have "extra" focus.) The "Exceeds Expectations" section of the rubric, therefore, contains only one bullet point that distinguishes it from the "Meets Expectations" section: "Details give the reader important, interesting information that goes well beyond the obvious or predictable." That phrase enables everyone in class to achieve a common understanding of what it means to exceed expectations on the *ideas* rubric and "speak the same language." At the same time, the wording honors the subjective nature of quality.

In the "Below Expectations" section, you will notice that each bullet point matches its counterpart in the "Meets Expectations" section, with one exception. Every "Below Expectations" bullet point contains the phrase "may or may not." These words acknowledge the reality that when a piece of writing earns a score of 2, it doesn't mean that every aspect of the writing falls below expectations. The writing could have made complete sense and had a clear focus, for example, yet did not include much detail. Constructing the "Below Expectations" section in this manner enables teachers to pinpoint which criteria may not have been met. The language in the "Significantly Below Expectations" sections is stronger, out of necessity, since the work is further below the level of quality.

Now let's take a look at the *conventions* rubric that enables us to assess the mechanical correctness of our writing. The "Meets Expectations" area in this rubric is slightly different from that of the *ideas* rubric in that the bullet points do not directly mirror the performance indicators. Instead, I modified the language to aid the children in understanding the differences among the four scores. When constructing this rubric, I felt I needed to include a general statement or principle that captured the essence of each level. To earn a score of 3, for example, a piece of writing can have some mistakes, as long as those errors do not interfere with the reader's ability to understand the text. The other two bullet points in this section build on and add specificity to that

Rubric for Ideas

The trait of Ideas focuses on the heart of the writer's message, namely the work's main ideas and the details that enrich, develop, and support the main ideas. The content should consist of clear, interesting, and important information.

Performance Indicators
- Makes sense
- Gets and holds the reader's attention/interesting
- Has a focus, a main idea, a thesis, or a sense of purpose
- Full of details that support the main idea
- Important information

4 = Exceeds Expectations
- It all makes sense.
- The writing has a clear focus or main idea.
- Details give the reader important, interesting information that goes well beyond the obvious or predictable.

---

3 = Meets Expectations
- **It all makes sense.**
- **The writing has a clear focus or main idea.**
- **The writing contains important, interesting details that support and adequately develop the main idea.**

---

2 = Below Expectations
- It may or may not make complete sense.
- The writing may or may not have a clear focus or main idea.
- The writing may or may not contain important, interesting details that support and adequately develop the main idea.

1 = Significantly Below Expectations
- It may or may not make sense.
- The writing may lack any sense of focus.
- Details may be completely lacking, irrelevant, or unimportant.

Figure 5.8 Ideas rubric.

overall idea. With a 2, on the other hand, mistakes are more frequent and may interfere with the reader's ability to understand. Over the years, this distinction between having some mistakes that don't interfere with comprehension and containing more frequent errors that do interfere has proven to resonate with children and allowed them to internalize a clear understanding of the difference between a 2 and a 3. The general principle undergirding a score of 4 is that there are few, if any, errors. Period. (Sorry, that pun was slightly intended.) The main identifier of a 1 is that the text is very difficult to read and understand and would need to undergo extensive editing to ready it for publication. As is the case with a 3, the additional bullet points in each section serve to expand on the general principle and offer a bit more detail.

A note of caution about the *conventions* rubric and other similar rubrics that mention the element of "frequency." With the *connections* rubric, for example, *frequency* refers to the number of errors a piece of writing may contain. For a descriptive writing activity, teachers may encourage children to incorporate many adjectives. As a result, a rubric for this topic may include a criterion related to the frequency with which a child uses describing words. In these situations we do not want to build any form of counting into our rubrics. Over the years, I have seen rubrics in which a child would earn a score of 4 for including five or more adjectives, a 3 for three or four, a 2 for one or two, and a 1 for no adjectives. It is easy to understand the rationale for this format. Counting is simple, it's quick, and it makes the task of assessment more objective. And that's the problem. Quality will always be subjective, and attempting to evaluate it objectively, tempting as it may be, throws a wrench into this process. Reducing the assessment of quality to a bean counting exercise will result in scores that do not accurately reflect the performance indicators or represent the rubric's various levels. In the case of descriptive writing, a piece of student work should not receive a higher or lower score simply because it contains a certain number of adjectives. Constructing a rubric with clearly defined levels based on thoughtful distinctions that acknowledge the subjective nature of quality is the way to go.

Math Problem-Solving Rubric

Let's further explore the inner workings of rubrics with the math problem-solving rubric shown in Figure 5.10. The quality criteria for this task, presented earlier in this chapter and phrased as action steps, have been inserted into the "Meets Expectations" section. With this rubric I would like to focus mainly on the "Exceeds Expectations" area, as it employs a useful tactic you

Rubric for <u>Conventions</u>

The trait of Conventions refers to the mechanical correctness of writing. Our writing should follow the rules of spelling, grammar, capitalization, punctuation, and paragraphing.

<u>Performance Indicators</u>
- Correct spelling & grammar
- Proper capitalization and punctuation (? . ! , " ")
- Indented paragraphs

<u>4 = Exceeds Expectations</u>
- There are few, if any, errors with spelling, capitals, punctuations, grammar, and indenting.
- Conventions may be used creatively to enhance the writing.
- Difficult spelling words and other above-grade-level-conventions are well done.

<u>3 = Meets Expectations</u>
- **The writing is clean and polished. It looks proofread.**
- **There may be some mistakes with spelling, capitals, punctuation, grammar, and indenting, but the mistakes do not interfere with the reader's ability to understand the writing.**
- **Errors may occur with difficult spelling words or other conventions that are beyond the grade level.**

<u>2 = Below Expectations</u>
- Conventions errors are frequent and may interfere with the reader's ability to understand the writing.
- Errors may occur with basic spelling words, beginning-of-sentence capitalization, and end punctuation.
- Errors may occur inconsistently. Writing may not look well proofread.

<u>1 = Significantly Below Expectations</u>
- Errors are so numerous that it is very difficult to read and understand the text.
- Extensive editing (virtually every line) would be required to polish the text for publication.

Figure 5.9 Conventions rubric.

Rubric for Math Problem Solving

With problem solving students are asked to identify the problem that needs solving, find the relevant facts and conditions, choose a strategy that will lead to a solution, and then carry out that strategy successfully.

Performance Indicators
- Understand the problem that needs to be solved
- Find the important facts and conditions needed to generate a solution
- Choose or create a strategy to solve the problem
- Determine a correct solution, label it, and check it for reasonableness

4 = Exceeds Expectations
- I did everything in the "Meets Expectations" box.
- I went the extra mile and showed more than one way to solve the problem.
- I used an unusually advanced strategy to solve the problem.

---

3 = Meets Expectations
- I wrote down the right question and used a question mark.
- I wrote down all the important facts and conditions.
- I chose a strategy and followed through with it from beginning to end.
- I wrote a correct solution, labeled it, and checked to see if it was reasonable.

---

2 = Below Expectations
- I may not have written down the right question.
- I may not have written down all the important facts and conditions.
- I chose a promising strategy, but I may have done it incorrectly.
- I may not have labeled my solution or checked to see if it was reasonable.

1 = Significantly Below Expectations
- I may not have written the question, or I may have missed most of the facts and conditions.
- I may have chosen a strategy that didn't make sense for this problem.
- I may have made serious mistakes with my strategy.

Figure 5.10 Math problem-solving rubric.

may want to apply to any rubrics you create. With this approach, the initial bullet point states that to earn a score of 4, the work must first satisfy all the requirements of a 3. This item saves us valuable space by eliminating the need to repeat each "Meets Expectations" criterion in the "Exceeds Expectations" section. The second and third bullet points in this section express specific ways a student can earn a score of 4.

In addition, the "Exceeds Expectations" section of this rubric, as well as the others my students and I employ, highlights one of the limits of relying only on quality criteria to assess quality. I mentioned previously how referring to quality criteria alone, with the help of a checklist, can serve as an adequate way to assess the quality of basic tasks, such as writing a paragraph. Though that is true, rubrics offer a superior approach. Perhaps the most important distinction between the two methods is that rubrics allow for the possibility that student work may exceed expectations. Plus, rubrics show children how to do so. Rubrics also provide more specific information as to whether a piece of work that doesn't conform to requirements falls just below or well below the score of 3. Rubrics enable us to make finer distinctions and provide more specific feedback. One final note: I created an entire set of 4-point rubrics for my TeachersPayTeachers page. You can find a few printable versions of these rubrics on the Routledge website.

Bringing Quality to Life With Models and Anchors

As essential as it is to define *quality* as conformance to requirements and build rubrics around those requirements to measure quality, we need one additional piece to complete this puzzle. The third and final step in the process of helping children produce quality work on a consistent basis is to exemplify quality, a teacher move that involves providing work samples (also known as models or anchors) that meet or exceed requirements for a given rubric. Without a doubt, clear performance indicators and well-constructed rubrics are absolute necessities. But there's nothing like seeing with our own eyes an actual piece of quality work for a task we are about to begin.

Models and anchors bring a rubric to life. I once heard an educator go so far as to claim that even the most well-constructed rubrics will have little meaning to children until they have the opportunity to see a sample representing each level. I discovered many years ago that some schools have amplified this point—placing so much emphasis on models that they employ the same rubric across multiple grade levels, with each grade level developing its own set of anchors. For children, analyzing models in detail can transform teacher instructions and rubric descriptors that can sometimes seem a bit abstract into something far more concrete. Studying work that other kids have done builds confidence, boosts motivation, reduces anxiety, and makes challenging tasks seem more doable. The goal during these moments is for kids to believe that they can be just as successful as the students whose work is being featured, and based on my observations, that's frequently what happens. In addition, establishing robust criteria and accompanying them with anchors and models raise the bar for all. Every time I share with my students one or more pieces of quality work, engagement is high and focus is strong. That's when the light bulb really goes on for kids. It is during these moments when children develop a fuller understanding of what quality looks like for a given task. At this point, the requirements of a task truly begin to sink in.

These work samples can come from a variety of places. The ideal way to accumulate these models is to keep high-quality examples from each class you teach and show them in the years that follow. "Homegrown" models are pure gold. The good news is, the longer we teach, the more models we can accrue. With this and many other aspects of classroom teaching, experience is a significant advantage—a gift that keeps on giving. Homegrown samples are always preferred because the children who created them likely worked with the same quality criteria that each new group of students will use and operated within a similar classroom structure and culture. Thus, we are able to compare apples to apples. That type of continuity matters to kids, especially when your students may be only a year or two younger than the creators of the work and may know them.

Of course, when we are brand new teachers, we don't yet possess any samples of our own. Not to worry! As we begin compiling models for the future, we have a few terrific options for our initial year. My first action would be to approach grade level colleagues to see if they would be willing to share any models they have collected over the years. Your school's curricular adoptions are another promising source of anchors. Many years ago, for example, my school embraced the reading and writing workshop approach pioneered at Teachers College, Columbia University. The planning resources my staff uses are loaded with student writing samples I routinely share with my class. Even if the quality criteria differ slightly from mine, my students still benefit greatly from analyzing these texts. Should those two curricular trees not bear any fruit, I recommend a couple of additional options. The first is the internet. If you enter search terms featuring specific grade levels, subject areas, and project topics, you may well hit pay dirt. Finally, if you continue to find yourself out of luck, there is absolutely nothing wrong with creating your own samples, either alone or with your grade level team, based on a given project's instructions and quality criteria.

Perhaps the most effective way to introduce anchors to your students is through an exercise known as a "norming activity." Begin by distributing an un-scored piece of work, a personal essay, for example, to each pair or small group. Working collaboratively, the kids read the essay and use the rubric to give it a score by measuring the work against the rubric criteria. Either through discussion or in writing, ask the kids to justify their scores by referring to at least three parts of the rubric. This step promotes thoroughness and accountability and enables the children to get to know the rubric on a deeper level. Encourage everyone to highlight, underline, or "mark up" both the rubric and essay to identify the evidence that undergirds their decisions. We want the kids to really dig into these sheets. The scores the kids choose are far less important than the reasons they give to support those numbers. The richness and power of this type of norming activity lie in the discussions the students have as they share their thinking and explain why they believe the writing deserves one score and not another. It is precisely because of these conversational opportunities that we ask the children to work cooperatively rather than individually.

When planning a norming activity, we can either give every group the same piece of work to examine or distribute different samples that represent each rubric level. Though both are effective options, I suggest the latter because it makes the end-of-lesson sharing period particularly valuable and interesting for the kids. As you display each sample piece of work on the board or document camera, invite the students who analyzed that sample to offer their thoughts as to which score they believed the work earned and explain why. Proceed through the anchors randomly so students can't easily predict that you are first showing them a 1, for example, followed by a 2, a 3, and a 4. Children are experts at noticing these types of patterns, and we don't want to be predictable. Kids tend to be extremely curious when we display the samples that groups other than theirs analyzed. As a result, engagement and focus are usually quite high.

Important note: If the anchors were created by older children your students may know, remove the names from any papers representing a 1 or a 2. We want to avoid any situation in which current students may tease, judge, or criticize former ones. We never want anyone to be publicly embarrassed about their schoolwork. Ever. Remember, teaching the whole child means looking out for the whole child. If we include names on the pieces of work we display, it is only for the purpose of celebrating that work and building connections among current and former students. Of course, if you prefer, you can omit the names from every paper.

In addition to helping children develop a better understanding of what quality looks like for specific tasks, norming activities also offer a sneak preview of various scoring situations and decisions we are all (teachers and students) likely to encounter when using rubrics. Many of these occurrences relate to the fact that several different ways exist for an assessor to arrive at a given score. For example, with the math problem-solving rubric, children may initially think that to earn a 3, a paper simply needs to include the four bullet points found in the "Meets Expectations" section. That's one way to achieve a 3, but rarely is the path to that score so neatly packaged. More commonly, bullet points from two to three levels of the rubric will match that piece of work. A given math paper, for instance, might feature two methods of solving the problem (an "Exceeds Expectations" bullet point), the right question and correct answer (two "Meets Expectations" items), and a couple missing important facts and conditions (a "Below Expectations" criterion). In this case, if we were to "average out" these bullet points, a score of 3 would be entirely reasonable. Discussing these and other possibilities during norming activities sets the stage for clear, fair, and accurate scoring.

Once you introduce anchors and models to your students, keep these resources visible so they can serve as consistent reference points throughout the length of the project or unit. Post them on the wall and/or create a file to display on an interactive whiteboard. Distribute hard copies if you want students to have the ability to highlight, underline, or add notes. We want to encourage this type of diligence as often as possible. Such thoroughness facilitates the development of useful habits and leads to higher-quality work.

Fostering a Quality Mindset With Our Students

In a whole-child classroom, becoming a highly successful student encompasses more than acquiring knowledge and learning skills across the curriculum. It also involves developing the habits, attitudes, and mindsets that empower kids to take charge of their learning and perform well both independently and collaboratively. In Chapter 2, I described several steps we can take to build into our classroom culture entities such as passion and creativity, as well as Habits of Mind and Habits of Character, such as kindness and respect. The pursuit of quality requires its own special mindset, and we want to begin focusing on this endeavor as early as possible.

The first time students will likely encounter the term *quality* in our classrooms is during the initial week of school, when we start reading and highlighting sample mission statements. The word will pretty much be in every sample we discuss, and that's a good thing. Children will associate the term with companies and organizations they know and like, and the word will develop credibility quickly and organically. Since it's the mission statements supplying the word all this attention, we won't need to give it the hard sell. Our role is simply to say, "Gee, is anyone else noticing how often we are seeing the word *quality*? Must be important." Because of its frequent appearances in the samples, the word will inevitably end up in our class mission statement, giving us many natural opportunities to refer to it over the course of the school year.

Launching our effort to define, measure, and exemplify quality will also serve a significant role in encouraging our students to value quality and commit themselves to its pursuit. From there, we can make several additional moves to develop a "quality mindset" in our students. Some children, of course, will enter the room on the first day already possessing this mindset. (Bless their hearts.) Others may be on the verge, while still others may be new to the concept or unfamiliar with what the pursuit of it looks like or entails. Every effort we make to shine a spotlight on quality and describe the amazing chain reaction that results once we embrace it as a top priority increases the likelihood that all our students will become *quality* students. Of course, we can never know which moves will resonate with which children. So we try a variety of approaches to maximize the chances that all our students will build a quality mindset.

Use Quotes to Inspire Children to Pursue Quality

Quote of the Day discussions, mentioned in Chapter 2, constitute another valuable tool we can employ to encourage children to embrace the pursuit of quality as an important goal. In what follows you will see three quotes that specifically focus on quality. The first comes from Robert Pirsig's (1974) classic *Zen and the Art of Motorcycle Maintenance*, a book that was rejected by 121 publishing houses. (That fact gives me hope as I sit here typing Chapter 5.)

> "Quality = Caring."
>
> —Robert Pirsig

Each year this quote is one of my students' favorites to discuss. I think kids are initially drawn to it because it's so brief and scores high on novelty since it looks like a math equation with words. When our goal is to produce quality in school and elsewhere, the quote suggests that our attitude about the work is just as important as our knowledge and skills, if not more so. Furthermore, achieving quality may depend less on our methods or techniques than our motivation, our "want to," and our determination. Pirsig's words can also be reassuring to students, who often become nervous and worry about whether their best efforts will be good enough to get the job done. Many kids may think, "Boy, my teacher sure seems to talk about quality a lot. I'd like my work to reach this level, but I'm not sure if I can do it." This quote can put children at ease and help them realize that if we care enough about what we are doing and if we are willing to invest the necessary time, effort, and passion, we will eventually obtain quality results.

> *"Quality is the first thing you think about, the last thing you think about, and what you think about in between."*
> —Author unknown

My former teaching partner and I liked this quote so much that we displayed it on a wall for an entire year. We wanted to emphasize the idea that in order to produce quality work, one must always keep that goal in mind, from the beginning of a project to the end. In addition, we can use this quote to highlight the difference between quality and quantity. It is common for elementary students to believe that more is always better, that a four-page story, for example, is superior to a two-page story. It is critical for kids to understand that the quality of what they produce and the amount of care they put into their work matter far more than how much they produce.

> *"Quality means a demanding, difficult, never-ending effort to improve."*
> —Lloyd Dobyns and Clare Crawford-Mason

This straightforward quote describes exactly what lies ahead for individuals and groups who embrace quality as a top priority. Pursuing quality is a journey with no endpoint. Even when things are going well and we feel highly successful in our chosen endeavors, we understand that we must keep getting better, no matter how difficult or demanding that improvement effort becomes. The world around isn't slowing down; neither can we.

Use Visuals to Inspire Children to Pursue Quality

In Chapter 2, I introduced the benefits of supporting our initial culture-building efforts with the use of visuals. Because these images engage children's attention, their messages often resonate with students in ways that text alone does not. Classroom signs and posters serve as consistent reference points that enable foundational habits, traits, and concepts to remain "living ideas" in our students' hearts and minds. In this section I share several new visuals that are specifically designed to encourage and inspire children to develop a quality mindset.

"Making the Choice" Visual

I created the visual in Figure 5.11 to encourage children to make what I call "The Choice." When kids follow through with this decision, they are dedicating themselves to becoming quality students. You can find the visual on

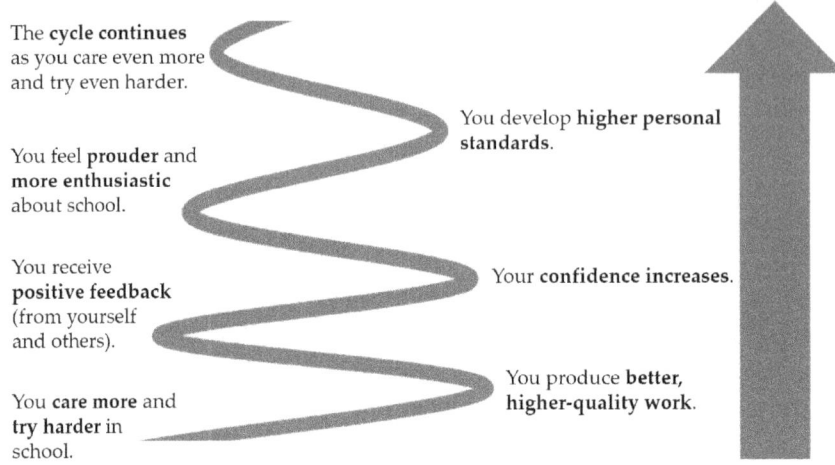

Figure 5.11 "Making the Choice" visual.

the "Teaching the Whole Child" board of my Pinterest page (https://www.pinterest.com/stevereifman/teaching-the-whole-child/).

The visual shows how making this choice can initiate a virtuous cycle that promises wonderful academic and social-emotional benefits. When students make the choice, they are committing themselves to caring more and trying harder in school. This decision leads them to produce better, higher-quality work. Once that happens, others take notice. Teachers will give them positive feedback. So will parents and classmates. The kids will even give themselves positive feedback as they realize the quality of their schoolwork is improving. That, in turn, boosts their confidence and causes them to feel prouder and more enthusiastic about school. That leads the kids to develop higher personal standards. The cycle continues as children care even more and try even harder.

Of course, the visual is especially powerful for children who have not yet made the choice. It is important to share the visual in class and at Back-to-School Night. On this evening I include a copy in the handouts I distribute and ask families to discuss these ideas at home and post the visual on a refrigerator, bulletin board, or other frequently visited location. No matter how many other efforts we make to inspire children, they are all unlikely to bear fruit until the kids have first made the choice to dedicate themselves to becoming quality students.

"Tug-o'-War" Visual

Sometimes, encouraging children to embrace the pursuit of quality involves addressing the private choices students make as they do their schoolwork.

Though these decisions remain hidden from public view, they exert an enormous influence on the quality of work students produce. By calling attention to this "internal thinking" and raising student awareness of their minute-to-minute choices, we can help everyone adopt attitudes, build habits, and take care of business in ways that increase the likelihood of quality and, in turn, facilitate the pride, confidence, and self-esteem boosts that come with it.

One example of this internal thinking relates to two conflicting goals children commonly have in mind as they begin a piece of work. First, they want to do a great job. Second, they want to get done. Throughout the year, I emphasize to my students that quality is always the most important priority, and we need to be willing to take our time, focus on the task at hand, and put forth our very best effort if we wish to be successful in school and in life. Of course, there will be times when all of us (children and adults) have spent considerable time on a task and we want to finish. The question, though, is, on a typical day, which desire usually wins?

The "Tug-o'-War" visual, shown in Figure 5.12, has proven to be an effective conversation starter over the years. You can find the visual on the "Teaching the Whole Child" board of my Pinterest page (https://www.pinterest.com/stevereifman/teaching-the-whole-child/). When introducing the image to students, I begin with the boy in the center, who's working on a task. Thinking bubbles extend out from both the left side and right side of his head,

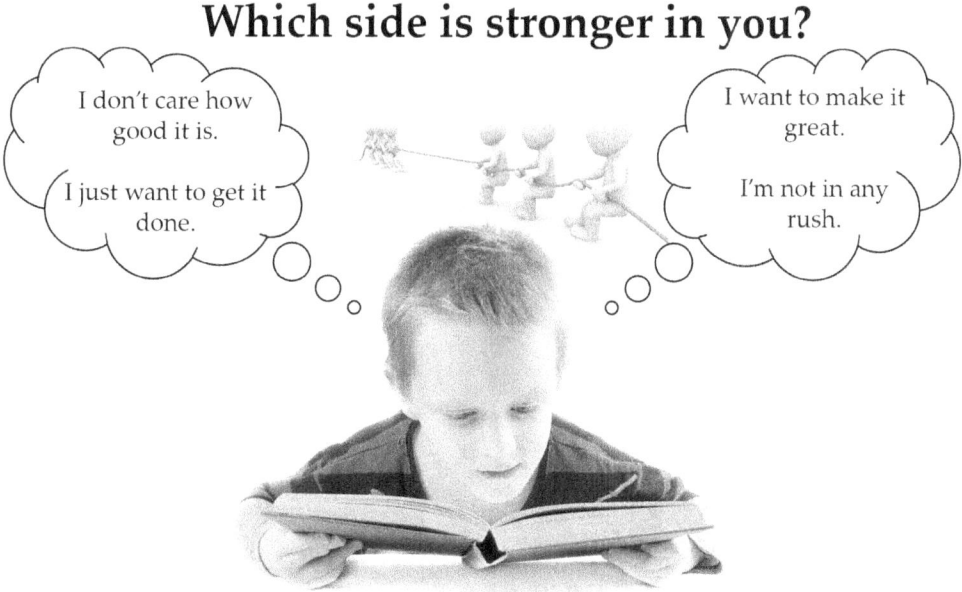

Figure 5.12 "Tug-O'-War" visual.

illustrating the two desires that might be guiding his actions. The bubble on the left side represents the "I just want to finish" approach; the bubble on the right, the "I want to make it great" approach. The image resonates with children and prompts them to reflect on a topic they may have never considered before.

Discussing the visual furthers our efforts to help students develop higher personal standards of quality with their schoolwork. Many kids tend to race through their work, pay little attention to its quality, and want only to get it done. When we rush, quality suffers, and children need to know that. The "Tug-o'-War" visual shines a spotlight on this issue and points out that while working on a task, we face an important decision. Do we just want to finish, or do we want to make it great? Do we want to complete the task as quickly as possible, or are we willing to slow down and invest the necessary time and effort to create something that makes us proud?

"Work Like a Champion Today" Sign

Every Notre Dame football player taps the legendary "Play Like a Champion Today" sign as they head from the locker room to the field on game day. Scan the following QR code (Figure 5.13) to watch a video of it. This ritual fires up the team and boosts motivation for the upcoming contest. After discovering this tradition, I decided to create the "Work Like a Champion Today" sign shown in Figure 5.14. For obvious reasons, I didn't want my students

Figure 5.13 QR code—Notre Dame's "Play Like a Champion Today" sign.

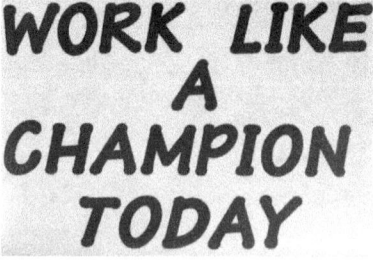

Figure 5.14 "Work Like a Champion Today" sign.

touching this sign every day (cooties could spread), so I placed it above one of our classroom doors. Ever since, the sign has served as a visual reminder of our class commitment to putting forth our best effort on a daily basis—a little jolt of inspiration. Over the years, many students have remarked how much they like that sign and how helpful they have found it. When introducing this sign, I recommend showing the Notre Dame version first.

The Challenge Bear

One year, I was seeking a way to help children develop a positive view of the difficult academic challenges they would inevitably face in school. Rather than worry about a challenge or try to hide from it, I wanted kids to embrace it. A short time later, the Challenge Bear was born. I borrowed a stuffed animal from a student and placed a "beauty pageant-like" sash with the word *challenge* around it. Annually, I tell the class that if anyone is feeling a bit nervous about a challenging academic situation, they are free to approach the bear and give it a squeeze before sitting down to get started on it. The kids love the lighthearted, playful tone that we use when discussing the bear, and it has come to represent our team's commitment to embracing tough challenges with confidence—an important life lesson.

D-Fence Sign

After seeing the positive impact of the Challenge Bear and understanding through my other teaching experiences how powerful a learning catalyst novelty can be, I continued to search for unique (even off-the-wall) objects, images, and ideas that had the potential to capture student attention and help important learning "stick" in their minds.

Typically, I will choose the instructional objective or larger life lesson first and then search for a novel way to convey it to children. That's how it worked when I created the "Tower of Opportunity" to express the idea that education is the key that opens doors and when I came up with the movement, song, and story activities that would later comprise my book *Rock It!: Transform Classroom Learning with Movement, Songs, and Stories*.

Sometimes, though, the order is reversed. That was the case roughly ten years ago when I was watching an NFL football game and saw a fan in the stands holding up the "D-fence" sign shown in Figure 5.15 with their team's logo on it. For years, crowds have been chanting "Defense" to give their team an edge, and this was the first time I had ever seen an actual team-specific sign that fans could wear on one hand while they were chanting.

I knew I had to have one. My plan was to bring the sign to class to share it with my students and have it on display for the rest of the year as a consistent reference point. What was the sign going to refer to? I had no idea. So

Figure 5.15 "D-Fence" sign.

I started thinking of a way the sign could help me communicate something important to the kids, and after a while, I came up with the following. As you read, imagine I'm talking to a group of children.

> When I was your age, I loved to play sports. One of my favorites was basketball, and I would spend hours outside, practicing my shooting. Like most kids, my friends and I loved playing offense. We loved to shoot the ball and score. Even though we knew defense was important, it wasn't as much fun as playing offense, and we didn't devote the same time and effort to improving our defense as we did to our offense. As we got older, we realized that for our teams to be successful, we needed to give equal attention to defense. Moving our feet, boxing out for rebounds, and other aspects of defense, no matter how small, aren't glamorous, yet they are necessary ingredients for success.
>
> The same idea holds true with baseball and football, in which hitting home runs and scoring touchdowns are fun and exciting, yet they represent only a small part of the game. Success requires a serious, ongoing commitment to the little things. The fans in the stands may not notice these little things, and they certainly aren't likely to show up on TV highlight shows. But they matter.
>
> This is also the case in school. In Writing Workshop, for example, you may love to come up with story ideas and love to draft. You may not feel the same way about revising or editing, but if you want to be a successful writer, you need to give these areas equal attention. Sometimes, these tasks may not be fun, and they may feel like a grind, but committing to doing them with a high level of effort and with attention to detail is necessary. These habits will stay with you and help you become successful in whatever you choose to do when you get older.
>
> Starting today, every time you see the sign I'm about to unveil, let it remind you of the effort we need to bring to the little things, the small tasks that may not be your favorite but that are so important for your success, in school and in other parts of your life.

Since I introduced the defense sign to my students, it has become an important class symbol. In fact, many kids do a small sketch of it at the top of their math assessments before starting their work. One young girl who, before learning of the sign, experienced great difficulty paying attention to detail with her math work actually started earning higher scores after she began to draw the sign on her math assessments. This ritual reminded her to slow down and work more carefully.

You and Future You

This brief video features a story, told through a series of simple drawings I made (*primitive* might be more accurate), that helps kids better understand why it is so important to work hard in school and take their education seriously. In many ways, the video brings to life the educational chain reaction mentioned earlier in this chapter. This project was inspired by Dan Roam (2016), author of the amazing book *Draw to Win*, and a New Zealand indie band called The Beths. You can find the video at *https://www.youtube.com/watch?v=RkmE7mkeJsI*. In addition to showing the video in class and discussing its main messages with my students, I email the link to parents so they can have a follow-up viewing and conversation at home.

Closing

One of the reasons I initially wanted to become a principal was so I could have the authority to manage our school's electronic message board. My first idea was a take on an ACDC lyric that I would post at the start of every summer: "For those about to read, we salute you." Here's another: "Welcome to Roosevelt School, where quality always has the right of way." Making quality the driving force of our teaching and learning does a massive, lifelong service for the students in our care and leads to a tremendous amount of success, joy, and fulfillment for everyone involved. Pursuing quality appeals to the best within us and brings the best out of us. It focuses our efforts, elevates our expectations, and offers engaging challenges. When team members (students and teachers) begin to achieve quality on a consistent basis, we experience a feeling of accomplishment that nobody can give us and nobody can take away.

Reference List

Crosby, P. (1984). *Quality without Tears*. New York: McGraw-Hill.
Glasser, W. (1990). *The Quality School*. New York: Harper & Row.
Kilian, C. S. (1992). *The World of W. Edwards Deming*. Knoxville, TN: SPC Press, Inc.

Pirsig, R. (1974). *Zen and the Art of Motorcycle Maintenance.* New York: William Morrow and Company, Inc.

Reifman, S. (2008). *Eight Essentials for Empowered Teaching & Learning, K-8.* Thousand Oaks, CA: Corwin Press.

Roam, D. (2016). *Draw to Win.* New York: Penguin Random House.

Walton, M. (1986). *The Deming Management Method.* New York: Perigee Books.

6

Motivation

After spending a couple of years early in my career studying W. Edwards Deming's quality principles and applying them to my teaching, I was pleased and encouraged by the initial results I was observing with regard to both student learning and classroom culture. At that time, I was teaching a "Home–School Communication" course at UCLA Extension for elementary educators. When I asked if I could offer a second course focused on implementing Deming's philosophy, my supervisor gave the green light. Deming's ideas eventually became known as the 14 Points of Quality, a set of integrated principles that provide a comprehensive framework for improvement. As a tribute to Deming, his work, and his profound impact on my teaching practice, I titled the new course "Eight Keys to Classroom Quality." (See the note at the end of this chapter.)

A few years earlier, I had watched a documentary about a band, and the lead singer described the difference between recording a song in the studio and playing it to a live audience. With no fans around, he pointed out, there's no way to know during the recording process how people will feel about or react to the song. There's no feedback. In a concert, however, feedback is immediate and powerful. I thought about this difference when I launched my second extension course. I believed strongly in every one of the "eight keys" I presented to the elementary educators enrolled in the course, yet I couldn't know if the teachers in attendance would find them useful. As I proceeded from one key to the next, I was heartened by the positive feedback I received. Teachers seemed to like our first topic, establishing a sense of purpose, and its focus on creating a class mission statement each year with children. The next few sets of ideas also met with a kind response.

And then I shared my thoughts on the topic that serves as the initial focus of this chapter—the dangers of employing rewards and punishments to manage children's behavior. The mood of the room instantly changed, and an awkward period of silence ensued and lingered. I later realized that because the educators in the course had been using classroom management systems based on extrinsic motivation for their entire careers, they had come to rely on this approach and held it dear. The ideas I was presenting called these practices into question in a way they had never heard before. If their student teaching experiences were anything like mine, I was threatening the only way they had ever learned to supervise their classrooms. They were understandably uncomfortable. One gentleman even compared my criticism of extrinsic motivation to a destructive military act used in times of war. He felt that I was trying to take away the only method he knew of supervising student behavior. I remember his exact words as if he uttered them yesterday. Even though I followed that content with elements of an alternative approach more consistent with a whole-child philosophy, it was a difficult sell and a difficult evening. With this book, my aim is to offer you, as new educators, a fresh, effective approach to leading your classrooms and help you avoid becoming attached to methods that possess so many drawbacks.

Let's dig deeper into the topic of using rewards and punishments to manage student behavior and the concepts of intrinsic and extrinsic motivation. The eighth of Deming's 14 Points of Quality counsels managers to drive out fear from the workplace. Though Deming established these points while working in Japan, he developed point 8 after observing factory life in the United States. Managing by fear, according to Deming, was not an issue in Japan. It was chiefly an American way of supervising workers.

American managers used fear to control employees. They did this primarily through the application of the quota system, under which workers are responsible for producing a predetermined number or amount of output per day. The pressure placed on workers to meet their quotas made for a very stressful work environment. For example, assume I work in an auto parts factory, and my co-workers and I must produce 50 spark plugs each per day. Those who fail to meet the quota, or who otherwise displease the boss, are subject to intimidation, threats, pay deductions, and even termination. On the other hand, there's also strong pressure among employees not to exceed the quota. The thinking goes that if management sees some workers surpass the production target, they will then raise it for everyone.

According to Deming, whether workers are struggling to reach the quota or holding back in order not to surpass it, the fear associated with this approach presents serious problems to organizations concerned about quality. First, the constant stress prevents workers from feeling secure in their jobs. It also robs them of all pride in workmanship and destroys any joy they may experience from their efforts; workers can't enjoy their jobs when they are worried about losing their jobs. In addition, fear causes employees to focus on their own survival rather than on producing quality work. Quality must become and remain the emphasis if an organization and the individuals within it are going to live up to their full potential. Fear distracts workers from that emphasis.

As an outspoken critic of management by fear, Deming claims "the economic loss from fear is appalling." Fearful employees cannot produce quality work. As author Mary Walton (1986) explains in the *Deming Management Method*, "many employees are afraid to ask questions or take a position, even when they do not understand what the job is or what is right or wrong." Fearing that they will be blamed for the problem, fired, harassed, discriminated against, or given a less-desirable job assignment, workers will continue to perform their duties wrongly or not at all. They will be afraid to report broken equipment, ask for additional instructions, or call attention to conditions that interfere with quality.

Why did companies choose to manage by fear? Were managers just cruel, uncaring people who enjoyed exerting their power? Was it because their desire to earn profits overrode any concern for their employees' well-being? While these two possible answers may appeal to some, neither gets to the heart of the issue. Instead, the work of psychologist Douglas McGregor suggests another, more logical explanation why companies relied on fear to manage employees: They felt they *needed* to do so. In *The Human Side of Enterprise*, McGregor developed two contrasting sets of worker assumptions, known as theory X and theory Y. These theories are shown in Box 6.1. Management operating under theory X assumptions believed that without such a coercive approach, workers lacked the motivation of their own to put forth the effort required to get the job done. Because of this perceived lack of internal

---

Box 6.1 Douglas McGregor's Theory X and Theory Y

Douglas McGregor's Theory X and Theory Y

Theory X Assumptions of the Worker

1. The average human being has an inherent dislike of work and will avoid it if he can.
2. Because of this human characteristic of dislike of work, most people must be coerced, directed, threatened with punishment to get them to put forth adequate effort toward the achievement of organizational objectives.
3. The average human being prefers to be directed, wishes to avoid responsibility, has relatively little ambition, wants security above all.

> **Theory Y Assumptions of the Worker**
> 1. The expenditure of physical and mental effort in work is as natural as play or rest.
> 2. External control and the threat of punishment are not the only means for bringing about effort toward organizational objectives. Man will exercise self-direction and self-control in the service of objectives to which he is committed.
> 3. Commitment to objectives is a function of the rewards associated with their achievement.
> 4. The average human being learns, under proper conditions, not only to accept but to seek responsibility.
> 5. The capacity to exercise a relatively high degree of imagination, ingenuity, and creativity in the solution of organizational problems is widely, not narrowly, distributed in the population.
> 6. Under the conditions of modern industrial life, the intellectual potentialities of the average human being are only partially utilized.
>
> *Source*: From *The Human Side of Enterprise* by McGregor (1960). Reprinted with permission of McGraw Hill.

motivation, management felt the need to control their workers externally through the use of fear and punishment.

If managers truly embrace theory X assumptions, then using fear in the workplace serves a constructive purpose. If I genuinely believe that my employees dislike their work and will avoid it at all costs, then the survival of the firm depends upon my finding a way to get them, and keep them, motivated. If that's my situation, then intimidating, punishing, and creating daily quotas for everyone to meet in order to receive a paycheck strike me as advisable courses of action to take. Sure, there are negative side effects to this approach, but our need to get work done around here justifies it.

Classroom Parallels

In American education, just as in business, an emphasis on control and punishment, rooted in theory X assumptions, has dominated the way we manage our students. Punishment has traditionally come in a variety of forms. Without the ability to affect wages, as factory managers can, teachers have historically punished students by impacting two other commodities they hold dear: free time and grades. When kids misbehave, we take away their recess or send them to detention. Adding to the misery, we have them write standards during this time. We also punish by lowering their grades. Should the negative behavior become extreme, we suspend and expel. The fear created by such exercises of power is just as real and presents the same range of problems encountered by workers in the factory.

Over the years, however, the negative aspects of controlling students through the use of punishment have led educators to search for more positive ways to achieve the same effect. The result has been an increase in the use of rewards, both tangible and intangible. Throughout his well-known book *Punished by Rewards*, author Alfie Kohn (1993) defines a reward as any situation where the idea "if you do this, you will get that" is at work, such as telling students, "If you spell all your words correctly, you will get a sticker." The idea of using rewards, rather than punishments, has obvious appeal. Because students are working to earn something positive rather than to avoid something negative, the classroom becomes a happier, more exciting place to be. Rewards appear to offer a win–win situation for everybody. Students win because they have opportunities to earn items that they value, while teachers also win because kids have to do exactly what we say in order to attain these rewards. They have to behave well and put forth effort.

Now, instead of taking away our students' recess time when they don't line up properly, we put five marbles in the jar when they do. When the students earn 50 marbles, they get a popcorn party. Now, when we discover that our class performed poorly on the weekly spelling quiz, we offer a sticker to every student who gets all the words right. Now, in order to ensure that every table has a smooth transition from one activity to the next, we add another point to the board for each table that does a good job. Every time a table earns ten points, we treat those kids to a pizza party.

The Problems With Rewards

Though rewards may appear qualitatively different from punishments, both approaches suffer from the same underlying problems. Kohn, in *Punished by Rewards*, writes "that rewards and punishments are not opposites at all; they are two sides of the same coin. And it is a coin that does not buy very much." He points out that while the negative effects of punishment may appear obvious, those of rewards are harder to detect. He has identified five specific problems associated with the use of rewards.

Rewards Punish
Rewards punish in two ways. First, they have the effect of controlling students' behavior. By offering a sticker to every child who shows me they are ready to line up for recess, I can easily manipulate the class into

action. Controlling students in this manner whenever we expect them to perform a task diminishes their autonomy. It denies them opportunities to act on their own, make decisions, and exercise responsibility. If our mission involves developing self-directed, empowered learners, rewards thwart that process by placing control squarely in the hands of teachers, not students. Our kids can't exercise self-control when their actions are being controlled.

Second, Kohn notes that rewards punish because "some people do not get the rewards they were hoping to get, and the effect of this is, in practice, indistinguishable from punishment." For example, imagine I promise my class 20 extra minutes of PE at the end of the day if everyone behaves well up to that point. After the morning goes very smoothly, the kids head to recess talking about how great our longer PE period is going to be. The group then returns from recess and continues its outstanding effort until lunchtime. As we walk to the lunch benches, I sense everyone's confidence growing. I hear one student tell another, "We've made it through the hard part. After lunch there's only one hour left until PE. We've got it in the bag." But wouldn't you know it, just 15 minutes before PE, two students begin playing around during social studies. I ask them to stop, but they continue misbehaving. I have no choice but to tell the class that there'll be no extra PE today. Predictably, the kids are deflated. They feel as if they have just been punished even though I haven't, technically, taken anything away from them. They simply were unable to do what was necessary to obtain the reward.

Rewards Rupture Relationships

Rewards rupture two sets of classroom relationships. First, rewards harm the relationships that students have with one another. This damage occurs commonly in situations of artificial scarcity in which the teacher intentionally limits the number of rewards that will be given out. Imagine that I tell my kids that whoever constructs the best science project will receive a beautiful plaque. By turning this activity into a competition, I pit every child against their classmates. This type of system "sets people up as one another's rivals, [and] the predictable result is that each will view the others with suspicion and hostility and, depending on their relative status, perhaps with contempt or envy as well."

Competition created by artificial scarcity also leads to other problems. According to Kohn, it produces "anxiety of a type and level that typically interferes with performance," discourages and de-motivates those students who believe they have no chance of winning, and results in a diminished sense of empowerment and responsibility for future performance due to the fact that people tend to attribute the results of a contest to factors beyond their control, such as innate ability. Above all, competition destroys any sense of cooperation and community that teachers attempt to build in their classrooms. It replaces "the possibility that people will try to assist each other with the near certainty they will try to defeat each other."

Rewards also rupture relationships among students when teachers offer collective incentives, as in the preceding example, in which I promised extra PE to the whole class if all the kids behaved well. Whenever the attainment of a reward depends on the efforts of everyone in the room, students quickly come to understand that any one individual holds the power to spoil it for the group. Kohn considers this approach "one of the most transparently manipulative strategies used by people in power. It calls forth a particularly noxious sort of peer pressure rather than encouraging genuine concern about the well-being of others." Students watch over one another like hawks, snapping comments such as "Shh!" and "Do your work!" to ensure that nobody jeopardizes the promised reward. Should the class ultimately fail to earn the incentive, the kids will immediately turn on the individual causing, or suspected to have caused, the disappointment.

Second, rewards rupture the teacher–student relationship. As educators, we try to create relationships with our kids characterized by trust, caring, and open communication. We want students to feel comfortable asking for help with something they don't understand, admitting mistakes, and coming to us with problems. This type of relationship, Kohn argues,

> is precisely what rewards and punishments kill. If your . . . teacher . . . is sitting in judgment of you, and if that judgment will determine whether good things or bad things will happen to you, this cannot help but warp your relationship with that person. You will not be working collaboratively in order to learn or grow; you will be trying to get him or her to approve of what you are doing so you can get the goodies.

Rewards offer a strong incentive to hide problems, create an impression of total competence, and devote time and energy attempting to impress the person in power.

Rewards Ignore Reasons

For three straight days, one of my most reliable students has failed to turn in her homework. Wishing to put a stop to this emerging trend, I offer her a reward if she brings it tomorrow. In doing so, I'm paying no attention to the possible causes of this sudden change in behavior; I'm only attending to the symptoms, wasting an opportunity to use this occasion as a learnable moment. By failing to focus on the reasons she hasn't been turning in her homework, I'm unable to help her in an effective way. Kohn points out that when acting in this manner, we really don't know what's going on beneath the surface because using rewards as a solution doesn't require us to know. "Rewards are not actually solutions at all; they are gimmicks, shortcuts, quick fixes that mask problems and ignore reasons. They never look below the surface." There could be any number of reasons that she hasn't been turning in her homework, such as organizational difficulties or an illness. Until teachers stop using rewards to mask these deeper issues, we will never be able to address them in ways that lead to genuine solutions.

Rewards Discourage Risk-Taking

While rewards may increase the likelihood that individuals will engage in a certain behavior in the short run, they also change the way we engage in that behavior. Specifically, Kohn argues, when working for a reward, "we do exactly what is necessary to get it and no more." Because the objective is simply to attain the reward, people are "less likely to take chances, think creatively, challenge themselves, play with possibilities, and follow hunches that might not pay off." Psychologist John Condry has dubbed rewards "enemies of exploration."

Rewards cause individuals to choose the easiest, fastest, and most effortless route to completing a task. Because the task comes to be seen as something that stands between you and the reward, it's logical that people would attempt to get it over with as quickly as possible. The task loses any inherent meaning and becomes simply a stepping stone to the reward. For example, when I was in first grade, my teacher gave a prize to every student who read 30 books. My friend Dean and I found the shortest book in our class library and read it 30 times. We then filled out the record sheet by writing the title of the book 30 times. Our goal was not to become better or more enthusiastic readers but to read 30 books.

Rewards Decrease Interest

Kohn's fifth reason explaining why rewards fail deals with the relationship between two types of motivation, extrinsic and intrinsic. Rewards and punishments are both examples of extrinsic motivation. I define *extrinsic motivation* to mean that *an individual desires to engage in a task not because of any connection to the task itself but because of outside incentives.* (In fact, the Latin prefix *ex* means "out of.") For example, if I begin listening to a certain radio station only because it's giving away $10,000 to caller 12, then I am extrinsically motivated. I'm not listening to the station because I enjoy the music it plays or the personality of the DJs. My desire to engage in the task of listening has nothing to do with the act of listening itself; I listen so that I can win money.

I listen not for its own sake but because it is a stepping stone to a greater good. Listening is simply a means to an end.

In contrast, intrinsic motivation focuses on what lies within the task, not on what successful completion of the task will earn. By *intrinsically motivated* I mean that *an individual desires to engage in a task due to the nature of the task itself or because of something inherent in the task*. For example, I was initially attracted to the sport of paddle tennis as a child because I enjoyed running around, hitting the ball, and planning strategy. I began playing the game for its own sake, not for extrinsic incentives, such as prize money. For any task, whether it's playing a sport or solving a math problem, intrinsic motivation exists when one or more of the following conditions apply:

- I find the task interesting.
- I find meaning in it.
- The task is important to me.
- I feel a sense of mastery or accomplishment when I do it well.
- I enjoy the challenge the task provides.
- I take personal pride and satisfaction in doing the task well.
- I value the learning opportunity the task offers.
- The task offers opportunities for self-expression and creativity.

Extrinsic rewards reduce intrinsic motivation. Kohn shared this conclusion after reviewing scores of research studies examining the issue. The basic point is that "people's interest in what they are doing typically declines when they are rewarded for doing it." The examples supporting Kohn's contention are numerous. One comes from my personal experiences as a paddle tennis player. These events taught me, firsthand, how powerful the effects of rewards can be.

I first swung a paddle tennis racket at the age of 5. My father had a regular Sunday morning doubles game down at the beach, and I would sit on a bench and watch for two hours, just hoping he would have enough energy when they were done to hit the ball with me for 5 minutes. Once I began playing, I was hooked. Whenever my family spent the night at the beach, I would wear my shoes to sleep so that I could get right to the courts the next morning. There was no time to waste. I would play from early in the morning until dark. Lying in bed at night, I would visualize myself hitting shot after shot.

I started playing junior tournaments at the age of 7, and adult tournaments at 13. When I found out that participants received trophies for finishing in the top 3 places, I really wanted to finish in the top 3 places. As I began to win these prizes, I wanted more of them. Soon, my desire to build up a trophy collection had eclipsed my intrinsic love of the game. My interest in accumulating trophies became a preoccupation, then an obsession. And it wasn't just trophies; other "extrinsics," such as my placement in the rankings, drove me to keep playing. My outlook on the game changed dramatically during my late teens and early 20s. Paddle tennis was becoming a job, not a hobby. Instead of lying in bed visualizing myself hitting great shots, as I had done during my childhood, I stayed up calculating how many ranking points I needed to advance to a higher position. By the time I hit the age of 23, the enjoyment was completely gone, and I retired from competitive play. From that point, it took several months of recreational play to rediscover the joy I knew so well as a child.

The motion picture *Searching for Bobby Fischer* provides another example that demonstrates how extrinsic rewards can decrease intrinsic interest. (I have shown the film to my students to illustrate this point.) As the movie begins, 7-year-old Josh Waitzkin walks home from school with his mother and baby sister. They pass through a park where some men are playing chess. He surprises his mom by asking if he could sit down to play with them. Though his mother has no idea that her son even knows how to play chess, she arranges a game for him. Josh's style of play attracts the attention of Vinny, Lawrence Fishburn's character, who compares the boy to a young Bobby Fischer. Having had his first taste of chess, Josh quickly develops a love for the game. He even tries to teach his sister how to play.

Sensing his son's potential, Josh's father hires a professional chess teacher, Bruce, played by Ben Kingsley. As part of his lessons, Bruce creates a variety of game situations and challenges Josh to choose the correct moves. Every time Josh makes the proper decision, Bruce awards him a certain number of "master class points." Bruce tells Josh that if he earns enough of these points, he will receive a certificate declaring him a grand champion.

Soon, Josh begins entering and winning local tournaments. His trophy collection grows to an impressive size, and he becomes the number 1 ranked player in his age group. As the boy's ranking rises, the pressure that his father and teacher place on him intensifies. Gradually, Josh's desire to play chess has less to do with his love of the game and more to do with points, rankings, trophies, certificates, tournaments, and winning. Ultimately, Josh stops having fun with chess entirely and plays out of obligation to his father. In the end, the boy's mother insists that certain changes be made in her son's life to restore his love of the game, and the movie concludes with Josh having a happier, more balanced childhood.

The finding that extrinsic motivation decreases intrinsic motivation has serious educational implications. Currently, many teachers are offering students rewards thinking that they increase interest in an activity when they actually decrease it. The most well-known examples of this phenomenon are those programs that offer students incentives for reading. Libraries, corporations, and other concerned groups organize these programs all over the country. When I taught first grade, the school distributed calendars to the kids each month. Every night they would enter the number of minutes they read. If, by the end of the month, the students read a designated number of total minutes, they would receive a prize.

The creators of these programs have the noblest of intentions. In criticizing the use of rewards, I mean, in no way, to criticize the well-meaning people who organize the programs. These individuals sincerely want children to choose to read more often. And initially, that happens. Offered an incentive for reading, students, in the short run, will read more frequently. What happens, though, is that this level of reading activity doesn't last. Several months down the road, without the presence of the reward, the amount of reading declines significantly. In fact, a truly frightening research finding indicates that in the long run, students who were initially rewarded for reading not only choose to read less often than they did at the outset of the program but also choose to read less often than did children who never participated in these programs in the first place. The problem, according to Kohn, is not that the effects of the rewards don't last but that the effects are the opposite of what was intended. "What rewards do, and what they do with devastating effectiveness, is smother people's enthusiasm for activities they might otherwise enjoy."

Kohn offers two reasons to explain why rewards decrease interest. First, he believes that "rewards are usually experienced as controlling, and we tend to recoil from situations where our autonomy has been diminished." Second, he suggests that "anything presented as a prerequisite for something else—that is, as a means toward some other end—comes to be seen as less desirable. 'Do this and you'll get that' automatically devalues the 'this.'"

Returning to our reading program example, students will figure out that if others are offering a reward for reading, then it must not be something they would want to do on their own; it's just a stepping stone to getting what they truly want: food, toys, and tickets to amusement parks. Educator A. S. Neill adds that rewarding students in this manner is "tantamount to declaring that the activity is not worth doing for its own sake" (Kohn, 1993).

Coming to Grips With These Findings

Kohn's identification of these problems comes at a time when the use of classroom rewards is, in my estimation, at an all-time high. Rewarding has become so commonplace that when teachers discuss the issue, the conversations tend to focus on the what, when, and how of rewards rather than the why.

From the time we begin our teacher training programs, we are led to believe that rewarding students in order to maintain control of the classroom is the way to go. Often, we are shown no alternative to this method. We learn about the theory of behaviorism and the idea of positive reinforcement in our courses, we work with master teachers who reward their students, and then we begin our first job in a school where our colleagues use rewards. We see no reason to question this approach because the professionals we respect offer incentives to their kids. It's all around us. We begin to reach a comfort level with this practice. After a few years of teaching, we become so comfortable with rewarding students that we cannot imagine managing a classroom without them.

Understandably, teachers who have reached this comfort level will find Kohn's work unsettling. Because it calls into question practices they hold so dear, many educators will initially resist or reject his conclusions. The most common response to Kohn's findings from teachers who have enjoyed success with the use of rewards is, "But they work!" I have heard this reply numerous times.

If by "work" educators mean that rewards produce temporary obedience in students, then yes, extrinsic motivation may work. If, however, they mean that rewards lead to the development and internalization of effective habits, then they do anything but work. During my third year of teaching, for example, I met with a member of our school's special education team to discuss one of my fourth graders who was experiencing significant behavioral difficulties. My colleague suggested the use of a specific reward and mentioned that it worked well the prior year. I didn't want to respond sarcastically, but I did think to myself that if the reward truly did work, the student wouldn't be repeating the same behavior as the year before. Producing short-term obedience is a far cry from achieving effective, long-term solutions. Furthermore, bringing about this temporary obedience comes at a cost. It comes at the expense of autonomy, relationships, creativity, interest, meaning, challenge, and other valuable entities that lie at the core of a whole-child classroom.

Another common response to Kohn's work is, "But rewards motivate people!" There's truth in this statement, though not in the way most people interpret it. Rewards do not motivate individuals in any intrinsic sense. According to Kohn, "[t]hey motivate people to work for rewards." They narrow our focus and reduce tasks to mere stepping stones. Moreover, W. Edwards Deming, in his book *The New Economics for Business, Education, and Government* (1986), remarks that when children are rewarded for doing well in school, "they learn to expect rewards for good performance." They, in fact, can become addicted to rewards. My first experience with this phenomenon came that day during my student teaching when the boy whose help I requested responded with "What do you give me for it?"

Above all, rewards demonstrate a lack of confidence in our kids and sell them short. By relying on extrinsic incentives to control our students' behavior, it's almost as if we are announcing to our classes:

- We don't think you are willing or able to behave and perform well on your own.
- We need to use these tricks to manipulate you into doing the things you should be doing anyway.
- These rewards benefit us, not you, but without them, we just don't think we're going to get very much done in here.

Of course, teachers who administer rewards don't think like that, but that's the subconscious message rewards send.

A Different Approach

In light of the considerable research on the effects of rewards, it becomes clear that neither rewarding nor punishing students offers teachers a management approach consistent with whole-child principles. The choice that so many educators face of whether to emphasize punishments or rewards in their classrooms, we now understand, is not really a choice at all. Both methods are extrinsic. Both seek to control the actions of students based on the promise that if you do this, this will happen to you, and, as a result, present a similar array of problems. Both rest on the assumptions of theory X put forth by Douglas McGregor, and both exist because they are believed to be necessary to maintain order and effort.

If we step back and look at the bigger picture, we see, then, that the real choice is not between rewards and punishments but between theory X and theory Y. If we believe in the assumptions of theory X, our classroom management will center on the issue of control. According to Stephen Covey, we will "assume that people have to be tightly supervised if they're going to produce or perform well." As teachers, if we believe our students will not put forth adequate effort on their own, then we will deem it necessary to incorporate rewards and/or punishments into our management plans. We will find ourselves offering stickers to improve spelling scores, distributing table points in exchange for smooth transitions, and giving marbles to straighten our lines.

However, if we embrace the ideas of theory Y, then we will not rely on extrinsic motivators due to our belief that all students possess intrinsic motivation and due to our understanding of the dangers that extrinsic incentives present. A belief in theory Y means that we hold very different assumptions about our kids and will manage them accordingly. Rather than emphasizing control, our paradigm, according to Stephen Covey (1994) in *First Things First*, will be one of "release." Our priority: empowerment. Under this paradigm, we assume "that, given the freedom, opportunity, and support, people will bring out the highest and best within them and accomplish great things." We further assume that students can and will put forth substantial effort on their own in the service of objectives to which they are committed.

In the classic 1993 movie *The Fugitive*, Dr. Richard Kimble (played by Harrison Ford) escapes from prison and returns home to Chicago to prove his innocence and find his wife's killer. After discovering a critical piece of evidence in the culprit's apartment, Kimble calls the US marshal assigned to the case (played by Tommy Lee Jones) and informs him of this evidence. The marshal dismisses the discovery as irrelevant and says, "I am not trying to solve a puzzle here." Kimble responds by saying, "Well, I am trying to solve a puzzle, and I just found a big piece." I felt the exact same way when I learned of McGregor's two contrasting theories. I viewed his work as a crucial piece of the puzzle I was trying to assemble in my quest to develop a whole-child approach for elementary classroom teaching. The two situations are practically identical, except, of course, for the fact that a US marshal wasn't pursuing me at that time. (That didn't happen until a few years later.)

Each year I include a copy of McGregor's theory X and theory Y in the Back-to-School Night packet I distribute to parents. I also share that if the school limited me to a single sheet of paper on this evening, I would send home these theories. My choice would be an easy one. McGregor's work is that foundational to my overall philosophy.

In particular, it is the second sentence of theory Y that most deeply resonates with me. "Man will exercise self-direction and self-control in the service of objectives to which he is committed." Upon reading that, I realized that if I wanted my students to commit their hearts and minds to educational pursuits, put forth maximum effort, and willingly and enthusiastically invest themselves in their learning, I needed to make a concerted effort to help everyone identify objectives that resonated with them. Put differently, I needed to find a way to establish a powerful sense of purpose that would inspire children to take daily action. In Chapter 4, I emphasized the significance of the overall classroom aim, mission statement, and Tower of Opportunity. That second sentence of theory Y offers a larger context that enables us to understand why these tools are so critical. That sentence creates the demand and clarifies the need for our efforts to establish purpose. Helping children understand the purposes of their learning dramatically increases the likelihood that students will exercise self-direction and take charge of their learning.

Extrinsic motivators are commonly employed to restore order in moments when student behavior falters and things become chaotic. In the "Introduction," I described how one such situation occurred while I was visiting a class at a different school during my first year. Upon noticing that his students were beginning to lose focus and starting to fool around, the teacher walked over to the part of the board that listed each table's points and waited. Immediately, the kids turned to face the board, sat up taller, and looked at the teacher. In a very real sense, rewards held that class together. I certainly do not mean to single out that group. That was simply one example of a phenomenon that happens regularly. In that capacity, rewards are nothing more than Band-Aids.

It is our higher purposes, then, captured in our mission statements and supported by our culture and commitment to one another, that truly hold us together. When behavior falters, we have to dig deep, find our patience, and remember what it is we are trying to promote in our classrooms. When things appear to be falling apart all around us, we have to decide how we are going to keep everything together. I have learned that the best move in these situations is to gather everyone, much as a basketball coach does during a time-out. I need to call attention to what I see happening, explain why I believe that behavior to be problematic or counterproductive, and refer to our mission statement for guidance, support, and accountability. Better yet, I can launch this impromptu meeting by asking the children why they think I called the class together. Eliciting responses in this manner empowers the kids to take ownership of the problem and invest themselves in generating a solution. However we initiate these problem-solving sessions, we regain the group's focus by calling attention to those ideas that we ourselves created. Higher purposes, not rewards, hold our class together. Ideas guide us and hold us together, not carrots and sticks. Intrinsic motivation and higher purposes are intertwined. No such connection exists with rewards. Extrinsic motivators don't address purpose at all.

When difficult moments occur—and they inevitably will—we benefit from viewing them as learning opportunities, not as occasions to lose our temper and escalate the use of controlling carrots and sticks. Without a doubt, a theory Y approach is significantly more difficult to employ than traditional, extrinsic management methods. Our efforts require considerably more time, more patience, and more problem-solving discussions. The results, however, are far more effective, far more lasting, far more empowering, and far more satisfying.

Teachers and students will only achieve quality in classrooms and schools when they co-create a learning environment consistent with theory Y assumptions. In fact, it is impossible to implement many of the ideas described in this book in the type of coercive and controlling environment necessitated by a belief in theory X. How, for example, can we increase the enthusiasm of our students when rewards decrease interest? How can we build strong, trusting relationships among members of our team when rewards rupture relationships? How can we foster the development of self-directed, responsible learners when rewards control behavior and thwart the development of responsibility? How can we encourage kids to play with possibilities and follow hunches when rewards discourage risk-taking? How can we foster a spirit of group problem-solving and continuous improvement when rewards ignore reasons? The problems that rewards present only serve to undermine the worthwhile purposes set forth in our class mission statements.

Intrinsic motivation is the fuel that powers the "empowerment engine." The pursuit of quality requires a substantial amount of motivation, and the only true motivation comes from inside. As Kohn puts it, "[i]f our goal is quality, or lasting commitment to a value or behavior, no artificial incentive can match the power of intrinsic motivation." According to "Praise, Involvement, and Intrinsic Motivation" (Koestner, Zuckerman, and Koestner, 1987), intrinsically motivated people "pursue optimal challenges, display greater innovativeness, and tend to perform better under challenging conditions." Previously, I shared the story of the Enterprise School District and mentioned Superintendent Lee Jenkins's assertion that student enthusiasm is the number 1 asset that any school possesses. I believe intrinsic motivation to be just as important a commodity, worthy of similar attention, emphasis, and protection.

The good news is that we, as teachers, have tremendous influence over our students' level of intrinsic motivation. There are certain practices that nurture it and others that destroy it. Our job is to eliminate the forces that destroy intrinsic motivation (e.g., fear, coercion, competition, blaming, ranking, and failure) and commit ourselves to promoting those that strengthen it. I describe these nurturing forces in the next section. In the following chapter, I provide more detailed information about what a comprehensive, whole-child classroom management plan might look like.

One final note: The classroom practices we employ to manage student behavior are, themselves, teaching tools and can rightfully be viewed as part of the curriculum. It is essential that these practices be educative—that they bring out the best in children and empower everyone to become better students and better people. In short, we need our management practices to send the right messages and be consistent with our highest whole-child priorities. The forces described in what follows do just that. The nurturing forces of intrinsic motivation powerfully and positively affect work habits, relationships, enthusiasm for learning, and motivation—all the entities that extrinsic motivation damages. Using rewards sends the wrong messages. Reading Kohn's work helped me realize why I was so uncomfortable that afternoon during my student teaching when the fifth grader whose help I had requested asked what I would give him for it. Kohn's book also clarified why I was so uncomfortable implementing a rewards-based system during my initial year of teaching. At their core these extrinsic methods rely on coercion and control, and that simply didn't feel right.

The Nurturing Forces of Intrinsic Motivation

In this section I present several forces that nurture intrinsic motivation. In addition to promoting student desire to engage in specific tasks, these forces benefit a classroom more generally. Collectively, they build morale and enthusiasm for learning, enhance self-esteem, deepen the sense of connection individuals feel to the classroom and to one another, and increase student willingness to put forth sustained effort. Furthermore, these ten forces make it more likely that children will find a flow and "get lost" in their work.

These forces enable us, as teachers, to be proactive and effectively address many of the reasons that so many children are not motivated in school. Many kids, for example, do not see the purpose of their learning, are bored, find the work too difficult or too easy, don't feel trusted or valued, or don't feel connected to something larger than themselves.

Purpose

The first step to creating an empowering classroom environment, you will recall, involves establishing a sense of purpose with our students. This effort starts at the beginning of the school year and includes the introduction of an overall aim and the development of a class mission statement. In addition, we can incorporate the seven life roles to broaden and deepen this discussion and ask the kids to create personal mission statements to help them identify *their* most important purposes for attending and doing well in school. Investing time in these endeavors encourages children to find meaning in their work and betters their understanding of how learning can improve their lives now and in the future. The connection between establishing purpose and nurturing intrinsic motivation is a simple one. Kids who understand the multiple purposes of their learning are more motivated to learn and more willing to commit themselves to academic pursuits than students who don't.

Contribution

Students will be more motivated to engage in a task when their work contributes to the well-being of others. One example of this phenomenon is cross-age tutoring, where older students assist younger ones. I have heard many stories about struggling fifth or sixth grade students whose lives were turned around after having the opportunity to help younger students who were also experiencing difficulty. I have seen similar increases in motivation when classes stage performances for senior citizens' centers, become involved in environmental causes, or present safety tips to kindergartners. Helping others brings out the best in us and offers a win–win situation for everyone involved.

These "out of the classroom" occasions have the potential to add tremendous value to our students' lives, but many times the kids' best opportunities to contribute happen each day in the classroom. During partner and group work, children know they have the chance to assist their classmates, and kids love helping others. It satisfies their need for fun, friendship, and power.

I once heard about a study of military personnel who fought in wars, and researchers posed the following question: "What was your most powerful motivating force when you were in battle?" The creators of the study speculated that perhaps the soldiers were fighting primarily for the love of their country or for their superiors. Both, as it turned out, were important. But what the researchers learned was that the soldiers, more than anything, were fighting for the other members of their unit. They were fighting for one another—for their buddies. Because of the extraordinary bond that existed among unit members, they didn't want to let their fellow soldiers down.

Of course, life in the classroom is completely different from the situations soldiers face, but the bonds among teammates are often incredibly strong, and our students will go to great lengths to look out for and help their friends. So we can bring that "I'm doing it for my buddy" dynamic to life in the classroom by incorporating a significant amount of cooperative learning because that tends to showcase children at their best. After explaining the instructions for a cooperative activity, we can emphasize the "Do it for your buddy" message before everyone begins working. The more we can have the kids contribute, the more they know their work matters in the lives of others, and the more motivated they will be. Take advantage of these benefits by seeking out opportunities for your kids to put their learning to use in the service of others.

Speaking of messaging, I wanted to mention a terrific book called *Made to Stick* (2007) by Chip and Dan Heath. The two brothers focus on why some messages resonate with their intended audiences (stick) while others don't. These communications can be quite varied, including, for example, advertisements from companies to potential consumers or instructions from parents to their children or from teachers to their students. Reading this book led me to become more mindful of the words I use with students, particularly those that come at the end of lessons as I am preparing to send everyone off to do their work.

Imagine my students are about to begin working on a math activity in partnerships. If I were to announce, "I need you and your partner to keep your voices down because I said so," that message would be based on power, control, and authority. Not a very theory Y way to go. If I were to say, "I need you and your partner to keep your voices down, and if you do a great job, you will each earn two table points," that message would be based on extrinsic motivation and present the same range of problems described earlier in this chapter. Finally, I could say, "I need you and your partner to keep your voices down because that will allow the groups around you to focus and do their best work. When the groups around you keep their voices down, that will allow you to do your best work." That message would be based on kindness, consideration, and mutual support. As a general principle, I recommend crafting messages that appeal to the best in children—those related to satisfying needs, reaching goals, and reinforcing culture. Positive, inspirational, and aspirational messages resonate the most and feel the best to deliver.

Interest

Since intrinsic motivation is often defined in terms of the interest that individuals find in a task, it makes sense that in order to increase the motivation of our students, we should attempt to make tasks as interesting and engaging as possible. There's a direct relationship between the two concepts. In terms of academic learning, we can increase engagement by promoting a hands-on approach, providing for significant amounts of student choice with regard to what and how children learn, and making tasks as meaningful and relevant to the kids' lives as possible.

Interest can also be cultivated in non-academic tasks, such as the ones you will find on the list of training routines in the next chapter. My students and I are always looking for ways to add interest to tasks that may otherwise be quite mundane. My favorite example deals with how I excuse the kids to recess. When I taught first grade, I excused one table at a time with the standard "Table A, you may go, table D, you may go, etc." When I made the switch to third and fourth grade, I tried another approach.

Here's how it works. First, I select a student volunteer to pick a category, such as foods, animals, or sports. Next, I ask the kids to think of their favorite item in that category. Once the kids have all done so, I start naming individual items. The children have permission to leave the room as soon as I name their item. My goal is to see if I can name the favorites of every student in the room without any clues from them. I always call the most obvious items first, such as baseball, football, and basketball if the category is favorite sport. After I name the obvious items, most of the kids leave, but there are always a few remaining. (Oftentimes, the children stay to watch even after their favorites have been called.) I then proceed to the lesser-known ones to see who else leaves. Inevitably, there are two or three children left who experience great delight in knowing that I haven't called their favorite yet. The kids take great pride in their ability to stump me. At some point, I surrender and ask them to tell me their favorite. Because the category changes each time, every child has many chances to stump me.

This method of excusing students takes only a minute or two and gives us the opportunity to bond, learn more about one another, and express different aspects of our personalities. It's also fun. Sometimes, depending on the category, it's even educational. Above all, though, it's a way for us to generate interest where none existed before.

Challenge

Human beings will seek out challenging activities. The degree of challenge, though, must be appropriate. We have little desire to engage in tasks that are too simple, because they offer no stimulation. We also have little desire to engage in tasks that are too difficult, because we wish to avoid the discouragement. Situations of optimal challenge bring out the best in us; they motivate us to the fullest. If you think about the times in your life when your motivation to complete a task was at its highest, it was probably because the task was neither too difficult nor too easy for you but appropriately challenging. This realization, however, can be daunting for teachers, since our job involves providing optimal challenge for each of our students, of whom no two are alike. Because no teacher can hope to know their students better than they know themselves, this is yet another reason to allow children to make choices about what and how they learn.

Success

Closely related to the idea of challenge is that of success. Nothing motivates like success, and nothing de-motivates like failure. Finding an optimal degree of challenge for each of our students increases the likelihood that they will be successful. As teachers, we must do everything in our power to find a way for every child to achieve some degree of academic success initially, no matter how far away they may be from mastering year-end standards.

Initial success keeps intrinsic motivation alive and begins to build confidence. Once students realize their first success, they will develop an appetite for more. The key is getting that first one. Some of the kids who enter our rooms in the fall may have never experienced academic success before and may be on the verge of giving up. We can't let this happen. We must keep them in the game. For example, if an incoming fourth grader experiences serious difficulty as a reader, then we can't start him with a fourth-grade text; that would be overwhelming. Instead, we may choose to focus on the sounds of each letter of the alphabet. Let's assume the student knew these sounds. Now, rather than beginning the year experiencing immediate failure, he encounters success. We, by no means, stop at this point or lower standards for him. We simply select a different entry point because we understand that success builds on itself. Of course, a tremendously demanding road still awaits this child, but success is the key to ensuring that he decides to make the trip.

Inspiration

Inspiration has an incredible effect on motivation. Telling stories, discussing quotes, and reading aloud uplifting biographies appeal to the best within us, remind us what's possible with enough hard work and dedication, and strengthen our commitment to reaching our goals and maximizing our full potential.

Inspiration is all around us. We can find it in the human interest stories we see in the newspaper and on television, the sporting events we watch on the weekends, and the books we read. There's inspiration in poetry and song lyrics. Finding these examples one day and sharing them with my students the next is one of my favorite parts of being a teacher.

Kids need to hear these stories. Learning about people all over the world who overcame long odds to realize their dreams, make great lives for themselves, and contribute to society powerfully impacts their own motivation. Children will be better able to appreciate the value of perseverance and the other important qualities we promote when they see how others have benefited from them.

One terrific way to inspire children is to read aloud stories in which the main characters achieve success by committing themselves to education, demonstrating strong character, and overcoming obstacles. In his book *Crash Course*, entrepreneur Chris Whittle (2005) supports this idea when he advocates "methodically exposing children to greatness, excellence, success in many fields and then emphasizing how learning was important to each example. Every day every school should put excellence on display."

What's particularly important is to select a wide variety of individuals so that students everywhere can identify with at least a few whose life stories resonate with *their* life stories and whose backgrounds resemble their own. For children who believe that attending school and earning an education cannot make a difference for people like themselves, our choices need to provide abundant, inspiring examples that prove otherwise.

Whittle's powerful message about helping children see the usefulness of education inspired me to write the book *2-Minute Biographies for Kids* (2013). The resource contains one-page biographies of 19 well-known individuals who used education to make better lives for themselves. The biographies trace the learning paths of the featured men and women and emphasize the educational accomplishments that made their later successes possible. The stories also highlight the adversity these people faced, the obstacles they overcame, and the positive character traits they demonstrated. In addition, interesting facts, anecdotes, and quotes are included so children understand that these individuals were at one time kids just like themselves.

The individuals included in this book were chosen with great care. Collectively, they form a distinguished group, featuring pioneers who broke barriers and gained entry into fields where access had previously been denied, significant racial and ethnic diversity, multiple educational routes to success, a variety of career paths and occupational fields, and examples from different periods in history.

2-Minute Biographies for Kids is an advertisement for education. The book's primary goal is to encourage children everywhere to become more determined, more motivated, more purposeful learners. The idea is that children who understand the critical role that education played in empowering these people to achieve the greatness for which they are known today will work harder and be more likely to persevere through difficult times.

In each story, the featured individual is not initially identified, thus creating an engaging "riddle" scenario. As kids listen to the title and the biography, they are learning about the person's life story, but they are also attempting to determine the identity of the individual being described. The final sentence of each biography reveals the person's name.

You may want to stop before reading this concluding sentence and ask the children in your audience if they would like to guess the individual's identity. Once the identity is revealed, you can then engage children in a brief discussion in which interesting and important aspects of the person's life are highlighted and potential lessons learned are emphasized. In Resource F, you will find a sample biography from the book.

The individuals featured in the examples and stories we share, however, don't have to come from outside our classroom. Our students have the ability and desire to inspire one another with their caring, their kindness, their commitment, and with the rich family histories they bring to school. We, as teachers, have the opportunity to encourage, recognize, and celebrate this behavior every day. Symbols, visuals, and success tips can also play an important role in our quest to inspire young learners. Be on the lookout for stories, symbols, and ideas you can use to inspire your students. Invite them to do the same.

Cooperation

The type of classroom environment teachers create strongly affects student motivation and performance. Cooperation, according to Howard Gardner, author of *Multiple Intelligences* (1993), is one environmental component that research has "shown to have a positive effect on students' social and psychological well-being, which eventually leads to higher academic achievement." Cooperation nurtures intrinsic motivation because it satisfies our students' need for belonging and because it usually makes activities more enjoyable. In addition, when kids work together, they are more likely to be successful at a given task than they would be alone.

Trust

Trust is another vital component of classroom environments that nurture intrinsic motivation. In a low-trust culture, according to Covey, supervision is tight and takes the form of "snoopervising." Managers manipulate behavior with carrots and sticks. Rules and regulations are numerous and cumbersome to prevent loose cannons from wreaking havoc. The emphasis is on control. Initiative is low.

Conversely, in high-trust cultures, intrinsic motivation flourishes. People are internally driven by a sense of teamwork and purpose. The emphasis is on release, not control. People's energies are liberated. As Covey puts it, workers are "fueled by the fire within," not by carrots and sticks. They are able to pursue organizational objectives, free from burdensome rules and regulations. Individuals experience joy.

Feedback

Imagine for a moment that you are a student in my class. You have recently published a Writing Workshop story, and you're waiting for me to assess it and hand it back to you. When I do, you notice that I've scored it to be a 2 on our 4-point rubric for *ideas*. You decide to continue working on the story to improve your score to a 3, the standard. But before you can begin to improve it, you need to know which specific areas to address. You look all over for my comments, but you don't find any. I have given you no feedback indicating what you did well, where you had difficulty, and how you can bring your work up to the standard. Understandably, you are de-motivated because you don't know how to proceed.

On the other hand, imagine that I return your work with extensive comments pertaining to each aspect of the rubric. You now know exactly what you need to address in order to raise your score. This information guides you. It helps motivate you to put forth the effort required to improve the story. Feedback is motivating. Described by many as "the breakfast of champions," feedback contributes to success and represents a vital part of building a culture of continuous improvement and quality.

I once heard someone remark, "Man knows everything about his work, except how to improve it. After all, if he knew how to improve it, he would be doing it already." This is where feedback helps us. When we are sincerely trying to improve in a given area but are unsure how to do so, we benefit from the expertise, experience, and wisdom of others. As Covey puts it, "getting other perspectives will help us improve the quality of our own."

In an empowering classroom environment, feedback takes many forms and flows in many directions. Most commonly, feedback flows from teacher to student. This type of feedback allows us to provide helpful information to kids about both their academic work and behavior. We offer our comments in writing and, when we have time, during one-on-one conversations. Feedback can also flow from student to student. As teachers, we facilitate this exchange of feedback among team members by encouraging them to work cooperatively as frequently as possible, such as during Writing Workshop, when it comes time to revise an initial story draft. Promoting student-to-student feedback sends the message that we consider all kids to be resources, capable of contributing to the betterment of the classroom community. As I mentioned previously, throughout the year I tell my students that sometimes the most valuable knowledge and skills they learn will not come from me, a book, or a website; they will come from one of their classmates.

Finally, feedback flows from student to teacher. I strongly believe that if I expect the kids to listen to my feedback, then I should listen to theirs. I see this partially as an issue of fairness, but more than that, I actively solicit feedback because I know that the class as a whole benefits from the ideas the students offer. The insights they provide are usually quite keen. In addition, kids appreciate teachers who are willing to listen to them. Feedback, then, benefits students not only when they receive it but also when they have a chance to provide it. Such opportunities improve their morale, give them greater ownership of the classroom, and generally result in a more productive environment.

Many years ago, for example, the children and I conducted our first set of Student-Led Conferences, a variation of the traditional parent–teacher meetings I will describe in Chapter 10. At that time, I was planning a second set for May or June. Though the conferences went well and the attendance rate was high, I wanted to make the second round better than the first. I had some ideas of how we could improve these meetings, and I wanted feedback from the kids.

I used a simple tool called a "Plus/Delta Chart" to collect student feedback. On the "Plus" side I wrote down everything that the kids liked about how we first conducted the conferences and that they wanted to hold constant for next time. On the "Delta" side I recorded all the ways they thought we could improve our format for the second set. (*Delta* is the Greek letter used in science to mean "change in.") A Plus/Delta Chart, then, tells us what to preserve and what to modify. I found myself agreeing with the group's recommendations and made a commitment to act on them the next time we conducted Student-Led Conferences. The Plus/Delta Chart we created can be found in Table 6.1.

One last point: The sooner children receive feedback, the more motivating that feedback will be. For example, when the kids learn a new skill during a math lesson, we should circulate as the kids are working on their independent practice to help them correct mistakes and clarify misunderstandings. Having everyone turn in their work to me at the end of the period

Table 6.1 Plus/Delta Chart

1. Liked that they had the opportunity to lead the conference without help from the teacher. 2. Thought the outline was helpful in getting organized for the conference. 3. Appreciated the freedom to choose the order in which they presented all the work to their parents. 4. Believed we did a good job of decorating the room for the conferences, including displaying all the science projects throughout the class so that parents could observe them. 5. Enjoyed using the computer to show their parents some of the work they had done recently. 6. Felt that the work they showed thoroughly addressed all the major subject areas.	1. Should conduct these meetings on more than one day in case any parents are unable to attend. 2. Should include Reading Notebooks as part of the work students show to parents. 3. Should use technology even more during the conferences. 4. Should invite other school personnel, with whom the students work, to meet with parents. 5. Teachers should participate in these conferences with their own families.

so I can take it home, correct it that night, and go over it the next day isn't as useful or motivating. (Plus, it takes the responsibility for improvement away from the students.) Cursive writing offers another example of this phenomenon. Many years ago, somebody remarked that one of the reasons children usually love learning to write in cursive is that they receive immediate feedback. They know instantly whether the letter they crafted matches the model provided, and if it doesn't, they know exactly how to make it better next time.

Recognition
A survey by the Council of Communication Management sought to discover what single factor had the greatest effect on worker motivation. According to author Bob Nelson in his book *1001 Ways to Reward Employees* (1994), it wasn't money. It was recognition. He reports, "While money is important to employees, what tends to motivate them to perform—and to perform at higher levels—is the thoughtful, personal kind of recognition that signifies true appreciation for a job well done."

The effects of recognition are just as powerful in the classroom as they are in the workplace. Acknowledging team members for noteworthy achievements makes them feel valued, boosts self-esteem, and builds confidence. When recognized, students realize that other people notice their hard work and care about the effort they put forth. They also feel a greater sense of connection to the classroom. As a result, intrinsic motivation thrives.

Because the benefits of recognition are so numerous, it's important for members of a team to acknowledge one another's efforts frequently. Like feedback, recognition should take many forms and flow in all directions. The following list contains several ways, formal and informal, in which teachers and students can offer recognition on a regular basis. Try as many of these options as you can. You will notice an immediate change in your classroom environment.

Statements of Recognition
In Chapter 3, I described the benefits of devoting the last few minutes of a class period to the sharing of recognitions. Whether these acknowledgments focus on academic achievements, Habits of Mind or Character, or gestures of friendship, the kind words allow every child to experience the pride that comes from being recognized.

"Way to Go" Notes
These are notes that any team member can give to any other team member for a job well done. "Way to Go" notes truly bring out the best in kids, both

those giving and those receiving the acknowledgments. In fact, many kids enjoy giving these notes more than they do receiving them. I'll never forget the day Sara was so excited to hand out a "Way to Go" that she built a wall of books around her desk to hide her blushing face. These papers take almost no time to fill out and to present, but the positive feelings they produce are lasting.

Kids develop very clever ways of delivering these sheets. Some will wait until after school and place a note in the recipient's desk so that they will discover it the following morning. Others will have me run interference for them as they transport the notes. For example, Chris once asked me if I could call Tiimo outside for a minute to discuss something so he could hide a "Way to Go" in Tiimo's backpack. Most kids, though, will just walk over and deliver the notes face-to-face. Seeing the fist bumps and smiles that accompany these exchanges is one of the highlights of my day.

Recognition Day

A formal event held every few months, Recognition Day is a time to honor the noteworthy efforts of all team members. At the ceremony, each student receives a certificate stating an accomplishment for which they are being recognized. Again, these acknowledgments can pertain to academic work, Habits of Mind or Character, or gestures of friendship. Every student is nominated either by a teacher, a classmate, a parent, or an administrator. To add a special feeling to the event and to accommodate parents and other guests, arrange, if you can, to have Recognition Day in the school auditorium or cafeteria. Students can even give speeches at the outset of the ceremony, act as emcees, and present the certificates to one another. The more student-run, the better.

Before closing out discussion of this topic, I want to distinguish between recognitions and rewards. Many consider them to be one and the same. In fact, I vividly recall a course I taught to a group of teachers in which I was pointing out the dangers of rewards and suggesting the nurturing of intrinsic motivation based on the ideas described in this section. One member of the group, however, drew the conclusion that, because some of the recognition ideas involve notes and certificates, now we are supposed to give students rewards but call them recognitions instead. He saw no clear difference between the two approaches.

My response was that recognitions are qualitatively different from rewards. The critical issue in separating the two is that of control. Rewards are used to control the behavior and effort of students. Recall Kohn's definition of a *reward*: "If you do this, you will get that." When children are offered a goody for completing a task, their energies are narrowly channeled in that direction. There's a controlling context when something is promised in advance. With recognitions, there's no effort to control students. Recognitions are meant to acknowledge a job well done and to express appreciation. Though recognitions often come in tangible form, they are never promised in advance and are not used to manipulate behavior. There's no "If you do this, you will get that" at work.

Confusion arises when we think of rewards as objects rather than as situations. A "Way to Go" note is not, in itself, a reward; it depends on the context in which the note is presented. For example, if I hold up a "Way to Go" at the beginning of the day and say, "Kids, I will present one of these sheets to every student who behaves well today," then that would be a reward because it fits Kohn's definition: If the kids behave well, they will get a "Way to Go" note. However, if I approach a student at the end of the day and say, "Alice, you really did great work today, and I'd like you to have this," then that's a recognition, because it's presented after the fact to acknowledge a job well done, with no attempt to control behavior.

I don't mean to imply that recognitions have no potential downside. It's certainly possible for a student to receive acknowledgment for a job well done and then to continue behaving that way for the sole purpose of receiving further acknowledgment. Students can become addicted to recognition just as they do to rewards. The answer, however, is not to eliminate recognition. I don't know too many people who would want to work in a classroom where teachers and students didn't acknowledge one another's efforts. You'd need a jacket in that kind of cold atmosphere. Rather, any difficulties associated with recognition should be dealt with honestly and openly through class or one-on-one discussions. Be proactive. By identifying and discussing potential problems before they occur, we greatly decrease the likelihood that they ever will.

Intrinsic Motivation: A Summary
Box 6.2, which follows, summarizes the forces that nurture intrinsic motivation. These forces work synergistically to create an environment where quality can flourish. No extrinsic motivators, either alone or in combination, can come close to producing such results. No student has ever been rewarded or punished into excellence. True success comes only when we bring out the very best in our students. And in order for us to bring the best *out* of our students, we must appeal to the best *in* them. These forces do just that.

> **Box 6.2 Summary of Forces That Nurture Intrinsic Motivation**
>
> *Summary of Forces That Nurture Intrinsic Motivation*
> 1. Purpose
> 2. Contribution
> 3. Interest
> 4. Challenge
> 5. Success
> 6. Inspiration
> 7. Cooperation
> 8. Trust
> 9. Feedback
> 10. Recognition
>
> *Source*: Adapted from *Eight Essentials for Empowered Teaching and Learning, K–8* (Corwin, 2008).

Introducing the Concept of Intrinsic Motivation to Children

Early each school year, I introduce the concept of intrinsic motivation to my students by conducting a special activity during our morning meeting time. I recruit a volunteer to sit at a desk off to the side of our rug area and pretend to read. (I say *pretend* because I am talking the whole time, and it's unlikely this child will be able to do any actual reading.) I mention to the class that our volunteer seems to be extremely focused on their book. That, we can see. What we are unable to determine visually, though, is *why* that child is doing such a great job. I ask everyone to brainstorm as many reasons as possible why the volunteer might be so into their book.

After a brief pair share, I open up the floor to anyone who thinks they have an idea why the reader is so *motivated*. I repeat that word several times during this activity so students can inductively learn its meaning. On the board I make two columns and ask the group to pay close attention to why they think I'm placing certain responses on the left and others on the right. Typically, the first few participants contribute statements such as, "She might really like her book," "Maybe she wants to get better at reading," and "Reading could be her favorite subject." I list these types of ideas on the right side of the board. Once the kids run out of ideas, I suggest a couple others that tend to catch everyone off guard. Maybe, I speculate, someone offered her a prize if she read for a certain number of minutes or threatened a consequence if she didn't read at all that day. I add those two ideas on the left side of the board. With all the possible reasons listed, I give the kids time to try to identify the difference between the two columns. There are usually some children who figure out that the reasons on the left really aren't about reading while those on the right are. At that point, I introduce the terms *intrinsic* and *extrinsic*.

I explain that when we are *intrinsically motivated* to complete a task, there's something within the task that appeals to or matters to us. For example, if I play a sport because I find it interesting and feel good when I play it well, my motivation is intrinsic. That means my desire is inside me and/or rooted in the task. I post the chart shown in what follows on the board and refer to it throughout my explanation. Usually, I am able to point out how many of the "right side" ideas the children suggested connect to items on the chart. On the other hand, I say, the items on the left side of the chart have nothing to do with the task itself. They relate only to what might happen to me if I do or do not complete the task. I then share the radio station example mentioned previously. I close out this brief introduction by emphasizing that the issue of motivation will be very important in our class, and we will return to this topic frequently.

Over the years I have learned that children take this intrinsic/extrinsic distinction seriously. During the 2020–21 pandemic year, for example, most of our days were spent on Zoom. We were able to return to in-person learning for just the final six weeks of the spring semester. Because our in-class time was so limited, I was able to post only a fraction of the visual reference points I typically display. During our final week, I was curious and asked the kids which visual they found the most impactful. The one that received the most votes was the Intrinsic Motivation Chart shown in Box 6.3. Many children

---

Box 6.3 Intrinsic Motivation Chart

Intrinsic Motivation

I find the task interesting.

I find meaning in it.

The task is important to me.

I feel a sense of mastery or accomplishment when I do it well.

I enjoy the challenge the task provides.

I take personal pride and satisfaction in doing the task well.

I value the learning opportunity the task offers.

The task offers opportunities for self-expression and creativity.

reported that the concept was completely new to them and that they looked at the chart frequently and found the various descriptors meaningful.

> **Box 6.4 Finding a Flow**
>
> *What Does It Mean to Find a Flow?*
> ★ You are working toward a goal.
> ★ The activity is so engaging that other things happening nearby go completely unnoticed.
> ★ You are lost in the experience.
> ★ You understand that something special is happening.
> ★ You remember this feeling and try to recapture it time and time again.

Fostering an "Intrinsic" Mindset With Our Students

At the end of the previous chapter, I shared several quotes and visuals designed to help children build a "quality mindset." I would like to make a similar effort in this section by presenting a couple of ideas, consistent with theory Y, that tap into children's desire to learn and grow, encourage self-direction, and appeal to the best in everyone.

"Finding a Flow" Chart

When many children work independently at their desks, their focus tends to waver. They can become easily distracted by other things happening in the room or experience difficulty sustaining their attention for an entire work period. Under a behaviorist approach, we might offer table points or other extrinsic incentives to remedy the situation. In a theory Y classroom, however, we seek genuine solutions that have the ability to produce long-term improvement and that avoid the drawbacks that extrinsic rewards present.

Introducing the concept of "flow," popularized by Hungarian psychologist Mihaly Csikszentmihalyi (1998) in his book *Finding Flow: The Psychology of Engagement with Everyday Life* (1998), gives kids encouraging descriptors that can serve as useful reference points. I like to introduce the bullet points shown in Box 6.4 a few weeks into the school year. Sometimes I will present this information earlier if several kids are experiencing difficulty with their focus at the same time. Periods in which multiple children simultaneously hit a low point are inevitable during the school year, and responding to these occurrences by sharing new, positive ideas is far more effective than becoming angry, punitive, or extrinsic.

When I first share these bullet points, I say that I know everyone is working hard to become a great student. I assume good intentions. I then announce that I'm excited to show them what researchers have found to be the highest-known level of focus—a flow. The kids are eager to test this concept over the next few days, and there's definitely an initial improvement in their performance as they strive to bring these criteria to life. Of course, it isn't possible for children or adults to achieve a flow state every time they sit down to work, but aiming high impacts productivity and leads to motivational benefits. Once the kids understand what "flow" means, I can mention it for the rest of the year, with individual children as well as the class as a whole. A cool, added bonus of this exercise is that it gives a nod to scientific research and exposes children to new academic fields and interests.

In the days following our introduction to flow, it is extremely helpful to review the bullet points both before the kids begin an independent activity and at the end of the period. Previewing these indicators plants a wonderful seed in the children's minds, enabling them to set a goal, select a specific bullet point to keep in mind, and begin their work on a high note. At the conclusion of the activity, I recommend asking student volunteers to share whether they felt they "found a flow" and, if so, which bullet points matched their experience. Offering extrinsic rewards is controlling; encouraging a flow state is empowering.

The Drive for 5

When children experience difficulty with their academic work on a consistent basis, it is easy to attribute that level of performance to a lack of effort or caring. In these situations, though, other factors might offer a better explanation. I have learned over the years that many kids genuinely do want to succeed academically but haven't yet learned the "nuts-and-bolts" skills and strategies that will help them level up. These "success tips" can pertain to work habits, attitudes, and other skills that support learning. As educators, we provide an incredible service to children by devoting instructional time to these areas. Operating under a theory Y approach, we assume good intentions on the part of our students and trust they will be receptive to any suggestions that can result in improved performance.

My favorite example of a success tip is a set of ideas I created many years ago called "The Drive for 5." This endeavor began one day when I was looking closely at our Habits of Mind and Habits of Character, two powerful sets of habits that have guided my work with students for most of my career. Together, the Habits of Mind and the Habits of Character show children the specific traits and behaviors needed to become better thinkers, better students, and better people. These 22 habits empower children to maximize their considerable potential, and I simply cannot imagine myself teaching in a classroom without using these ideas as daily reference points.

As I studied these habits carefully, I noticed that a few of the behaviors included among this larger list seem to have particular power in explaining why some students consistently achieve success in school and why others haven't yet been able to do so. Of course, factors that lie outside the control of teachers and schools most certainly impact how well children perform in the classroom, but the good news is that there are a small number of "high-leverage" behaviors that all children can learn and that all teachers can nurture and develop. With time, effort, and consistent attention paid to these five areas, every child can become a highly successful student and experience the greater confidence, higher self-esteem, and greater learning gains that result from this success.

I came to describe my quest to help children develop these behaviors as "The Drive for 5," due to the fact that (with only a small amount of linguistic gymnastics) the initial letters of each behavior can be combined to spell the word *drive*. I share this idea with students at the beginning of every school year and with families at Back-to-School Night. At our Parent Conferences in November, I give each family an "acronym" visual to place on a refrigerator or bulletin board so these ideas remain visible and accessible throughout the year. This has been one of my most ambitious endeavors, and I believe it to be the one with the greatest potential to impact student performance. It is my hope that, by giving attention to these high-leverage behaviors, we can empower all our students to be successful in school and beyond. Table 6.2 provides visuals to accompany each letter of the acronym.

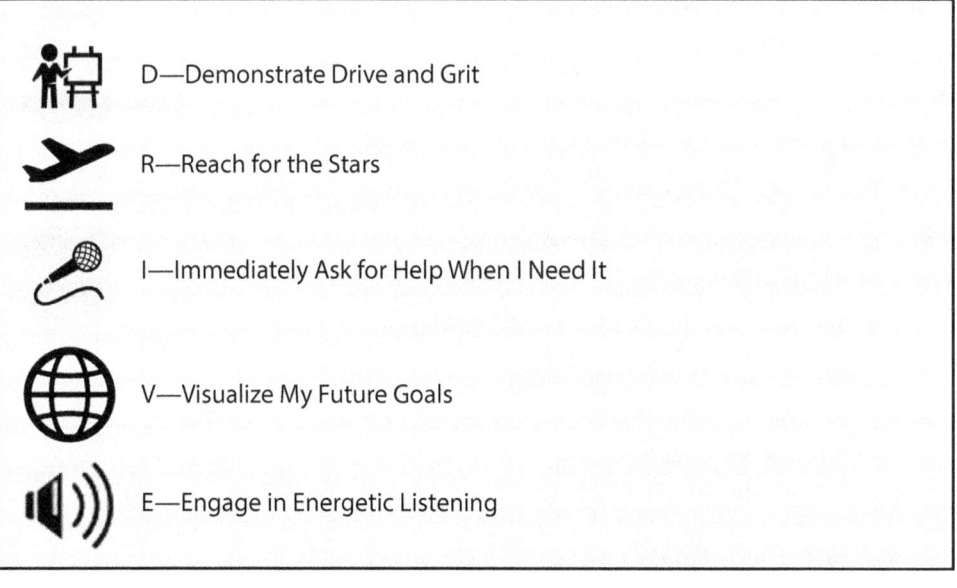

All children can be highly successful students. The key is to focus our attention on the right places. It turns out that there are five powerful steps kids can take to enjoy the greater confidence, higher self-esteem, and greater learning gains that come from being successful in school. Our quest to develop these behaviors is called "The Drive for 5."

Closing

The last few decades have produced incredible advances in the teaching and learning of several academic areas. In math, for example, approaches such as cognitively guided instruction (CGI) have changed the way children interact

Table 6.2 "Drive for 5" Visual

Demonstrate Drive and Grit
The first step in becoming a successful student is making a commitment to education and deciding that doing well in school matters to you. Once you've done this, you are excited to arrive at school each day, and you work with energy, enthusiasm, and passion. You take responsibility for your learning and don't need reminders to focus. You are disciplined. You invest yourself completely in your work and make productive use of your time. When difficult challenges arise, you enjoy and embrace them, and you persevere until the end. How you sit while working and while listening and how you carry yourself are important parts of demonstrating drive.
Reach for the Stars
Successful students hold themselves to impressively high personal standards with regard to their work, effort, and behavior. You reach this level by caring deeply about your work and not rushing through it. Your goal isn't simply to finish; it's to produce quality work. You take uncommon pride in what you do and only want to turn in work that represents your very best effort, even if it means putting in extra time. You understand that every piece of work you do is like a self-portrait. You won't settle for anything less than your best. An important part of having high personal standards is paying attention to detail while reading, answering questions, and proofreading written work.
Immediately Ask for Help When I Need It
Successful students expect to understand new information during lessons and while reading. When they don't, it's as if an alarm bell goes off in their heads, and after making an initial good-faith effort to make sense of the content, they raise their hands to ask questions and gain clarity. They're not shy, and they don't worry that classmates will judge them. They feel comfortable speaking up for themselves without any fear or worry. After all, there's nothing to worry about. We're all in this together.

> **Visualize My Future Goals**
>
> Successful students have a strong understanding of why they're in school and why it's important to work hard and do well academically. They know that doing well in school matters, both now and in the future. These kids understand the link between today's successes and tomorrow's opportunities. They think about such things as what types of careers and passions they might want to pursue and what areas they might want to study in college. Understanding the multiple purposes of doing well in school increases motivation to learn and leads to higher levels of maturity.

> **Engage in Energetic Listening**
>
> Successful students are attentive listeners. These kids listen closely when their teachers present lessons or give important directions, and they listen just as well when their classmates are sharing information and asking and answering questions. Successful students listen closely to everyone; they don't miss a thing. You can see it in the posture they take during instructional lessons and in the eye contact they consistently make with the speaker. They want to absorb as much information as possible during lessons and discussions, and they participate frequently. They involve themselves in the conversation, enthusiastically and confidently.

with and make sense of their learning, leading them to become more powerful, more engaged thinkers. In language arts, the workshop approach pioneered by the Teachers College, Columbia, has afforded students authentic opportunities to think, create, and deepen their understanding of reading and writing concepts by being real readers and writers. The time has come for a similar transformation in the way teachers lead their classrooms. Theory X approaches rooted in 19th-century factory methods are beyond outdated and present an array of problems that, to this day, remain largely unknown to those who employ them. I believe extrinsic motivation to be the most under-the-radar, under-examined issue in our classrooms today. This practice continues to thwart the development of many worthwhile ideals educators hold dear and wish to promote. Our 21st-century world requires individuals who exercise self-direction, collaborate well with others, solve complex problems, and follow their passions. We need classroom approaches that empower children's energies, not control them.

The education community has invested tremendous time and thought into improving curriculum and instruction. We need to invest that same amount of thought to modernize the way we supervise our classrooms and build culture. We need to subject our management methods to strict scrutiny, go deep under the hood with table points and prize boxes, and analyze if they are taking us where we want to go—if they are promoting or thwarting our highest priorities. It's imperative that we increase awareness of the devastating effects that theory X approaches are having on student learning, intrinsic motivation, and classroom culture while raising awareness of the tremendous opportunities that await us once we, as a community of educators, embrace theory Y approaches on a mass scale. Just as we did with CGI and Teachers College, we need to make our decisions based on what research shows us and not simply rely on tradition or do what we've always done. Action on this front is urgently needed.

Notes

I very much wanted my 2008 book *Eight Essentials for Empowered Teaching and Learning, K–8* to share the name of my UCLA Extension course, but it wasn't meant to be. My publisher didn't share my enthusiasm for the idea. It reminded me of the time I wanted to attend Stanford University. The admissions committee didn't share my enthusiasm for that idea either.

A. S. Neill's quote is found in A. Kohn, *Punished by Rewards* (New York: Houghton Mifflin, 1993), 76. Neill, the author of *Summerhill*, was quoted in M. Morgan, "Reward-Induced Decrements and Increments in Intrinsic Motivation," *Review of Educational Research* 54 (1984): 5.

Reference List

Covey, S. (1994). *First Things First*. New York: Fireside.
Csikszentmihaly, M. (1998). *Finding Flow: The Psychology of Engagement with Everyday Life*. Alexandria, VA: BasicBooks, 1993.
Deming, W. E. (1986). *The New Economics for Business, Education, and Government*. Cambridge, MA: MIT Center for Advanced Engineering Study, 110.
Gardner, H. (1993). *Multiple Intelligences: The Theory in Practice*. Alexandria, VA: BasicBooks.
Heath, C. and Heath, D. (2007). *Made to Stick*. New York: Random House.
Koestner, R., Zuckerman, M., and Koestner, J. (1987). "Praise, Involvement, and Intrinsic Motivation." *Journal of Personality and Social Psychology*, 53: 389.
Kohn, A. (1993). *Punished by Rewards*. New York: Houghton Mifflin.
McGregor, D. (1960). *The Human Side of Enterprise*. New York: McGraw-Hill.
Nelson, B. (1994). *1001 Ways to Reward Employees*. New York: Workman Publishing.
Reifman, S. (2008). *Eight Essentials for Empowered Teaching & Learning, K-8*. Thousand Oaks, CA: Corwin Press.
Reifman, S. (2013). *2-Minute Biographies for Kids*. Author.
Walton, M. (1986). *The Deming Management Method*. New York: Perigee Books.
Whittle, C. (2005). *Crash Course*. New York: Riverbed Books.

7

Expectation

In the previous chapter, I described the evening in which I first presented information on the dangers of extrinsic motivation to a group of educators who were enrolled in my "Eight Keys to Classroom Quality" UCLA Extension course. Once I had completed that section, one gentleman admitted to feeling totally deflated. He shared that he had always used rewards to manage student behavior and couldn't imagine getting through a school day without them. He then compared my delivery of these findings to a destructive military act. A bit later, he made a second military analogy by saying that if he did ever remove rewards from his teaching practice, he would feel as if he was "unilaterally disarming."

It was difficult seeing him react so strongly to my presentation, and I did my best to acknowledge his feelings, empathize with his situation, and encourage him to hang in there as we proceeded to the remainder of that section, which focused on the nurturing forces of intrinsic motivation, as well as the other course topics that would offer strategies and practices that, I believe, constituted a far more effective approach that he would be excited about. The phrase "unilaterally disarming," though, struck a deep chord with me. Those words conveyed a belief that working with kids was a type of battle, our relationship had to be adversarial, and we needed an arsenal to do our jobs successfully.

That occasion also marked the moment in which my whole-child approach received its first significant criticism—that a philosophy without rewards was unrealistic and inherently "soft." (Fortunately for me, I'm not the sensitive type, and I was not at all affected by those words that were delivered at 6:28

p.m. on a chilly Tuesday evening 27 years ago.) That criticism, in my view, carried the implication that teachers who choose not to use extrinsic motivation would automatically preside over classrooms lacking boundaries and structure and that if students misbehaved, they would face no consequences or accountability.

This chapter counters that implication and focuses on how we can build a theory Y environment in which children behave well on a daily basis without the use of rewards. We accomplish this task by providing thorough training, an endeavor that involves setting high behavioral expectations, practicing the routines and procedures we expect everyone to carry out, offering encouragement and support, and holding kids accountable whenever necessary. With these efforts, we set children up to be successful by following the old adage that says the best way to solve a problem is to prevent it from happening in the first place. In an atmosphere of clear, high expectations, encouragement and support, and consistent accountability, students thrive.

The Importance of Thorough Training

Before exploring what a classroom training period might look like, let's examine the topic of training in various areas of our society. Setting aside time for focused training efforts has long been an important part of professional sports, the armed forces, and the corporate world.

In professional football, America's most popular sport, players and coaches from the 32 National Football League (NFL) teams report every summer to Training Camp, where they spend nearly two months preparing and practicing for the season ahead. Although many of the athletes probably wish they could play their first game on the day they arrive in camp, they know a tremendous amount of work needs to be done before they are ready to take the field.

Each team member has important responsibilities to fulfill during Training Camp. The head coach must take a group of diverse individuals, many of whom are strangers to one another, and assemble them into a cohesive, functioning unit. He must establish an environment of teamwork and discipline so that each athlete can perform to his potential. Players must learn how to play their positions well and understand that the team, as a whole, will only be successful when each individual does his part.

Together, players and coaches make many critical decisions. Perhaps each team's most crucial decisions involve determining its goals for the upcoming season. Struggling teams may decide that their seasons will be successful if they win half their games. Stronger teams set their sights higher; they will settle for no less than a trip to the playoffs. Elite teams will consider their seasons a failure unless they reach the Super Bowl. Clear, ambitious goals provide focus for everyone's efforts. They remind players and coaches what they are determined to accomplish.

During Training Camp, players and coaches also establish routines, procedures, and guidelines that enable them to carry out their work in the most efficient and effective ways possible. For example, they determine where they will practice, what time practice will start, and how long practices will last. They reach agreement on where everyone stands in the huddle, what type of terminology they will use when calling the plays, and what kind of attire they will wear during practices, games, and road trips.

These expectations are set, reinforced, and rehearsed until they become second nature to the players. By the time Training Camp ends just prior to Opening Day, players will be prepared to succeed on the field because they will have accounted for nearly every situation that could arise during a game. Next time you watch the NFL on television, notice how well-trained players are in their routines. They know where to go, what to do, when to do it, and how to do it. Professional football players may make these routines look easy to perform, but keep in mind, this ease comes as a direct result of weeks of diligent practice.

In the military, new recruits spend several months learning what it takes to be a soldier. Down to the last detail, they learn how to perform such functions as eating, dressing, grooming, marching, and communicating. They are thoroughly trained in the routines and procedures of their jobs. Expectations pertaining to their performance and conduct are set and clarified. Before these individuals are ever asked to carry out the responsibilities of soldiers, they learn, practice, and internalize these responsibilities.

In the business world, quality-oriented companies pay careful attention to the issue of training. Specially designed programs help new workers learn the expectations of their jobs. According to Dr. W. Edwards Deming, the greatest strength of any organization lies in its people. Their skills, knowledge, and talents comprise a firm's most valuable assets. Before workers can contribute fully, however, they must be trained to do their jobs well. Trying one's best isn't enough. Recall author Mary Walton's quote from *The Deming Management Method* (1986) in Chapter 5: "You have to know what to do, *then* do your best." In the 1989 issue of the *Training and Development Journal*, writer Ted Cocheu adds, "Quality experts . . . all agree that a comprehensive training curricula is critical to providing everyone in the organization with the knowledge and skills to fulfill his or her quality-improvement responsibilities."

Cocheu believes such a training program addresses the following issues:

- Exploring the need for improvement as well as its individual and collective benefits
- Communicating the organization's quality goals
- Developing a common language to talk about quality-related issues
- Defining the structure and processes through which quality improvement will take place
- Clarifying everyone's responsibilities
- Providing people with the tools and techniques to manage the quality of their work

Launching a Classroom "Training Camp"

In this chapter I describe how we, as teachers, can apply the aforementioned ideas about training to the classroom setting. Because we genuinely want our students to be successful, we must initially invest the time to train them in the various responsibilities we expect them to fulfill. In an empowering classroom environment, such a training program includes:

- Introducing and discussing the class aim
- Creating a class mission statement
- Clearly defining a set of Habits of Mind and Habits of Character
- Determining and clarifying goals
- Establishing requirements, rubrics, standards, and scoring systems so students understand how their work will be assessed
- Building a culture of caring, trust, respect, and teamwork
- Establishing the routines, procedures, and expectations that will help you and your students complete tasks in the most efficient and effective ways possible

In general, four to six weeks of thorough training will be needed to address the priorities mentioned earlier. That time frame, of course, is simply a guideline. Yours may vary slightly due to such factors as the grade level you teach and the amount of prior experience your students have had working with one another, with you, or with teachers who share your basic teaching philosophy. Commonly, educators readily acknowledge the important benefits of training yet neglect to follow through with sufficient attention to these matters due to the very real pressure to start teaching standards right away so the kids aren't disadvantaged come testing time. Such a decision is understandable, but it's also shortsighted. The long-term benefits of training far outweigh the short-term costs.

Investing time during the beginning of the year to set our students up for success will save considerable time down the road. As an example, let's take the issue of playground behavior. Specifically, let's focus on how we expect our students to solve problems and settle disputes on the yard. Inevitably, there will be times when a couple of kids return to class from recess incredibly upset. At first glance, you can easily tell that they (1) argued with someone over a game or a piece of equipment, (2) had a fight, (3) got in trouble with the yard teacher, or (4) all of the above (usually progressing from 1 to 2 to 3). Without any training as to how to solve playground disputes, your students won't be equipped to handle them. As a result, problems will occur repeatedly, and you will be forced to spend valuable instructional time dealing with the aftermath all year long.

On the other hand, if you spend the first few weeks of the year discussing this issue with your students and empowering them with strategies to solve their problems constructively, you greatly reduce the likelihood that intense, unpleasant episodes will occur. These efforts begin the first day of school. A short time before recess, I gather the kids together to talk about appropriate playground behavior. I tell them that we all know there may be times on the yard when people bother or try to start trouble with us. I pose the question: "What should you do to handle this situation in a positive way?" Students usually suggest the following answers: ignore them, ask them to stop, walk away, or tell the yard teacher. I then call a student volunteer up to the front of the room to engage in a recess simulation. I pretend to bother that student in a variety of annoying ways. In response, she proceeds through our list of suggested remedies until I am ultimately hauled away by the yard teacher.

These simulation activities are incredibly effective for many reasons. First, they are enjoyable to do and entertaining to watch, so the students pay close attention to the points I'm trying to make. Second, because the playground incident isn't actually happening as we speak, we can analyze and respond to it with some emotional detachment. The heat of the moment isn't clouding our judgment. Finally, our efforts to solve the problem are proactive. Because I timed the simulation to occur before the class ever went out to recess, kids don't feel like they're being put on the spot for something they just got caught doing. Everyone can participate in the simulation with a clean conscience. This exercise exemplifies the principle of striving to solve a problem by preventing it from occurring in the first place.

As effective as they are, these simulations and discussions can't be one-shot deals. The power of a simulation is greatly diminished if it represents the only time students hear from us about important matters. Consistent follow-up efforts are needed if we expect our students to internalize these strategies and use them successfully. Returning to our recess example, I make sure to set aside a few minutes after the first recess ends to see how things went. We talk about how the kids spent their time, whether any problems arose, and if so, how they were solved. I continue to set aside time both before and after recess to discuss playground matters for the first few weeks of the year. We spend this time practicing how to respond to a wide variety of recess situations either that have occurred or that we believe are likely to occur. After repeated discussions, simulations, and practice activities, the kids understand what their options are, when they should be used, and why they're important.

There's no getting around the fact that these training efforts require time. In fact, if you figure that I set aside 10 minutes a day for the first few weeks of school to focus on proper playground behavior, then we're talking about a substantial investment of time, especially considering the amount of content the students are expected to learn. But there are worthy payoffs from this investment. As a result of these training efforts, the students will have safer, more enjoyable recesses. In addition, they become empowered with valuable communication and problem-solving skills that will help them handle a wide variety of situations in a constructive manner. Also, once I conclude that these efforts are no longer necessary, I know I won't have to devote significant time to this issue in the months ahead. So while it may seem that training activities are taking a large chunk out of your day, keep in mind the time you're saving yourself later in the year and the quality you're adding to each day.

Of course, proper playground behavior is not the only area in which we will need to train our students. The kids also need to learn the routines, procedures, and policies that we expect them to follow in the classroom. Such matters include how to sharpen a pencil, where to hang backpacks, and how to sit in a chair. These aspects of classroom management aren't glamorous, but they are important. If they aren't done well, there's the potential for injury, confusion, distraction, disruption, and wasted time.

Before you can train your students in these matters, however, you must take the time to identify them. To generate this list, I close my eyes and pretend the bell has just rung to begin a typical school day. I visualize a complete day's worth of activities from start to finish. As I think about each one, I write down all the things students need to know in order to perform that activity effectively. For example, when the bell rings, the students line up in our designated spot. Immediately, I know that I have to teach my students where and how to stand in line. Next, I envision the kids walking peacefully inside the room and putting away their belongings. I note that I must show my kids how to walk in line, how to enter the room quietly, and how to put away their materials. Then, imagine that the first academic task I ask my kids to do is silent reading. As I picture the students reading quietly, I add to my list that I need to teach them how to sit in a chair, how to hold a book, and how to record the title, author, minutes read, and pages read in their Reading Notebooks for each book they read.

When I finish my virtual tour of the school day, I wind up with a list similar to the one shown in Box 7.1. It includes the routines, procedures, and policies that I use to organize my training efforts at the beginning of each year. (You can find a printable copy on the Routledge website.) Where appropriate, I have also included methods, strategies, and ideas that have proven to be effective.

Box 7.1 List of Training Routines

List of Training Routines

Self-Management

- ★ How to sit in a chair
  Bottoms on chairs, sitting tall with excellent posture.
- ★ How to push in a chair
- ★ How to sit on the rug
  Cross-sitting or hook-sitting, with eyes on speaker.
- ★ How to raise your hand
  Hands up high (so I don't have to guess if they're actually up).
- ★ How to follow the silent signal
  Eyes on teacher, hands empty, hands touching forehead. (I will provide more information about this topic later in the chapter.)
- ★ How to follow the Acceptable Volume Indicator (AVI)
  I will describe the AVI in detail later in the chapter.
- ★ When to ask questions during an instructional lesson
  I ask the kids to hold their questions until the end of the lesson so the flow of instruction isn't interrupted.
- ★ How to use hand signals
  I frequently ask students to use hand signals during a lesson so that I can check their understanding. In response to my statements, kids show thumbs up if they agree with a statement I make about the content, thumbs down if

they disagree, or thumbs to the side if they're not sure. Their responses help me determine whether I should move on with the lesson, spend more time reviewing key points, or follow up with the individual children after the lesson.

Getting Around
- ★ How to enter and leave class quietly
- ★ How to line up and walk in line
- ★ How to transition quickly and quietly from one activity to the next
- ★ How to carry a chair
  I ask my students to use two hands and carry it in front of them for safety purposes.
- ★ When to use the bathroom
  Preferably before and after school and during recess and lunch
- ★ When to use the drinking fountain
  Before and after school and during recess and lunch

Materials
- ★ Where to put backpacks, jackets, and lunches
- ★ Where all class materials are stored
- ★ What to keep in your desk
  Only books, folders, and pencil boxes that I provide all students on the first day of school. In the pencil boxes I provide two pencils, a large eraser, a glue stick, scissors, and a box of crayons. I give kids their own materials to teach responsibility and to avoid disputes.
- ★ How to hold and care for books
  Books should never be left open facedown, because it ruins the spines. Instead, students should use bookmarks. Each child has a bookmark that contains a list of reading strategies so the kids have easy access to these ideas while they are reading.
- ★ When and how to sharpen pencils
  We don't use the electric sharpener during instructional time because the noise is disruptive. Instead, the student leader sharpens a bunch after school or in the morning before class and puts them in a can labeled "Sharpened." Throughout the day, when a pencil no longer works, the kids trade it for a better one by putting it in the "Unsharpened" can and taking one from the "Sharpened" can. The two cans sit side by side on the counter in the back of the room.
- ★ Tissue policy
- ★ How to pass out and collect materials

- ★ How to distribute the lunch cards
- ★ How to put papers into folders
  Tuck papers all the way into the pocket so they don't become wrinkled or stick out of the top
- ★ Where to turn in homework

Classwork

- ★ How to head your paper
  Name and date in the top right-hand corner of the paper, and the title of the activity centered on the top line of the paper
- ★ What to do when you finish work early
- ★ How to use Writing Notebooks
  I glue a sample Writing Notebook page to the inside cover of these resources so, at a glance, students can see how to title each new entry and conclude each day's work.
- ★ How to use class computers

Policies

- ★ What students are allowed to bring to class (toys, gum, candy, water bottles, food?)
  I encourage students to keep water bottles at the foot of their desks in order to remain hydrated throughout the day. The bottles must be filled during their free time.

Relating With Others

- ★ How to get the teacher's attention
  Rather than approach me when they need help, the students raise their hands so I can come to them or call them up to me. This prevents a group of kids from coming up to me at once. (That can be scary.)
- ★ How to work in cooperative groups
- ★ How to greet visitors
- ★ How to act when delivering a message to another class or to the office
- ★ How to answer phone or intercom

Subject- or Activity-Specific Expectations

- ★ How to record the book title, author, and pages and minutes read in their Reading Notebooks
- ★ How to progress through the stages of Writing Workshop
- ★ When it's necessary to skip lines while writing and when it isn't
  As a general rule, I ask the kids to skip lines only when we're going to revise our written work. During these times, the extra space is helpful.

> **General Class Business**
> ★ How to take attendance
> ★ How to do the lunch count
> ★ How to perform the various monitor jobs
> ★ How to perform the responsibilities of a student leader
>
> **Safety**
> ★ How to use the first-aid kit
> ★ How to handle problems on the playground
> Many schools have adopted formal conflict resolution programs to address this need. If yours hasn't, you and your students can generate your own list of effective problem-solving strategies.

No detail is too small. Though some items on the Training Routines list may appear trivial or unworthy of your time and some of the explanations may seem overly explicit, it's important for the kids to understand your expectations unambiguously. Often we assume that our students already know how to do many of the tasks on this list, only to discover later that we had assumed incorrectly. When it comes to routines, don't assume that the children have mastered *anything*. Save yourself the aggravation and start at square one.

Developing your list before the school year begins puts you in a terrific position to provide your kids with thorough training in these expectations. Once the year starts, I make sure that as I introduce each aspect of the curriculum, I also teach students the routines, procedures, and policies that relate to it. Taking the kids step-by-step through each new feature of the classroom leads to greater success, and over time, completion of the routines becomes more and more automatic. For example, early in the school year, I ask my students to copy a paragraph from a health textbook so that I can have a baseline sample of their printing. Before the children begin their copying, though, I explain how they should head their paper and then model the procedure I expect them to follow. I show them where to write their names, the date, and the title of the activity. I indent the first sentence and write from margin to margin. Then, I answer all their questions so they are clear about my expectations. In addition, as the kids are working, I walk around the room to check everyone's paper. Finally, I follow-up on this initial effort for the next few weeks until the procedure becomes second nature to them.

The list of training routines itself can become an effective teaching tool. If you leave sufficient space between each item and provide your students with a copy, the list serves as an advance organizer on which the kids can take notes. During the first few weeks of the year, every time the students learn a new routine, procedure, or expectation, they can add it to the organizer. In addition, you can enlarge the list and create a poster-size advance organizer that you keep in front of the room. With either of these options, you and your students can write detailed definitions of each new routine, jot down key words, or represent ideas with pictures or symbols. However you ask the students to fill out their organizers, the simple act of committing something to paper will help them learn and remember what you expect of them and understand that you take these expectations seriously. When complete, the organizers can function as a type of training manual to which your class can refer when necessary. You may also want to leave it for the substitute on the days you're out of the classroom. Finally, should a new student arrive later in the year, your organizer can help that child make a smoother transition to their new surroundings.

Holding students accountable for their performance with these expectations is perhaps the most important aspect of our training efforts. For example, when the kids are working quietly at their seats, how quiet do they need to be? Does the room have to be completely silent? Can the kids talk softly? Can they talk loudly? To address this issue, I created a chart called the Acceptable Volume Indicator, AVI for short. The AVI includes three levels of noise: conversational tone, whisper, and complete silence. During the first week of school, I introduce the AVI to the kids, explain its purpose, model each level, and describe the types of activities for which each level will be used. Then, as the kids begin their work, we practice all three levels. Once we have practiced the levels sufficiently, the students need to know that I mean what I say. The first time students exceed the acceptable noise level, I call their attention to it. If it continues to happen, we take a few moments to discuss the issue as a class. I continue to model what I expect, hold more simulation activities, give them more opportunities to practice, and explain why it's important to adjust to each level. When students understand the purpose of a procedure or routine and see the value in it, they will commit themselves to performing it better.

Don't accept unacceptable performance. Once you do, you're sending a message, loudly and clearly, that such conduct will be tolerated. There's no room for indecisiveness or vacillating. Decide how good is good enough and stick with your decisions. Be consistent and firm. As author Philip Crosby puts it in his book *Quality Without Tears* (1984):

> The determined . . . [teacher] has no recourse except to make the same point over and over until everyone believes. The first time a deviation

is agreed upon, everyone will know about it before the ink is dry. "Oh," people will say, "there are some things that don't have to be right."

If, for example, a student hands you a paper without their name on it, hand it back. If your kids return to the room from lunch making too much noise, have them go back outside and line up again. Such actions are not punishments; they are effective responses to let your students know that you mean what you say. Over time, the students will rise to your expectations. By holding them accountable early in the year, you will make the rest of the year much smoother.

An effective way to help students improve their ability to perform these routines is to use what legendary educator Madeline Hunter, in her book *Discipline That Develops Self-Discipline* (1990), calls "think-starters." I learned of this technique during my UCLA training program when Hunter was one of my professors. Imagine Randy has just handed me a paper with no name on it. If I told him, "Put your name on it," that would be a "think-stopper" because I'm the one pointing out his mistake. On the other hand, imagine that I asked, "What do you need to do before handing me this paper?" In this case I'm helping Randy discover his own mistake. That would be a think-starter. Asking him instead of telling him shifts the responsibility to Randy. Think-starters give students ownership of their behavior. By encouraging kids to reflect on their actions, think-starters help them internalize these habits and build their capacity for the future. While Randy may have forgotten to put his name on the paper this time, think-starters increase the chances that he will remember to do it next time.

I recommend taking the following steps every time you introduce a new routine or procedure to your students:

1. Introduce the new routine.
2. Describe the importance of performing the routine correctly so students understand its purpose and, perhaps, how it positively affects culture.
3. Explain how to perform the routine in a step-by-step manner.
4. Model the steps of the routine.
5. Hold simulation activities whenever possible.
6. Provide multiple opportunities for your students to practice the routine until it becomes second nature to them.
7. Hold students accountable for proper performance of the routine.
8. Use think-starters to help students internalize these habits and behaviors.

Four to six weeks into the year, you and your students will be ready to conclude your training period. To culminate and reinforce these efforts, ask your students to prepare brief skits about the items on your Training Routines list. These presentations fit neatly with the classroom aim because they entertain the kids while also bringing their understanding to a new level. If you have the ability to do so, consider taking videos of the skits. You can then use these performances, or at least some of them, as instructional videos for the following year's students.

The most common mistake teachers make with regard to training is ending the training period prematurely. Sometimes we start a school year fully committed to training our students thoroughly, and the first two weeks go extremely smoothly. The kids respond well to our efforts, and they don't appear to need additional practice. After three weeks, the routines become more automatic, and we are tempted to bring our training period to a halt. After all, there's a great deal of content for the kids to learn, and the thought of using the time we had earmarked for additional training to get to that content a bit faster is an attractive one. As attractive as this thought may be, however, resist this temptation. The extra time you take to build a foundation for quality learning will pay off. Effective training cannot be rushed.

Another common mistake involves the approach many educators take when establishing expectations with students. Sometimes, especially as new teachers, we want to start things off on a relaxed note with the goal of "easing" children into the higher expectations we will ultimately hold for them. The rationale for this way of thinking makes sense. We're new teachers, we want to make our students happy, and we don't want to ask too much of them too soon. Though understandable, that method is doomed to failure. Once children are accustomed to behaving in a certain way, it's extremely difficult to change those behaviors. The most effective approach is to begin the year, as Crosby suggests, setting and reinforcing high expectations. That isn't always fun, and it can be a grind, but it's a necessary step for creating the type of environment in which children function at their best. Perhaps, several months into the school year, if the children are consistently performing and behaving at a high level, we can consider proceeding a bit more loosely. But the other way doesn't ever seem to work.

There's an old teaching adage that says, "Don't smile until November." We don't need to go to that extreme when establishing high expectations, but we do need to remain resolute in our commitment to creating a high-performing culture. By the way, in a recent poll (conducted by me), that adage ranked right up there with "Sticks and stones may break my bones, but names will never hurt me" as the most inaccurate mantra in history.

Commit yourself to making the training of your students a high priority during the beginning of each school year. By February or March, you will be glad you did. An initial investment of time will not only save you considerable time down the road but also result in a more productive, more focused classroom environment. As any quality expert will tell you, individuals and teams simply cannot perform their jobs well without proper training.

Additional Points About Training

- Among the routines and procedures we ask our students to perform, we want to pay special attention to those related to partner and group work. You will recall William Glasser's assertion that cooperative learning should be the default mode in our classrooms due to the fact that it satisfies our need for friendship and belonging, usually leads to greater success, and tends to be more enjoyable for children. As valuable as cooperative learning may be, however, it can also be complicated. Partners may disagree, argue, attempt to make decisions unilaterally, or withdraw. Children must develop a variety of communication and problem-solving skills to carry out this type of learning smoothly and successfully. This endeavor takes time, practice, empathy, and patience. Consequently, our students will benefit from multiple demonstrations, simulations, and post-lesson discussions. In addition, we want to provide opportunities early in the year for students to reflect on and self-evaluate their performance, as well as celebrate the great work of their partners with Statements of Recognition. Another great technique is the "fishbowl," in which a volunteer pair goes about its business as the other kids watch. We conclude the fishbowl with a conversation in which everyone offers compliments to the featured students and, perhaps, suggestions for improvement.
- Following the class signal is another routine that typically requires extra attention and practice. As educators, we have many choices as to how we call for children's attention when they are in the middle of a task. No matter which option we select, however, many children tend to experience difficulty with this expectation. I have seen many children in many classrooms continue with their work when their teacher signals for their attention, and in a way, that's admirable. The kids are often immersed in the task at hand and don't want to stop. Having said that, though, when we need everyone's attention, we need a reliable method of gaining that attention quickly.

Here are a few suggestions to help students improve their ability to follow the signal and help you remove the stress from what can often be a frustrating endeavor. First, follow your signal with a gentle countdown that gives the kids time to remove their attention from their classwork and transfer it to you. I gain everyone's attention by clapping three times. When my students hear that, they put down their materials and respond with three claps of their own. They then turn towards me, make eye contact, and place their hands on their forehead. Asking the kids to place their hands on their forehead ensures that they won't return to their work as I am speaking. After I clap, I use a soft voice to say, "And empty hands on forehead, with eyes on me, in 5, 4, 3, 2, 1." That calming tone, combined with the additional time, greatly eases this transition.

Second, don't begin giving instructions until the room is quiet and all eyes are on you. We don't want the kids thinking it is acceptable to keep working or talking with their partners and ignore our words. Even if they protest and say they are still listening, we explain that we need the eye contact as well as the listening. Eye contact improves listening and shows respect. Sometimes, I will start talking and then immediately stop. Silence is powerful, even if it's only for a couple of seconds. A brief pause generally heightens everyone's listening. Third, if you will be asking the children to follow a multi-step direction (three steps, max), preface those directions with the words, "When I say 'Go.'" That way, the kids know to wait until you finish speaking and say "Go" before executing your instructions. Oftentimes, several children will bolt into action while we're still talking, and we want everyone to begin following the directions only after we have finished.

Finally, avoid "over-signaling." Calling for student attention too frequently prevents the kids from finding a rhythm and can lead to a choppy work session. Responding to the signal every ten minutes or so can be difficult enough for children. It's significantly harder for the kids when we call for their attention every minute or two. Before administering your signal, decide if the information you wish to share needs to be done right at that moment or whether it can wait.

◆ In the previous chapter, I described how teachers and students will only be able to achieve quality when they co-create a learning environment consistent with theory Y assumptions. Specifically, I pointed out how the type of coercive and controlling environment necessitated by a belief in theory X can damage many of the whole-child priorities we hold dear, such as enthusiasm for learning, trusting relationships, self-direction and responsibility, group problem-solving, and continuous improvement. Another entity that theory X practices can negatively impact is training. I have emphasized the importance of investing 4–6 weeks in this priority because it builds student capacity, helps everyone become more independent and interdependent, and enables us to create a productive work environment. In a theory X environment, we wouldn't need to spend one minute on training. After all, we could always offer a reward to elicit desired behavior whenever the need arises. Without training, a tremendous amount of personal and collective growth and development would be lost.

- As important as it is to be consistent with class procedures, it's perfectly fine to shake things up periodically and put a fresh face on those routines that have become a bit stale. Most commonly, this happens during the last few months of a school year. If students stop performing a given procedure with the same gusto they showed in our initial weeks, that's not necessarily a sign that the kids have done anything wrong. It may simply mean that it's time for a change. For example, I like to begin the school year with the "PACE" acronym to help everyone become better listeners. The acronym breaks down the task of listening into the following parts: posture, attention, careful listening, eye contact. Identifying the core aspects of attentive listening provides specific criteria for the students and enables me to provide clear feedback when I want to recognize positive behavior or need to hold kids accountable. When I say "PACE" at the beginning of an instructional lesson, the kids know exactly what to do.

  A few years ago, when we spent much of the school year on Zoom, I noticed the quality of listening start to wane as spring approached. (Perhaps, like me, the kids were merely distracted by the excitement of the upcoming baseball season.) I decided to replace "PACE" with "SEE," which stood for shoulders squared to the screen, eyes straight ahead, and ear contact—a new term I invented to add a little novelty and humor to our days. (It was a challenging year. Sometimes we need to amuse ourselves in this line of work.) As your school year progresses, be on the lookout for any routines that might benefit from a little variety.

- On the list of Training Routines shown in Figure 7.1, I mentioned that on the first day of school I provide each child with a pencil box that includes two pencils, a large eraser, a glue stick, scissors, and a box of crayons. Giving kids their own materials teaches responsibility and helps avoid disputes. It produces another benefit as well. This practice also ensures a level playing field with regard to supplies. When students bring in their own materials, a subtle competition can develop to see who has the coolest, most elaborate, or best supplies. That can lead to issues of status, distraction, and even hurt feelings. Of course, obtaining a class set of each item requires money. If you are fortunate to work in a school in which you receive an annual budget, I recommend this approach. If not, then asking the kids to bring in their own supplies may be the way to go, perhaps with specific brand suggestions to ensure equity. I consider it a shame that educators often have to spend their own money on classroom supplies, and I would never ask any teacher to do this.

- Educator Angela Watson, author of such books as *Fewer Things, Better*; *Unshakeable*; *Awakened*; and *The Cornerstone*, once shared an idea during an online presentation that I found so profound I began using it on the first day of school every year. Her idea offers a way to set high expectations and couple opportunity with accountability to help children reach them. Specifically, she tells her students that their actions and choices influence her actions and choices. I imagine that many educators may operate their classrooms with this idea in mind, but prior to Watson's session, I had never known anyone to announce this message to students explicitly. At the conclusion of her presentation, I opened the file containing our "Norms for Discussion" and added a new slide with a quote that reads: "Your actions and choices influence my actions and choices."

    When I introduce this concept to students on the first day, I offer the following scenario: Imagine you and your best friend want to be desk partners. When you express this desire to me, I become concerned that the two of you may experience difficulty maintaining focus on your work without becoming chatty, silly, or distracted. If I were to make every important classroom decision by myself, I would probably say no. With this idea (*I say pointing to the slide*), I will first give you two a chance to show you can handle the responsibility of being desk partners. That way, you have a say in the matter and can invest your energies to achieve your desired outcome. Perhaps, this opportunity will fail spectacularly. Or maybe it will bring the best out of you both. Maybe your focus, your productivity, and your work will be better than ever. The only way I can know for sure is to provide you with the opportunity to give it a shot. If you can make it work, then you can be desk partners. If not, one or both of you will move to a different seat. It's up to you two. And (*I *continue*) this practice doesn't apply only to seating locations. If you want us to do more cooperative learning activities, try new ideas, or change something else about our class, I will give you the chance to make it work. Your actions and choices will help me make my decision. In this classroom I will not be the only one making important decisions. All of you will have a major role to play, and together, we can create the class we want—with effort, motivation, and accountability.

- In *The Quality School* (1990), William Glasser recommends a classroom environment that can be described as one of "unanxious expectation." That means we consistently expect a lot from our students, but we don't reach the point in which our supervision puts undue pressure on the kids or produces significant stress. During my interactions with children, I think about Glasser's guidance quite a bit and use it as a self-check to help me determine if a specific expectation I hold is reasonable. If it is, I maintain that expectation. If not, I modify it. For example, after the morning bell, I might ask myself, "Is it reasonable that I expect everyone to enter the room quietly and put away their belongings within a short time without reminder?" Yes. "Is it reasonable that I expect everyone to arrive ready to learn with their best focus?" Yes. "Is it reasonable that I expect everyone to work silently and independently at their desks for an hour?" No. In addition, if I discover that numerous reminders and heavy accountability are required to keep students on track during an activity, it's probably a sign that I am expecting too much and/or creating significant stress for the group.

  One question that frequently arises when discussing accountability in a theory Y environment concerns whether rewards and punishments should ever occupy a place in our management repertoire. My view—and I know my philosophy is unusually strict on this issue—is that students should never see, experience, or be offered an extrinsic reward for meeting a class expectation. Punishments, or consequences, on the other hand, are a bit trickier. I believe teachers and administrators should incorporate punishments only as a last resort. Hopefully, all our efforts to build a need-satisfying culture, promote caring and kindness, develop trusting relationships with children and parents, and engage in problem-solving when problems occur will produce a learning environment in which serious offenses are rare. Will they still happen? Of course. And when they do, the last thing we would ever want is for a child to commit a serious offense and face no accountability.

Setting High Personal Expectations

So far, this chapter has focused primarily on setting high *behavioral* expectations and helping children reach them. We accomplish this task with a 4- to 6-week culture-building and training period that enables kids to learn class routines and procedures and develop the mindsets and attitudes that bring out our best and increase the likelihood of academic success. In this section I expand that focus to the setting of high *personal* expectations—for academics and other aspects of whole-child learning, for our lives in school and our lives outside of school.

One of the most valuable lessons I have learned as both a teacher and an athlete is that the most powerful first step any of us can take to boost performance in a given area is to set higher expectations. That will be the rising tide that lifts all boats and the catalyst that leads to meaningful change. I introduce the concept of high personal expectations by sharing that, in my view, we are very fortunate in life if we have parents and teachers who set high expectations for us. That is a gift. The real magic, however, doesn't begin until we make these expectations our own—when they become *personal* expectations. Once that happens, buckle up. That's when we begin to take off. As teachers, we encourage this commitment with the "Making the Choice" visual, the "Reach for the Stars" component of the Drive for 5, and our morning meetings that feature the Quote of the Day, class mission statement discussions, and Tower Talks.

We continue promoting the benefits of setting high personal expectations by sharing stories from our own lives or the lives of others. For example, starting in seventh grade, science was the subject area in which my grades were the lowest. That remained true for the first few months of eighth grade, when I would consistently earn lower scores on my Introduction to Physical Science tests. After seeing roughly the same score on all my tests, it was easy to think that was how it was always going to be. But one day the stars aligned. I completed a test that Dr. Cook took a few days to grade. He eventually handed me a paper that said 94% at the top. Of course, I checked to see if it also said Steve Reifman at the top. (It did!) That 94% represented a breakthrough and changed everything for me in science. Seeing that score was a powerful "shaping" moment that launched a chain reaction. Once I earned my first A, I realized I was capable of earning that score again and again. I believed I could earn As consistently. With that higher expectation, I studied harder and approached my work with greater motivation and confidence. The higher scores soon became more common. In the previous chapter, when describing the ten nurturing forces of intrinsic motivation, I mentioned success. Specifically, I emphasized the importance of helping children, especially those who tend to experience difficulty academically, achieve initial success. My eighth-grade science story is an example of this phenomenon. Finding success early in the school year boosts enthusiasm, motivation, confidence, and commitment. It also leads to higher personal expectations—a gift that keeps on giving. In addition, you will notice more subtle indicators of children's progress. You will observe growth in how students carry themselves in class, the volume of their voices when they participate in group discussions, how they handle adversity, and how they pay attention to detail.

I have long believed that human beings will perform at whatever expectation level they set for themselves. In school, if we earn Cs and we're okay with that, we will work hard enough to get a C and no harder. Our expectations are that powerful and lay the groundwork for the effort and commitment that follow. All in all, I view this human tendency as good news. It reminds us that when we set higher expectations, we can achieve more and perform better. Resolving to improve leads to improvement. Earning low scores doesn't have to be permanent. Things can change, and they can change quickly once we decide we want better for ourselves. This is a message our students need to hear frequently and, hopefully, experience for themselves.

Setting high personal expectations is a skill. Once we raise student awareness of this topic, some really fun conversations ensue. Each fall I share with the group that this year we will talk a lot about the importance of developing great reading skills, math skills, and writing skills, just to name a few. But how good are you at thinking big? At expecting epic things from yourself? How well do you dream, aim high, and reach for the stars? After children get a taste for this endeavor, they delight in dazzling classmates with their lofty hopes. That brings me to Jesse, a Hall of Fame setter of high personal expectations. When introducing the Habits of Character, along with its rubric, to Jesse's third- and fourth-grade class in 1996, I asked everyone to begin thinking of a goal they would like to reach in the coming weeks. During follow-up discussions, many children would say they wanted, for example, to be a 3 in *responsibility*, a 4 in *kindness*, a 3 in *respect*, or a 4 in *service*. One day Jesse shocked the world by announcing that his goal was to be a 4 in everything. Bless his heart. Immediately, eyebrows rose all throughout the room. If Twitter were around back then, kids would have posted about Jesse's boldness as soon as they got home. To his credit, Jesse matched his words with world-class motivation and actions. The effect on our classroom culture was powerful and lasting.

Introducing high personal standards also affords us the opportunity to follow up with individual children when we notice them setting less lofty expectations or settling for less than their best. One of my tutoring students, for example, was preparing for an upcoming quiz and shared that he would be happy if he scored 8 out of 10. My response: "Why? Why not 10 out of 10? Why settle for less than your best?" Interactions such as these provide incredible learnable moments. Through our words and actions we can convey to children just how capable we think all of them are and how they can reach the highest levels of learning by believing in themselves, aiming higher, and following up on those higher hopes with consistent effort, motivation, and determination. Sometimes we have deep-seated beliefs regarding our own potential in a given area, and these beliefs can lead us to build mental barriers that keep us from achieving our actual potential. Discussing the setting of high personal standards and following up on these conversations as needed can help kids overcome these barriers and unleash newfound energy and initiative that can bring tremendous satisfaction and joy, especially during those moments when they realize they accomplished something that, a few months earlier, they didn't think they could.

On a lighter note, we can also follow up with children about their personal expectations using a bit of humor and novelty to get our point across. Humor is especially effective later in the school year, when our culture is well established and students have already developed positive habits and mindsets. My favorite approach involves calling a child up to my chair to see how they're doing on a piece of work. Imagine, for example, that the kids are drafting realistic fiction stories in Writing Workshop. "So," I'll begin, "how are you doing with your story?" Assume they respond with, "It's pretty good." That's my cue. "Oh, really," I say, "that's what we're going for these days? Just pretty good?" Kids usually laugh, a couple might roll their eyes, but they get the message. One last note: If you decide to sink to this level and incorporate juvenile humor, be sure the child is someone who can take a joke. I've learned the hard way that not all kids appreciate humor directed their way and might not react favorably to it.

Look to reinforce the significance of high personal expectations as often as you can. One terrific way to follow up is to conclude instructional lessons with positive messages that students hear as they prepare to begin their work. Phrases such as "Aim high," "Reach for the stars," and "Be extraordinary" take just seconds to say yet, over time, can make a meaningful difference in how children approach their schoolwork and how they perceive their own abilities. In addition, post a sign on a classroom wall that asks the question: "How high are your personal standards?" Refer to it frequently as you attempt to create a classroom culture where children strive to be the best they can be, aim high, and never settle for less than their highest-quality work.

The ultimate payoff to this emphasis on setting high personal expectations occurs when children bring up this topic without adult prompting and combine their words with consistent motivation and action. That's when we know our efforts are paying off and our messages are sinking in. For example, another of my tutoring students was a member of my fourth-grade class the year before we began our one-on-one sessions. On our very first evening, I asked whether she had already started thinking of goals for the new school year. Her first goal, she relayed, was to reach for the stars. She repeated that goal every time we met during the first couple months of the year. Those moments are some of the most gratifying for us, as educators, because they remind us of the value we are adding to children's lives.

Individual Case Studies

Sarah

In Chapter 3, I emphasized the importance of speaking one-on-one with students on a regular basis. One excellent reason to initiate a private meeting is to encourage a child to set higher personal expectations. My favorite example of this type of conversation occurred with Sarah, a third grader who was performing at grade level in math yet would include comments in her explanations such as "I don't know very much about math." When the two of us met, I showed her our most recent math assessment. The directions asked everyone to write a narrative explaining what they knew about division, and her paper was strong. As we began analyzing her assessment, I underlined a few excellent pieces of information she included. (I always recommend launching a meeting with positive comments. It relieves any anxiety a child might be feeling and creates a more relaxed atmosphere.) Then, I read aloud the three sentences, scattered throughout her paragraph, in which she either doubted or minimized her knowledge or ability. I proceeded to (dramatically) cross those sentences out. I made the point that she definitely does know quite a bit about math and had every reason to believe in herself. Sarah smiled. Using specific examples from student work samples to make larger points is a terrific strategy. Providing specific recognition and feedback can do wonders to build children's confidence because the proof is as clear as day. After this conversation, Sarah began to display greater self-belief and expect more from herself. Some students don't need much of this "building up," while others may need quite a bit. Many children don't expect much from themselves because they believe they lack the intelligence or skills to succeed, and it's important for us to serve as cheerleaders whenever possible to forcefully counter that notion.

Riley

As important as it is to recognize students' work and academic skills, it's more impactful to recognize work habits, effort, and attitude. Ideally, we will be capturing only positive examples so that students can have a "feel good" moment that reinforces these entities. Real life, however, doesn't always work this way, and we can't be hesitant to step in and call attention to times when effort and attitude are suboptimal. It's not that we are scolding kids or trying to make them feel bad. Many times, though, we need to be firm, especially with middle- and upper-grade children who, over the years, have developed work habits and traits that are not serving them well and that are resistant to change. These matters tend not to improve on their own. Even when our words and tone may be firm, our messages are always coming from a good place and always born from our view that students who are currently performing poorly are capable of so much more and have greatness inside of them—if they are willing to work a little harder, put more time and effort into their schoolwork, and expect more from themselves. From these difficult conversations can spring tremendous growth.

One example of this type of conversation occurred the day after I was subbed out for a special school activity. I was present at school that day, but I was only in the classroom with my kids for the first hour of the morning. I then popped into the room a few times throughout the day as my schedule allowed.

In the plan I left for the substitute, I gave the kids approximately an hour in the afternoon to work on a writing project that was due the following morning. At the end of the day, I learned from our substitute that one student accomplished very little during that time and gave an excuse as to why. He then found me after school to ask if he could take the project home to have it typed. In my mind, he was seeking to have someone do his work for him and enable him to meet the deadline without having to put forth effort on his own.

I spoke with that student right then and there, and we spoke again the next day. This child was talented and kind, yet he was working below grade level in all subject areas. Even though the focus of the activity was writing, our conversation was not about writing. It was about honesty, work ethic, and expecting more from ourselves. I explained that he had a choice to make about how he went about completing this project. He could have used the ample class time provided to dig into his work, produce as much as he could, and finish his project independently. Or he could waste his time, make excuses, and look for a way out. Unfortunately, he chose the latter.

I explained that if he was ever going to reach his considerable potential, he needed to make better choices. He needed to embrace challenges, not avoid them. He needed to look to do the most, not the least. He had made choices like this one before, and if he was ever going to break this habit, it was going to be because the adults in his life held him accountable, inspired him to expect more from himself, and encouraged him not to settle for less than his best. He needed to know that the adults in his life believed in him, were encouraging him, and knew he could do better. Our unconditional support and high standards gave him the best chance of developing his own higher personal standards. He may not alter his expectations tomorrow or next week, but if he heard this message enough times, ultimately it would sink in.

It takes time for major attitudinal changes to occur, and though it requires tremendous patience and perseverance on our part, this is arguably the greatest service we, as teachers, can provide to our students. We demonstrate our commitment by following up with a child for as long as it takes, even into the next school year, when they are in somebody else's class. As I mentioned, these issues tend not to get better on their own. Strong action needs to be taken. This action needs to combine positivity and encouragement with a firm resolve to maintain a high expectation level. For many students, we may be the only people in their lives who communicate this openly and honestly and who provide this type of consistent support.

Jessica

In the type of cooperative classroom environment we try to create, we never want children to feel as if they are in competition with one another. Rather than focus on whether they are doing better than or "ahead" of anyone else, students should value "personal bests." I do think, though, that kids can learn from one another's example. If one student raises the bar—with regard to the quality of their work, effort, or behavior—that can encourage everyone else to perform at a higher level too.

One time I wanted to recognize the efforts of a particular student while also hoping that her success story would inspire others. Her overall improvement was phenomenal, and she was basically a living embodiment of the "Making the Choice" diagram mentioned previously. This girl was usually extremely quiet in class, and it felt good to shine the spotlight on a student who sought no attention for herself. It is easy sometimes for quieter kids to go unnoticed, and I make a consistent effort not to let this happen.

Privately, I asked in advance if she would give me permission to share her progress with the class (including the struggles), and she willingly agreed. Her face lit up a few minutes later when I introduced her story to the class. I told everyone that we had been talking a great deal about setting high personal expectations during the year and that I wanted to feature one of our students who had done exactly that.

I explained that in the beginning of the year, Jessica experienced difficulty taking responsibility for her homework and even missed a few important writing deadlines. She and I had a meeting with her parents about this situation, and then things changed. She began taking school more seriously and working harder. The quality of her work improved, and she began to receive positive feedback from her parents and me. She started to feel proud of herself, and her confidence increased. The cycle then continued. Her initial success, combined with the positive feelings the success produced, led her to work harder, which made the work better. The feedback became more positive, and the feelings of pride and confidence grew.

All this happened because she decided she wanted more for herself. She wanted to do better. Her success didn't happen because of her parents or because of me. Nothing occurred due to luck, magic, or an accident. It happened because she made a choice and followed up that choice with consistent action. Perhaps other students who had not yet made that same commitment would become inspired by her triumphs and decide they are ready and willing to make this type of effort.

A Final Thought: Understanding Student Vulnerability

Several years ago at one of my school's monthly professional development sessions, the presenter gave each staff member a few minutes to solve a challenging math word problem involving fractions. One teacher, who normally pays obsessive attention to detail, misread the question and then, during the share-out, unwittingly revealed the result of this error with the group. Of course, that teacher was me, and I was a bit embarrassed at what I had done.

We open all our professional development sessions with these types of questions, and they are great because they remind us what it is like to be a student. Because, as teachers, we are typically the ones posing the questions, rather than the ones attempting to answer them, it is easy to forget how it feels to make a mistake in front of your peers and feel vulnerable. Children feel this way all the time, and though I try to be sensitive to this fact, my experience at that meeting brought my understanding of student vulnerability to a new level.

Since then, I have noticed some subtle changes in how I communicate with my kids during academic lessons. When introducing challenging material, for example, I find myself prefacing my instruction with sentences such as, "I know this part may be a bit tricky" and "Be careful when you're doing this step because I sometimes have trouble, and I need to remind myself to slow down and be extra careful."

Communicating in this manner helps students relax, gain comfort with the idea of making mistakes, and realize that both adults and children struggle sometimes. As a result, I believe I am creating a more understanding learning environment. There are many well-known quotes about mistakes and the importance of seeing them not as negative outcomes to avoid but as valuable learning opportunities to embrace. As teachers, we all know this, but I have learned that this positive view of mistakes becomes even more relevant when we have just made one publicly ourselves.

I share these thoughts about student vulnerability in this section because, after spending much of the chapter focusing on setting high behavioral expectations, remaining firm, and holding kids accountable, I wanted to balance out this "tough talk" with sensitivity and empathy. I began this chapter by relaying my UCLA Extension student's criticism of my whole-child approach as soft. At first, I admit, that characterization upset me. Over the years, though, I have come to realize that his words were accurate, and I now view them as a compliment. At its core, this is a soft approach, one that shows an appreciation for the feelings and emotions of all team members and for what's it like to be in a situation in which we make a mistake in front of others or don't understand something right away while those around us seem to grasp it immediately. As important as it is to hold students accountable and be firm, we want to couple that emphasis with the ability to see matters through our students' eyes, appreciate their perspective, and understand the "user experience" of being a child in our classroom. If your school doesn't provide opportunities for you to occupy the role of student, I recommend that, as your schedule allows, you take a yoga class, enroll in an after-school course, or seek out some other type of experience that reminds you what it's like to be a learner.

Reference List

Cocheu, T. (1989). *Training and Development Journal.* January issue.
Crosby, P. (1984). *Quality without Tears.* New York: McGraw-Hill.
Glasser, W. (1990). *The Quality School.* New York: Harper & Row.
Hunter, M. (1990). *Discipline That Develops Self-Discipline.* El Segundo, CA: TIP Publications.
Reifman, S. (2008). *Eight Essentials for Empowered Teaching & Learning, K-8.* Thousand Oaks, CA: Corwin Press.
Walton, M. (1986). *The Deming Management Method.* New York: Perigee Books.

8
Empowerment

No matter how busy we may become as educators, it is critical for us to take sufficient time on a regular basis for self-care. In order for us to expend the necessary energy and effort to help our students thrive, we need to preserve and strengthen our own physical and mental health. By ensuring that we address our own needs, we put ourselves in a position to best serve our students and help meet their needs. One of the primary ways I manage stress and take the time for self-care is by working out at the gym a few days per week.

Occasionally, when I am in the middle of a strength training workout, someone will ask for a "spot" when performing the bench press exercise in which people lie on a flat bench and attempt to push a barbell from their chests into the air for a certain number of repetitions.

If, for example, my friend is trying to bench-press 20 lb ten times, the weight is so light that he can easily complete the set on his own. When the amount of weight increases, however, he needs me to spot for him so that the barbell doesn't remain on his chest when he reaches the point of muscle failure.

Assume that when trying to bench press 185 pounds, my friend's goal is to complete eight repetitions. He finishes the first six reps on his own yet struggles halfway through his seventh. I am standing behind him the entire time, with my hands underneath the bar, ready to assist. In this situation I have a choice to make, and I basically have three options. First, I can do nothing. If I choose this approach, the barbell will eventually come down on his chest, an injury is likely to occur, and our friendship will likely end.

On the other hand, I can take over and finish the rep for him. If I simply grab the bar at the first sign of struggle and return it to the weight rack on my own, I ensure his safety, but I have done nothing to help him improve his strength. As a result, the next time he bench presses, there is no reason to expect that he will be able to lift any more weight than he did this time.

The best approach in this situation is for me to put my hands under the barbell and do as little work as possible to help him keep the bar moving. If he's able to do most of the work himself, my effort will be very gentle. If his struggle increases, I will assume more of the workload. I will continue to adjust the amount of assistance I provide based on the amount of work he is able to do for himself.

If he needs only a small amount of assistance on the seventh rep, he may choose to try for an eighth. On that rep I will probably have to increase the amount of support I provide. The strength gains this set produces occur mostly in these final two reps, not the first six he could do independently. My performance as a spotter helps him move beyond what he could do independently to that next level of strength. When he bench presses again the following week, he will probably be able to do more of the work on his own because of the assistance I provided this time around.

These moments of productive struggle are crucial growth opportunities. By offering just enough guidance to keep the bar moving, I am helping my friend move beyond his current capacity to a larger future capacity.

That is the essence of empowerment.

The same principle I describe for spotting a bench presser in the gym also holds true in the classroom and should govern our interactions with students. Establishing empowerment as an important "class culture" priority needs to occur at the beginning of a new school year. Dictionary definitions of *empower* tend to include words such as *give*, *enable*, or *permit*. I prefer a more "kid-friendly" and more inspiring term that I share with students and explicitly state as one of our classroom goals. To be *empowered* means that we are *becoming more powerful learners*.

Once students embrace the concept of empowerment, they become more active learners and begin to display the initiative, independence, and motivation that will help them soar, both now and as they get older. Ideally, all our students would enter our classrooms on day 1 already demonstrating these traits, and typically, a portion of our class will. These kids will emerge as leaders by setting a tremendous daily example and exerting a significant positive influence on their peers. In all likelihood, though, there will also be children who tend to be passive learners, display little to no motivation or enthusiasm for academic pursuits, and put forth minimal effort. These students will likely present our greatest challenge. Rather than view this situation negatively, I prefer to adopt a different perspective and consider it our greatest opportunity to make a difference and gain fulfillment. All children possess these empowerment "muscles." By introducing the concept of empowerment, including it in our class mission statement, emphasizing its importance to parents at Back-to-School Night, and remaining focused on it throughout the school year, we help everyone develop these muscles and maximize their amazing potential. When that happens, I tell the group, we will possess more knowledge, do things for ourselves that we used to need help with, make better decisions, take charge of our learning to a greater degree, and operate with more confidence. We will be unstoppable.

In the next section, I share a set of strategies we can employ to build an empowering learning environment.

10 Teacher Moves to Create an Empowering Learning Environment

Don't Do Things for Children That They Can Do for Themselves

Every day I walk with a group of students down the hall to the cafeteria. When we arrive, the first two kids in line retrieve our lunch cards and pass them out to everybody else. I could easily distribute the cards myself, but I believe it is important for the children to take on as much responsibility as they can handle throughout the school day, even for seemingly small tasks. By empowering them in this manner, we provide natural opportunities for children to take initiative, develop manners and other communication skills, solve problems independently, and demonstrate responsibility and leadership. In the classroom, similar tasks would include sharpening pencils, distributing and collecting papers, and maintaining a neat, organized desk. Once you identify these tasks, be sure to add them to your Training Routines list.

This idea of not doing things for children that they can do for themselves also applies, of course, to situations in which we provide academic support to students working independently or in groups. These occasions, more than any other type of classroom interaction, most closely resemble the bench-pressing scenario described earlier. Assume a pair of students experiences significant difficulty with a science investigation. If we provide too much assistance, students may complete their work successfully, but in the process, we may deny them opportunities to think for themselves and develop as independent thinkers and problem solvers. On the other hand, we certainly don't want to abandon them when the pair genuinely requires assistance. Instead, we offer as little help as necessary "to keep the bar moving."

Stepping back and taking a yearlong perspective, I realize teaching for empowerment means asking children to demonstrate more independence and take greater and greater responsibility for their learning as the school year progresses while relying on adult assistance less and less. It's the classroom application of the well-known fishing analogy: Give a person a fish, they eat for a day. Teach that person to fish, they eat for a lifetime. Educator Madeline Hunter, during one of my graduate school courses in 1993, once emphasized this same point by saying that, in many ways, a teacher should be like a doctor. A doctor's job, she asserted, is complete once the patient no longer needs them. Of course, we will always be there to guide children's learning, but once students have embraced the concept of empowerment, they will no longer need us to remind them to put forth effort, exercise initiative, demonstrate independence and responsibility, and accomplish other tasks that they can and should complete on their own. The "swing set" metaphor also comes in handy, especially when attempting to help kids understand the meaning of empowerment. As very young children, we aren't yet able to generate enough power on our own to soar into the sky. So we ask (sometimes beg) adults to give us a push. When we grow older and stronger, that assistance is no longer necessary. We possess all the power we will ever need to reach great heights.

Another reason we don't want to do too much for students relates to our emphasis on helping children develop Habits of Mind and Habits of Character. Those moments when children experience academic difficulty are golden opportunities to develop critical habits, such as patience, perseverance, thoughtfulness, and cooperation, to name just a few. If we offer too much assistance, we may be unwittingly blocking those opportunities. In the process, a tremendous amount of potential growth may be lost. Those times when children become frustrated and find themselves tempted to quit may actually be blessings in disguise. By adopting a long-term view, letting these situations play out, giving students more time to work through a challenging situation, and offering just enough support to keep the bar moving, we are laying the groundwork for students to develop robust habits and approach future endeavors with greater confidence.

Close your eyes and think through a day's worth of learning activities, routines, and procedures. Ask yourself if there are currently some things you are doing for children that they can do for themselves. In addition, should you have a quiet moment to observe your students at work, be on the lookout for things they aren't currently doing for themselves but could be.

One final note: I'm sure I don't need to say what I am about to say, but I would rather err on the side of caution whenever potential confusion about a topic might arise. (Having said that, I'm shocked that this paragraph survived my editor's red pen.) When I state that we shouldn't do things for kids that they can do for themselves, that concept should never preclude us from doing favors for our students or showing kindness on a regular basis. Imagine, for example, a child sneezes and clearly needs a tissue. If I notice the sneeze and happen to be standing by the tissue box, I'm not going to stand my ground, shake my head, and snap, "Get it yourself!" Of course, I will bring over a tissue. Creating a culture of kindness and teamwork is a million times more important than insisting that children do things for themselves 100% of the time.

Ask, Don't Tell

A well-known teaching tip in the area of writing encourages children to "show, not tell." That means, for example, that if we introduce the main character's 5-year-old brother in the opening paragraph of Chapter 2, we wouldn't want to include the following sentence: "He is annoying." Rather, we would attempt to show through the younger child's actions and words that he is annoying. Showing is considered a stronger form of writing than telling. The same idea holds true for teachers when we interact with students experiencing difficulty. Instead of telling kids what to do, it's (almost always) a stronger form of teaching to ask questions. "Ask, don't tell" can become a powerful mantra for us to follow in our effort to empower children. For many of us in the profession, however, this can be challenging. After all, we're educators. We tend to enjoy dispensing information and see that as a critical part of our classroom role. During instructional lessons and at other times, we will have many opportunities to do just that. When seeking to support a student experiencing difficulty, however, asking questions should be our default mode. Asking instead of telling is an important rule of empowerment.

Perhaps the most practical, effective application of "Ask, don't tell" can be found in Madeline Hunter's "think-starter" concept. Think-starters not only exemplify the "Ask, don't tell" strategy but also bring to life the "Don't do things for children that they can do for themselves" concept. These two teacher moves work hand in hand. Recall the situation I described in the last chapter in which Randy hands me a paper without his name at the top. Telling him to write his name before turning in his work would solve the short-term issue but do nothing to increase his long-term capability. Telling him what to do would be a "think-stopper" by thwarting his chance to think for himself and eliminating the possibility of using this moment as a learning opportunity.

Instead, were I to follow the "Ask, don't tell" rule, I would say, "Randy, what do you need to do before turning in your work?" That puts the responsibility on Randy and invites him to invest some time and thought to discover a solution. I resist the temptation to provide him with a solution, because it's so much more valuable to give Randy the chance to think of one for himself. Furthermore, by asking rather than telling, I increase Randy's future capacity and make it more likely that he will take responsibility next time for remembering what to do.

Think-starters are one of those ideas that seem so simple yet are incredibly profound when we consider the combined effect of using it consistently over time. Let's look at another example of how we can incorporate think-starters into our teaching. This time, rather than focusing on the performance of a single classroom routine, let's delve deeper and analyze a situation in the area of math in which my fourth graders are working in pairs to solve the following problem from my *Math Problem Solving Menus* (2013)

> *Sam, Sarah, Arielle, and Alex are members of a Little League Baseball team. They are the first four hitters to bat in each game. Sarah does not bat first. Sam bats between Alex and Arielle. Alex bats between Sarah and Sam. What is the batting order for these four players?*

One pair is unsure which strategy to employ, and the two kids approach me, seeking help. Several strategies can lead to the correct solution, such as Guess and Check, Process of Elimination, and Make a Chart. The last thing I want to do is impose a strategy choice, tell them too much, or do their thinking for them. My goal, as the bench-press analogy suggests, is to keep the bar moving. I want the students assuming ownership of the problem-solving process, and I will offer the lightest assistance possible when they are unable to keep the bar moving on their own.

During these times when students are not able to achieve immediate success, it is tempting for teachers, both new and experienced, to step in and offer too much support. Kids may become frustrated and discouraged, and that can be difficult to watch. As teachers, we tend to be nurturers and pleasers. We care about our students and want them to be happy. We worry that if we don't offer enough assistance, students will continue to struggle and perhaps shut down. Our instinct is to remove them from unpleasant situations. Our motives are good.

As noble and understandable as these desires may be, we must resist the temptation to say or do too much. Experience has taught me that children aren't fragile. Challenging situations won't break them. Quite the opposite. Working through tough times makes kids stronger. These are occasions that offer children the potential to become powerful learners and boost their confidence. Kids need these moments of productive struggle to build resilience and grit. Students can only develop these traits when their teachers embrace these occasions and view them as opportunities, not as crises to end as quickly as possible.

Returning to my conversation with the two students, the first question I would ask is whether they have thought of any strategies they have used successfully in the past that they think might work for this problem. If they say yes, I would follow up by having them tell me what they have accomplished thus far. As long as the kids are able to demonstrate progress, I can continue asking questions, offering encouragement, and keeping the assistance gentle.

Only when they are unable to keep the bar moving on their own would I suggest specific strategies or next steps, and even then I would mention a few ideas and have the kids pick one. I'm trying to say as little as I can to preserve their opportunity to generate ideas and maintain ownership of the process.

Embrace Moments of Productive Struggle

As a college student, I was fortunate to take a sports psychology class taught by Dr. Bob Rotella, professor and author of such books as *Golf Is Not a Game of Perfect* and *Putting Out of Your Mind*. Rotella helped many professional golfers develop the mental skills required for success on the PGA Tour. One of my favorite principles I learned from his course and his books involves what are typically regarded as pressure situations. Having to sink a 12 ft birdie putt on the 18th hole to tie for the lead is an example of this type of occurrence. Commonly, we view these occasions in negative terms—stressful, nerve-racking, or anxiety-filled. How we label these moments, however, is a choice, as there is typically nothing inherently positive or negative about them. What one player sees as a pressure shot can just as easily be viewed as an opportunity shot.

Ever since I sold my soul to the sport of pickleball in the summer of 2021, I have revisited my sports psychology materials and made a concerted effort to improve my mental skills just as much as my physical skills. Now, when my partner and I are serving 10–11, I try to embrace this moment as an opportunity point, not a pressure situation.

I share this information to extend and amplify the point I made about moments of productive struggle in the classroom. These situations happen all the time in schools, and there's nothing inherently positive or negative about them. As educators, though, we often tend to regard them as unpleasant episodes from which children need to be saved. I strongly believe we must adopt a different view and attach a positive association to these times. Put simply, we must embrace moments of productive struggle as valuable growth opportunities. With this more positive view, observing productive struggle can be exciting because we believe it has the potential to provide some of the most incredible moments that will occur in our classrooms. With time, experience, and encouragement, students can eventually develop this mindset as well.

Incentivize Empowerment and Choice With More Empowerment and Choice

In the previous chapter I described how educator Angela Watson announces to her students that their actions and choices influence her actions and choices. That practice doesn't just help educators set and reinforce high classroom expectations; it's also a major empowerment move. *Empowerment* is the opposite of coercion and control. In an environment characterized by coercion and control, we feel constrained and limited, sometimes even helpless and trapped. In such an atmosphere, our spirit and motivation suffer and our performance declines.

Launching each school year with Watson's approach, on the other hand, achieves the opposite effect. Explicitly stating to students that their actions and choices influence ours contributes significantly to the creation of an empowering environment and helps children understand the power they have to shape the direction of the class. This message produces an incredibly positive effect on students by letting them know they have the incentive to take initiative and conveying how important their current actions and choices are in determining their future opportunities. Kids come to understand they have the ability to control, to a large extent, their own destiny—whether that means more frequent group learning activities or the opportunity to sit next to a close friend, just to name a few desired outcomes—and create the type of classroom environment they prefer, provided that they "make it work" by behaving responsibly and knocking their initial opportunities out of the park. Kids who are able to achieve their desired outcomes can generate additional opportunities for themselves, kick-starting a virtuous cycle that results in higher and higher levels of opportunity, responsibility, and empowerment. As a result, motivation and enthusiasm blast off.

Look for opportunities for students to make as many meaningful choices about classroom life as possible. Commonly, kids enter a new classroom at the start of the school year and assume their teachers will make most, if not all, of the big decisions about how the class will operate. By combining encouragement and opportunity with high expectations and accountability, we counter this notion and help everyone realize that they will have a large say in their user experience and that their actions and choices matter. Ultimately, our job as educators is to create the conditions that bring the best out of our students. We empower children to go as far as their initiative, hard work, and effort will take them. Watson's approach plays an important role in this endeavor.

As teachers, striving to empower our students may require us to relinquish some control, but in the process, we gain children's commitment, buy-in, and loyalty. In addition, by placing our trust in the children and demonstrating our deep belief that they have the ability to make wise decisions, we earn their trust in return. Plus, when we are able to operate in an empowering environment, our spirit soars. Student motivation skyrockets when they know the choices they make matter and know they will be held accountable for their behavior.

One final note about incentivizing empowerment and choice with more empowerment and choice: Whenever I use the word *incentive*, I am sensitive to the fact that the term tends to be employed to refer to extrinsic motivation.

The approach I describe in this section is not extrinsic or based on McGregor's theory X assumptions. Extrinsic motivators are about control, unrelated to the task at hand, and damaging to our goal of encouraging children to take initiative, demonstrate responsibility, and develop self-control. In contrast, incentivizing choice with more choice is directly related to the task at hand, emphasizes release, and promotes the taking of initiative and the development of responsibility. Encouraging choice and opportunity empowers children to achieve self-control.

Structure Student Choice Thoughtfully

In a 1994 episode of the Simpsons, Principal Skinner announces: "All students proceed immediately to an assembly in the Butthead Memorial Auditorium . . . I wish we hadn't let the students name that." Of course, an outcome like this is hardly surprising when children have total say over a given matter. As teachers, we know that affording kids opportunities to make meaningful choices about their learning is important and empowering, yet sometimes it's difficult to know how much choice is appropriate. Unlimited choice can be problematic. With academic matters, for instance, kids who have unlimited choices can easily make decisions that result in their work being too easy, too challenging, or off-topic. On the other hand, no choice at all is de-motivating and stifling.

Fortunately for us, a third alternative exists. In between "total teacher control" and "total student control" lies one of the most useful constructs I have learned in my career. Many years ago I attended a workshop presentation led by educator Sandra Kaplan, author of such books as *Differentiated Curriculum and Instruction for Advanced and Gifted Learners* and *Project CHANGE*. In her session, Kaplan described a framework called "choices within parameters." This structure offers a win–win scenario for both teachers and students and can be applied to a wide variety of situations.

Let's look at a few examples of how *choices within parameters* works. The first relates to life outside of school, while the two that follow apply to the classroom setting. Imagine you have two 10-year-old twins, and you take them to a restaurant for dinner. You notice that the menu is huge and contains several healthy and less-than-healthy options. You don't want to order for your kids because you want them to learn how to make healthy food choices for themselves. You also don't want them ordering pancakes topped with whipped cream, strawberry syrup, chocolate chips, and Fruity Pebbles (even though it's the best-tasting cereal of all time—that's indisputable). Instead you support your children's choices by establishing parameters—they must order a protein and two vegetables. You decide on the food groups, and the kids choose foods within those parameters. In other words, we structure the choices. The children choose items within those categories. One child might choose chicken with broccoli and corn; the other, a turkey burger with spinach and carrots. *Win–win.*

In the classroom, some of the most meaningful content choices children make involve essays and research projects. In California, fourth graders learn the five-paragraph structure for both personal and persuasive essays. Since personal essays relate directly to the children's lives, the kids tend to make their choices easily and without any stress or controversy. Typically, students will craft such thesis statements as "Soccer is my favorite sport," "I have a great big sister," and "I love my mom."

Persuasive essays, on the other hand, are more challenging because the kids are trying to convince others to adopt their viewpoint and because their reasons and evidence need to go beyond their personal experience. The first few years I taught this writing unit, many children experienced significant difficulty selecting a topic that was appropriate for their age level or that enabled them to generate enough reasons and examples to support their thesis. Despite my and their best efforts, this project led to a fair amount of frustration.

All that changed, however, after I attended my first International Society for Technology in Education (ISTE) conference during the summer of 2018 in Chicago. It was there I discovered the United Nations Sustainable Development Goals that serve as a call to action by all countries to create a global partnership to end poverty, reduce inequality, address climate change, and focus on other urgent worldwide priorities. Scan the QR code in Figure 8.1 to read about the 17 Global Goals. As I learned more about this initiative, I knew I needed to incorporate it into my teaching and began searching for ways to integrate the goals into my curriculum. The first opportunity I found was our persuasive essay unit.

Now, at the outset of the project, I announce that everyone's selection needs to relate directly to one of the Global Goals. Not to worry, though! There will still be tons of topic choices. Because I like to introduce these goals early in the school year, the kids already have familiarity with this information by the time we launch our persuasive essay unit and are ready to jump

Figure 8.1 QR code—United Nations Sustainable Development Goals.

right in and start brainstorming possible thesis statements. In what follows you will see a list of ideas students have generated in recent years, with the related goal in parentheses.

- There should be a Smartboard in every classroom in America. (Quality Education)
- Girls should be allowed to play on boys' sports teams. (Gender Equality)
- We should all use sustainable energy. (Affordable and Clean Energy)
- Laws against killing sharks should be better enforced. (Life Below Water)
- Poaching shouldn't happen to animals. (Life on Land)

When compared to "unlimited choice" persuasive essays, structuring students' topic choices using the Global Goals has resulted in higher-quality work and more enjoyable writing experiences. Students are more enthusiastic and engaged. In addition, crafting thesis statements has been a smoother process, and the kids have found greater success generating reasons for these thesis statements and identifying age-appropriate research articles. Integrating the Global Goals in this manner also raises student awareness of important world issues, inspires the kids to take action to achieve worthwhile aims, and encourages everyone to spend time thinking about larger societal purposes. Employing the *choices within parameters* framework leads to similar outcomes for other types of projects as well. Even though we, as teachers, establish the parameters, the children still have plenty of choices to get excited about.

Another writing project that features the *choices within parameters* approach is the California Information Book Project my students begin each January. The California State Framework for social studies lists the topics that children in each grade are expected to learn. These expectations are divided into a few sections. One section, "California's Growth and Development After 1850," includes way too many specific items for fourth graders to explore in depth. It's never a good idea to give surface-level treatment to any curricular focus, so I knew I needed to find a way for my students to study these items in a way that promoted depth over breadth. Fortunately, as part of our Writing Workshop, my students complete one major research project during our time together. One year I came up with the idea of integrating social studies into our writing and turning the long list of topics into project choices for the kids. Now, the categories shown in Figure 8.2 represent our parameters, and the children each choose a specific item from one of the categories for their research project. These topics relate to various aspects of California's growth and development. Once the kids had completed their research projects, we would achieve depth over breadth by participating in a series of activities in which everyone would share their projects with the group.

In Box 8.1, you will find the list of categories and specific topic choices I present to my class.

Box 8.1 Project Choices for California Information Book Project

Focus Question: How Did California Develop Economically, Politically, and Culturally After 1850?

Topic Choices

California's Connection to Major Events
- ★ The Great Depression
- ★ The Dust Bowl
- ★ World War II

Industry
- ★ Aerospace industry
- ★ Electronics industry
- ★ Large-scale commercial agriculture
- ★ Large irrigation projects
- ★ Oil industry
- ★ Automobile industry
- ★ Communications industry
- ★ Defense industry
- ★ Trade with the Pacific Basin

Communications
- ★ Pony Express
- ★ Overland Mail Service
- ★ Western Union
- ★ Building of the Transcontinental Railroad

Education
- ★ K–12 public education system
- ★ California's public universities

Immigration
- ★ Immigration from other countries
- ★ Migration from other states

Growth of Towns and Cities
- ★ Los Angeles
- ★ Sacramento
- ★ San Francisco
- ★ San Diego

Water System

Trace the evolution of California's network of dams, aqueducts, and reservoirs.

Arts and Entertainment
- ★ The rise of the entertainment industry
- ★ Walt Disney
- ★ Louis Mayer (head of a movie studio)
- ★ John Steinbeck (award-winning writer)
- ★ Ansel Adams (photographer and environmentalist)
- ★ Dorothea Lange (photographer and photojournalist)
- ★ John Wayne

There is one aspect of the California Information Book project that distinguishes it from the persuasive essays described previously. If students experience difficulty finding a topic that's personally meaningful and engaging, they have the ability to suggest an additional topic—as long as they can show that it genuinely played an important role in California's growth and development after 1850. (On the classic game show *The Joker's Wild*, host Jack Berry referred to this move as "going off the board.") Offering the kids this option is a form of "Your actions and choices influence my actions and choices" since it provides the incentive to take ownership of their learning, display initiative, and shape the direction of their project in a way that works best for them. Over the years, many children have gone off the board and produced excellent information books about such topics as the Apple Corporation, the history of health care in California, and Stanford University. A few have even gone off the rails and done a project about USC. (I must have been in an exceptionally good mood the day I approved that idea.)

Keep an eye out for times when the *choices within parameters* approach may benefit you and your students. If you are able to empower children further by providing the ability for them to suggest additional parameters or choices, even better. Making these options available promises an incredible payoff in terms of student ownership, initiative, motivation, engagement, and performance.

Capitalize on Potential Empowering Moments
In previous chapters, I have emphasized the importance of taking advantage of learnable moments—opportunities that present themselves to strengthen culture, develop habits, or further progress toward valued aims. That practice applies to the focus of this chapter as well. We also want to be on the lookout for "empowering moments." What exactly does that mean? In daily classroom life, situations naturally arise when students find themselves in the middle of a dilemma or experience difficulty. As educators, we could easily make a decision for them, but that would rob the children of ownership and thwart their potential opportunity to exercise initiative and develop valuable problem-solving skills.

When this type of situation occurs, we need to step back, seek the child's perspective, and ask how *they* think they should proceed. Our goal is to build character, foster independence, and increase students' capacity for the future.

Focusing on the students' view of a situation creates the conditions in which they have the chance to take initiative and ownership, and we are not. This may seem like a simple point, but it's another of those occasions when the results of following this practice consistently over time are powerful.

The first time I experienced a potential empowering moment came during my graduate training at UCLA and a few classmates and I had the tremendous opportunity to observe a middle-grade class at a nearby elementary school. I remember enjoying my visits to that classroom greatly. The teachers were terrific; the students, amazing. One morning, the lead teacher opened the class meeting by reviewing an incident that happened the day before at lunchtime. I wasn't there to witness it, but apparently, several members of the class either teased, frightened, or bothered a group of younger children. The teacher asked her class what she thought they should do to remedy the situation. The children suggested walking downstairs to the primary classroom to apologize and came up with a couple other constructive solutions as well. The teacher then replied, "Good, because I have already arranged with the [primary grade teacher] for us to go down there later today." The two steps the teacher had taken up to that point had been empowering: seeking the children's perspective and soliciting their input. The only recommendation I would have made in that situation would have been to refrain from arranging a class visit before the middle-grade students made that decision themselves.

One example from my own classroom happened before laptops entered the picture and my students still published their Writing Workshop projects by hand. On this day, the kids were rewriting their stories in preparation for our upcoming celebration. In our school, writing celebrations are a big deal; they are the times when we share the projects we have worked on for weeks with classmates, parent visitors, and administrators.

The day before our celebration, one of my students (whom we will call Heather) was sitting on the rug, copying her edited first draft onto our nice green publishing paper. Accidentally, another student walked by her without realizing she was down there, and he stepped on her work. The sheet didn't tear, but it was noticeably bent and damaged. Heather was a conscientious worker who took great pride in the appearance of her projects, and she was understandably upset.

At this moment, I needed to accomplish a few things. First, I talked with the boy who stepped on her paper to make sure he knew that Heather and I knew what he did was an accident. He understood that, remained calm, and then apologized to her. Next, I needed to speak with Heather. It is so easy for teachers to insert themselves into situations like these, take over, and make decisions on behalf of the child involved. I didn't want to do that.

Instead, I wanted this to be an empowering moment for Heather. After I had ensured that she was calm and willing and able to speak with me, the two of us discussed her options. I told her that I knew how much time and care she put into her written work, and in this situation, if she wanted to finish her publishing on the damaged paper, I would understand and accept her project. I didn't want to require her to start over, especially since the celebration was the next day.

Another option was for Heather to get a new piece of paper and start that sheet again from the beginning. After thinking it over for a short time, she decided to start over. I asked if she was sure she wanted to do this. She didn't hesitate. Heather said she wanted to have a beautifully published project for the celebration. I have learned that, in these moments, we cannot force students into the decisions we believe are best; we can only talk about their options, discuss the pros and cons, and trust that, over time, students will make great choices.

At the end of the period, I called the class together to share what had just happened. I wanted to take Heather's empowering moment and have it be an empowering moment for the whole class. I explained to everyone that, in this situation, Heather had a choice to make, and it is a choice that all of us have several times every day. We can choose to take the fastest path to being done, or we can do everything in our power to make our work the best it can be, even when doing so may require extra time, extra effort, and personal sacrifice. With this example, Heather could have chosen to finish the damaged paper and call it a day, or she could start again on a new piece of paper, even though she did nothing to cause the damage to her paper.

I made a big deal out of the choice she made, and everyone in the class looked at her with tremendous respect. I wanted to emphasize the choice she made, and I also wanted her to walk away from this experience feeling like a winner, considering she easily could have walked away feeling like a victim. In addition, taking advantage of these empowering moments goes a long way in helping us build character in our students and create a classroom culture of quality.

Another example of an empowering moment occurred just over ten years ago during our school's annual round of Parent Conferences. During each conference, I met individually with children and their parents for 20 minutes. We began by discussing a self-evaluation sheet the students completed in class regarding the 13 Habits of Character that form the foundation of everything we do. We then analyzed work samples and discussed each child's academic progress in all the major subject areas. I also like to build in agenda items in which we focus on nutrition, hydration, sleep, and exercise. By addressing each child's work habits, social skills, academic progress, and health, I know I'm being faithful to my goal of teaching the whole child.

To tie these individual components together, I conclude every meeting with a goal-setting activity that I mentioned in Chapter 3 and will also highlight in Chapter 9. Each child, with help from their parents and me, sets three goals to guide our work over the next few months. Typically, the goals pertain to academic concerns, such as reading comprehension or math problem-solving, but they don't have to. Specific Habits of Character and Habits of Mind also make for great goals. Students who are already performing at a high level in all academic areas may benefit the most from a goal focused on reducing their stress level, getting more exercise, making a new friend, or trying to enjoy certain subjects more than they currently do. Other kids, who may not yet be performing at grade level, frequently gain the most from goals that may not seem directly connected to academics but are critical in building a foundation of work habits that will ultimately lead to academic success. Goals such as becoming more disciplined, more responsible, or more organized exemplify this idea. During this conversation, I ask everyone to focus on only the most important factors affecting their overall progress and happiness.

When approached thoughtfully, goal setting is perhaps the most empowering activity in which any of us participate because it affords us the opportunity to look at ourselves in depth, make worthwhile decisions, and choose our own path. It is personal. It is meaningful. It is motivating. It can also be potentially life-changing. Setting goals brings out our best and helps us envision our best selves. Goal setting helps us address our weaker areas and turn them into strengths. Plus, the goal-setting process helps us become more reflective, more self-aware, and more honest with ourselves. Sometimes it is uncomfortable for students, and it needs to be uncomfortable if we are going to step out of our comfort zones, form lasting habits, and produce genuine change.

I have asked students and their families to set goals during their conferences for many years. As a follow-up step, I request that families write or type the goals and put the sheets at home in a prominent place, such as on a desk, bulletin board, or refrigerator, so that the kids refer to them often. Prior to that year, the results had been mixed, with some students taking their goals to heart and making impressive progress, while others invested significantly less effort and made significantly less progress. Over time I have learned that few things are more discouraging than to set aside the time and make the effort to create goals and then have those goals be forgotten after the conference. As a result, I am always on the lookout for ways to keep the goals relevant and motivating.

That year, something wonderful occurred that took our goal setting exercise to a level I had never before experienced. I relay the story in this section because it shows what can happen when we encourage children to invest their energies in an endeavor and then turn them loose. First, some background. Each year our school creates a conference schedule that gives one pupil-free day for these meetings, followed by four consecutive minimum days. A majority of families choose to have their conferences on the pupil-free day, and the pivotal moment in our goal setting exercise came the morning after that day.

On that Thursday morning, two children brought to class their typed list of goals to display on their desks. I asked their permission to share these sheets during our morning meeting. I was thrilled to share these lists with the group for a few reasons. First, this type of sharing typically creates a strong sense of momentum and gets a new endeavor off to a great start. All important team initiatives need initial momentum and early successes to thrive and grow, and I wanted to capitalize on this moment and use these goal sheets as a catalyst to spur further action.

Second, I had a feeling that the students who hadn't yet had their conferences were going to be intrigued with this exercise and impressed that two students had already followed up on their conferences by bringing in the goal lists so quickly. Third, once students saw the first lists, I knew we could recognize those efforts and then find ways to make these lists even more effective.

That is exactly what happened.

We discussed how awesome it was that some students were already taping their goals to the top of their desks for easy reference. Then, we discussed how we could make these sheets even more helpful. Over the next two days, some kids began bringing in sheets that not only included their goals but also contained sections where the kids could write down daily evaluations. A few children chose to self-evaluate with our 1–4 scale, while others drew happy, neutral, or sad faces to rate their performance for that day.

Other kids jumped on this idea, and each day several more students brought in new, improved, and more ambitious goal sheets that included mini-calendars, where they could record daily or weekly self-evaluations. Each time new sheets arrived, I shared them during the morning circle, and the commitment and enthusiasm for goal setting kept growing. Though the goal setting process had led many children to make substantial progress in previous years, that year's group seemed to be approaching their goals with an uncommonly high level of commitment.

Every day the bar kept getting raised, not in a competitive way, but with a spirit of cooperation and continuous improvement. As more and more students brought in their goal setting sheets to share with the class, new ideas continued to emerge about how we could make this process more effective. It was clearly evident after a short period of time that students who were evaluating their progress on a daily basis were making rapid progress with regard to each of their goals. One day, though, as we were discussing this process as a class, another new idea emerged that enabled us to take our goal setting and self-evaluation to a higher level.

As one student was describing his sheet, we came up with the idea of evaluating our progress not once but several times per day. I asked if I could borrow his sheet, and in front of the group, we divided the boxes he made for his daily self-evaluation into four smaller boxes. Now, rather than evaluate his progress only at the end of the day, he would assess his performance four times: before recess, before lunch, before afternoon recess, and at the end of the day. (His revised sheet is shown in Figure 8.2.) Frequent self-evaluations help children keep their goals fresh in their minds throughout the day. In addition, collecting this data allows us to analyze whether performance remains consistent throughout the day, improves, or weakens. Furthermore, many interesting questions and critical thinking opportunities arose as we analyzed this data.

Eventually, every child had attached to their desk either a list of personal learning goals or a thoughtfully developed self-evaluation sheet, which they looked at or completed at least once per day. I didn't require students to perform any specific type of self-evaluation. I have tried that in the past, and though there were definite benefits that resulted, I now prefer a more voluntary, grassroots approach, where improvements arise more organically, powerful ideas and practices spread on their own, and students commit

Self-Evaluation Sheet

Self-Discipline

- Working quietly at seat
- Lining up on time
- Entering the room quietly

Focus

- Pausing to give eye contact and listen carefully to instructions the first time
- Thoughtful responses to questions
- Pay attention to details and take pride in work habits
- More important to read and understand information rather than race to finish the sentence or paragraph
- More important to get the answers correct rather than hurry to finish the problem or task
- Review work and complete task

Transitions

- Pause to listen to the beginning of directions
- Quickly and patiently switch to new activity
- Wait patiently with good posture for next instructions

Pride

- Driven by intrinsic motivation
- Caring deeply about my work
- Keep trying to improve

	Monday	Tuesday	Wednesday	Thursday	Friday
Self-Discipline					
Focus					
Transitions					
Pride					
Scale of 1-5...	5 = Excellent		3 = Good Effort		1 = Poorest Effort

Figure 8.2 Self-evaluation sheet for student goals.

themselves because they see the value in it, not because they have to do it. What began as a 5-minute exercise at the conclusion of each Parent Conference had grown tremendously and taken on a life of its own to become one of the core features of our team.

When the kids are learning from one another, innovating, and finding ways to take our work to the next level, it is one of the best things that can happen in a classroom. It is one thing for teachers to talk about how everyone matters and everyone has the opportunity to contribute to the betterment of the group, but throughout a process like this one, the kids see this idea in action. Team bonding grows. Mutual respect increases. Expectations elevate. An infectious energy takes over the room as students take an idea and run with it. Children become genuinely excited about finding ways to do better in school and take pride in the fact that something they did influenced how other kids approached their schoolwork. Children do better in school because of something that someone else brought to the table. It's voluntary, it's contagious, and it's amazing. This is what can happen when children feel empowered to take action.

Be a Consistent Model

The next three sections of this chapter revisit strategies I first mentioned in the "Culture" chapter and apply them to the concept of empowerment. Leading the way: modeling. Just as with every other trait or habit we wish to promote in the classroom, the most powerful, effective way for adults to encourage empowerment is to serve as a living embodiment of that idea. Children are paying close attention to us, and our actions speak louder than our words.

With entities such as honesty and kindness, modeling desired behavior is fairly straightforward. We model honesty, for example, by telling the truth, even when doing so may be uncomfortable. We model kindness by caring about our students, showing empathy, offering compliments, and valuing their perspectives. Modeling empowerment, however, can be a bit trickier. How do we model empowerment? To start, let's think of specific actions that fall under the larger "umbrella" of *empowerment*. Such a list might include the following:

- Demonstrating initiative
- Setting goals and striving to reach them
- Doing as much as possible by ourselves without relying on others
- Seeking out and conquering challenges
- Embracing moments of productive struggle

- Taking action to right a wrong or address a meaningful personal or societal issue
- Facing issues and problems head-on rather than complaining, placing blame, making excuses, or feeling sorry for ourselves
- Realizing that sometimes the only thing holding us back is ourselves and fighting through moments of doubt, discouragement, or inertia

Once we have identified various expressions of empowerment, we keep an eye out for opportunities to demonstrate "empowering behaviors" in the classroom. Unexpected situations happen all the time in our work, and we will no doubt find ourselves with numerous chances to model empowerment. When leading a challenging instructional lesson, for instance, we can be honest with the kids about the difficulty we are experiencing, embrace it without complaint, and share how excited we are to work through it and reach a successful conclusion. When technology goes on the fritz or the art, music, or PE teacher doesn't show up, we stay calm, maintain a positive attitude, and search for a solution that enables us to make the best of the situation. When a new educational resource we purchased doesn't work as advertised, we contact the manufacturer and take the necessary steps to obtain a replacement. Children benefit from seeing adults take action in this manner.

In addition to reacting and responding to situations, we can be proactive as well. We can create opportunities to model empowerment. Goal setting offers tremendous potential in this regard. If you're beginning a new workout regimen, seeking to learn new recipes, planting a garden, or launching some other personal endeavor, bring the kids with you (metaphorically). Set a goal, post it in the classroom, convey excitement as you get started, and provide updates on your progress, the ups as well as the downs.

Share Inspirational Stories

We can build on our efforts to model empowerment behaviors by sharing stories that are likely to resonate with students, whether they be personal in nature or related to the lives of well-known individuals children may know and admire. Storytelling is an incredibly powerful teaching strategy because kids form an emotional connection with our messages and, consequently, remember our words for a long time. These stories can pertain to any of the bullet points mentioned in the previous section. The best opportunities to share stories usually occur during our Quote of the Day discussions, as these sayings provide natural "launching pads" for us.

The following quote by George Bernard Shaw inspired one of my favorite empowerment stories: "The real moment of success is not the moment apparent to the crowd." I tell my students that this quote reminds me of a movie I saw many years ago about legendary Romanian gymnast Nadia Comaneci, who captured the world's attention with her gold medal performances in the 1976 Montreal Olympics. Comaneci, at the age of 14, became the first gymnast to be awarded a perfect 10 at the Olympic Games and earned a staggering 7 such scores on her way to winning three gold medals.

It's easy to think, I say to the class, that Nadia's moment of success occurred in Montreal when a worldwide audience watched her routines. What the quote is telling us, in my view, is that her real moment of triumph happened well before she arrived at the Olympics. It took place behind the scenes, during those long years of training, when nobody was watching. I conclude my story by relaying a scene from the movie that shined a spotlight on her rigorous training. One evening, Nadia was practicing one of her routines. It was late, probably around 9:00 p.m. The gym was empty, with only Nadia and her coach inside. The girl's father walked in the door and announced it was time for her to go home. Nadia had just completed a routine and wasn't happy with it. She told her father that she couldn't leave because the routine wasn't perfect yet. Nadia performed the sequence again, nailed it, and then informed her father that the two could now head home. I point out to my students that Nadia took the initiative in this situation. She didn't need her coach or father to evaluate her performance and suggest next steps. Nadia did it herself. She was empowered. The young gymnast had a goal that was personally meaningful and wasn't going to stop until she reached it.

Consider sharing stories from your own life or the lives of others anytime you or they took action to solve a problem, reached a goal, or overcame an obstacle. Sharing personal stories deepens the bond we have with our students and leaves a lasting impression. Think of times when you didn't want to accept something the way it was and took action or when you realized you had the power and ability to improve some aspect of your life and initiated steps to make it happen.

Recognize Noteworthy Student Efforts
I mentioned previously that each year we will likely have a few students who tend to sit passively at their desks when they encounter difficulty rather than take responsibility to solve their own problems or seek assistance. One great way to show these children an alternative approach is to recognize examples of students who take charge and demonstrate responsibility and initiative. Hearing about how their classmates handled challenging situations can be far more powerful than listening to a teacher's explanation. Plus, this type of

recognition can have a terrific effect on class chemistry and help the kids see one another as resources.

In Chapter 2, I shared the story of two kids who took charge on Picture Day when I was still inside the auditorium, taking my individual snapshot, and several students had already made their way outside for the group photo. I was worried that the unsupervised students would be running around, climbing trees, and disturbing other classes. When I saw that two students had taken charge and already positioned their classmates in order from tallest to shortest, I was thrilled. My sense is that most children wouldn't have taken initiative in that situation. If a few classmates had started fooling around, it's likely that the others would have just sat by or joined in. They might have become uncomfortable by what they saw, but I would not have expected anyone to intervene. Some kids might think to get involved but would hesitate out of fear of getting in trouble for interfering with the teacher's job. The fact that these two kids felt empowered to solve the problem was special and certainly deserving of recognition.

When kids demonstrate this kind of initiative, responsibility, and leadership, without being asked or prompted, we seize the opportunity to recognize that behavior, especially when it links directly to an idea from our class mission statement. We can provide this type of recognition ourselves or encourage students to call attention to these deeds whenever we gather on the rug for the Statements of Recognition mentioned in Chapter 3. Recognizing this type of behavior is one of the most powerful ways to spread it.

Another important type of student conduct we can improve through recognition is playground behavior. Helping children develop the communication and problem-solving skills required for positive playground interactions and safe, enjoyable recess periods can be particularly challenging for elementary educators. Since we are generally not outside with the kids at these times, it can also be stressful. Playground supervisors will frequently bring recess incidents to our attention. We want and need to hold follow-up conversations with the involved students, but we can't be completely sure what actually happened. Many times kids will deny the alleged behavior, focus on the conduct of other children, or place blame. On other occasions kids will demonstrate honesty about their involvement in a situation, own up to what they did, or skillfully employ a strategy to solve a problem or diffuse a situation to keep it from escalating. Whenever we learn of that type of exemplary conduct, it benefits the group to hear about the positive choices their classmates made, with those children's permission, of course. It also provides a well-deserved shoutout to the individuals who made such great decisions.

Shine a Spotlight on Empowerment

At the 2019 SHAPE America Conference in Tampa, Florida, I learned about "Spotlight Days," a fun, clever way for teachers to give greater attention and "free advertising" to important concepts, habits, and/or traits. The basic idea involves selecting five high-priority focus areas that we want to feature throughout the school year and assigning each to a different day of the week. In Figure 8.4, you will find an image displaying the five concepts I chose to include once I returned home (mindfulness, kindness, empowerment, service, and gratitude). You will also notice my attempts at catchy names for these "theme" days.

When choosing our five concepts, I recommend steering clear of terms such as *quality*, *teamwork*, and others that we will likely be mentioning every day. Instead, we should aim to choose worthwhile ideas, such as mindfulness and gratitude, that, amid the hustle and bustle of classroom life, may not always receive the time and emphasis they deserve. Unfortunately, these concepts can end up on the back burner. We can prevent that from happening by including them among our spotlight categories.

Assigning a different theme to each day of the week is an interesting form of "branding." This approach gives the individual days their own identity that can bring a fresh excitement to our mornings. By associating each concept with its own weekday, we can build them into the fabric of our classrooms and provide meaningful opportunities for children to develop valuable habits and skills in a way that works with our busy schedules. Introducing the five "spotlight ideas" in this manner creates situations in which students won't just be *learning* these concepts; they will be *living* them. The activities I describe in what follows blend smoothly into daily classroom life and enhance the learning our classes are already doing. Children, therefore, will experience these ideas as a seamless part of their school day, not as an "add-on" or one-shot deal.

Incorporating this approach into our teaching can produce many positive outcomes and add tremendous value to children's lives. Specifically, Spotlight Days have the potential to powerfully impact kids' overall happiness and sense of well-being while also taking their academic learning to a new level. Developing specific habits associated with the five concepts can boost confidence, foster independence, increase focus and productivity, and encourage students to become more thoughtful, both in their interactions with others and with how they engage in their schoolwork. In addition, students are more likely to work with greater enthusiasm and purpose and find more meaning and joy in their learning.

Choose the themes that you believe to be the most relevant and meaningful for your teaching. Sometimes it's difficult to narrow down our wish list to only five choices. Should you find yourself in this situation, feel free to select five at the outset and swap out one or more when you start another round, say, a few months into the school year, at the start of a new semester, or once you feel the original five are part of your students' "functioning selves" and the kids are ready for something new.

I recommend scheduling a "kickoff" week to introduce your five concepts and bring each one to life with one of the suggested activities I describe in what follows. After that, brief mentions or reminders each morning over the next week or two may be all your students need in order to remember and act on these concepts. Because our schedules during the initial part of each school year tend to be so jam-packed, it is perfectly fine if you wait a few months before adding Spotlight Days to your repertoire. In addition, once you have introduced your five themes, taking an occasional break from this activity will not diminish its effectiveness in any way. In fact, it might even keep the Spotlight categories fresh as you progress through the school year. Even the most engaging activities and ideas can become a bit stale if we feature them every day for months and months.

In Boxes 8.2 through 8.6, you will find the sequence of Spotlight visuals that introduce the emphases of each theme. I follow each visual with detailed implementation suggestions.

Table 8.1 "Spotlight Days" Themes

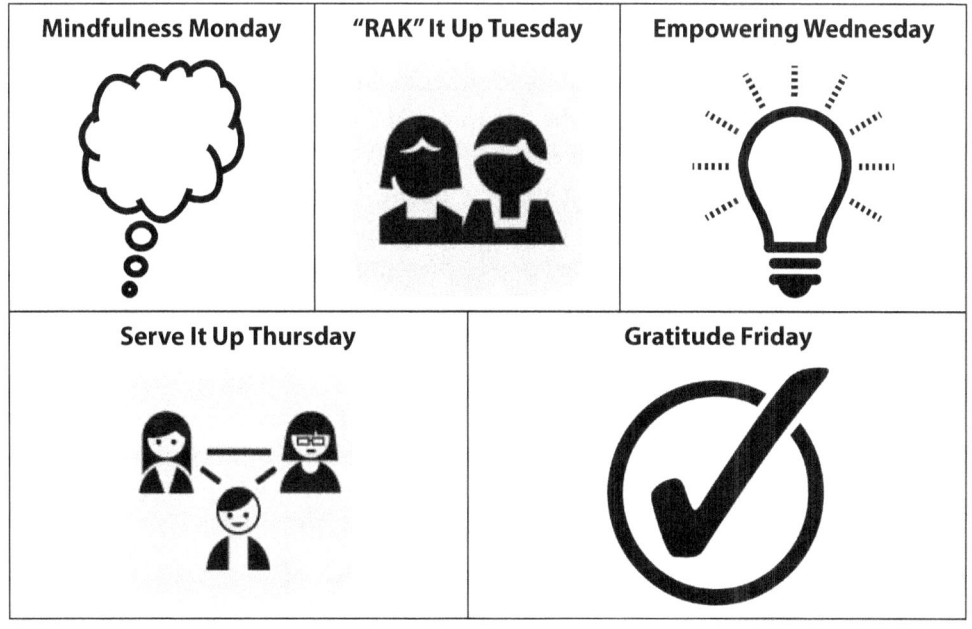

> **Box 8.2 Spotlight Day 1: Mindfulness Monday**
>
>
>
> *Spotlight Day 1: Mindfulness Monday*
> ★ Pay attention to present-moment experiences with curiosity and openness.
> ★ Be aware of other people's feelings
> ★ Stay calm and relaxed, no matter what happens.

Mindfulness has become a popular topic in schools in recent years. Developing habits associated with mindfulness will benefit children both inside and outside of school for years to come. In my view, teachers need to raise student awareness of two critical aspects of mindfulness—building habits and then applying them. (Sometimes I use the analogy of earning and spending our "mindfulness capital," as we do with money.)

Common exercises that are designed to raise awareness of mindfulness and build habits include deep breathing, mindfulness walks, and observing (and perhaps journaling about) what we are sensing at the present moment without judging or reacting to those thoughts and feelings. These activities can be effective in helping children pay greater attention to what is happening in the here and now, avoid distractions, and stay calm during difficult situations. Morning circle time is a terrific time to engage in brief mindfulness exercises. The transition from the playground to the classroom after recess, lunch, and other breaks can be challenging for many children, and these times also offer great opportunities to practice mindfulness.

Once children understand the meaning of mindfulness and have participated in practice activities, we need to make a concerted effort to help our students apply their skills on a regular basis. That's where the real added value lies. Consider an activity I use with my class called the "Mindful Minute." During that time, I ask everyone to pay attention to what they see, hear, feel, smell, and taste. The goal is to help them concentrate and fill their minds with what is happening right now.

I often joke with the group afterward about how, even though that exercise is a valuable one, practicing mindfulness does not mean that we are mindful for only one minute a day. Rather, we want to become mindful as a matter of habit and apply what we learn *throughout* the day—when it's needed the most and when calling upon our skills is the most difficult.

My initial effort to promote this type of mindful approach to daily classroom life involves the social-emotional check-in we do as part of our morning routine. One at a time, you will recall, my students go around the circle and share a number between 1 and 10 to indicate how they are feeling. While each person is sharing, I encourage everyone to pay close attention so they notice when a classmate's number is low. That way, we can make an effort to cheer them up and be a great friend during the day so that person's number increases as the day progresses. That's being a good teammate. In a class of 30, it's easy to lose focus as people are saying their numbers and have our thoughts drift to other topics. Our morning check-in, therefore, is a terrific time to emphasize mindfulness, because it increases class bonding, strengthens teamwork, builds friendships, and offers children an easy-to-understand way in which mindfulness can pay immediate dividends for all of us. Moreover, it doesn't require any additional instructional time.

Building upon that effort, I began looking for other opportunities to make mindfulness a natural part of our school day, and I encourage you to do the same with your students. When we define *mindfulness* as "focusing our attention on the present moment," we can integrate it seamlessly into both academic and non-academic aspects of our classroom. Here are some academic examples. At the start of a math lesson, we can encourage students to be mindful of the pros and cons of the various strategies we will be using for multiplying one-digit numbers by three-digit numbers. Before launching into the day's read-aloud, we can ask everyone to be mindful of the techniques the author of our book uses to create drama and suspense. Before drafting our persuasive essays, we can emphasize the importance of being mindful of our audience to ensure that our arguments are convincing.

Examples of incorporating mindfulness into social-emotional learning are also numerous. As the kids head outside to the playground, we can ask them to be mindful of their friends' feelings when they're playing a group game at recess and be mindful of how their words might affect the feelings of others at the table during lunch. We can also bring the focus to ourselves. For example, before students begin a challenging activity, we can encourage everyone to be mindful of their reactions when something doesn't go their way. Are we able to stay calm and manage our emotions, or do we become angry, raise our voice to someone, or say something that we might later regret?

Seeking and capitalizing on opportunities to develop and apply skills and habits of mindfulness can have a profound effect on our students and our overall classroom environment.

> **Box 8.3 Spotlight Day 2: "RAK" It Up Tuesday**
>
> *Spotlight Day 2: "RAK" It Up Tuesday*
>
> Commit Random Acts of Kindness
> Examples:
>
> ★ Let someone stand in front of you in line.
> ★ Compliment someone for their great work, effort, or behavior.
> ★ Invite people to have lunch with you or to play games at recess.

"RAK" is short for "random acts of kindness." The purpose of this second Spotlight Day is to accumulate or "rack up" kind gestures throughout the day so students can enjoy the benefits of both giving and receiving them and understand the powerful impact these acts can have on our self-esteem, our feeling of belonging, and the overall classroom environment. I have always liked the idea of "random" acts of kindness because, in my mind, it captures the spirit of being kind to people for its own sake, because it's the right thing to do, and because we don't ever need a reason to display kindness towards others.

As with the other Spotlight Days, the most effective approach is to introduce "RAK" It Up Tuesday during our morning meeting or morning circle time and then follow up a few times, if possible, throughout the day. One great way to share this concept with your class is to present the visual shown earlier and then give students a few moments to brainstorm other examples of kindness as part of a think-pair-share exercise. I recommend creating an ongoing list that can serve as a long-term reference point. It's important to brainstorm examples of kind acts that can be done in school as well as those that can be performed outside of school with family and friends. After introducing this Spotlight Day during our kickoff week, I like to follow up the following Tuesday morning by asking each child to select a specific kind act and commit to doing it sometime that day. Kids are excited by this short-term endeavor and can gain immediate gratification for doing a kind act for someone else.

Creating a "Looks Like/Sounds Like" chart is another terrific exercise to complete with your students so they know what exactly they might see or hear when people are being kind to one another. Sharing brief articles and showing short videos can also deepen student understanding of kindness. (Of course, you can use these strategies for the other Spotlight Days as well.)

In an earlier chapter, I shared how author Stephen Covey once said that after every interaction we have with other people, we leave something behind. Hopefully, that something is kindness, positivity, and joy. Discussing this idea with children helps them understand the power that our words and actions can have on our classmates, teachers, family, and friends. Before students begin any pair or group activity, encourage everyone to show kindness, patience, and understanding with their partners. At the conclusion of these activities, or in the last few moments before recess, lunch, or the end of the day, add to your ongoing list of examples or "Looks Like/Sounds Like" charts or ask for volunteers to share aloud something that someone did that day that made their day better.

> **Box 8.4 Spotlight Day 3: Empowering Wednesday**
>
>
>
> *Spotlight Day 3: Empowering Wednesday*
> ★ Feel confident and powerful as a student.
> ★ Try to do more and more things independently.
> ★ Take charge of your learning to a greater degree and be a problem-solver.

Since this chapter focuses on empowerment and already contains suggestions for bringing this concept to life in the classroom, I would like to use this space to recommend "Stuck on an Escalator," a hilarious YouTube video you can watch with your students. When the escalator that two adults are riding on their way to work shuts down, they become completely helpless and complain without doing anything to solve their problem. Kids love the absurdity of this situation, and showing them the opposite of empowerment helps them better understand what the concept truly means. I recommend watching the video two to three weeks after you've introduced this third Spotlight Day. The viewing experience sets the stage for an engaging follow-up conversation.

> **Box 8.5 Spotlight Day 4: Serve It Up Thursday**
>
>
>
> *Spotlight Day 4: Serve It Up Thursday*
> ★ Look for ways to help one of your classmates.
> ★ Find a way to help your teacher or another adult at school.
> ★ Do chores at home to help out your family.

When designing our distance learning schedule for the 2020–21 school year, my district built in a 20-minute period at the end of each day for teachers to meet with their English-language learners in a small group setting, while the rest of the class began their asynchronous work. I was supposed to have two English-language learners on my roster. Just prior to the first day of school, however, within a 24-hour period, I received emails from both families saying they were going to head back home to Europe for the duration of the pandemic. (Not the first time parents have fled the country upon discovering their children would be in my class.)

Without any English-language learners, I received permission to use that time to provide additional help to students as soon as a need arose. During one week in the fall, I met with three children to focus on improving the structure of their personal essays. A fourth child, whom we will call Serena, asked if she could join us and work one-on-one in a breakout room with a member of the small group to offer personalized assistance.

That kind of gesture is the essence of "Serve It Up Thursday"—a fourth Spotlight Day that focuses on service. With Serena's permission, I told the rest of the class about her kind act the following morning. Soon, other kids made the same offer, and whenever possible, I implemented this form of peer tutoring because the benefits of this type of service are so powerful, for both those providing the assistance and those receiving it. Children's understanding of academic material increases when they teach it to others, and students often learn more effectively when someone their age (who speaks their "language") is doing the explaining. Service increases class bonding, strengthens teamwork, and boosts self-esteem. Plus, taking some time to help a classmate, because we care and because we want to, simply feels good.

We can help the idea of service spread throughout our classes by brainstorming a variety of examples, creating and reviewing ongoing lists, and encouraging students to look for opportunities to be of service at school and at home. Pointing out examples of service in books we read and articles we come across also helps kids get excited about serving others. Our goal as educators is to create a classroom culture in which service matters and where service is practiced and valued.

Box 8.6 Spotlight Day 5: Gratitude Friday

Spotlight Day 5: Gratitude Friday
- ★ Be grateful for all the positive things in your life.
- ★ Thank a member of your family for everything they do for you.
- ★ Thank someone at school for the work they do to help you.
- ★ Thank a friend for the kind things they do for you.

In 2011, Shawn Achor, CEO of Good Think Inc., delivered an inspiring TED Talk titled "The Happy Secret to Better Work." A big idea in his 12-minute presentation is that in our society people tend to believe that we should work hard in order to be happy. Achor suggests that this way of thinking could be backward. He argues that happiness makes us more productive, creative, and successful. In short, happiness should come first. At the end of his talk, Achor shares some strategies that people can use to focus on the positive aspects of their lives and become happier.

My favorite suggestion is one that I've used with my students for the past few years. Achor asserts that individuals who try this idea for 21 straight days can train themselves to think differently about their lives and actually re-wire their brains. I don't think Achor was speaking specifically to a group of educators, but I think teachers everywhere can benefit from his approach.

His idea involves thinking of things in our lives for which we are grateful. Each day we think of three new ideas, and over time we realize just how much we have in our lives to be grateful for. For three weeks each school year, I have conducted this "Happiness Project" at the end of our morning routine. I give everyone a minute of "quiet think time" to come up with their "three gratitudes" and then ask for volunteers to share one or more of their ideas with the class.

During the first few days, volunteers tend to mention such things as family, friends, school, food, and shelter. I originally thought the kids might have difficulty generating new ideas after the first week, but that has never happened. Instead, when we encourage everyone to think more deeply and focus on various aspects of their lives, large and small, they share amazing gratitudes.

I have seen the Happiness Project lead to positive changes in students' moods, attitudes, and productivity, especially with kids who have a tendency to pout or complain when things don't go their way. Of course, informing parents about this project and encouraging follow-up at home strengthens the power of this activity.

There are three "teaching moves" I make when leading this exercise that I believe yield important benefits. First, when I introduce the activity each morning, I start by announcing the "day number" and the number of ideas we have generated thus far. On day 10, for example, I say that we are thinking of gratitudes 28, 29, and 30. That seems to resonate with the kids, and I think they realize to a greater degree how fortunate we all are when we can find that many positive things in our lives.

Second, I try to share examples from my own life. One time I told the kids I was at a concert the night before and felt so happy to see one of my favorite bands. Right at that moment, I thought of three things about that night that made me grateful, and I was excited to share them the next day in class. When the kids heard that I planned my list the night before, they got excited and came in the next couple of days with great ideas ready to share.

Finally, during the three weeks of our Happiness Project, anytime I meet one-on-one with students who appear to be sad or lacking confidence, I don't start talking about the task at hand right away. Instead, I first ask them to tell me their three gratitudes from that morning. Doing that seems to bolster their spirits, and then we can address the schoolwork.

Transitioning from the "15 consecutive school day" structure to a weekly "Gratitude Friday" is a smooth process. I recommend starting by introducing the visual shown in Figure 8.9 and describing Achor's "Happiness Project." Then, the kids can jump right in with their first three gratitudes. If you wish, and if you have the time, everyone can write their gratitudes in a notebook or journal so they can keep adding to their lists for the next few Fridays. Putting their ideas on paper will also help everyone remember their gratitudes from one week to the next and avoid repeating any. Providing time for your students to elaborate on their gratitudes, perhaps add drawings, and then discuss their ideas with a partner or small group is also useful. At the end of the activity, volunteers can share their gratitudes with the whole class.

With this "weekly spotlight approach," the kids wouldn't be thinking of their gratitudes on consecutive days, as Achor suggests, but I don't see that as a big deal. Continue for as many Fridays as you wish—enough to provide an in-depth experience, but not so many that the activity loses meaning. Even though your students will be adding gratitudes only once a week, I still suggest beginning each session with the "day number" and "gratitude numbers."

When the initiative concludes, we can use it as a reference point for the remainder of the year. The Happiness Project becomes something we can revisit on a regular basis to help us build and maintain a sense of gratitude in our lives. During those inevitable times when things don't go our way and the bad seems to outweigh the good, we can remember coming up with a few dozen positive things for which each of us feels grateful. The goal is for that realization to help us ride out the challenging times and maintain a positive attitude, even when it can be difficult to do so.

Here's another suggestion for how we can build the idea of gratitude into the fabric of our classrooms. Before opening a math lesson, for example, or starting a new piece of work, stop for a moment and acknowledge how fortunate we all are to be able to do what we are about to do. Voice an idea, such as: "I'm grateful for the opportunity to solve this problem, conduct this science investigation, or read this book because I know not everyone has this opportunity. I know that many kids around the world may not have the books, supplies, or technology that we do, and I appreciate our situation." A statement like that will set a tremendous tone as your group begins the learning.

Closing Thought: If it ever comes up, please emphasize to your students that even though Spotlight Days focus on only one concept per day, we should make an effort to act in these ways every day. That way, a child will never say, "Oh, I'm supposed to be nice to people on Wednesdays? I thought kindness was just a Tuesday thing."

Note

http://www.ted.com/talks/shawn_achor_the_happy_secret_to_better_work.html

Reference List

Reifman, S. (2013). *Math Problem Solving Menus*. Author.

9

Improvement

I may be dating myself, but it wasn't *that* long ago when accessing the internet required a small modem and big patience. After dialing up a phone number, I would cross my fingers and hope it wouldn't be too long before that distinctive combination of beeps and white noise arrived to indicate a successful attempt. Connecting could take several minutes and was never a guarantee. Fast-forward approximately 30 years. Nowadays, children will describe a 2-second lag in internet access as "forever." Technology has exploded in recent decades, and with that rapid progress have come higher standards and increased expectations for what we, as a society, deem acceptable and desirable.

Technology, of course, is not the only area that has seen rising standards and loftier expectations. Sports is another. Baseball pitchers are throwing harder, pole vaulters are soaring higher, and swimmers and runners are getting faster. In swimming, for instance, race times that would have earned Olympic gold medals a few decades ago no longer earn athletes a spot on their nation's team. College admissions is a third area. Grade point averages, test scores, and number of high school honors classes keep increasing for incoming freshman cohorts, and student profiles that would have once earned a high school senior a spot at the college of their choice no longer merit admission. Taken together, these examples illustrate that what was once good enough to survive and succeed in our society often no longer suffices.

As standards, expectations, and circumstances change all across our landscape, we must adapt to keep pace. Our success as individuals and as a society depends on our ability to learn and improve. Continuous improvement is one of the central tenets of W. Edwards Deming's quality philosophy and a hallmark of whole-child teaching. Although progress in a given area tends to be measured in numerical terms, I believe continuous improvement is primarily a way of thinking. An attitude, a mindset. The Japanese have a word for it, *kaizen*, meaning the spirit of continuous improvement. At the beginning of each school year, it's important for us, as educators, to build this spirit into our classroom culture and encourage children to find a way to get a little bit better at what they do every day. Our goal involves helping students understand that the world around us demands improvement and that committing to this pursuit has value—it feels good, generates an incredible sense of pride and satisfaction, and serves as the primary vehicle that empowers us to produce quality work and fulfill our amazing potential. There's a certain thrill and confidence we experience when we realize we are achieving at a higher level with our habits and skills than we were just a short time ago, and we want kids to pursue and embrace that feeling.

Introducing Children to Continuous Improvement

I first introduce the concept of continuous improvement to my students early each school year during our *Leo the Late Bloomer* read-aloud and follow-up discussion. As I mentioned in Chapter 2, once the kids learn all the ways Leo blooms, I ask for volunteers who wish to share an important academic area in which they want to bloom during our time together. My objective with this exercise is to whet the children's appetite for the learning we'll do throughout the year and build excitement about getting better at something personally meaningful. When I ask everyone what they "want to bloom in the most," I'm really trying to determine how they want to improve. Previously, I shared my belief that improvement cannot be forced. The desire to learn and grow must come from inside, from the children themselves. In my view, the more we create a sense of excitement with our words and actions and the more we nurture students' intrinsic motivation, the greater that desire will become.

My next effort to convey the importance of continuous improvement comes from the work of author Christopher Whittle, whose *Crash Course* (2005) inspired my e-book *2-Minute Biographies for Kids*. One of the important topics Whittle addresses is student engagement. In our quest to make schools more engaging and exciting places for kids, he suggests that educators look closely at children's favorite activities outside of school and try to incorporate features of those activities into the school day. Right at the top of the list: video games. When playing video games, kids are never bored. They are engrossed in a current level that's neither too easy nor too difficult. The amount of challenge is just right. As soon as players succeed at a given level and move eagerly to the next, they feel on top of the world, and they want to feel that way again. The quest to advance to higher levels is exciting and motivating. Children display impressive determination to conquer the demands of one level and advance to the next. Once players achieve a new level, they want to keep "leveling up." Kids love the term "leveling up." Because this term resonates with children on a deep level, it provides a great entry point for introducing and discussing the concept of improvement.

Of course, schools are not video games. That doesn't mean, however, that we can't make schools *more like* video games by integrating the concept of "leveling up" into our daily classroom learning. Doing so enables us to realize the same psychological, enthusiasm, and motivational benefits that the quest to level up in a video game produces. Over the years, I have identified three primary ways to structure student learning through the use of levels. The first involves independent reading. My school has adopted the well-known Fountas and Pinnell system to level the books our students read. Each year our staff encourages everyone to embrace the challenge of trying to advance multiple levels, and kids feel tremendous pride and satisfaction every time they pass a reading assessment.

I'd like to add a note of caution at this point. In Chapter 6, I shared how the use of extrinsic rewards can have the effect of reducing important tasks and activities to mere stepping stones as children become laser-focused on acquiring prizes. In the process, a great deal of exploration, thinking, joy, and learning can be lost. If we are not careful, the same can be true if we reduce the awesomeness of reading, and other academic areas, to a mere sprint from one level to another for the sake of accelerating improvement. We need to be mindful of these potential dangers. Of course, we want kids to enjoy reading for its own sake and become immersed in the texts they encounter and connect with the characters, storylines, and themes. Books offer incredible experiences full of emotion, wonder, richness, and adventure. As teachers, we want to preserve these entities at all costs and encourage children to improve their skills at the same time. We can do both.

A second example of how to incorporate "leveling up" into classroom learning involves the addition, subtraction, multiplication, and division facts that my students are expected to learn by June. Every two weeks my students take a 50-problem quiz focused on one of these operations. The kids have 2 1/2 minutes to complete all the problems. The quizzes are sequenced to create a four-level "video game." Everyone begins with addition. Those scoring 49 or 50 pass the quiz and advance to subtraction. Students who score below 49 continue taking the addition quiz until they pass. The process is entirely self-paced, and just like in a video game, students advance to the next level once they have mastered the current one.

Until recently, my students used a basic "Math Facts Progress Sheet" to record the date of each quiz and their scores. The sheet contained four sections, one for each operation, with enough space in each section for everyone to record the results of several quizzes. There was nothing wrong with this sheet, but there was nothing particularly interesting or motivating about it either.

Then, I created the format shown in Figure 9.1 and noticed an immediate change in my students. They got a kick out of the baseball theme and loved the "hitting a home run" metaphor in which each passed quiz represents another base on their trip around the diamond. Rounding each base was like mastering the next level of a video game. The new format seemed to resonate with my students in a lasting way.

In addition to the baseball diamond image, the new sheet also includes three features not found on the original one. Once the students recorded the date and score after each quiz, I would meet with them individually to share their projected score for next time. (Each meeting is super quick.) I based these projections on the "typical" jumps students have made in the past with these operations, usually 5–10 problems. Once a student saw my projection, I asked what their goal was for the next quiz. Here's where we, as teachers, have a tremendous opportunity to help kids develop a championship mindset by choosing a goal that's higher than the projection. By encouraging everyone to do this, we help create an environment in which we reach for the stars and hold high expectations for ourselves. The hope is that higher expectations lead to more diligent studying. Finally, the section at the bottom enables us and our students to write notes, share strategy suggestions, and record any feedback we discussed during our one-on-one meetings.

I created an item for TeachersPayTeachers that contains a few variations of the baseball diamond sheet I described. That way, you can use the baseball diamond format without the projection and goal sections, should you wish to do so, create headings of your own, and even use the sheet for other academic areas. (You can find a printable version of the math baseball diamond on the Routledge site.)

A final example of how to incorporate "leveling up" into classroom learning represents my attempt to solve one of the most vexing challenges new teachers face: how to keep children productively occupied and engaged when they complete their main math activity early. Whenever my students finish their daily math activity before the end of the period, they proceed directly to their Math Problem Solving Menus. Since I discovered this idea several years ago, it has been one of the most effective parts of our overall

Name:

Figure 9.1 "Baseball Diamond" math facts progress sheet.

math curriculum. Each menu is a sheet with four open-ended story problems that call on students to employ a wide variety of strategies.

There are nine menus in the set, and the kids strive to complete as many of the nine as possible by the end of the year. The menus begin with straightforward, multi-step problems involving addition and subtraction. From there, the menus increase in difficulty and complexity. Many of the problems connect to and extend concepts we are learning in class, while others feature concepts and require strategies that go beyond our state's content standards.

Using Math Problem Solving Menus helps me accomplish four primary objectives. First, the menus keep my students productively engaged and occupied during the entire math period. Many times, kids can lose focus at the end of a math period because they know they have completed the important work and think that anything they do after that is less important. That doesn't happen with the menus.

Second, many of the menu problems offer valuable reinforcement, extra practice, and meaningful review of important content that we learned earlier in the year. Plus, because each menu problem features an engaging story or situation, the kids are applying their skills and using them in context.

Third, the menus are differentiated. Because high-achieving math students tend to finish daily math work faster than their classmates, they will spend more time working on their menus and progress to the more difficult ones sooner. Kids who struggle with core concepts usually spend less time on their menus, and that's okay, because these students need more time to master the basics. So in a typical math period, everyone is working at an appropriate level of challenge for the entire time. (Note: Students who aren't spending much class time on their menus are welcome to take them home so that they don't lose out on this valuable experience, and many children have done so over the years.)

Finally, because each menu is part of the larger set of nine, there is a yearlong cohesiveness to this activity. The progression from one menu to the next is designed to resemble the move from one video game level to the next. As I mentioned previously, the step-by-step nature of video games ensures that kids are optimally challenged and never bored. Progressing through the nine menus offers children this same experience in school. In addition, it promotes goal setting and an achievement orientation. Trying to complete all nine menus before the end of the year becomes a meaningful, shared classroom goal.

Math Problem-Solving Menus are the focus of another item I created for TeachersPayTeachers. The pdf contains the menus themselves, along with the template students use to complete the steps of our process, a scoring rubric, answer key, and implementation suggestions. I also published this resource as an ebook on Amazon.com (2013). (You can find a printable copy of the Problem-Solving Organizer, the first three menus, and the answer key for these menus on the Routledge website.)

Look for ways to harness the power of "leveling up" with your students. If the independent reading, math fact, and math problem-solving examples fit your pedagogical style and are appropriate for the age and grade you teach, consider implementing them in your classroom. Try to find others as well. Structuring learning through the use of levels promises significant benefits in terms of engagement, motivation, and performance.

Continuous Improvement: Key Principles

The remainder of this chapter focuses on useful principles, practices, and tools we can employ throughout the year to maximize our opportunities to promote continuous improvement in the classroom. Continuous improvement is an indispensable component of learning environments that embrace quality as a top priority. Through the following examples I examine the concept of improvement on the individual and class level, pertaining to both process and product and addressing a variety of whole-child objectives. Let's begin with a set of key improvement principles.

Cultivate a Growth Mindset

In an article posted in *Entrepreneur* on December 17, 2012 (17 Dec 12), Jennifer Foster relays a well-known story in which a man encounters an elephant tethered to a small post with a short piece of rope. The observer is shocked that this big, strong creature doesn't simply break the rope and escape his predicament. The man asks the elephant's trainer how such a thin rope could possibly contain the animal. The trainer shares that the elephant was unable to break the rope as a baby and developed the enduring belief that he would never be able to break the rope, even though the creature now clearly possessed the power to do so. Foster points out that although the elephant had grown physically, "his mindset kept him believing" that a different outcome was impossible. The animal had concluded there was no point in ever trying again. Foster refers to this limiting way of thinking as the "elephant mindset."

Stanford psychologist Carol Dweck, author of *Mindset: The New Psychology of Success* (2007), uses a different term to describe the elephant's outlook—a *fixed mindset*. Throughout my career, I have learned that even at young ages, many children have adopted a fixed mindset regarding their skills, aptitudes, and potential. During our private conversations, these kids have expressed their belief that, for example, they have never understood math or been good at reading and figure that will always be the case. Children operating under a fixed mindset paradigm think that since they're not good at some things now, it's never going to change. Sadly, it's not uncommon for students to utter statements such as "I've never been good at reading," "Writing isn't my thing," or "I'm not a math person."

To create a classroom culture of continuous improvement, educators must strongly counter manifestations of a fixed mindset and, instead, promote the development of a growth mindset, another powerful concept Dweck describes. It's important to introduce students to these opposing ways of thinking early each school year. We raise awareness of these concepts through the same vehicles I have mentioned when referring to other culture-building priorities: modeling, storytelling, read-alouds, videos, recognizing student successes, and capitalizing on learnable moments. Before we can focus on specific improvement practices in our classrooms, kids need to embrace the larger idea that improvement is always possible. Children need to know that with hard work, belief, and determination, tomorrow can always be better than today, our next assessment score can always be higher than our last, and our past performances don't have to limit or dictate our future efforts. Progress is always possible. When we invest our hearts and minds in a sincere effort to improve, such change is not just possible; it's inevitable.

Should you ever hear a child express a negative belief about their skills, aptitude, or potential, respond with one of the most powerful words we have in our teaching vocabularies—*yet*. Student: "I'm not good at subtracting large numbers." Teacher: "You may not feel that you're very good *yet*." Using this word consistently will lead to its spread throughout your classroom. You may even hear the children using it in their conversations with one another. *Yet* reaffirms a growth mindset and unconditional belief. *Yet* focuses not on what students might be capable of doing now but well into the future. *Yet* takes a long-term view of student learning. *Yet* conveys confidence. *Yet* expresses a belief in future learning, future production, and future achievement. Later in this chapter, I will describe a teaching practice we can incorporate that brings to life the "power of yet" in a tangible way.

Foster a Realistic View of Improvement

In addition to promoting a growth mindset, another service we can provide students involves fostering a realistic sense of how the improvement process typically works. Quite often, children who commit themselves to continuous improvement expect massive jumps in performance to occur quickly and expect that progress to continue without setbacks. To counter these notions, it's important for us to convey two important points: (1) Improvement is usually achieved through small, incremental steps, and (2) human progress is not linear. Let's explore both of these ideas on a deeper level, beginning in the next paragraph with a focus on incremental improvement.

Imagine a student earns a score of 10 out of 50 on an addition facts quiz and sets a goal to reach 50 out of 50. That's an admirable, ambitious goal, though it's unlikely the child would achieve it by the next quiz. Expecting to score a 50 on the heels of a 10 would likely overwhelm the student and create stress. Our role in this process is to encourage the setting of reasonable short-term goals and recognize incremental improvement from week to week. Whereas the child may view a follow-up score of 23 as a failure, we point out an increase of 13 problems—meaningful progress. A 31 on the following quiz would represent another step in the right direction. Every step forward shrinks the original gap.

As students achieve short-term successes, they develop a hunger for more success. Initial success fuels the desire for more success. Throughout this process, kids feel better about themselves and take greater pride in their work. Their confidence increases. They begin to believe they can do hard things and achieve demanding goals. By recognizing the value of improvement and emphasizing it constantly, we break the long journey toward the accomplishment of these goals into more manageable trips, empowering children to work hard, persevere, and perform to their potential. The spirit of continuous improvement takes students from where they start to where they want to get.

Share with your class any stories you hear about the value of incremental progress. In the past I have told my students about Major League Baseball executives who traded the 24th man on a 26-player roster for a slight upgrade at the backup catcher position, car companies that implemented a few dozen employee suggestions to create its next model, and businesses who improved their profitability by shaving a few cents off their costs. Celebrate the small jumps. They add up to produce large results.

Let's shift our focus to the idea of linear versus non-linear improvement. The diagonal arrow shown in Figure 9.2 represents an ideal "growth path." The arrow climbs steadily higher, without any pauses or dips along the way. We need to explain to our classes that progress in a given endeavor doesn't generally proceed on that trajectory. The reason: We're human beings. Inevitably, despite our best efforts and intentions, we plateau, we have lags, we have off days. A more realistic picture of improvement can be seen in the "lightning bolt" image underneath the arrow. Strong upward movement, followed by a small dip, with that pattern repeating a few times. Raising students' awareness of this view of improvement can help everyone manage their expectations, offer reassurance, and keep spirits high when an inevitable dip occurs. Kids need to understand that in the face of a setback, there's no reason to panic. We are still on the right track.

Understanding the "human path" to improvement also enables us to steer our classes through behavioral rough patches that occur throughout the school year. Sometimes these stretches happen at predictable times, such as the week or two before an extended break, the afternoons that follow standardized testing sessions, and windy or rainy days. Oh, and Halloween.

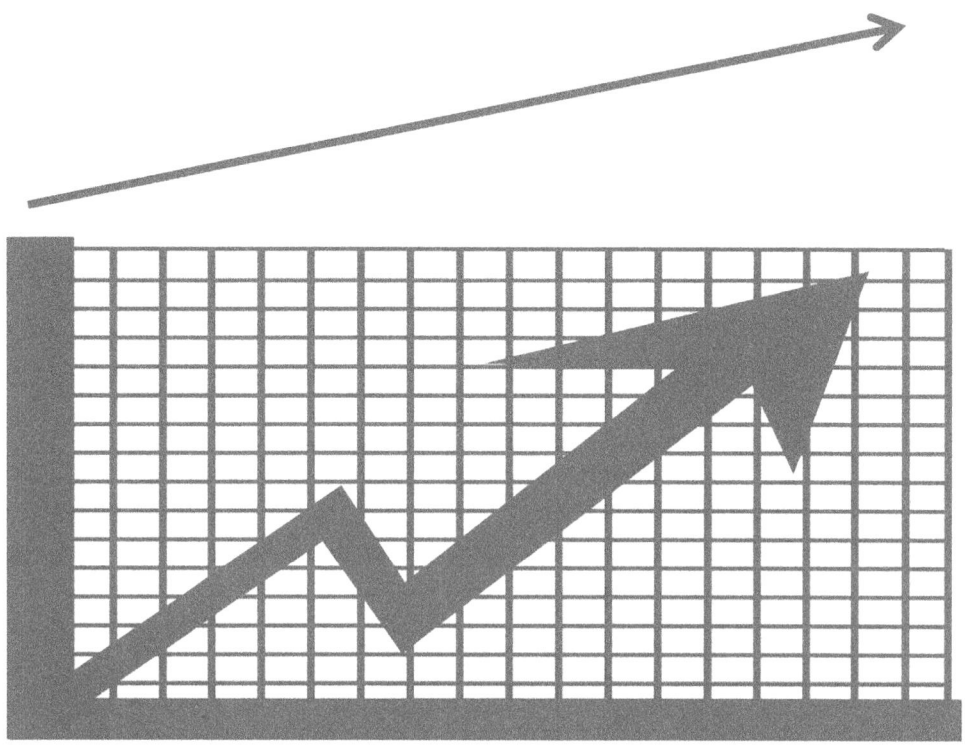

Figure 9.2 Linear and non-linear improvement.

Other times, difficult moments can arise out of nowhere with no clear cause. If we can be that wise leader who sees the big picture and doesn't overreact to these situations, because we know they are simply speed bumps on the road to improvement, we can stay calm and cool and ride it out, without letting the behaviors we're witnessing ruin our day or lead us to become overly punitive.

One of my favorite examples of this type of situation took place nearly 25 years ago. Usually, I teach every class of students for one year, but because of some enrollment oddities, many of the kids were with me for a second year. Ours was a combined group of third and fourth graders. As a whole, this class was incredibly well-behaved. But on the day in question, very little seemed to go right. Many kids were out of their seats during independent work time, others were off task, and there seemed to be a great deal of distraction. (And it wasn't even Halloween.) I remember this day vividly. When my most well-behaved students started participating in the mayhem, I knew it was just one of those days. I took a deep breath and decided to take a step back and watch, almost as an outside observer. After a while, I called everyone to the rug. Tempting as it might be sometimes to yell, blame, or lecture,

I was able to stay calm and remind myself that human progress isn't linear. I pointed out what I was noticing, and I held the group accountable, but I was able to do so with some emotional detachment. As teachers, if we can address moments such as these using wisdom, experience, and perhaps a bit of humor as our guide, it's better for us and sends a tremendous message to children about how to handle difficulties as thoughtful leaders and problem solvers.

Encourage Personal Bests

Once students commit themselves to continuous improvement, it is very common for them to become competitive with their classmates. Each year I strongly emphasize to my group that never will they hear me compare one person's assessment score, reading level, or any other academic measure with somebody else's. Why? First, public comparisons have a destructive impact on the child with the lower score and create an uncomfortable feeling for everyone involved. The self-esteem damage that comes from being on the short end of a public comparison announced by a teacher can last forever. Two cases in point. Seventh-grade algebra and college philosophy. I can describe both situations in vivid detail and quote the speakers' exact words, even though these events occurred more than three decades ago. Regularly comparing ourselves to others can decrease joy and enthusiasm for learning and affect our willingness to participate in future endeavors. Second, public comparison sends the wrong message about what our culture is all about. Rather than promoting cooperation and teamwork, comparisons signal competition. All of a sudden, children can start to see classmates as rivals and threats instead of friends and resources.

To avoid the powerful negative effects of competition and bring the best out in our students, we fill our classroom environment with the spirit of personal bests. That means, we dedicate ourselves to putting forth maximum effort, day in and day out. Along the way, we have fun finding out how good we can become at any given activity or in any given area. Our goal is to be better "every next time," to set a standard the first time we engage in an activity and then attempt to exceed or surpass that performance in the future. If we want to compete, we do so with only ourselves. I once heard someone remark that real victories lie not with outdoing others but with trying our best, arriving at the finish line with no regrets, and accepting the consequences, satisfied by the fact we gave it everything we had.

As part of our messaging to students, we need to be direct and honest about the fact that in any endeavor, there will be some people who are more skilled and talented or who are just better than we are, and others who are not as good. That's how life is, whether we are talking about singing, painting, running, soccer, or any of the thousands of other activities we may attempt.

I often share the example of 5K races I used to run. Whether I crossed the finish line before the others in my vicinity is irrelevant. They're them, and I'm me. What matters is whether I ran the best I could that day and, perhaps, whether I set a new personal best time.

Of course, no matter how strongly we discourage kids from caring about their classmates' scores after an assessment, they will remain curious. We can't change that. What we can do is emphasize personal bests and discourage the temptation to care how everyone else did. They're them. We're us. The only meaningful competition is the one with ourselves.

Facilitate Peer-Inspired Improvement
This section builds on the previous notion of personal bests. When I emphasize to children the importance of putting forth our best effort and avoiding the urge to outperform our classmates, that doesn't mean each of us has to go it alone. Quite the opposite. As teachers, we can facilitate a positive peer dynamic in which every child seeks out opportunities to learn from, inspire, and serve as a meaningful influence on their classmates. We can join forces in our learning while avoiding the harmful effects of competition.

The goal-setting process from the previous chapter is a prime example of this phenomenon. I described how many kids started bringing lists of goals and self-assessment sheets to class following their Parent Conferences. As we shared these creations and discussed how we could make these resources even more useful, more and more students kept building on their classmates' ideas. The spirit of improvement and innovation was amazing. The kids were designing their own sheets, yet the process was truly a team effort. Every day the quality of student output kept elevating, not in a competitive way, but in a let's-raise-the-bar-together-and-see-where-this-can-go type of way.

With this grassroots approach, improvements arise organically and powerful ideas and practices spread on their own. Students commit themselves to this endeavor because they see the value in it, not because we are establishing mandates. I also mentioned in the previous chapter that when the kids are learning from one another, innovating, and finding ways to take their work to the next level, it is one of the best things that can happen in a classroom.

Fortunately, opportunities present themselves across the curriculum to capitalize on the infectious energy that fills the room as students take an idea and run with it. Math problem-solving strategies, responses to literature, and story writing techniques in Writing Workshop represent just a few of these possibilities. Our role is to keep an eye out for interesting, novel strategies and techniques and share them with the group. Instructions such as, "Check out how Heather described the setting of her story" and "Look closely at how Omar solved this multi-step word problem" draw the children in and get the gears in their minds turning. Facilitating this kind of peer-inspired improvement is yet another reminder of how teamwork empowers the whole to become greater than the sum of the parts.

Appreciate the Harmony Between the Individual and the Group
During the first year of my career, I was meeting one morning with my mentor teacher who noticed the Student of the Week certificate displayed on the wall. A mild look of disapproval appeared on her face. "Steve," she began, "at this school we focus more on the group as a whole than the individual." Those words surprised me, and I was taken aback. I had never before encountered the notion that a conflict existed between the needs of the individual and those of the group. Rather than view these two entities as mutually exclusive, I had always believed them to be mutually beneficial and enriching. In terms of continuous improvement, we want to promote the growth and development of each individual and the class as a collective. Both of these "lenses" demand our full attention.

To capture my commitment to foster both individual and team improvement, I coined the term the "Metallica Principle." When I mention during my workshop presentations that I'm a big believer in the "Metallica Principle," eyebrows tend to rise throughout the room, and people think that my students and I blast heavy metal music during math time or bang our heads during the playing of our school song. (Though both options are tempting, neither is true. At least not yet.) I created this concept many years ago after watching a 1998 "Behind the Music" documentary about the band and hearing a story shared by lead singer James Hetfield. Members of the group, according to Hetfield, were becoming extremely frustrated during the recording of one of their albums because he was dictating, down to the note, exactly how everyone was to play their instruments, leaving them no freedom, flexibility, or opportunity to offer input. From this process, Hetfield realized that for the band, as a whole, to thrive, everyone's ideas and involvement mattered. Nobody wants to have their actions tightly controlled or their initiative stifled. Everyone had to perform their roles in a way that felt right to them and made them happy. Motivated, empowered band members led to a motivated, empowered band.

In the classroom, the Metallica Principle simply means that for the group to be enthusiastic, productive, and successful, every student must be valued as an irreplaceable team member because of the ideas, energy, and uniqueness they bring to the group. The goal of personalizing each child's school experience (the focus of the next chapter) begins with this understanding. Dedicating ourselves to facilitating both individual and group improvement and fulfillment offers a win–win situation to everyone involved. As we help each child improve their behavior, for example, the behavior of the entire class also improves, making our independent work time and instructional lessons smoother and more enjoyable. Fostering the reading growth of each child leads to deeper and richer class discussions. The same idea holds true for every other academic area. A rising tide lifts all boats.

"Coach 'Em Up"

The final key principle in this section is actually more than a key principle. It represents the essence of our mission to bring the best out of each child, foster continuous improvement, and empower children to reach their amazing potential. Borrowed from the world of sports, "Coach 'Em Up" is a term that describes our daily quest to help children achieve incremental progress with their academics, behavior, and other whole-child priorities. Much as athletic coaches do with their players, we embrace the opportunity to work closely with each individual child, one-on-one, meeting them where they are and proceeding from there, bit by bit. Our goal is to make the most of each day and facilitate small jumps. Baby steps. A new reading strategy here. Better understanding of a math concept there. A more consistent work ethic one day. Improved listening the next. These incremental moves may seem minor on any given day, but they add up to massive achievements over the course of an entire school year.

"Coaching 'Em Up" can be one of the most fulfilling aspects of our job while also being one of the most challenging, sometimes frustrating. There are times when the work can seem tedious and repetitive, and signs of progress are difficult to find. It can be a grind. Some days we feel like a million dollars; others we may bang our heads against a wall, but we commit to this ongoing process because we trust that setbacks will be temporary and accomplishments will be lasting. Most victories in teaching are private ones, and we savor these moments. When obstacles arise, we learn from them, problem-solve, and strive to do better the next day.

The one-on-one time we spend with kids, coaching 'em up, often produces some of the best bonding moments we will experience in the classroom. Each day, one meeting at a time, we embark on a quest together, overcome obstacles together, and perhaps achieve results students didn't think were possible. My favorite example of this phenomenon came while working on a phonics activity with a few first graders during my initial year of teaching. One boy, whom we'll call Jesse, experienced significant difficulty with the focus of the lesson and screamed out, "I am the stupidest kid in the world." Then, for the only time in my 28-year career, I raised my voice to a child—100% intentionally. I replied, "No, you're not." My instinct told me that Jesse needed to hear a sharp rebuke to what he had just said, and I trusted my instinct. In the weeks that followed, I coached Jesse up as well as I could. Then, all his reading practice culminated in a beautiful moment one day when, in a similar small-group setting, something clicked in his mind and he shouted, "I am the smartest kid in the world!" Priceless.

The primary challenge regarding one-on-one "Coach 'Em Up" sessions involves finding the time to lead them. These meetings can only occur when the rest of the class is productively occupied and we can focus our attention on just one child. Achieving this level of independence may take several weeks. A necessary step in this process involves emphasizing to the kids how important and valuable these one-on-one sessions are for everyone's development. Of course, we want children focused on their work because it's critical for their personal growth. We also want everyone to realize that being independent and quiet is a sign of courtesy toward the student next to me, a favor that will be returned when it's their turn. I attempt to conduct most one-on-one sessions during our daily independent reading period because that's the time when the kids are most engaged and least likely to need assistance. Independent work time during math and Writing Workshop offers other potential meeting times, but these periods are not as reliable since we will frequently need to help students. In preparation for these meetings, I keep recent student work samples nearby so I can seize opportunities as they present themselves. My quest to meet one-on-one with kids takes on greater urgency after I have scored a round of math assessments or writing pieces and want to provide feedback in as timely a manner as possible. During these periods, I have student papers stacked up and ready to go. I do my best to conduct as many meetings as I can in the time I have available, without rushing or stressing.

Continuous Improvement: Key Practices

In this section I offer practical, tangible ways to bring to life the principles described in the previous section. These practices have the potential to greatly impact academic learning, student enthusiasm, and classroom behavior.

Retakes

In his book *The Quality School Teacher* (1993), William Glasser encourages schools to adopt an evaluation system based on the notion of improvement. Using an approach he calls "concurrent evaluation," Glasser states that students should have frequent opportunities to meet with teachers to discuss their work. During these discussions, students explain what they have done and how they believe they can improve their work. After continuing to improve the work, the students repeat the evaluation, explaining how the revised piece of work represents an improvement over the prior one. Students stop the process when they believe that further attempts to improve the work will no longer bring about significant change. Glasser asserts that under this system, "students would learn much more than now and begin to do quality work." He goes on to say that "students would be better able to appreciate that education can increase the quality of their lives, and teachers would find their job much more enjoyable than they do now."

Students working in this type of classroom culture will become far more likely to want to improve their own work, far less likely to settle for less than their best, and far more aware of the learning gains they are making. The Habit of Character "pride" contributes greatly in the effort to build this mindset in students. Specifically, the parts of the definition relating to "caring deeply about my work" and "trying my best to improve" play a significant role in keeping this message alive and well throughout the school year.

Glasser's "concurrent evaluation" concept promotes the development of a growth mindset and takes full advantage of that wonderful three-letter word: *yet*. As I mentioned in Chapter 5, our overall academic goal is for children to produce quality work on a consistent basis. As William Glasser explains in *The Quality School* (1990), any piece of work at any given time can be described as either "quality" or "not yet quality." If the work conforms to our requirements for quality work, then that child may very well decide to stop at that point. But if the work can't yet be considered quality and quality is the expectation, then we need to ask that student, "Why would you want to stop now when this isn't yet your best work?" Posing this question to kids reinforces the high expectations we hold for our class and sends the subtle yet powerful message that all children are capable of producing quality if they are willing to invest the necessary time and effort. In this situation, improving work until it can accurately be called *quality work* should become a natural part of the way our classes conduct business.

Love isn't strong enough of a word to capture my feelings for Glasser's "concurrent evaluation" system. Over the years I have experimented with several ways to incorporate its spirit and substance into my classroom practice and achieved varying results, in terms of student success, ease of implementation, and my mental health. I have learned that implementing this approach with too many students and/or too many pieces of work at any given time can quickly become overwhelming. It can be difficult enough to keep up with every child's current academic work. Adding in the kids' attempts to improve previous work often gets to be too much.

To preserve the benefits of Glasser's approach while addressing its challenges, I streamlined this process to make the goals more achievable given the demands and time constraints of an elementary school classroom. Now, I guide my students' improvement efforts through the use of a simple, straightforward practice known as a "retake." To keep everything manageable, I focus exclusively on the areas of math and writing and allow retakes only on "major" pieces of work, not daily classwork. Specifically, I offer children the opportunity to do a retake after they complete each math assessment and published writing piece. If students earn a higher score on the retake, I happily count that higher score.

Here's how the process works. After the kids take a math assessment or publish a writing piece, I score both on a 4-point scale. Any student whose overall score falls below a 3 is eligible for a retake. It's awesome when children who have earned a 3 ask to do a retake to raise their score to a 4, but to keep things manageable, I offer retakes only to kids whose score is below standard or, in Glasser's words, whose work cannot yet be considered quality work. Once I am finished scoring a round of math assessments or published writing pieces, I review the work, one-on-one, with each student as part of my efforts to coach 'em up. That generally takes a few minutes per child. Depending on the conferring time I have available, this follow-up can take anywhere from a few days to a couple of weeks.

After concluding the one-on-one conferences, I email the parents whose children are eligible for a retake. Sometimes I will email the parents individually. Other times, I will send a group email. To preserve both parent and student confidentiality in a group email, I will not mention any child's name. In addition, I will send the message to myself and "bcc" all the parents. My decision on which type of email to send depends on how many kids are eligible for a retake and how much time I have available at that moment. When possible, though, individual emails are always preferred. Parents appreciate the personal attention, and as a result, their children are more likely to do a retake. Once I know which children are on board for the retake, I provide a reasonable period of time to complete it. Math retakes occur in class during silent reading time; students do writing retakes at home, ideally without adult assistance.

Without getting too deep in the weeds, I wanted to provide a few additional retake details. On a math assessment, the overall 1–4 score is determined by averaging the 1–4 scores I give to each question. To make matters easier for the kids, they only need to retake the individual questions in which they scored a 1 or 2. It really doesn't make sense for anyone to redo a question in which they already earned a 3 or 4. Improving their scores on those problems enables students to improve their overall score. With regard to the writing, student work is scored on one or more rubrics, such as the Ideas and Conventions rubrics I presented in Chapter 5. When scoring student writing pieces, I underline or highlight the bullet points that reflect how well a given child does with regard to each of the performance indicators featured on the rubric. On the retake students revise their work by addressing any bullet point(s) that fall below a score of 3.

Offering retakes does require additional time on our part. I know that some teachers may not wish to score an assessment or writing project more than once, may not feel that students should receive a second chance, or believe that they should have studied harder or done better the first time around. I understand these sentiments. If we are truly devoted to the concept of continuous improvement, though, I believe that the additional time required to carry out this process is worth its weight in gold. The benefits that accrue in terms of student learning, motivation, perseverance, and pride are real and lasting. The more frequently kids produce work that rises to the level of quality, the better it is for their long-term growth and development. Retakes can help us increase this frequency.

Ideally, all children will jump at the opportunity for a retake every time we offer it and demonstrate the desire to retake a piece of work as many times as necessary to achieve quality. In my experience, though, that ideal is not yet reality. Some kids will, indeed, opt for a retake every chance they get, others won't, while still others will participate occasionally. I don't mandate retakes, but I do heavily encourage them. In my emails to parents and conversations with students, I try to avoid the temptation of guilt trips and hard sells and instead highlight the benefits of choosing to do a retake. I try to appeal to and tap into the intrinsic motivation to learn and grow that all children possess. In addition, I focus on how proud the children will feel when they improve their work and point out what an impressive sign of dedication it is when kids accept a retake invite. Afterward, if kids are able to improve the score to the level of quality, I make a big deal about recognizing their progress and commend them on choosing to take on additional work that they didn't have to do.

Analyze One Round of Assessment Results to Improve the Next

When my school adopted the Columbia Teachers College approach to Writing Workshop, I carefully read through the Units of Study to familiarize myself with the new curriculum. During that initial year, our writing calendar kicked off with Small Moment Narratives—true, personal stories that take place within a short time period, say, 5–15 minutes. This project enables children to bring their ideas to life with details and develop their stories bit by bit. To create an engaging narrative, students are expected to include a balance of the following "ingredients": character description, setting description, action, dialogue, and internal thinking. During the lessons that began each writing period, we learned the meaning of each term, studied samples from the unit overview, and participated in practice exercises as a group. A few weeks later, as I scored each child's published story, I identified the ingredients that featured prominently in the work (quality) as well as those that were either missing entirely or included in only a limited way (not yet quality).

Because the kids would produce a second Small Moment story in the next writing unit ("Improving the Quality of Personal Narratives"), my goal was to analyze the data I collected so I could focus my instruction in round 2 on the ingredients that needed the most attention. The data collection process was nothing fancy. I listed the ingredients on a sheet of paper and kept a simple tally as I read all the student work. When we began round 2, I explained my process to the class so they understood why we were spending more time on some ingredients than on others. Because the kids understood the need for this instruction, the group's focus during the lessons was strong, and the quality of their second Small Moment Narratives far exceeded that of the first.

It's perfectly fine if you explain the emphases of round 2 briefly and informally. Your students may be more engaged in this process, however, if you accompany your explanation with a visual. Showing the list of ingredients along with the tally you kept can be an effective option. That way, the class can see exactly why some ingredients will be receiving more instructional time than others. Since no child's name is included on this list, there are no confidentiality issues to worry about. Should you wish to take your visual presentation to a higher level, consider the Pareto chart, a quality tool named after Italian sociologist and economist Vilfredo Pareto. A Pareto chart represents data ranked by category. See the sample in Figure 9.3. Proceeding from left to right, the growth areas are listed in bar form from most to least common. As authors Barbara Cleary and Sally Duncan point out in their book *Tools and Techniques to Inspire Classroom Learning* (1997), this visual approach focuses attention on the right things. Please note that the sample I provide is not a "textbook" Pareto chart. For the sake of simplicity, I omitted the numerical information this tool typically contains.

Since that experience, I have tried to mine other opportunities in which my students would be completing similar, comparable, or related projects back-to-back. Examples include math problem-solving challenges, responses to literature, essay writing, and science investigations. Each time, I followed the same process: gathering data pertaining to strengths and growth areas after the initial effort so that I can improve instruction and boost performance the second time around. Without applying the lessons learned from one round to improve instruction the next, the kids would, in all likelihood, continue to encounter similar difficulties or make the same mistakes, and I would miss valuable opportunities to add value to their learning.

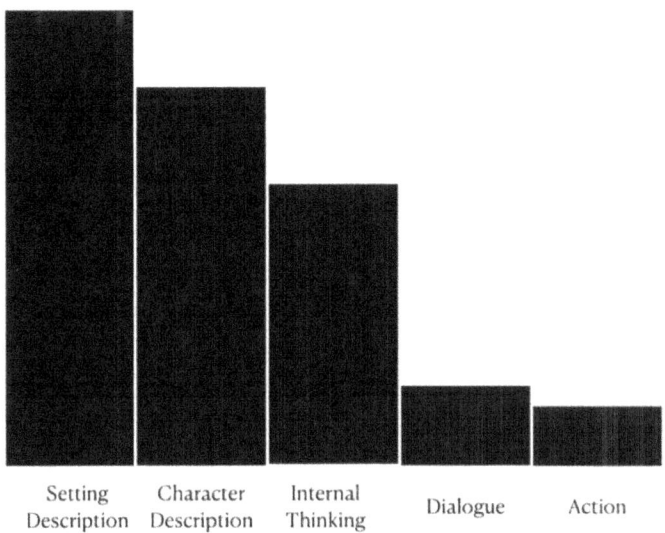

Figure 9.3 Pareto chart.

Engage Your Students in Group Brainstorming

In Chapter 4, I introduced my classroom's overall aim of "Increasing Learning While Increasing Enthusiasm." To determine how we are doing in our quest to boost enthusiasm, my students complete a short survey three to four times throughout the year. For each subject area, the kids choose either a happy face if they enjoy a subject, neutral face if it's "just okay," or sad face if they do not enjoy it. Ideally, every child will enjoy every subject by the end of the school year. Unfortunately, though, the goal of 100% happy faces may not be attainable because students often enter our classrooms with strong negative feelings about certain subjects due to prior experiences, both in school and out of school, and these feelings are resistant to change, particularly with older students. What matters most is improvement, not perfection, and aiming for all happy faces serves a valuable purpose because it charts a direction in which we would like to move with the kids.

Suppose we administer the Fall Enthusiasm Survey and find that 14 out of 26 students enjoy math. The next time around in December, 17 students enjoy math. Even though we have not yet reached the point in which every child enjoys math, the group has made genuine progress—exactly the type of progress we wish to foster throughout the year. Later, at the end of the year, we still may not have all happy faces. That's to be expected. Our hope is to have more happy faces and fewer sad faces in June than we did in September.

I would like to turn our attention to the initial survey in the beginning of the school year. If I were to compile the results, analyze the data for ways to boost enthusiasm, and report back to the class with a few suggestions, quite a bit of good could result from my efforts. However, if we dug into the data *together*, discussed it openly and thoughtfully, and brainstormed recommendations for improvement as a group, that would be exponentially better. Certainly, the investment, ownership, and buy-in would be much stronger. Just as significant, the suggestions would be far better than any I could have come up with on my own. Seek to involve your class in this type of group brainstorming anytime you find yourselves with an issue to resolve or an aspect of classroom life you would like to improve. The Plus/Delta Charts I described in Chapter 6, in which children share what they like about a given project, event, or aspect of their learning and what they wish to change, can often serve as a launching point for these "improvement discussions."

Let's take a deeper dive into the challenge of increasing student enthusiasm for learning throughout a school year. The results of the Fall Survey from a few years ago are shown in Figure 9.4. Generally, art, computers, and reading receive the highest number of happy faces. (By the way, I know that counting "computers" as a subject must sound terribly dated. But back when I started the survey, this technology was brand new to our school, and I wanted to get a sense of how the kids felt about using it. "Computers" has remained on the survey ever since.) On the other hand, drama, social studies, and spelling tend to fare poorly. This sample is consistent with that pattern.

Increasing the number of happy faces for a given subject doesn't happen naturally or automatically. It requires a concerted, consistent effort from all team members to bring about meaningful change. Even though it can be tempting to jump right in and begin deep analysis of the survey results, start from square one. Ask the children to identify the subjects that received the greatest and least amount of happy faces. The first year I conducted this whole-class discussion, one child raised his hand and offered an idea that his classmates quickly built on. Before you knew it, the kids were producing one of the best improvement conversations I have ever witnessed. The main point the kids generated was that we should focus on the one or two subjects that had the most happy faces and try to figure out why so many kids found these subjects enjoyable. Then, once we identified the most appealing features of these subjects, we could look for ways to spread them throughout the curriculum. Brilliant. In other words, we should take the most enjoyable features of one subject and look for ways to apply them to others.

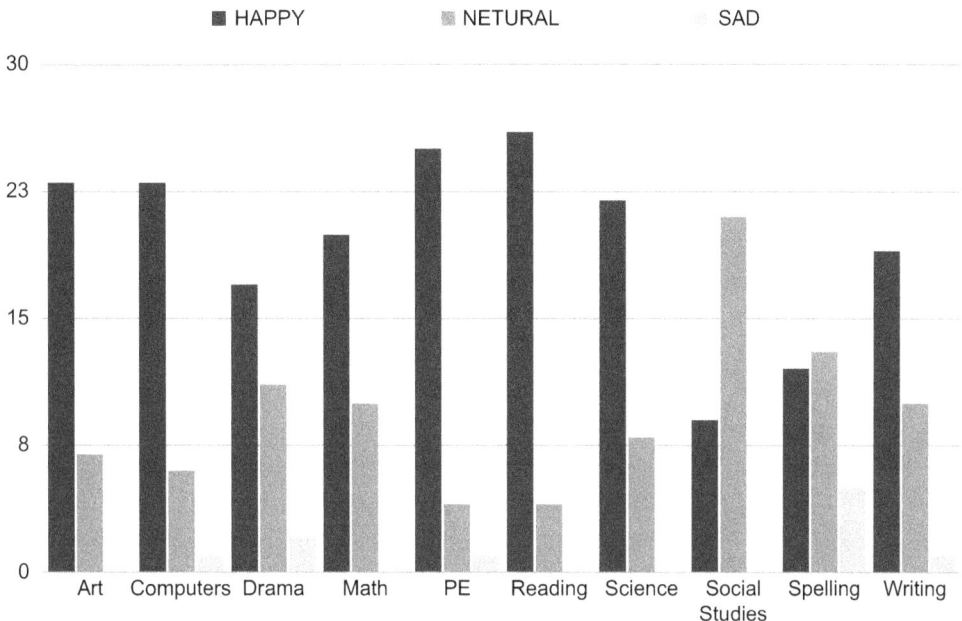

Figure 9.4 Enthusiasm Survey display.

From the discussions I have conducted over the years, I have learned that there are three primary ways to increase enthusiasm for any given subject. First, make learning as hands-on as possible. According to my students, the main reason computers receives so many happy faces stems from the fact that the devices allow for hands-on learning. Children have repeatedly expressed the belief that activities are more enjoyable when you get to do something rather than simply read or hear or talk about it. Once we initially established that hands-on learning makes using computers more enjoyable, I encouraged everyone to search for ways to use this information to make other subjects more enjoyable. Soon, they began finding novel ways to incorporate hands-on learning into areas such as spelling (by bouncing balls to practice new words), science (by participating in more frequent experiments and investigations), and art (by creating sculptures, prints, and architectural models). Every subject that we made "more hands-on" experienced an immediate increase in enthusiasm.

Second, whenever possible, give kids choices about what they will study. In art, for example, during the last few weeks of one school year, I wanted the children to have authentic experiences as artists. I didn't particularly care what they made; I simply wanted them to create works of art they considered meaningful. When students choose for themselves, their motivation increases and greater learning gains result. In addition, when everyone in the room works on something different, the students learn a great deal from one another, and they gain exposure to a much wider variety of disciplines than if I, the teacher, would have had everybody do the same thing. For example, one boy decided to make a Japanese woodblock print. When he announced his decision, the rest of us didn't know what woodblock prints were. But when we saw what he had created, the kids were impressed by his work, and I was glad that I had provided the opportunity for him to explore his own interests. During the mini Open House we held to display these projects, he even brought along his supplies and made a copy of his print for everyone who visited his table.

There are also multicultural benefits to this approach. Many teachers experience difficulty with the topic of multiculturalism because it can be such a challenge to incorporate the contributions of so many cultures into the curriculum in meaningful ways. By transferring responsibility for choosing project topics to the students, we allow the multiculturalism that already exists in our classrooms to manifest itself. In fact, I strongly believe that a classroom where children are making choices about what they study will naturally become a multicultural classroom due to the fact that the kids will have regular opportunities to explore and share ideas that are important to them.

Third, children will enjoy a subject more when they can decide not only *what* to study but also *how* to study it. Because students all learn in different ways, we should encourage everyone to determine how they learn best and then allow them to use those methods and learning styles as often as possible. I once taught a child with dyslexia who used his drawing ability and creativity to help him learn to spell new words. Playing to his strengths enabled him to be successful at a task with which he had always struggled. Furthermore, making choices empowered him to use an area of strength to develop an area of weakness, thus boosting his confidence and preventing discouragement from overwhelming him. Such customization also fits neatly into our overall classroom aim because it increases both learning and enthusiasm. Hold children accountable for results. Let them choose the methods.

Beyond these three ways to increase enthusiasm, another fact needs to be mentioned at this point. I have learned that a tight connection exists between how children feel about a subject and how capable they believe themselves to be in that area. Whenever a child puts a sad face for a given subject, it is often because that person experiences difficulty with that subject. Thus, over the long term, as kids improve their skills in a subject and develop more confidence, an increase in enthusiasm for that subject should inevitably occur.

At the end of the school year, take a minute to place your academic assessment results and your enthusiasm data side by side. For any subject, if you notice that your students' academic performance improved *and* they enjoy their work more than they did at the beginning of the year, then you have every reason to take pride in a job well done.

Use "Before and After" Samples to Point Out Improvement

Collecting student work samples on a regular basis throughout the year serves a variety of important purposes. The first time we will need a representative set of assessments, writing pieces, and math problem-solving activities, for example, will likely be Parent Conference Week, when we'll want to support our evaluations and observations with evidence. These work samples will also come in handy when completing report cards. Another lesser-known, yet extremely powerful, reason to gather samples is that this step enables us to make side-by-side comparisons featuring work from different times in the year.

There are two types of occasions when we would want to meet one-on-one with a child and show work samples from September and December, for example. First, we may notice that a child has made noteworthy academic progress over an extended period yet still expresses doubts about their skills and abilities or doesn't seem to recognize their growth. To counter these notions, we want to explicitly point out their impressive improvement. In this case, our goal involves boosting that student's confidence, expanding their perspective, and increasing their awareness of how far they have come as a learner. I'm not sure if this is a universal human phenomenon, but in my experience, when children know something or are able to perform a skill, it is very difficult for them to recall a time when they didn't possess that knowledge or couldn't yet perform that skill. In other words, once we know something, it is easy to think that we have always known it.

Improvement can often be an ambiguous, intangible concept, and showing "before and after" work samples helps students clearly observe their growth. Typically, I employ this practice with math assessments, writing projects, and printing samples, yet there's certainly no limit to the types of learning we can compare. It is always interesting to witness a child's reaction when we point out the growth in their math skill level, the greater detail in their written pieces, or the neatness of their printing. Kids appreciate seeing the change from the first piece of work to the second. Many are even jolted by the starkness of the contrast. Once we gather enough pieces of work, pointing out student improvement in this manner can produce tremendous benefits without requiring significant time or effort. Plus, we don't really need to do any planning. As a general rule, whenever a child earns their highest assessment score to date or demonstrates a significant jump with a given skill, invite them to a one-on-one meeting in which you show the "breakthrough" piece of work side by side with their initial effort in that area. According to an old expression, "Nothing motivates like success." Showing side-by-side work samples enables us to capitalize on that success.

In contrast, we can also invite students to observe a side-by-side comparison in situations when, quite honestly, we haven't seen meaningful progress over time. Throughout the year I emphasize to my class that once we embrace the spirit of continuous improvement, we don't want to be spending our time talking about the same issues and challenges over and over again. If, for example, the group experiences difficulty following the silent signal in September, that's fine. It happens. After further practice, encouragement, and accountability, however, we shouldn't need to devote significant time to this issue on a daily basis. The same idea holds true with specific aspects of individual students' learning. If a child's writing is very difficult to read in September, for example, we offer encouragement, additional practice, and accountability. That writing should look neater weeks and months later. If it doesn't, a side-by-side comparison can do wonders. Seeing the two printing samples look the same can be very revealing to the child. Perhaps the student genuinely believed the writing had been improving, or maybe they hoped we had forgotten about the issue. These conversations may be difficult ones to conduct, but they hold kids accountable and can serve as the catalyst for future improvement.

Incorporate Storytelling to Improve Student Behavior

Throughout the book I have described many benefits of storytelling. In this section I would like to apply the practice to the specific issue of improving student behavior. No matter how well-behaved any of our classes might be, inevitably there will be times during the year when many children seem to be going through a rough stretch all at once. Having a bunch of students experience a bump in the road at the same time should not be taken as a reflection of our management skills. It simply means that our students are human. As teachers, we can't predict or control when these ups and downs will occur, but we can control how we respond to them.

Over the years, I have learned that when many kids are having trouble focusing on their work in class or finding themselves getting into an unusually high number of arguments on the playground, the most effective response is often storytelling.

When telling a story, the key is to feature a student who isn't involved in the incident(s) happening at that time, who experienced something similar in the past, and who overcame that difficulty using an approach that others can emulate. That way, everyone can relate to and benefit from the story's messages, yet nobody feels as if they are being singled out, put on the spot, or made to feel guilty about something they just got caught doing. This approach is non-threatening, and kids can listen to our stories with some emotional detachment.

As the kids listen to me, they will naturally put themselves in the shoes of the featured student, think through the given situation, and absorb the lessons I am embedding in the story. The storytelling approach is far more effective than lecturing, rewarding, or punishing.

For example, about ten years ago, a few children were having difficulty taking responsibility for their actions on the playground. When situations occurred, they tended to deny their involvement or shift the blame to others. When I found out what was happening, I immediately thought of one boy in class who wasn't involved in these incidents but who demonstrated the type of honesty and responsibility I wanted the other children to develop. We'll call this child Tim, and with his permission I told the following story to my class as part of our morning circle time.

I started the story by telling everyone that throughout the year, we will all have our ups and downs, and there will be times when we're simply not performing at our best. It could be happening in class, on the playground, or elsewhere. When we're in the middle of one of these rough patches, there are certain things we can do to move through it and come out stronger than we were before. I then said that someone in this class went through one of these difficult times a while back, and he handled everything so well that I wanted to share his story with them. So I asked his permission to do so, and he gave it to me. That student is Tim. Instantly, the kids are curious. Because the story features someone they know, I have their full attention.

Here's the story. At Tim's Parent Conference, I told him and his mother that after an outstanding third-grade year, he was off to a bit of a tough start this year. (I taught this group for two years.) His work wasn't quite as strong as it was the year before, his writing tended to be very messy, and he wasn't showing the same level of self-discipline in class. After he heard me say these things to his mother, Tim had a few choices. His first option was to deny. He could have said, "No, Mom, this isn't true. My work is fine. I'm doing as well as I did last year, and I'm not really sure what my teacher is talking about." Tim didn't do that.

Second, he could have deflected. He could have said, "Yeah, Mom, it's true. I'm not doing as well as I did in third grade, but it's because my neighbors keep distracting me. Every time I try to do my work, someone keeps talking to me or preventing me from focusing. Plus, a whole bunch of other kids are struggling too." Tim didn't do that either.

Instead, Tim made a different choice. After I described the situation, he stopped and thought for a moment. Then, he said, "You know what, it's true. I haven't been doing as well as I could have, and I'm going to make a change. I'm going to start working harder, being neater, and showing more self-discipline." The next day, Tim responded like a champion. There was an immediate improvement with his work and behavior that lasted until the end of the school year.

I concluded my story by making a big deal about how impressed I was with Tim's honesty and responsibility and how much respect I gained for him after seeing how admirably he handled himself during the conference. The class listened intently to this entire story, and the ones who were involved in our recent incidents learned some valuable lessons from Tim's experience without being singled out or put on the spot.

As teachers, we can't go back and change any of our students' negative behavior. All we can do is focus on decreasing the likelihood that such behavior will recur. Our goal is to increase our students' future capacity by imparting valuable lessons that will resonate with them. Storytelling is a terrific way to do that.

Deliver a Good Old-Fashioned "Pep Talk"

Each spring, schools around the country typically participate in some form of standardized state testing. Though valid concerns exist regarding the effectiveness of the testing and the stress it can cause children, I have always encouraged my students to adopt a positive view of the exercise and see it as a chance to demonstrate all we've learned during our time together. Over the years, some children have expressed concerns that a poor test score will ruin their report card or affect their ability to advance to the next grade level in the fall. I assure them that none of that is true. I make a concerted effort to calm everyone's nerves and, instead, help everyone see the testing as something to get excited about. I do that by seizing a golden opportunity to incorporate an engaging sports metaphor into my teaching. I tell my students, "I'm the coach, you're the players, and the testing is our version of the big game. Together we're charging toward the playoffs!"

Most years, my efforts pay off. The kids genuinely do become excited for the testing and embrace the challenge it provides. One year, however, things were different. In the weeks leading up to the testing, as we were reviewing and prepping, the group seemed down. I couldn't quite put my finger on what was happening. I wasn't sure if it was nerves, a lack of confidence, or something else. What I did know was that when these moments occur, we, as teachers, can improve the overall mood of the class, boost enthusiasm and motivation, and energize the environment with a good old-fashioned pep talk. Delivering a short, inspiring address doesn't just produce real benefits; it's also a lot of fun. We get to channel our inner Knute Rockne, the legendary Notre Dame football coach who led his Fighting Irish to a comeback win in a 1928 game versus Army with his famous "Win one for the Gipper" halftime speech. Or if you prefer a lighter, more humorous reference, we can channel our inner Bill Murray, who, in the 1979 classic *Meatballs*, filled his Camp North Star charges with the confidence to come from behind to defeat archrival Camp Mohawk in their annual two-day Olympiad.

Opting to go more Rockne than Murray on this occasion, I delivered a pre-testing pep talk that I consider my favorite of my career. The year was 2012. I remember that because the New York Giants had beaten the heavily favored New England Patriots in the Super Bowl just a few months earlier. Also, a parent volunteer was in the room at that time, and he was a huge sports fan and friend. It was a blast to tell a sports story with him listening in. I shared with my students that even though the Giants won the Super Bowl, that didn't mean the team was dominant for the entire season. They had their ups and downs along the way. As I spoke, I drew the team's season-long "timeline" on the board from left to right. The design strongly resembled the image I presented earlier in this chapter to demonstrate how human progress isn't linear. I described the Giants' regular season triumphs and challenges. With only a few games remaining on their schedule, it wasn't a sure thing that the team would even make the playoffs. Then, an amazing thing happened. The Giants peaked at the right time. They summoned all their energy, effort, and motivation and ended up winning their division by playing their best when their best was needed.

I then connected that idea of peaking at the right time to our situation of prepping for the upcoming state testing. Sure, I said, we have had our ups and downs this year, our triumphs and our challenges. And wherever we find ourselves now, we have a couple of weeks to do what the Giants did—peak at the right time. Play our best when our best is needed. If we take advantage of our opportunities leading up to the testing, we'll be just fine. No reason to worry; every reason to relax and feel confident. I used the next two weeks to guide the kids—mentally, emotionally, strategically, and tactically—so they could have a positive testing experience and perform to their potential. Kids love these moments because they are so positive, uplifting, and novel. Pep talks bring out our best and our students' best.

As part of our effort to build morale, boost confidence, and increase motivation, we can also give our class an inspiring, engaging nickname. We can either introduce it during a pep talk or mention it at a different time. Aaron Boone, manager of the New York Yankees, once referred to the team's hitting lineup as a bunch of *savages*, eager to attack opponents' pitching and do damage. That nickname is attention-getting and gives the team a powerful identity. Consider giving your students an identity that's engaging and inspiring and conveys the identity you want the group to exemplify. I don't recommend *savages*. Better alternatives include *All-Stars*, *Go-Getters*, *Battery Chargers*, or some term from your mission statement.

Continuous Improvement: Effective Tools

In previous sections of this chapter, as well as in earlier chapters, I have described useful "improvement tools" that we can employ to facilitate both whole-group and individual progress. With regard to collective improvement, effective options include the Plus/Delta Chart (first mentioned in Chapter 6) and the Pareto chart from this chapter. Plus/Delta Charts enable the group to brainstorm strengths and suggestions as we conclude a class activity, such as Student-Led Conferences, and plan for future experiences with that same activity. Pareto charts allow for clear, visual representations of growth areas as we wrap up a class unit or project, such as Small Moment stories, and plan for future rounds.

Any list of individual improvement tools must, by law, begin with the big 3: goal setting, reflection, and self-evaluation. Goal setting is believed by many to be the most powerful human motivator to take action and initiate improvement. Goal setting can be either formal or informal. A formal goal setting process, such as the one described in Chapter 8, involves selecting and writing a small number of goals, posting the list at home and perhaps at school, and following up over a period of weeks with reflection and self-evaluation. Writing and sharing our goals holds us accountable and increases the likelihood that we will follow through with what we'd like to accomplish. Ideally, we would initiate a formal process every time we ask students to set goals. Due to time constraints, however, goal setting may not always work this way, and that's fine. A combination of formal and informal goal setting, done mentally, orally, and in writing, works well given the realities of classroom life and will produce tremendous results over the course of a school year.

Informal goals can also be powerful, even though they may be unwritten and focus on a much shorter period of time. I believe the most effective example of an informal process to be the goals I ask kids to set each day at the conclusion of our morning routine (Reifman, 2016). At this time, the children are standing in "hook-up position," a relaxing stance that comes from Paul Dennison's well-known Brain Gym program (Hannaford, 1995). In this position the students close their eyes and set a goal for the day related to a Habit of Character, Habit of Mind, work habit, or social skill. This exercise is beneficial because it asks everyone to look ahead. Many times, when teachers bring up the issue of behavior, it is because someone just got caught doing something negative. When I mention habits first thing in the morning, however, nobody feels as if they are being put on the spot as a consequence of poor behavior. Proactive goal setting is about planting a positive seed in children's minds. Since all eyes are closed during this time, I can walk around and check in privately with certain students about various behavioral issues they may be having and offer encouragement.

This type of goal setting helps each person identify the area in which successful performance will make the biggest difference in their day. For example, if I know that my greatest difficulty in school involves working with others, I will set a goal about cooperation and think about the specific steps I need to take to make that happen. If maintaining eye contact during instructional lessons is something I struggle with, I will make that my goal. This process is quick, it's private, it's personal, and it allows everyone to start the day on a positive note. Plus, it teaches a valuable life lesson—when we experience difficulty in a given area, we need to commit ourselves to addressing that area. We don't try to hide from it or pretend the issue doesn't exist. Adding an element of goal setting to our mornings is an important step in facilitating student improvement.

Some papers the kids use in class are not specifically designed for the purpose of goal setting, but we can easily include an element of goal setting to make the sheet more effective. The baseball diamond image shown earlier in this chapter is an example. The main purpose of that sheet is for the kids to record the date and results of each of their math quizzes. Adding the "Goal" column encourages the kids to think about their next quiz and plan ahead. Later in this section, I describe another sheet that has specific purposes other than improvement yet features an element of goal setting.

Reflection and self-evaluation are related processes, as performing one often involves carrying out the other. Both play a vital role in promoting a culture of quality and improvement. We can facilitate thoughtful self-evaluation through the use of checklists and rubrics, such as the Habits of Character and Habits of Mind Rubric shown in Chapter 2 and the writing rubrics presented in Chapter 5. Written reflection questions, also contained in Chapter 5, enable children to take time at the conclusion of a significant project to think about what went well and how they would like to improve in the future.

Just prior to the start of Parent Conference Week, I ask the children to complete a self-evaluation sheet related to our Habits of Character. On it, the kids use our Habits of Character rubric to give themselves a score (1–4) for each habit. To help everyone proceed thoughtfully and carefully through this exercise, I structure the activity as a directed lesson. On the board I show one Habit of Character at a time, along with the indicators, and provide a few moments for the kids to think about how well they have recently been performing in that area. Then I ask them to record a score for that habit in writing. We continue in this manner until everyone has completed the entire evaluation. Finally, I have the kids identify what they believe to be their best habit (by circling that score) and the one in which they want to improve the most (by putting a box around that score). Identifying their greatest strength builds confidence and awareness, and identifying their area of greatest need prepares them for the goal-setting process that will occur during the conference. The students know they will be attending the conferences and sharing these scores with their parents and me, and they take this self-evaluation seriously.

The self-evaluation sheet becomes the first item I share with families at each conference. I tell the parents that we look at this page first, before any piece of academic work, because the habits form the foundation of everything we do in class, and I believe it is important to highlight areas of student strength and address areas of concern before we move to the academic items on our agenda. In my experience, any patterns that we notice with the children's academic performance, both positive and negative, can usually be traced to at least a few of the Habits of Character, such as self-discipline and responsibility. So, discussing the self-evaluation sheet at the outset sets the tone for a productive meeting and gives us a terrific lens to use as we analyze the work in the various disciplines. I seek student input as much as possible during this discussion.

In the remainder of this section, I introduce a few new individual improvement tools. You may wish to use them "as is," or perhaps they will inspire your own adaptations or creations.

End-of-day Flowcharts
Alan Blankstein, author of *Failure Is Not an Option* (2004), writes, "Ensuring achievement for *all* learners means having an overarching strategy that encompasses the majority of learners—and then having specific strategies aimed at those who need extra support." This idea and the next two describe specific strategies that can help students who may need additional assistance in their quest to meet classroom expectations.

Freddie, an organizationally challenged student of mine, had a habit of leaving class each afternoon without some important items: his homework, his backpack, his jacket, and his books. He meant to take all these things home; they just rarely found their way into his hands. One morning, I sat down with him and suggested that we create a flowchart to help him remember what he needed to do before he left school each day.

Together, we constructed a step-by-step plan, whose steps are shown in Figure 9.5. (We taped the flowchart to the top of his desk.) Now, Freddie had a clear procedure to follow. The flowchart transformed what had been a confusing array of tasks into a visible sequence of simple steps. The flowchart empowered Freddie to take charge of his behavior. After reading this procedure day after day, he would eventually internalize it, and organization would soon become a habit. This approach builds his capacity while also sparing him some nagging from his parents and teacher.

Consider using a flowchart anytime you and your students need to organize your thinking sequentially. For example, when you are absent, you can leave your lesson plan on the board in the form of a flowchart so the kids know how to proceed from one activity to the next without needing much guidance from the substitute teacher.

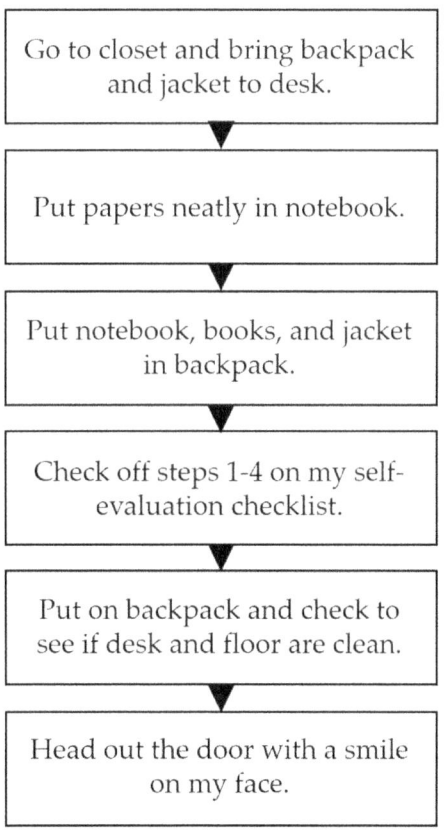

Figure 9.5 Freddie's end-of-day checklist.

Check Sheets (Version 1)

Serena was having trouble staying focused at her desk. During independent work time, she would frequently look around the room and try to start conversations with other students. I suggested that she keep a check sheet by her side to record the number of times she found herself losing focus each day. I figured that if she became more aware of this tendency, her focus would improve. Boy, was I wrong. After a week or so, the two of us sat down to talk. The check sheet hadn't been working. We realized that it wasn't serving a useful purpose because it required her to make a check whenever she did something that was viewed as negative. Not surprisingly, she wasn't too enthusiastic about commemorating her losses of focus with check marks.

We then tried a different approach. She would now keep a check sheet by her side to record happier occasions. Every time she lost her focus and then regained it without anyone having to remind her, she would put a check on her paper. Slowly, her focus began to get better. As she saw the number of check marks grow day by day, her attitude improved, and her confidence increased because she knew she was the one controlling her behavior. See her check sheet in what follows in Figure 9.6. Serena's improvement also had a positive impact on those around her. Because she was no longer distracting her neighbors as much, they could focus better on their work. She made my job easier as well since I didn't have to keep as close of an eye on her.

Suddenly, other kids began asking me if they could create check sheets of their own. Some, like Serena, wanted to improve their focus, while others wanted to improve a different aspect of their behavior, such as attentive listening. Because this approach was flexible, the kids could apply it to any Habit of Character, Habit of Mind, work habit, or social skill. Before long, half the class proudly displayed check sheets on their desks. I had a check sheet epidemic on my hands. As these events unfolded, I took great pride in the fact that all of it was completely voluntary. The commitment was coming from the students themselves.

Check Sheets (Version 2)

Over the past year, I have been employing a second type of check sheet with children I tutor after school and getting excellent results. A sample is shown in Figure 9.7. Even though I haven't yet used it in a classroom setting, I'm confident this format would work well. Before starting an independent work period, the child sets two to three goals that can relate to any Habit of Character, Habit of Mind, work habit, or social skill. Initially, we may need to guide the kids during this step and give suggestions. Including the indicators beneath each goal is helpful, but not mandatory. At the bottom, write

Improvement ◆ 279

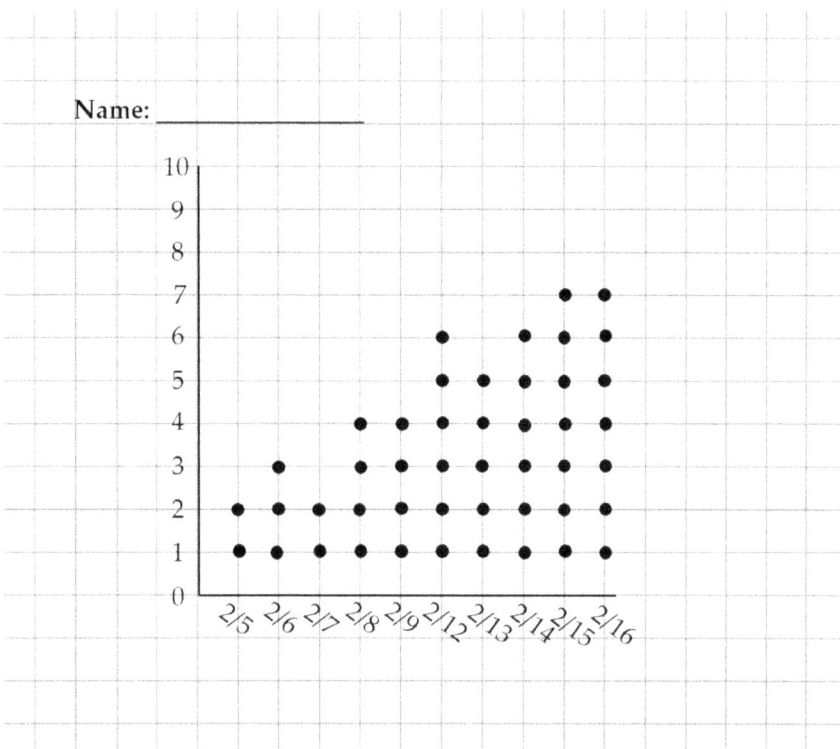

Figure 9.6 Serena's check sheet.

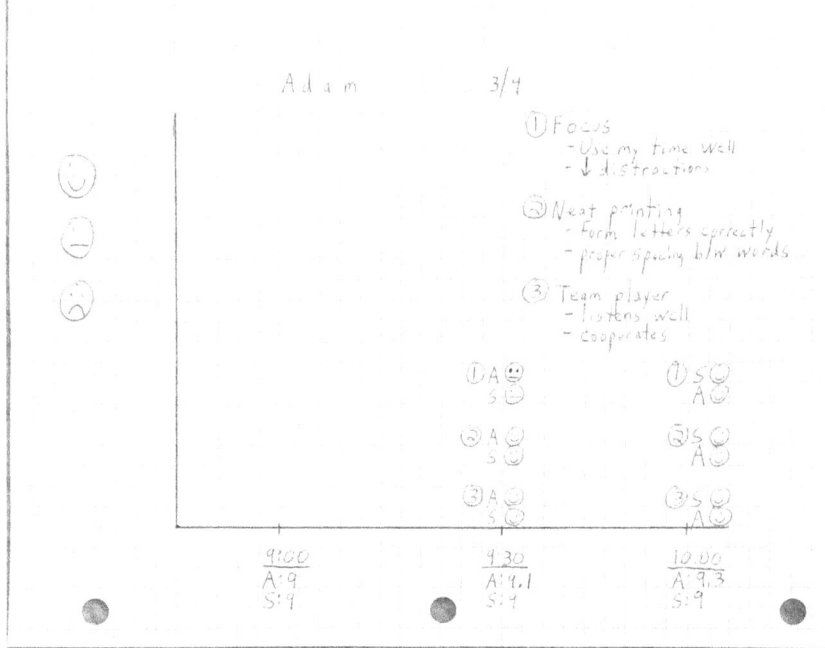

Figure 9.7 Sample check sheet (version 2).

the starting time, the "halfway" time, and ending time. Halfway through the period, both you and the child complete a quick self-evaluation using the same "happy face, neutral face, sad face" system associated with the enthusiasm surveys. Assessing halfway and at the end provides the opportunity for the child to improve their performance during the second half of the period. Thus, it's a formative assessment, not a summative one that offers a final evaluation without any chance for the child to demonstrate growth. I like to have the child go first when assessing each goal at the halfway point and then switch the order for the final assessment. That way, we each have a chance to lead the process. Feel free to switch this order or have the same person go first each time. To add a social-emotional component to this exercise, include at the bottom the same 1–10 scale from the morning check-in activity.

Of course, the elephant in the room with this approach is that we need to be available to participate in this process with the student and observe their performance from time-to-time as they work independently. In a one-on-one tutoring session, that's no problem. In a classroom setting, it is much more difficult. If you're available for a quick drop-in at the beginning of the process, halfway through, and at the end, that's awesome. If not, it's not necessarily a deal-breaker. After some initial training, the child can complete many, if not all, of the steps independently and check in with you afterward. Whatever time you are able to devote to this exercise is worth it, as it leads to substantial benefits. Kids take greater ownership of their learning, increase awareness of their strengths and growth areas, become more committed to success, and raise their personal expectations.

Math Cover Sheets

Originally, I created the Place Value Cover Sheet shown in Figure 9.8 so students could have an easy way to keep track of their math problem sets and organize them sequentially in their math folders. Then, I had the idea of including space for a brief self-evaluation that everyone would complete after each lesson. Using the 1–4 scale shown in Figure 9.9, the kids circle the number indicating how they felt about the lesson and how confident they were in their grasp of the content. Later, when the children took home their problem sets to study for the unit assessment, I encouraged them to look at the numbers they circled to see which lessons might require additional review. Our daily, end-of-lesson self-assessment provided tremendous bang for the buck, providing valuable information in very little time. I was so pleased with this practice that I designed the same type of cover sheet for the rest of our math units.

Name_____

Place Value Unit Cover Sheet

Date	Lesson #	Self-Evaluation				Location
_____	_____	1	2	3	4	_____
_____	_____	1	2	3	4	_____
_____	_____	1	2	3	4	_____
_____	_____	1	2	3	4	_____
_____	_____	1	2	3	4	_____
_____	_____	1	2	3	4	_____
_____	_____	1	2	3	4	_____
_____	_____	1	2	3	4	_____
_____	_____	1	2	3	4	_____
_____	_____	1	2	3	4	_____

Comments, Notes, Reminders: _____

_____

_____

Figure 9.8 Math cover sheet.

How Did It Go?

1	2	3	4
This is new to me. I don't get it at all.	I get it a little bit. I'm close to understanding.	I understand it well.	I can teach others.

Figure 9.9 Math cover sheet self-assessment scale.

My Day in a Nutshell

The "My Day in a Nutshell" half-sheet shown in Figure 9.10 offers a simple, effective way for children to assess themselves at the end of the day on essential indicators of health and classroom performance. The top half promotes the importance of making healthy choices. Anytime I can advertise these aspects of health, I feel as if I am doing my students an important service. The bottom focuses on cooperation, listening, focus, and enthusiasm. Completing this sheet a few minutes before they leave for the day helps kids reinforce what they're doing well, determine possible goals for the following day, and perhaps notice cause-and-effect relationships between the two parts. Feel free to substitute other priorities that you believe deserve additional attention.

Group Work Evaluation Sheet

Similar to "My Day in a Nutshell," the "Group Work Evaluation Sheet" (Figure 9.11) offers a simple, effective way for children to assess themselves on essential indicators, except this form is designed to be used at the conclusion of cooperative learning activities. The top half relates to work habits, while the bottom focuses mostly on social skills. Using this sheet the first few times students work in groups of three or more heightens their awareness of your expectations, holds them accountable, and results in more frequent, more positive participation among team members. You can ask the kids to

Name_____ Date_____

My Day in a Nutshell

I slept at least 8-9 hours last night.	1	2	3	4
I drank plenty of water today.	1	2	3	4
I ate healthy foods today.	1	2	3	4
Besides PE class, I exercised today.	1	2	3	4
I got along well with others today.	1	2	3	4
I was a great listener today.	1	2	3	4
My work focus was strong today.	1	2	3	4
I enjoyed myself at school today.	1	2	3	4

Comments: _____

_____

Figure 9.10 "My Day in a Nutshell" self-assessment sheet.

do this exercise individually or work together to determine an overall group evaluation.

How Was My DRIVE-ing Today?

To keep the "Drive for 5" concept alive in the minds of students, we can have them complete the half-sheet shown in Figure 9.12 every few days or once a week after we have introduced the five parts.

Reading Goals

The first experience my students have with written goal setting comes a few weeks into the school year during our Reading Workshop (Reifman, 2016). One of the main emphases at this time of year is to help children learn to live the life of a reader and develop effective habits. To facilitate this type of growth, I ask students to write on an index card at least three goals that they would like to reach as a reader. We share these goals aloud, bring the cards home so the kids can discuss them with their families, and then post the cards

Name_____   Partner_____

Date_____

Group Work Evaluation Sheet

Focus

My focus was strong.   1   2   **3**   4

I used my time appropriately.   1   2   **3**   4

I contributed energy and ideas to my group.   1   2   **3**   4

Cooperation

I listened with respect to my partner.   1   2   **3**   4

I cared about my partner's needs as well as my own.   1   2   **3**   4

We solved problems quickly and fairly.   1   2   **3**   4

Comments: _____

_____

Figure 9.11 Group Work Evaluation Sheet.

Name_____   Date_____

How Was My DRIVE-ing Today?

D - Demonstrate drive & grit   1   2   3   4

R - Reach for the stars   1   2   3   4

I - Immediately ask for help when I need it   1   2   3   4

V - Visualize my future goals   1   2   3   4

E - Engage in energetic listening   1   2   3   4

Comments: _____

_____

Figure 9.12 "Drive for 5" self-assessment sheet.

on a bulletin board for easy reference and consistent follow-up. A sample is shown in Box 9.1. Here are some types of goals students like to set:

- Read for a certain amount of time each day outside of school
- Work on a specific reading skill (e.g., inferring, summarizing)
- Finish a series or start a new series
- Expand into new genres to have a greater variety of reading experiences
- Make reading more of a social activity (e.g., start a book club or read to a sibling)
- Improve reading focus or stamina
- Write ideas on Post-its while reading
- Move up a certain number of levels during the upcoming year
- Try to enjoy reading more than in the past

Box 9.1 Reading Goals Card

My Reading Goals Card

1. I want to be an intelligent reader.
2. I want to read a few Harry Potter books.
3. I want to read with my family more often.

Informal Reflection and Self-Evaluation Options

When time does not allow for formal, written reflection and self-evaluation, you and your students can still accomplish a great deal through discussion, hand signals, and "private thinking." Imagine, for example, that the kids have just finished using a new math problem-solving strategy and 3 minutes remain before the start of recess. Give everyone 30 seconds of "quiet think time" to reflect on what went well, what was challenging, and what they might do differently next time. Have the children turn and talk to a neighbor about how the experience went for them. Ask them to rate their comfort level with the strategy by showing one to four fingers at chin level.

In the event you run out of time in Writing Workshop before the children have a chance to complete the written reflection questions you wanted them to answer, conduct the activity orally, giving the group some time to do a think-pair-share for each question. Any type of reflection and self-evaluation is valuable.

As the kids participate in these various informal options, use "think-alouds" to model the process for them. Doing so will greatly increase their comfort level and proficiency. If, for example, we are reflecting on our recently published fiction stories, I can share the following:

> "I'm happy with all the dialogue I included in my story, and I think I put in exciting action. Next time, though, I can add more character and setting description. I'm not sure if my readers really knew that much about my main character or could envision the setting clearly. I can definitely do better next time."

By opening the door to my thinking in this manner, the children can see what a thoughtful, detailed reflection looks like. As a result, they will be more likely to offer this type of comment the next time we reflect on our work.

Our Development as Professional Educators

In this chapter's final section, I would like to focus on how the concept of continuous improvement applies to our growth as professional educators. As teachers, we spend countless hours helping our students get a little bit better at everything they do. As I have mentioned previously, this type of progress involves various strategies and techniques, but more than anything else, continuous improvement is an attitude, a mindset. It's important for us to embrace this spirit throughout the length of our careers. Since I think, talk, and understand the world in terms of sports, let's begin with a basketball analogy.

Many fans consider Michael Jordan to be the most outstanding basketball player of all time. (These people are right.) It's difficult to argue with his credentials. Jordan earned two Olympic gold medals, led the NBA in scoring 10 times, won five Most Valuable Player awards, participated in 13 All-Star Games, and led the Chicago Bulls to six NBA Championships.

Though he excelled as a player during each of his professional seasons, Jordan at the age of 32 was far superior to Jordan at 22. In no way did he arrive in the NBA as a finished product. Of course, natural talent played a large role in his success, but hard work played an even larger one.

Every summer, during the league's off-season, Jordan committed himself to improving specific aspects of his game. One summer, he would focus on his three-point shooting, another on his defense, still another on his free throws. By purposefully working to develop into a complete player, Jordan made the most of his vast potential.

Similarly, as teachers, we have the opportunity and, I believe, the responsibility to develop our skills over time so that we can fulfill our potential as educators and maximize the learning gains of our students. Of course, instead of basketball skills, our focus lies in developing our pedagogical, instructional, and leadership skills.

In some cases, our schools and districts take the lead in providing consistent, thorough training in these areas. For those of us who may not receive such opportunities, we take it upon ourselves to build our repertoires—we read, reflect, plan, attend conferences, connect with colleagues in person and via social media, and participate in continuing education. Ultimately, responsibility for our own professional development lies with us as individuals.

Over time, our hard work pays off. All our data collection, discussions with students, and efforts to build a culture of quality and improvement will yield substantial dividends. We will know more about how to do our jobs better. We will be more familiar with a wider variety of instructional and curricular approaches and have a better sense of how to use them for the greatest benefit. We will know more about what works, what doesn't, and why. We will get a little bit better every day and significantly better every year. As a result, more students will demonstrate proficiency with the content standards, more children will enjoy more subjects, and more students will demonstrate the Habits of Mind and Habits of Character that distinguish them as quality learners. The progress will not come right away, but it will be steady and consistent.

Each summer I encourage you to enjoy the relaxation time you have earned and fully deserve. To the greatest extent possible, however, try to find time to identify aspects of your teaching practice that you would like to improve and invest the time to make it happen. In the end, we will all be able to take pride and satisfaction in a job well done and experience deep joy and fulfillment.

Reference List

Blankstein, A. (2004). *Failure Is Not an Option*. Thousand Oaks, CA: Corwin Press.
Cleary, B. and Duncan, S. (1997). *Tools and Techniques to Inspire Classroom Learning*. Milwaukee, WI: ASQC Quality Press.
Dweck, C. (2007). *Mindset: The New Psychology of Success*. New York: Ballantine Books.
Foster, Jennifer. (17 December, 2012). "The Elephant Mindset." *Entrepreneur*.
Glasser, W. (1990). *The Quality School*. New York: Harper & Row.
Glasser, W. (1993). *The Quality School Teacher*. New York: Harper Perennial.

Hannaford, C. (1995). *Smart Moves: Why Learning Is Not All in Your Head*. Marshall, NC: Great Ocean Publishers. For additional information regarding Brain Gym please consult the following: D. E. Wilson, *Minute Moves for the Classroom*, or any of the Brain Gym instructional materials developed by Paul Dennison.

"Metallica 'Behind the Music' Documentary." Original air date: November 22, 1998. Production Companies: Gay Rosenthal Productions & Santo Domingo Film & Music Video.

Reifman, S. (2008). *Eight Essentials for Empowered Teaching & Learning, K-8*. Thousand Oaks, CA: Corwin Press.

Reifman, S. (2013). *Math Problem Solving Menus*. Author.

Reifman, S. (2016). *15 1/2 Ways to Personalize Learning*. Author.

Whittle, C. (2005). *Crash Course*. New York: Riverbed Books.

10
Personalization

In Chapter 1, I emphasized that "whole-child" teaching begins with the belief that all children are unique and special and possess unlimited potential. Because teaching the whole child involves understanding that each "whole child" is different from every other whole child, it's important for us to treat our students as the unique individuals they are. Viewing our role through this lens will help us maximize their specific strengths, talents, and abilities and create an enthusiastic, need-satisfying classroom environment that empowers everyone to thrive. The Metallica Principle, introduced in the previous chapter, ties in well with this endeavor. For the group to be happy, productive, and successful, each child must feel valued as an irreplaceable team member because of the ideas, energy, and personality they bring to the class.

Our goal, then, is to personalize the learning experience of our students to the greatest extent possible. Though we may hold common academic and behavioral expectations for members of the group, we must always strive to treat each child as an individual. At first, this may appear to be a daunting, perhaps even overwhelming, task, given all the responsibilities and demands we face on a daily basis. In this chapter I present several ways to make the task of personalizing learning a little less daunting and a ton of fun.

Taken together, our efforts to personalize the learning experience of our students yield valuable academic and social-emotional benefits. First, children who feel appreciated, recognized, and valued work harder, learn better, and become more likely to develop an achievement orientation. They invest themselves more deeply in classroom activities and display a greater sense of ownership. During class discussions, they freely share knowledge, ideas, and strategies with their peers. In addition, our efforts foster positive feelings and increase motivation and buy-in. Personalizing the learning environment helps children establish a positive identity within the classroom community and increases both group bonding and individuals' sense of belonging. Children feel more comfortable being themselves and expressing their personalities. As the theme song of the classic sitcom *Cheers* expresses, "[s]ometimes you want to go where everybody knows your name." Our classrooms can become one of those places.

In addition, personalizing our learning environment boosts pride and self-esteem and gives kids their moment in the sun. It produces smiles and makes kids feel special. As a teacher, there may not be anything more joyful and satisfying than that.

Student Leader Tributes

The next two ideas put a smile on the faces of all children, yet they particularly benefit those quiet, shy kids who tend to fly under the radar. The primary appeal of these ideas is simple—both guarantee that every learner receives a highly personalized form of individual attention that is 100% positive. The first affords each child the chance to become a student leader. (This position is commonly known as "student of the week," but I prefer the term *student leader* because of the leadership opportunities and responsibilities I have built into the role.)

Every Friday before recess, I draw a popsicle stick from the cup I keep by the whiteboard, and the person whose name is chosen becomes student leader for the following week. That child gets to answer the phone, take the attendance sheet to the office, deliver materials to other classes, and handle a variety of classroom monitor jobs. Each morning that child stands outside the door and greets the rest of the kids as they enter the room. In addition, they lead everybody in the Pledge of Allegiance and our morning movement warm-up routine. I also fill out a colorful certificate and hang it on a bulletin board where the kids can put up pictures of their family and friends and share the photos at the end of their week. At that time, students can also share a special object from home, similar to how they did during the opening week of school.

A few years ago, my students and I added a new twist to this weekly feature when I selected Tracy's name from the cup. I can get a bit silly before recess, and I joked that as a tribute to our new student leader, everybody needed to show up on Monday wearing a flower in their hair, as Tracy routinely did. I completely forgot about my little joke and was shocked when six kids showed up on Monday with flowers in their hair. Tracy was absolutely beaming when she saw this, and a new tradition was born.

The following week, a boy named Danny became student leader. Because he didn't routinely wear a flower in his hair, we needed a different way to honor him during his special week. He said that he liked wearing blue shirts to school, so the following week, many kids wore blue shirts to school. These tributes, which began as a throwaway joke before recess, have become a quick, simple, and powerful way to give kids their moment in the sun and make them feel like an important part of the team.

Before I leave school on Fridays, I send an email to the class parents announcing the name of our next student leader and sharing that child's "tribute choice." Many kids have followed Danny's lead and invited classmates to wear clothing of a certain type or color. Others have simply asked everyone to join them for lunch or play a game with them at recess. Communicating with families in this manner spreads positivity and increases the likelihood that the kids will remember the tributes the following week.

Give All Your Students Their Own "Thing"

Beyond offering each child a turn as student leader, we can personalize everyone's classroom experience and guarantee positive attention by giving learners their own *thing*. I know that's not the most elegant or precise word choice, but I'm intentionally employing a vague term because, in this section, *thing* can mean so many different, well, things. When we give kids their own thing, it can be a nickname, a job, a gesture, a signal, or a private joke—anything that makes a child feel special and acknowledged as an individual. The goal is for every child to have or be known for something that is uniquely theirs.

Typically, these examples are lighthearted and playful, yet they have the potential to produce incredibly powerful bonding moments—between teacher and student or among the whole team. Frequently, my interactions with children regarding these *things* are the best parts of my day because they're so much fun.

Let me share a few examples with you. First, several years ago, I taught a terrific young man named Bobby. He has a heart of gold and a strong desire to do well academically. Once or twice a day, however, he would lose focus during independent work time and rest his head on his desk. When this happened, I whispered his name from my chair in the front of the room, and he would look my way. I then pretended to throw him an energy bar that he would pretend to catch and eat. That was all he needed to return to work.

Besides being a bit silly, this strategy follows the effective management practice of intervening only as much as necessary when children stray off task. Eating virtual energy bars in class became Bobby's thing.

Another gesture-related idea is one I like to call "Flipping My Student the Bird." (It's not what you think.) Gary is kind, good-natured, polite, and knowledgeable about a wide variety of topics. On a typical school day, he would have trouble maintaining his attention during instructional lessons and produce little to no work once he began his independent practice. I am convinced that he never meant to cause any problems and always had the best of intentions when he entered class each day. Still, he would frequently sit idly at his desk for extended periods of time and have little to show for it.

One day I was sitting in class with Gary, and I came up with an idea. Never would this idea be found in an education textbook, but I trusted my judgment and felt it was worth a try. I asked him what he was currently most passionate about. He responded that he loved birds. He even told me that his mom said she might get him a bird one day, and that thought made him happy.

I asked if he would be willing to try an idea. He agreed. I curled my fingers into the shape of a bird. It didn't really look like a bird at all, but I referred to my curved hand as a bird, and Gary was happy to play along. After all, kids who experience behavioral or academic difficulties often become frustrated as well, and they are usually more than willing to try a fresh approach.

I told Gary that my "bird hand" would be our new private communication signal. If he was working well at his desk and I showed him the bird from my spot in the front of the room, that meant he should keep up the good work and show me the bird in return to acknowledge my positive message.

If he wasn't working well at his desk when I flipped him the bird, it was my way of inspiring him and encouraging him to think of something positive in his life so that he would begin to become more productive. He liked that I would show him the bird in both of these situations because if he was doing well, he would get a confidence boost and a feeling of pride and recognition. If he wasn't, he would get the redirection he needed. Many times it's so easy to focus on the negative, and I really wanted to emphasize the positive.

When I went home later that afternoon, I had no idea what to expect once I returned to school the next day. Then I realized that whether or not our new bird signal paid dividends, at least no harm would result. Our signal was not extrinsic, had no side effects, and had no downside. There was no fear of punishment and no promise of an extrinsic reward that bore no connection to the task at hand. It was meant as a purely inspirational gesture. Nothing but positivity.

The darndest thing is, it actually helped. He slowly became more productive, and more than that, it strengthened our bond (unlike extrinsic motivators, which rupture relationships) and kept everything positive. Of course, simple gestures like flipping the bird do not constitute a comprehensive plan that will solve all problems. These gestures are, however, part of an overall approach that seeks to inspire students by appealing to the best in them. Flipping the bird became Gary's thing.

Next, on most days, before our morning circle time, I ask the children to stand behind their desks with the previous night's homework in front of them. (Usually, the kids turn in a math activity plus one other piece of written work.) To ensure that the students put their names on their papers, I have everyone point to the top of both pages. Until that year, every time we did this, the kids would extend their arms straight out in front of them and touch the top of the paper on the left with their left index finger and the sheet on their right with their right index finger. All that changed one day when Cindy touched the sheet on the left with her right hand and the paper on the right with her left hand. This innovative maneuver soon became known as the Cindy Tuttle Cross-Handed Grip (patent pending). Other kids, with Cindy's permission, soon adopted it. This independent thinker was proud that her idea was spreading throughout the classroom, and the cross-handed grip became Cindy's thing.

These *things* can be especially valuable with children who experience daily difficulties with behavior and whose conduct can sometimes frustrate us. Focusing on something positive, such as a nickname, can lighten the mood, change the way we interact with that child, and ultimately, change the outcome of those interactions. One year, a girl who sat in the front row of the rug during instructional lessons often lacked energy and drifted off while I was talking. I wanted to find her a nickname that captured the spirit of the active approach I was encouraging her to develop. With her permission, I began to call her Spark. This nickname didn't completely solve her difficulties, but it definitely helped her perform better. During those times when she had trouble, the nickname kept the tone positive. After all, it's hard to be frustrated with someone when you're calling them Spark.

Sometimes, a nickname or gesture will be effective for only a short while; other times, it can last the whole year and beyond. With regard to the former, Tracy (with the flower in her hair) was on a roll one morning. Everything she did was 100% correct. During math, I remarked, "Tracy, you really nailed that problem." When it happened again a short time later, I repeated that phrase. After a while, I said, "Tracy, we should call you the Hammer, because you're nailing everything." She laughed, and that became her nickname—for another hour or so. I initially liked the name because it was so preposterous, so *not* who she was, but it turned out that the idea of a little girl with a flower in her hair being named after a construction tool just didn't have staying power.

One idea that did stand the test of time originated approximately 25 years ago, and it's my all-time favorite example of giving kids their own thing. Early in the school year, I noticed that a girl named Sara Evans always seemed to be smiling. After a while, I started calling her Smiley. (Not as original as the Hammer, I know, but it seemed to do the trick.) 20 years later, I was talking with a young assistant at a doctor's office who mentioned that she went to high school not far from where I taught. I started throwing out a few names to see if she might have known any of my former students. When I asked if she knew Sara Evans, she replied, "Oh, you mean Smiley?"

Nicknames can also work well with pairs or small groups. The year we spent on Zoom during the pandemic, two boys joined forces on a Reading Workshop project. The duo got off to a bit of a rough start and didn't seem to be gelling or having much fun. I wanted to make the project more enjoyable for them and help them form a bond. So I started thinking of possible nicknames for the team. One day, while I was meeting with them in a breakout room, they answered all my questions correctly and seemed particularly sharp. Thus, "The Blades" were born. From them on, I referred to them by that name so they would see themselves as a cohesive unit capable of incisive thinking.

The first year my students and I used the ideas from our class mission statement to create a corresponding visual, I hadn't yet figured out how to turn our pencil sketches into a professional-looking design. I thought the visual looked great, even in pencil, but I wanted it to serve as the front of our class T-shirt and knew I needed it in digital form. I voiced that desire one morning to the kids (without mentioning the T-shirt part), and in one of those moments when a potential problem is actually a potential opportunity in disguise, Oscar raised his hand. "I'm really good at Google Draw," he announced. *Phew,* I thought to myself. Within a couple of days, Oscar had transformed our sketch into a digital design that looked awesome on the front of our shirts. The best part: He loved doing it and offered to revise the image and create new ones, for any purpose, anytime we wanted. Using his tech and artistic skills to contribute to the class became Oscar's thing.

Brian was another student whose tech skills saved the group's collective bacon. One year I wanted to integrate coding into our curriculum, and the kids had the opportunity to create a variety of projects using Scratch, an amazing free coding app. Fortunately, the grandfather of one of the kids possessed expertise in this area and was available to volunteer during each of our coding sessions. The following year, right when we were set to launch this project, I found out he wasn't available. I wasn't too panicked, however, since I thought I had learned enough the prior year to offer whatever assistance the children might need. Boy, was I wrong. Luckily, Brian was a nationally, perhaps internationally, known and respected contributor on Scratch. He was incredibly generous with his time and bounced around the room, providing support to classmates in need. And once he taught a skill to someone, that person then started teaching it to others. The group's knowledge of coding grew organically all because of Brian. Offering tech knowledge and support became his thing.

When trying to give your students their own thing, let ideas arise organically. Have fun with this endeavor, and don't put any pressure on yourself to complete the task within a specific time period. Don't announce this initiative or promise anything in advance. That would only create stress. As you notice opportunities for jobs, nicknames, private jokes, and the like, capitalize on them. These things don't need to be anything fancy. If, for example, a child loves sharpening pencils before class each morning, that becomes their thing.

Who I Am as a Learner

In the beginning of the year, it is important to gather information about children's individual strengths, challenges, and any factors that may impact their learning. Many kids, for example, need to sit at a desk near the front of the room to listen better, have many ideas to share during class discussions yet are too shy to raise their hands, or require extra time to complete classwork. The sooner we learn this information, the better. Once we are aware of these issues, we can work with kids and their families to problem-solve and put everyone in the best position to be successful.

The "Who I Am as a Learner" activity is flexible and can assume a number of forms. One approach is to structure the exercise as a letter writing activity in which students respond to a prompt, such as: "Use the space below to share anything about yourself that will help me do a better job as your teacher. You are free to include strengths, challenges, previous school experiences, or any other factors that may affect your learning."

A more structured approach is to provide students with the "Strengths and Challenges" sheets shown In Figure 10.1. (The back displays a sample I made.) The chart contains several categories and asks the kids to list at least one strength and one challenge in each category. Because the categories are specific and the boxes fairly small, this option may be less daunting for students and, as a result, yield more useful information than an open-ended letter. The categories found on the chart are simply suggestions. While I do recommend including both academic (e.g., "math") and non-academic (e.g., "Habits of Character") categories, the choice of items is up to you. Feel free to swap out any of mine for whole-child priorities that you believe might be more appropriate for your teaching.

Name _____   Date _____

Strengths & Challenges

Directions: This week we will check in with ourselves to see how things are going with various aspects of our learning. Write at least 1 strength and 1 challenge for each of the areas below. Use the examples on the back to help you.

Strengths	**Challenges**
Math	
Reading	
Writing	
Homework	
Habits of Character	

Figure 10.1 Strengths and Challenges sheet (front and back).

Name _____   Date _____

Strengths & Challenges

<u>Directions:</u> This week we will check in with ourselves to see how things are going with various aspects of our learning. <u>Write at least 1 strength and 1 challenge for each of the areas below.</u> Use the examples on the back to help you.

Strengths	**Challenges**
Math I have a strong understanding of fractions and geometry.	I have to work on paying more attention to detail.
Reading My productivity is good. I usually read 25-30 pages every time I read 40 minutes.	I need to record my minutes, date, and pages more carefully.
Writing I have a lot of creative, interesting ideas.	It's hard for me sometimes to elaborate on my ideas.
Homework I'm really good at doing homework by myself.	I don't always practice my math facts enough.
Habits of Character I'm always trying to be kind and honest.	Self-Discipline is a challenge for me.

Figure 10.1 (Continued)

This type of reflective thinking is always valuable, yet it can be difficult for those children who may have never before thought about their learning on such a deep level. Consider making this a homework activity. That way, the children can talk with family members who may be able to help them produce higher-quality responses than the ones they would have come up with on their own in class. Because instructional time is at such a premium these days, sending home this activity will free up some time as you plan the first couple weeks of your school year.

I mentioned in Chapter 3 that during the first week of school, I send a letter to families introducing myself, sharing my educational approach, explaining how important it is for all of us to work together closely, and describing my plans for the year. To this note I attach a page inviting families to share with me anything about their children that they think will help me perform my duties as a teacher more effectively. Specifically, I ask for information about the kids' strengths, challenges, likes, dislikes, areas of special sensitivity, and anything else they feel I should know. Hearing from both parents and the students themselves about these matters provides me with extremely useful information.

Personal Mission Statements

Personal mission statements represent the fourth and final ring of the "organizational target" described in Chapter 4. Starting from the overall aim and moving to the class mission statement, 7 Life Roles, and now personal mission statements, we proceed inside-out from the general to the specific, from the group level to the individual level. Each successive ring advances our cause to establish a sense of purpose in our classrooms.

Like the class compositions discussed earlier, personal mission statements express hopes, purposes, and guiding principles. The document, however, focuses on the individual student, not the group as a whole. Creating a personal mission statement affords children the chance to identify their most important priorities and set meaningful, well-rounded goals that can motivate them to achieve at higher levels. It empowers team members to chart their own directions, declaring who they are, whom they want to become, and what they are determined to accomplish. This process requires careful reflection. For many children, it will be the first time they have thought about their lives on such a deep level.

The personal missioning process offers kids a chance to discover important goals and priorities that can channel their energies in a positive direction. In addition, this exercise helps children better understand the purposes of their learning, improve their behavior, work with greater motivation and enthusiasm, and find greater meaning in their work. In *First Things First* (1994), author Stephen Covey comments that one of the unique characteristics of humans is that no matter our circumstances, we have "the creative imagination to envision a better way and the independent will to create change." We can choose our attitude in any given set of circumstances, choose our own way. Furthermore, he argues, developing a compelling vision of the future

> is the best manifestation of creative imagination and the primary motivation of human action. It's the ability to see beyond our present reality, to create, to invent what does not yet exist, to become what we not yet are. It gives us capacity to live out of our imagination, instead of our memory.

Asking students to chart their own directions also shows them that we value each as a unique and special person. Trusting kids with this responsibility sends the message that we believe the work they do is important, that they are all valuable resources to their community, and that the world needs them to make it a better place. We express our faith that they have the potential to make a difference in the lives of people and have the ideas, energy, and ability to improve the quality of life of their communities. According to Covey,

> everyone has his specific vocation or mission in life; everyone must carry out a concrete assignment that demands fulfillment. Therein he cannot be replaced, nor can his life be repeated. Thus, everyone's task is unique as his specific opportunity to implement it.

Unlike class mission statements, which must be done early in the year to maximize their effectiveness, there's no best time for your kids to create these personal constitutions. Students should begin defining their personal missions when you believe they are comfortable with the concept of a mission statement and understand how it can help them think about and shape their futures. Generally, I like my students to start in January, right after winter break. That way, I can make a big deal about the project and take advantage of the fact that kids usually return from vacations more focused, more open to new ideas, and more ready for a challenge than usual.

Students create their personal mission statements in Writing Workshop. The process generally takes a week. Step 1 is the most recent addition to this endeavor and, for many children, has been the most valuable. On an 8.5" × 14" sheet of paper, the kids create personal timelines that begin on the left with their births and continue to the right until the age of 80 (to match the "80th Birthday Celebration" activity that I have them complete after the timeline). At specific ages or stages of life (e.g., middle school, college, after college), the children write bullet points indicating what they would like to do, experience, or accomplish. For example, a child may write that she wants to study programming in college, travel to Spain in the years immediately following graduation, start a business at 25, run a marathon at 30, learn to sculpt at 35, and retire at 65. The level of explicit detail involved in this activity really helps children with the later stages of the process. In Figure 10.2, you will find two timelines. I filled the first with a variety of "whole-child" examples to serve as a sample; a student made the second. Children who need additional time to complete their timeline are more than welcome to bring it home and return it to class the following day.

In step 2, the kids have a couple of days to complete the following imagination-stretching activity, a variation of one suggested by Stephen Covey in his book *First Things First*. I ask my students to write at least a page and a half in response to this prompt:

> *Pretend that you have just turned 80 years old. To celebrate this milestone, your family, friends, and people from all walks of your life have organized a special dinner in your honor and will give speeches about the kind of person you have been in your life. Imagine the event in as much detail as you can—the setting, the people, the decorations. What would you like them to say about you? What personality characteristics would you like them to emphasize? What achievements, contributions, memories, and stories would you like them to share? Assume that you have accomplished everything that you ever dreamed of accomplishing and reached all the goals you ever set for yourself. Finally, as you look around the room, think about the difference you have made in these people's lives.*

To support students with this step, I first give them time to brainstorm a list of speakers and write a few bullet points indicating what each speaker will say in their speech. This type of "pre-writing" stage is usually incredibly helpful for kids, especially those who tend to have difficulty getting started on a substantial piece of writing. Whether they draw a box for each speaker or create a chart or web, investing time to gather and organize ideas greatly increases student enjoyment and productivity.

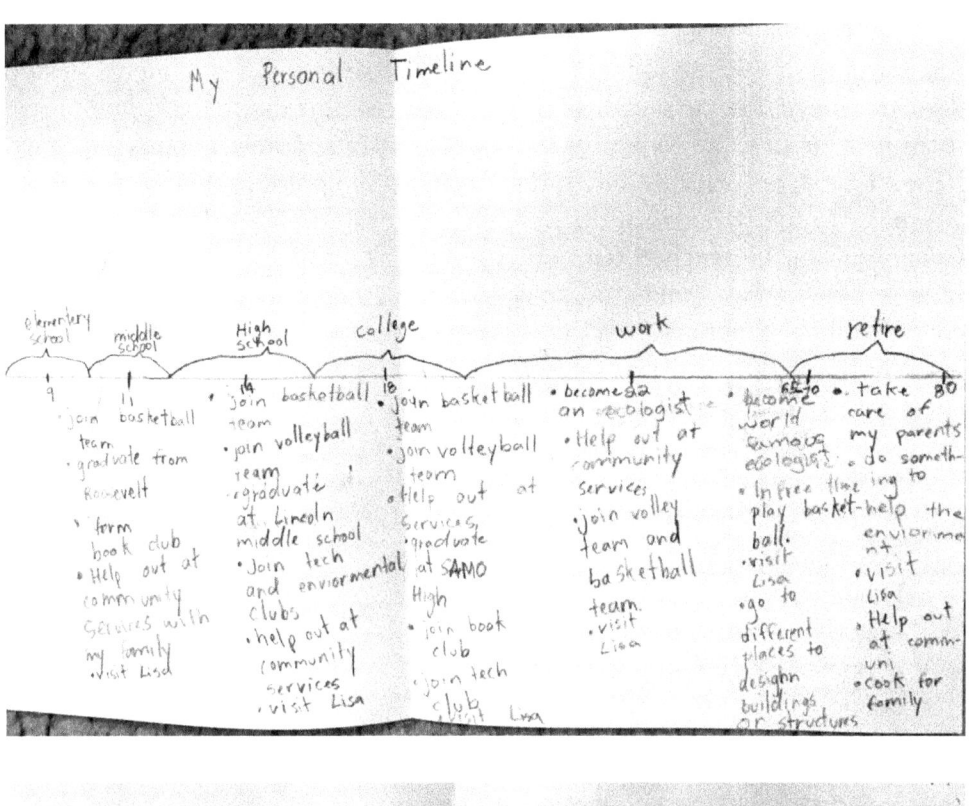
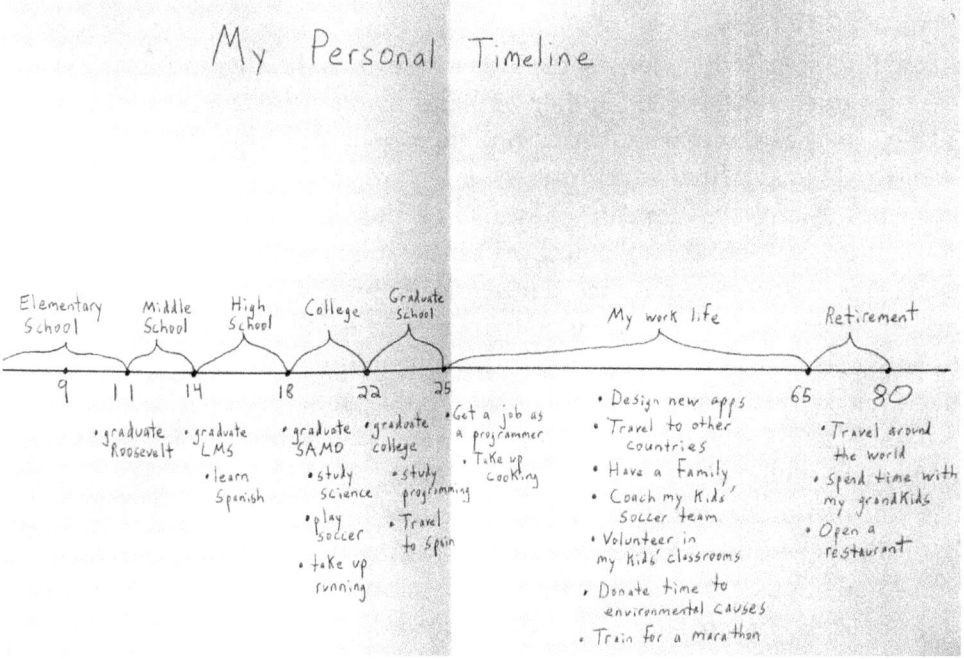

Figure 10.2 Personal timelines.

The timeline entries from step 1 and tributes from step 2 become the raw material from which the kids draft their personal mission statements in step 3. At this stage it is the responsibility of each child to shape these two sets of ideas into ten or more sentences that begin with the phrase "I choose." Starting each sentence with these words reinforces the point that it is the choices we make in life that will ultimately determine our success and happiness. Goals will not be reached, and success will not be attained by accident or luck. Only when we make the choice to act a certain way or pursue a specific course will we give ourselves the best chance to fulfill our mission.

What follows is a list of sentences that have appeared on students' personal mission statements.

"I choose to be a veterinarian."
"I choose to help save the environment."
"I choose to study foreign languages."
"I choose to go to college."
"I choose to help support my family."
"I choose to be responsible and respectful."
"I choose to be an excellent mother."
"I choose to open a restaurant with my family."
"I choose to be a basketball and soccer player."

In the final step of this process, the kids revise and edit their initial drafts and then produce a clean copy, either by hand or on a device. Besides emphasizing correct grammar, punctuation, and spelling at this stage, I also use this step to ensure that each mission statement contains a "balanced" set of priorities. By *balanced* I mean that the ten sentences address a variety of life roles and whole-child habits and priorities, such as setting higher personal expectations and becoming more intrinsically motivated. For example, I will ask students who focused their statements exclusively on career and educational goals to add sentences about the contributions to society they would like to make or the type of people they would like to become. Because these sentences tend to be short and follow the same structure, combining revising, editing, and publishing into one step is doable.

You may not need to supervise students heavily during this missioning process because of their experience crafting the class mission statement and referring to it throughout the year. Be sure, however, to remind everyone about the importance of word choice and phrasing. Once the students complete the process, it is important that they have regular opportunities to revisit their personal statements in order to internalize the ideas they contain.

Culminate the process of creating personal mission statements with an engaging art activity. Have the kids design their own personal mission boxes. (I have found that 9″ × 9″ × 9″ white gift boxes work best.) The project calls for students to visually represent the ideas in their personal mission statements using photographs from home, pictures cut from magazines, and any other stickers, images, and available materials they can attach to their boxes. Each side of the box features a specific aspect of the personal mission statements. These six areas are listed thus:

1. Who I am
2. Important people in my life
3. My contribution to society
4. My interests and hobbies
5. My goals for the future
6. Ideas and beliefs that are important to me

I give my students a sheet of paper with the labels for these six sides. The kids then cut the sheet into strips and attach the strips to the boxes. This

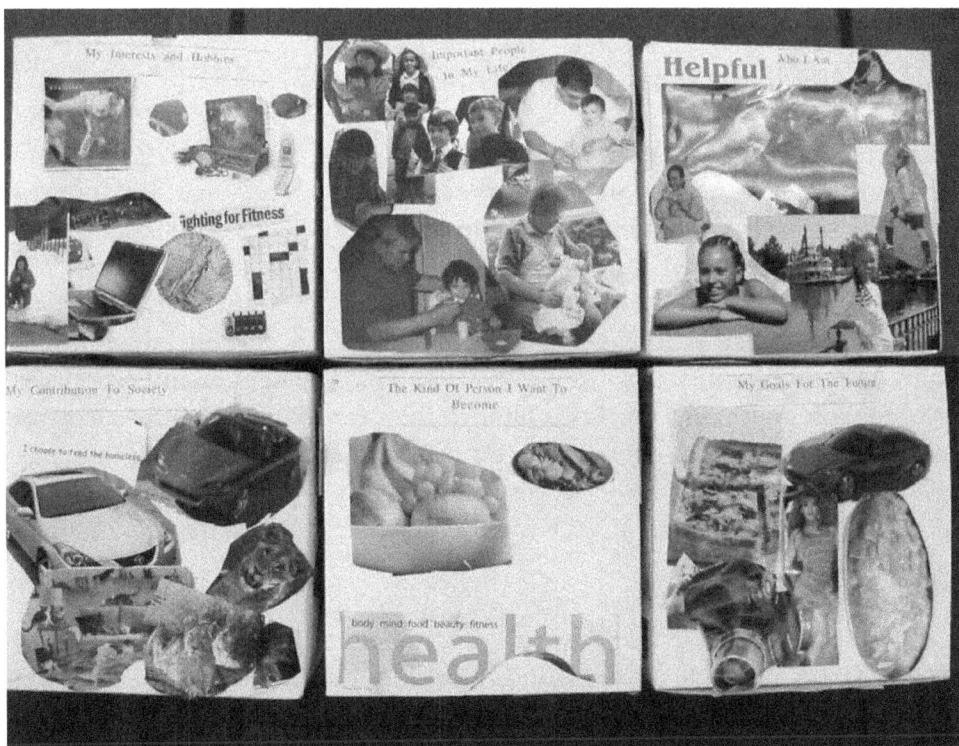

Figure 10.3 Sample sides from personal mission boxes.

project is time-consuming. I generally block out an hour-and-a-half period on consecutive days so the kids have plenty of time to complete each side. Students who finish early can partner up with a classmate who may not be progressing as quickly.

Expressing these hopes and thoughts artistically, as well as verbally, both broadens and deepens student understanding of what they want to accomplish. In addition, observing the kids trying to determine how best to communicate their ideas visually is fascinating. The experience also has a wonderful effect on class cohesiveness and morale. It helps the kids learn more about one another and better appreciate one another's uniqueness.

If you find that you're unable to devote this much class time to the project, there is always the option of making it a homework activity. The obvious drawback, of course, is that the kids will be creating their boxes away from their classmates, and the bonding and mutual sharing of materials that occurs in class will be lost.

At our school's annual Open House, I have students place their personal mission statements and personal mission boxes side by side on their desks. Without fail, parents and other visitors share with me that these projects are one of the highlights of their evening.

Student-Led Conferences

Elementary and middle schools often schedule Parent Conferences in November, or roughly a third of the way into each new school year. I view these meetings as indispensable parts of the home–school connection and greatly value the quality time I can spend with kids and their families. During the conferences, we work as a team to discuss areas of strength, address areas of need, solve problems, and set goals for the future. Because meeting individually with each family is so time-consuming for teachers, many schools do not schedule follow-up meetings later in the year to continue these conversations. Student-Led Conferences offer teachers a wonderful way to extend and strengthen the home–school connection, because when compared to traditional Parent Conferences, they require only a fraction of the work and the time.

Student-Led Conferences offer kids meaningful opportunities to take ownership of their own learning and become more independent and self-directed. These meetings work like traditional Parent Conferences, except that the student assumes the role of teacher. Because the kids have taken our place, we have no active involvement in these conferences. We are not at the table, watching; family members only. Our job is to stay out of the way. We don't even walk around to take a peek. Our presence may interrupt the flow of the meeting and take the spotlight off the student. This is their moment. Our role involves greeting families as they enter the room, thanking them for coming, and talking with them briefly when the conference concludes.

Because we're not involved in these meetings, many can occur simultaneously. Whereas a complete round of Parent Conferences can take a week or more to finish, an entire set of Student-Led Conferences can be conducted in one day. Pick one afternoon, and block off 2–3 hours, say, from 3:30 to 6:30. Because Parent Conferences typically occur one-third of the way into the school year, I like to schedule my Student-Led Conferences in early March to give parents an opportunity to see their children's work roughly two-thirds of the way through the year.

Send home a sign-up sheet asking parents to choose a half-hour time slot within this window. At any given time, as long as there are enough tables in the room to accommodate each family, space will not be an issue. Of course, some parents may need to reschedule for a different day due to work or other commitments. (When this happens, I make sure to offer a time when I was already planning to be in the room.)

Families first learn about Student-Led Conferences early in the school year. Inform parents by sending home a newsletter sometime in October or November. (The sample newsletter included in Chapter 3 serves this purpose.) Also at this time, introduce your kids to the concept of a Student-Led Conference by explaining what they are, how they will work, and how they connect to the class mission. Informing the students about these conferences well in advance will encourage them to take greater pride in their work because they know that they will ultimately be the ones sharing the work with their families. In addition, the first round of Parent Conferences becomes more meaningful to the kids because it serves as a form of dress rehearsal for the Student-Led Conferences.

Preparation for Student-Led Conferences begins approximately 1–2 weeks before the event. I recommend starting earlier if you want your students to create handmade invitations for their parents. With instructional time being at such a premium these days, my students and I start our preparation about a week and a half before the big day. I send home a conference sign-up sheet about a month prior to Student-Led Conferences.

There are two main ways to structure Student-Led Conferences. The first offers a simple, straightforward introduction to this endeavor, while the second requires a bit more time, effort, and preparation. I find that the additional time and effort are well worth it, however, because the latter option allows me to shine a spotlight on specific Habits of Mind and Habits of Character. Whichever option you choose, the first important task that the kids undertake is assembling their work portfolios. These portfolios may include any combination of the following:

- Work samples from the different disciplines
- Academic assessments showing progress toward the content standards
- Reflections, self-evaluations, journals, and/or learning logs focusing on work and/or behavior
- Personal mission statements
- Photographs or videos of performances or presentations
- Special papers or projects

If you choose option 1, you must decide which portfolio items you will select and which you will ask the students to select. One way to achieve a balance is for you to determine broad categories of work and then let students pick specific examples of work from these categories. (An example of the *choices within parameters* approach.) For instance, within the category of Writing Workshop projects, have the kids choose their favorite piece of writing to share with their families. Once you and your students have decided which items the portfolios will include, organize the assembly process by using the "What Should Be in My Portfolio?" sheet shown in Figure 10.4. (All the sheets my students use during our preparation process can be found in a TeachersPayTeachers item I created called "The Student-Led Conference Starter Kit.") Once the kids write the name of each piece of work they select, this form becomes the table of contents they keep in the manila folders that serve as their portfolios, along with the work itself.

After the students assemble their portfolios, the next step involves deciding what they are going to say about these items during the meetings. To help the children accomplish this task, use the "Student-Led Conference Outline" shown in Figure 10.5. This advance organizer enables everyone to put the items in the order the kids wish to present them and includes two blank lines under the spot where students write the name of each item. On these lines the kids write two specific points or comments they would like to make about each item. There is also space on the outline for brief introductory and concluding remarks. When completed, the "Student-Led Conference Outline" serves as each student's personal conference agenda.

A few days before the conferences, have the kids practice giving their presentations to a partner. By first rehearsing with peers, your students can work out the kinks and gain confidence. Some children will choose to follow their outlines closely as they share their work; others will not. Either way is

Name_____ Date_____

What Should Be in My Portfolio?

<u>Directions</u>: Put a check on the appropriate line for each item.

	Complete	Not Yet	Missing
1. _____	_____	_____	_____
2. _____	_____	_____	_____
3. _____	_____	_____	_____
4. _____	_____	_____	_____
5. _____	_____	_____	_____
6. _____	_____	_____	_____
7. _____	_____	_____	_____
8. _____	_____	_____	_____
9. _____	_____	_____	_____

(Optional)

| 10. _____ | _____ | _____ | _____ |
| 11. _____ | _____ | _____ | _____ |

Figure 10.4 "What Should Be in My Portfolio?" sheet.

Name_____ Date_____

Student-led Conference Outline

I. Introduction
    A. Greet family and thank them for coming

    B. _____

II. First Item _____

    A. _____

    B. _____

III. Second Item _____

    A. _____

    C. _____

IV. Third Item _____

    A. _____

    B. _____

V. Fourth Item _____

    A. _____

    B. _____

VI. Fifth Item _____

    A. _____

    B. _____

Figure 10.5 Student-Led Conference Outline.

VII. Sixth Item _____

    A. _____

    B. _____

VIII. Seventh Item _____

    A. _____

    D. _____

IX. Eighth Item _____

    A. _____

    B. _____

X. Ninth Item _____

    A. _____

    B. _____

XI. Tenth Item _____

    A. _____

    E. _____

XII. Eleventh Item _____

    A. _____

    B. _____

XIII. Conclusion
    A. Thank your family for coming and ask if there are any questions.

    B. _____

Figure 10.5 (Continued)

fine, as long as the kids address the main points they wanted to make. I have even had students go a step further and prepare their entire presentations on index cards for a more professional look. Brainstorm other such possibilities with your kids so that they can benefit from one another's clever ideas.

On the day of the conference, lay out all the portfolios on the children's desks. Greet the families as they arrive, and once they locate their child's portfolio, show them to an empty table. Most families will stay for approximately 30 minutes, while others will stay for well over an hour. It is wonderful to watch the kids share their work with pride. Being a fly on the wall enables us to hear a number of interesting comments from parents and students alike.

Make a special effort to speak with all the families before they leave. Thank them for coming, and ask for their feedback. In addition, remind them that you are always available should they ever want to schedule a meeting with you. I learned this lesson the hard way. The only negative reaction I've ever heard in over 25 years of conducting Student-Led Conferences came from a parent who felt that I was abdicating my responsibility as a teacher by having her daughter lead the conference. The mother felt that I should have led it. Her comment caught me completely off guard. I had always viewed Student-Led Conferences as a supplement to my communications with parents, not a replacement.

Follow up on these meetings by asking your students to reflect on their presentations, either in class or for homework. Have them write what they liked, what challenges they faced, how they would improve these conferences in the future, and what advice they would give to a student about to conduct a Student-Led Conference for the first time. In addition, invite the parents to write their children a letter expressing what they enjoyed about the meeting, what they learned, and how much they appreciated being able to spend that time together. I have seen many heartwarming letters that significantly strengthened the parent–child bond.

A more advanced and targeted form of Student-Led Conferencing shines a spotlight on the 9 Habits of Mind and 13 Habits of Character that comprise the foundation of my teaching. I strongly believe that an integral part of my job involves helping students become better people and better thinkers, and these habits help me do just that. The Habits of Character, you will recall, focus on specific work habits, social skills, and attitudes. The Habits of Mind focus on specific ways of thinking and ways of acting. I try to build these habits into the fabric of my students' daily experience in a variety of ways. Featuring these two sets of habits in our annual Student-Led Conferences is an important part of this effort.

For approximately the last 10 years, I have used the Habits of Character and Habits of Mind to structure our Student-Led Conferences because the meetings offer a wonderful opportunity to reinforce these valuable ideas. The steps that students follow to prepare for these conferences are similar to those I just described, except that this approach puts the habits front and center.

I wish I could shine a spotlight on all the habits during the Student-Led Conferences, but there are simply too many. From the 13 Habits of Character (cooperation, courage, fairness, honesty, kindness, patience, perseverance, pride, positive attitude, respect, responsibility, self-discipline, and service), I choose to focus on 6. From the nine Habits of Mind (bias, connections, craftsmanship, evidence, judgment, openness, relevance, thoughtfulness, viewpoint), I choose three. Thus, our conferences focus on nine habits in all. Feel free to increase or decrease this number based on the age and readiness of your students.

The preparation process for option 2 begins when I distribute a list of the nine habits to my students. I then explain that everyone will build their portfolios by choosing one piece of work that best represents each habit. This is a higher-level thinking challenge that requires evaluation, judgment, and a solid understanding of what each habit means.

Here is a numbered list of the nine habits I selected for my students.

Habits of Character

1. Courage
2. Perseverance
3. Pride
4. Positive attitude
5. Responsibility
6. Self-discipline

Habits of Mind

7. Craftsmanship
8. Judgment
9. Thoughtfulness

To help guide the students in their selections, I distribute a second sheet listing the major projects and activities that occurred during the preceding few months. This sheet, with the projects organized by subject area or some other guiding idea, reminds me of the song list of a greatest hits album because it includes only the best and most important things we have done since Parent Conferences in November.

After the kids make their nine selections, we then proceed through the same steps I described in the first option: (1) placing the work inside the portfolios and (2) completing the Student-Led Conference Outline sheet. As a final preparation step, I ask the kids to reflect on and describe the rationale for each of their nine choices. Specifically, using simple reflection strips, students explain how a given piece of work exemplifies the habit to which they matched it. For example, a child might say, "I chose my realistic fiction story to represent the habit of pride because I cared deeply about it, and I think it's a better story than the one I wrote in the fall." The comment needs to connect to the definition of the habit. We clip these strips to the work samples so parents can see them during the conferences. Reflecting on their choices in this manner promotes thoughtfulness and judgment and also reinforces the meaning of each habit.

At the Student-Led Conferences, children and their families have quite a bit to discuss. Not only are the participants discussing the work itself, but also they are talking about the various habits and how the different pieces of work bring these habits to life. The preparation process may seem like a substantial amount of work, and it is. I have found this experience, however, to be so powerful in so many ways that I cannot imagine myself teaching children without incorporating Student-Led Conferences into our school year.

Personalized Motivational Visuals

One of the most difficult challenges teachers face involves motivating students who haven't yet committed themselves fully to academic pursuits, who may never before have had positive experiences in school, and who may not yet demonstrate the drive and work ethic required to be successful. As I have discussed, throughout my career I have incorporated "Quote of the Day" discussions into our morning routine, used storytelling, and implemented other steps to help children tap into their internal motivation, and these efforts have had a significant impact on how students perform in the classroom. With some kids, however, we need to take additional action due to the severity of their situations.

In recent years, I've started creating personalized, inspirational visuals for some of my students. When I decided to make the first one for a child who was having an extremely difficult start to the year, I knew that his favorite football player was Seattle Seahawks running back Marshawn Lynch. Normally tough to tackle, Lynch (now retired) frequently took his game to the next level and got into what's known as "beast mode," in which he was nearly impossible to bring down. I thought "beast mode" would be a perfect new nickname for this child, as it exemplified the active, determined, unstoppable mindset I was trying to help him adopt as a student.

Creating the visual was a lot of fun and didn't take that long. After finding images of the Seahawks logo, Lynch, and our team name (THQ) on Google, I located a photo of my student, at his best, working at his desk. Figure 10.6 shows a version of this with stock photos for the football player, logos, and student, and with placeholders for names, but I think you get the idea.

I was eager to present the visual to him the next morning in class. I didn't know how he would react when seeing it for the first time. He was usually very quiet and tended not to show any emotion. Right away, I noticed two things. Anytime he worked in a different part of the classroom, he brought the visual with him and put it on the table next to his work. That continued until the end of the year. Second, at dismissal time, the visual was always on the top middle section of his desk. Typically, to put it kindly, neatness wasn't this child's highest priority. Papers were often lost or seen falling out of his desk and backpack. But the visual was respected and cared for.

Whenever he did a great job focusing on his work and using his time well, he was exemplifying his version of "beast mode." I loved capturing these moments by calling him by his new nickname and recognizing his fine effort. Did the visual and nickname, by themselves, lead to dramatic changes and make his difficulties disappear? Of course not. But did having something positive to look at each day that shows him at his best

Figure 10.6 Personalized motivational visual.

and on equal footing with his favorite athlete begin to make a difference for him and help him start to view school and himself more favorably? I believe it did.

Shortly after I presented the visual to this student, his best friend in class asked me to make one for him too. This second child also experienced great difficulty with his learning, and I was thrilled that he took the initiative and requested a visual. Unlike his buddy Beast Mode, he didn't follow sports closely and didn't have a favorite player. He said he liked the Oakland (now Las Vegas) Raiders, though, so I found a picture of Derek Carr, their quarterback at that time. Instead of the words "Beast Mode," the boy suggested that we use "Touchdown," the idea being that anytime he did a great job in class, it was like he was scoring a "learning touchdown." This visual, like that of his friend, could always be found neatly arranged on his desk at the end of each school day.

Students can also create their own desktop displays and receive a boost of inspiration by placing small flat items on the top corners of their tables. If you use nameplates in your class, attaching images to the back is a great way to ensure privacy if that's what a child wishes. One student recently wanted to put a picture of his dog on his desk because when he looked at it, the photo put him in a good mood and reduced the feelings of stress he often experienced in school. As long as kids don't become distracted by a given item, they can gain significant emotional benefits that can lead to improved focus and better academic performance. Plus, incorporating this strategy affords children some ownership of their workspace.

Classroom Display Case

On the back wall of my classroom, I have set aside a large rectangular space for students to display their favorite pieces of work. In this area, known as the "Display Case," the kids each have their own dedicated spots that are roughly 15" × 15". While the idea of displaying student work on a classroom wall is certainly not new, there are two aspects of this suggestion that I believe offer a twist on how work is traditionally shown.

First, the students are in charge of deciding what work is displayed in their individual areas, and they may update their displays at any time. This freedom and flexibility enable students to capture moments of personal triumph in "real time" in a tangible way. For example, if a student solves a difficult math problem that took a long time to complete, she may post it in her spot right then and there. Pride, confidence, and self-esteem soar when students realize what they have accomplished and know they can place their work somewhere prominent and look at it whenever they need a boost. Families do this all the time on their refrigerators, and we can do the same in the classroom.

Second, because the kids are choosing what appears on the wall, the Display Case always features a wide variety of work at any given time. There is absolutely nothing wrong with bulletin boards that feature work samples from a single project or subject, but there's something especially cool about seeing many different types of samples that the students themselves chose. Giving children the opportunity to select their Display Case items and update them at any time builds student ownership of the classroom and reinforces the point that everyone is an important, valued part of the team. Plus, it's a terrific way to spotlight high-quality academic work.

Keys to Victory

Before the kickoff of a televised football game, you are likely to hear the announcers discuss each team's "keys to victory." For example, Tony Romo of CBS may describe how the Kansas City Chiefs need to run the ball effectively, protect Patrick Mahomes so he has time to pass, and play tough defense.

In the classroom, children have their own keys to victory. Over the past few years, I've discussed this idea with my students at assessment time. Before we take an end-of-unit math assessment, for example, I ask everyone to identify the single most important thing they need to do to earn a high score. For some kids, it is paying close attention to detail. For others, it's reading the directions carefully, making sure they show all their work, or checking their work thoroughly at the end.

Once the kids have each identified their individual key to victory, I encourage them to write or sketch that idea at the top of their papers before they begin working. (By the way, my current favorite is the advice one boy gives to himself to "be smart.") That visual reminder has made a significant difference for many students, providing a quick, simple form of guidance, motivation, and inspiration. Plus, this process helps children understand themselves better as learners and promotes reflective thinking. My students and I establish several class symbols throughout the year, such as the "D-fence" sign (shown in Figure 10.7) that reaffirms our commitment to paying attention to detail, as football players must do when playing defense. Many kids like to sketch one of these symbols at the top of their papers or create their own.

Figure 10.7 Sample "key to victory."

POPP Time

Over the years, I have experimented with various ways to incorporate into my teaching a version of Google's "10% time," a policy that affords employees the opportunity to use a portion of their week to pursue personally meaningful projects, even those that don't directly relate to their job descriptions. The appeal of this practice is obvious. Individuals become highly engaged and motivated to learn new knowledge and skills in an area of personal interest, stretch themselves beyond their comfort zones, and tackle new challenges while experiencing greater joy and satisfaction at work.

As much as I wanted students to realize these same benefits, none of the initial options I implemented seemed to click. I tried different incarnations with different names: Choice Time, Enrichment Time, and Genius Hour. During this period of trial and error, I always began a new iteration with high hopes, yet I struggled to determine clear goals for this time, the type and amount of structure to provide, and specific outcomes and expectations. The kids consistently enjoyed these class periods, but I always felt that we could be getting greater bang for our buck.

Ultimately, I figured out my goals for this endeavor. I wanted children to choose an area of personal interest and proceed through a flexible process in which they determined a project focus, conducted research, and created a final product to share with others. The projects would proceed over a period of weeks. That aspect really appealed to me because in previous years the kids would often move from one activity to the next without investing much time and energy. I wanted them to commit to something more long-term. I also believed including research would add to this endeavor by ensuring that valuable learning would occur. Throughout these stages, the kids would receive numerous opportunities to think and plan for themselves, develop better judgment and decision-making skills, and learn how to use unstructured time well. All I needed was a new name!

In the spring of 2021, "POPP Time" was officially born! I introduced Projects of Personal Passion to my students a few weeks before we would actually begin choosing topics. That year, the kids would have regular class time once state testing concluded. POPP Time can also begin much earlier in the school year with periods once a week or whenever you have available time in your schedule. To whet the kids' appetite, build excitement, and give everyone time to brainstorm ideas, I shared a series of vignettes (1–2 per day) to highlight a variety of possible projects. Each year I create new vignettes based on what the previous year's students did. You will find a few of these vignettes in what follows.

I love baseball, and I have been playing my whole life. When I watch games on TV, the announcers talk a lot about how the pros use advanced math to help them become better hitters. I thought that was cool. I really want to become a better hitter. I want to learn about launch angle, exit velocity, and the other statistics that players are using. I want to start by making a video of my swing showing how it looks right now. Then, I want to read articles about these statistics, take notes, and change my swing based on what I learn. For my final project, I want to make a second video showing how my swing looks after I have made changes based on what I learned. In the video I will describe what changes I made and why I made them.

I want to become a doctor when I get older. I am especially interested in studying diseases. I want to be somebody who helps cure a disease. I will pick a disease and read articles about it. I will organize my notes into different categories. For my final project, I will make a three-sided poster board with information and pictures showing what I learned. I might also write a few letters to patients at local hospitals who have the disease, to let them know that I am thinking about them and wish them well.

I really enjoyed doing the Climate Action Project earlier this year. I didn't know much about what people around the world are doing to solve the climate crisis, and I want to learn more about these possibilities. I will research different solutions and take notes. My goal is to take what I learn and make a list of the "top 10 climate change solutions" that the world should do. For my final project, I will write an article about these solutions and try to get it into a local newspaper. I might also make posters to place around the school, if the school will let me.

The Global Goal that means the most to me is gender equality. I am amazed that in 2021 there are still such big difference between men and women in so many aspects of life. I want to focus on jobs and salaries. I will research the major differences that still exist in terms of what types of jobs men and women do, what their salaries are, and other aspects of the work world.

Once I find these differences, I want to raise awareness around my community, so more people know about it. I'm pretty good with technology, so I might create a website that draws attention to gender equality.

When I grow up, I want to be an architect. My dream is to design the coolest "green" home in Santa Monica. I will research various strategies and innovations that architects are now using to build environmentally friendly homes. I will also research strategies that people are working on but that haven't been invented yet. Once I take notes and organize them, I want to make blueprints and floor plans showing what the house will look like from the outside, on each floor, and in each room. It will be the coolest thing I have ever done.

Aviation is a passion of mine. I want to design planes when I get older. Airplane design will be the focus of my project. I will find books and articles that teach me how to design an airplane. As I read, I will take lots of notes and organize them into helpful sections. Once I finish doing my research and organizing my notes, I will make detailed plans and sketches of my airplane. The plans will show the outside from different angles, the inside, the cockpit, and other areas of the plane.

In addition to the vignettes, I prepared students for POPP Time with a slideshow I created. In what follows you will see the various elements of the slideshow.

POPP Time

Projects of Personal Passion

Each of you will design a project that you will spend time on over the next few weeks.

The project should be . . .
- ★ Personally meaningful and important to you
- ★ Connected to one or more of your passions
- ★ Something you are VERY excited to work on

Begins with . . .
- ★ A question
- ★ A goal
- ★ Something you want to learn

Then we plan our process: a thoughtful series of steps that take place over many weeks . . .
- ★ What kind of research will you conduct for your topic?
- ★ How will you take notes and organize your ideas?

> - ★ What steps will take you from the beginning of your project to the end?
> - ★ What schedule or structure will you follow?
> - ★ Might there be a service component to your project?
> - ★ What final product will you create that has value to you and maybe others?
>
> **When you finish planning, start your process . . .**
> - ★ Conduct your research.
> - ★ Take notes and organize your ideas.
> - ★ Figure out the steps of your project.
> - ★ Create a schedule or structure for the steps of your project.
> - ★ Begin making your final product.
>
> POPP Time might just be your favorite part of the school day!
>
> What are you waiting for?
>
> Let's get POPPin'!

On the day of our first POPP Time class period, the kids were ready to go! Step 1 involved completing the project sheet shown in Figure 10.8. Once I approved each child's project sheet, they then created an action plan (Figure 10.9) to guide their process. Though my goal was to empower everyone to take charge of their project from beginning to end, I decided that I would check each child's progress every time they completed a step. I believed this was a necessary "quality control" and accountability move.

One of the best signs of student engagement occurs when kids enter class on a given morning asking if we're going to be working on a specific project that day. That's what happens with POPP Time. Engagement, motivation, and productivity are as high as they are for any project or activity we do during the school year. Who knows where these interests may take a child? If this project simply provides a cool classroom experience, that's terrific. If it leads to a college major, future career, or lifelong passion, even better.

A final note about POPP Time. The journey from my first attempt at incorporating "10% time" into our classroom to the launch of POPP Time took several years and featured its share of ups and downs. Should you discover that an idea you want to implement doesn't initially bring you the results you seek, no worries. Keep trying. Consider putting it away for a while, letting the idea percolate in your mind, and giving it another shot down the road. Sometimes the best results come from this way of thinking.

Name_____ Date_____

My POPPin' Plan

1) My overall topic (1-2 words): _____

2) I want to (1 sentence): _____

_____

3) To learn more about my topic, I will do the following research:

_____

_____

_____

4) Is there a service component to your project?

_____

_____

5) For my final product, I will make: _____

_____

_____

*Other notes or details about my project:

_____

Figure 10.8 POPP Time project sheet.

Name_____ Date_____

"POPP Time" Action Plan

Use the space below to write all the steps you need to complete for this project. Be sure to look at your planning sheet to help you remember all the things you need to do before you begin making your final product. You must get checked every time you finish a step. Once you get checked, you will move to the next step.

Step	Approved
1) _____	_____
_____	_____
_____	_____
_____	_____
_____	_____
_____	_____
_____	_____
_____	_____
_____	_____
_____	_____
_____	_____
_____	_____
_____	_____

Figure 10.9 POPP Time action plan.

One approach I recommend for implementing new strategies, projects, and units involves using the last 4–6 weeks of the school year as a valuable "R&D" period. If your school's standardized testing sessions end sometime in May, start a research and development endeavor the following week. The atmosphere tends to be more relaxed at that time, and the kids are usually ready for something new and different. Besides POPP Time, another important aspect of my class that was born in this manner was our current seating arrangement. One year, I decided to take a break from having a set of tables with four to eight students each and play around with a U shape. Immediately, I loved how this structure allowed every child to see every other child and opened up a space in the front of the room for a large rug. Cooperative learning was no problem since the kids could easily move chairs to create space for groups of four to collaborate.

Personalized Academic Projects

Derek was the first student I taught who earned the highest possible score on every one of our major math assessments. His mom asked for a meeting so the three of us could discuss enrichment options for him. There were several possibilities I could have employed to offer differentiation, and I believe that the highest form of *differentiation* is *personalization*. In this case, that meant creating a project that would empower him to grow as a mathematician by combining this discipline with an area of particular interest. This child's number one passion—baseball, specifically the Dodgers. (This child and I got along well.)

Here's what I suggested to the child and his mom. First, since he wasn't finding the homework challenging enough, I extended him the option of replacing it with something more interesting and challenging. That was the initial time I made that offer to a family. In the years that followed, I established a policy that any student earning a 4 out of 4 on our first five math assessments could either continue doing the homework or opt for a personalized, replacement activity they might find more challenging. (Everyone would still work on our Math Problem Solving Menus in class if they finished their work early.) Interestingly, most kids in that situation have chosen to keep doing the homework because they believe it played a large role in enabling them to earn those high scores.

Specifically, I suggested to Derek's mom that he create a project focusing on "advanced analytics" that baseball teams were using to evaluate players and plan game strategy. Derek and I had spoken about these statistical measures many times, and I thought that launching a project in which he could capitalize on his love of baseball to learn more about higher-level mathematics would be amazing. Derek's face lit up when he heard this idea. His mom agreed to give it a try, even though she seemed a bit skeptical.

Derek ended up crafting a plan in which he would research a set of statistical measures and then employ them to both evaluate the previous season's Dodgers roster and project the performance of the following season's team. His guiding question: Will next year's Dodgers be better than last year's? Derek willingly and enthusiastically devoted hours and hours to this passion project. He worked on it at home and, because he had already completed all nine math menus, in class as well. After sharing his results with classmates, I encouraged him to send his report to the team. A few weeks later, he received a nice response from a member of the Dodgers staff. Though it wasn't exactly the response I had hoped for—a job offer for him and season tickets for me—it was a kind gesture.

While every child participates in POPP Time, only a small number of students will likely perform at a level high enough to trigger this type of individual academic project. Still, we should feel free to offer this type of opportunity to any child who wants it. This kind of project doesn't have to focus only on math. Reading, writing, and science are just a few areas that lend themselves well to a self-selected, self-directed project. Sometimes kids will launch a self-selected topic on their own and tell us about it in class. When this happens, ask them to share details, progress updates, and final products with the group. Make a big deal about the initiative, motivation, and enthusiasm these children are displaying when they undertake an endeavor because they want to, not because they have to. Celebrating these efforts promotes intrinsic motivation. Whether student projects involve writing, coding, art, music, or some other area, the drive, passion, and discipline they summon will help them soar now and into the future, both in and out of school.

Conclusion

We are living in a time when content standards and standardized testing are exerting an enormous influence on America's schools. To help children meet these common expectations and score well on common assessments, it may appear that teachers need to treat students the same way and use common methods. This couldn't be further from the truth. Increased standardization will not lead to better academic performance. In fact, the opposite is true. If our nation's students are to raise their collective level of achievement, it will come as the result of greater personalization.

Children perform their best academically in an environment where they are known well by their teachers, cared for, acknowledged for the unique talents and gifts they possess, and encouraged to make meaningful choices about their learning. In addition to better academic learning, valuing and honoring the uniqueness of each child will lead more kids to have positive school experiences, develop higher self-esteem, and feel more connected to their schools and to the people in them. Parents genuinely appreciate this type of personalization as well and express gratitude when they believe we give everyone special attention and really "get" their child.

Our efforts to personalize the learning experience of our students begin week 1 with the Passion Survey we ask kids to complete and the First-Day Letter we send home so parents can provide information specific to their child. This process continues with our daily observations and interactions with the kids and through implementing the strategies described in this chapter. Getting to know our students well is perhaps the most joyful and fulfilling aspect of our job.

Reference List

Covey, S. (1994). *First Things First*. New York: Fireside.
Reifman, S. (2008). *Eight Essentials for Empowered Teaching & Learning, K-8*. Thousand Oaks, CA: Corwin Press.
Reifman, S. (2016). *15 1/2 Ways to Personalize Learning*. Author.
Reifman, S. (2020). *107 Awesome Elementary Teaching Ideas You Can Implement Tomorrow*. New York: Routledge.

Resource A

Habits of Mind List and Information

The Habits of Mind

1. Bias
   - Understanding how our preferences, experiences, and attitudes may hinder our ability to address issues objectively
2. Connections
   - Understanding cause and effect
   - Seeing the big picture (how people, places, and events fit together)
3. Craftsmanship
   - Paying attention to detail
   - Possessing a passion for excellence
   - Displaying thoroughness
4. Evidence
   - Maintaining a reasonable skepticism
   - Articulating reasoned arguments
   - Differentiating between fact and opinion
5. Judgment
   - Weighing and evaluating evidence
   - Choosing among alternatives
   - Having a sense of the relative values of the various features of a complex situation
6. Openness
   - Admitting mistakes freely
   - Being willing to consider seriously the thoughts and ideas of others
   - Being curious to learn new things and asking questions out of personal interest
7. Relevance
   - Distinguishing between the important and unimportant
8. Thoughtfulness
   - Thinking deeply in an informed, disciplined, and logical manner
   - Taking time before answering questions and stating opinions
   - Reflecting on past performance to improve future performance

9. Viewpoint
   - Understanding events, issues, problems, and phenomena from multiple perspectives

The most effective way to incorporate these habits into your teaching is simply by taking advantage of natural opportunities that present themselves on a daily basis. Building the Habits of Mind into your repertoire should not feel like a burden for you or like another demand added to your already-overcrowded plate. The habits fit nicely with what you are already doing.

During read-aloud, for example, encourage your students to make *connections*. They may want to connect one aspect of the plot to another that occurred several chapters earlier, or they may choose to connect the personality of the protagonist to that of a character in a different book. Pretty soon, after encouraging our kids to expand the types of connections they make, students will become comfortable raising their hands and saying, "I'd like to make a connection." Furthermore, they will become more competent with cause and effect, foreshadowing, and other literary features that require them to focus on the big picture. Eventually, the kids will be making connections in other subjects, and you will have added a valuable disposition to their repertoires with very little time and effort.

Opportunities to introduce other Habits of Mind are just as plentiful. I like to introduce *craftsmanship* before the kids use rulers to create graphs for the first time during math or before art projects in which they need to pay attention to important details. *Viewpoint* is a useful habit to discuss when addressing arguments that occur on the playground or when students are first learning to work in cooperative groups. As part of my overall effort to help students become more independent and less reliant on teacher assistance, we talk about the importance of developing and trusting our *judgment* to solve our own problems. *Evidence* becomes important during literature and social studies, when we need to refer to the text to find support for our inferences or conclusions.

Over time, these habits will become an indispensable part of your classroom vocabulary; they will become powerful reference points that you and your students revisit frequently. You will find that your students' development as thinkers far exceeds what it would have been had you focused exclusively on knowledge and skills. Eventually, as you become more comfortable with the Habits of Mind, you will be ready to move beyond spontaneous use of them and begin incorporating them purposefully into your curricular and instructional planning.

Once you have decided which Habits of Mind to incorporate into your instruction, consider using one or both of the following visual aids when introducing these ideas to your students. The first is a set of signs that includes background information about each habit, along with the indicators shown earlier. A sample sign for the habit of connections is shown in what follows.

Connections

The human brain is constantly seeking to make connections. It wants to understand the patterns that exist in the world. The brain searches for patterns and connections in books, in math, in history, and in every other part of our daily lives. Looking for connections helps us make better sense of the world around us.

Indicators:

- Understanding cause and effect
- Seeing the big picture (how people, places, and events fit together)

I display this set of signs on the front wall of my classroom so the habits can maintain an important presence throughout the year. The signs serve as a constant visual reminder of these ideas.

The second visual aid contains a series of slides. Each one focuses on a specific habit and includes such information as the bullet-pointed indicators shown on the Definitions list, a sentence that uses the word in context, related words, unrelated words, and examples of the habits in action. Taken together, these various parts provide a thorough introduction to each habit. In what follows you will find the slide for evidence.

Slide for Evidence

- Maintaining a reasonable skepticism
- Articulating reasoned arguments
- Differentiating between fact and opinion
  - The kids believed what David said about history because he provided so much strong <u>evidence</u> to support his ideas.
  - Related words: *proof, facts, convincing, persuading*
  - Some people who rely on evidence: jurors, scientists, historians, police officers, readers

I am fortunate to have a Smartboard in my classroom, and I present these slides to my students using Notebook software. (You can find a Notebook file containing all nine Habits of Mind slides on my TeachersPayTeachers page.)

Should you not have a Smartboard, you can print out the slides and show them on a document camera or create signs for your wall.

Since I use all nine Habits of Mind with my students, I introduce one habit per week early each school year, usually on Monday mornings, because I have found that discussing big ideas like these is a great way to start the week. The order in which we introduce the habits generally doesn't matter, but sometimes we can be strategic with our timing. For example, if I know that my students will be using rulers for the first time during a given week, I will introduce craftsmanship that Monday.

Resource B

Beginning-of-the-Year Activities

Here is a complete list of beginning-of-the-year activities from Chapters 2 and 3.

Introduced in Chapter 2

- Norms for Discussion
- Passion Survey
- Human Health Hunt
- Play-Doh Activity
- Picture Book Read-Alouds
- Compliments
- Habits of Character and Habits of Mind

Introduced in Chapter 3

- High Fives
- Cooperative Handshake
- Meet Me in the Middle
- Roller Coaster
- Special Object Sharing
- Appointment Clocks
- Resource Board

Resource C

Parent Involvement Information

Ways to Promote Working Together

- Assemble a list of community organizations whose addresses and phone numbers parents may need.
- Invite parents to participate in special class events, such as holiday parties and cooking activities.
- Organize workshops and arrange for guest speakers on matters of interest to parents.
- Have a potluck meal in your classroom. You may want to schedule it to coincide with one of the workshops mentioned earlier.
- Incorporate the expertise that parents possess into your curriculum. Whenever you begin a new unit of study, ask parents if they have any knowledge or experience in that area that they would like to share. Your effort to include parents in this manner shows that you are truly committed to building a classroom community where every team member is valued as an important resource.
- Consider making a home visit. Parents are often more comfortable relating to teachers at home, where the setting is more familiar and the atmosphere more informal.
- Survey students and parents periodically about various aspects of your classroom. This is another way to demonstrate that you value their input.
- Actively solicit parents to volunteer in your classroom. Their labor helps out tremendously while their mere presence shows students that they care about the education of young people.
- Distribute a homework sheet for parents to sign in order to show that they have monitored their child's efforts. Many teachers attach a sheet of this kind to a homework packet that contains all the activities for a given week.
- Have your students write invitations to their families for major class events. Invitations written by students are more personal and more meaningful to parents than those done by the teacher.
- Maintain a reasonable open-door policy in your classroom. Parents should feel comfortable approaching you, but they need to know

that it must be done during non-school time.
- Try to become involved in neighborhood and community events. Participating in community clean-ups, canned food drives, and recycling rallies sends the message that you view the school as not just the place where you work but as part of a larger community about which you care deeply.
- Encourage parents to observe in your class. They are more likely to want to volunteer and more likely to understand your point of view once they have seen part of an actual school day.
- Distribute a calendar of major school and class events. Doing so gives parents the advance notice they need to organize their schedules around these occasions.
- Establish a phone tree and/or class email list. Both serve as quick, effective ways to communicate important messages to all parents.

Helping Parents Help Their Children

A significant aspect of the home–school relationship involves helping parents help their children at home. Parents are usually eager to play a major role in the education of their children, but they are rarely shown how to do so. Unfortunately, teachers often interpret this parental uncertainty as unwillingness or apathy. Share the following suggestions with parents to assist them in this endeavor.

- Commit yourselves to playing an active role in your child's education. Many parents leave the responsibility for their child's education with the teacher. No matter how dedicated your child's teacher may be, this practice is unwise. Parents must remain involved on a consistent basis.
- Repeatedly express to your child that doing well in school and getting an excellent education are essential prerequisites for living a happy, productive life. You can never repeat this message too many times.
- Develop a homework policy with your child. No television until all homework is complete? No playtime? Discuss questions such as these with your child so that both of you are clear about your expectations for home study.
- Provide your child with a quiet study area. If possible, supply a desk and a spot to keep all necessary books and materials organized. With or without a desk, however, it's critical that children have a consis-

tent place to study where nobody will disturb them. Providing such an atmosphere will not only enable your child to have an easier time studying but also let him or her know that you think doing homework is an important priority.
- Encourage your child to complete homework activities as independently as possible; offer help only when necessary. Giving too much assistance can cause your child to become dependent on you, while not giving enough can cause frustration. Strive to achieve the right balance so that your child exercises responsibility and you still remain actively involved in overseeing his or her efforts, both on daily homework activities and during long-term projects and test preparation.
- Respond promptly to all paperwork and notices that your child's teacher and the school office send home.
- Discuss school events and happenings with your child as often as possible.
- Don't hesitate to express to the teacher any concerns you may have about your child's progress.
- Make sure that your child takes all needed supplies to school every day.

Open House

I have mixed feelings about Open House. On one hand, I believe it can be a valuable opportunity for teachers and students to display with pride the work they've done during the preceding months. On the other hand, Open House often becomes a big show, a form of end-of-the-line inspection where visitors walk through your room to evaluate you and your students. At its best, Open House shows the school community what you are all about. Visitors learn about your mission and goals and what you did to bring these ideas to life. There is a sense of celebration and accomplishment in the air as you and your students highlight the quality work you did together. At its worst, Open House resembles a fashion show. An emphasis on making things look good overrides any attempt to inform observers about the important work that occurred in the classroom. Too often, an informal competition develops as to who has the most attractive bulletin boards or the most attention-getting art projects.

One way of maintaining the focus on student work and moving away from the idea of Open House as end-of-the-line inspection is to host a series of mini Open Houses throughout the school year. A mini Open House is an exhibition of student work that occurs at the completion of a specific unit of study. It is an exciting, enjoyable way to culminate any unit. Mini Open Houses can be held for any subject area or for any type of long-term project. They focus directly on the quality of student work and offer parents a clear view of the kinds of learning activities you believe to be most beneficial. In addition, they require very little time to plan and stage. If you hold enough of them regularly, by the time Open House rolls around, visitors will already have a strong understanding of your approach and philosophy.

When my third and fourth graders finished a math unit on patterns and functions a few years ago, we held a mini Open House to show parents what the kids had learned. We also invited administrators and other classes to attend the event. Each student described a real-life situation in which a numerical pattern existed and made a table representing this pattern mathematically. We divided the event into two parts. During the first part, half the students stayed at their desks, presenting their work and answering questions, while the other half walked around, visiting each project. The two groups switched roles halfway through. By the end, every child had an opportunity to demonstrate their learning to a genuine audience in an authentic manner.

Reference List

Reifman, S. (2008). *Eight Essentials for Empowered Teaching & Learning, K-8.* Thousand Oaks, CA: Corwin Press.

Resource D

The 7 Life Roles

This section contains the priorities associated with each of Dale Parnell's 7 life roles (*Why Do I Have to Learn This?*, 1995). Thoroughly discussing these roles with your students will help them better comprehend the purposes of their learning. You may want to spread these conversations out over time, focusing on one role per day or per week. To deepen student understanding of the seven roles, consider some creative way of bringing these responsibilities to life, such as a skit, poster, or puppet show.

Lifelong Learner: writing, reading, listening, speaking, arithmetic and math, solving problems, thinking creatively, seeing things in the mind's eye, critical thinking

Citizen: understanding responsibilities of a citizen, understanding local and state operations, coping with bureaucracies, understanding basic principles of taxes and the economy, locating community resources, understanding principles in the conservation of natural resources, understanding human diversity

Consumer: understanding principles of goods and services; evaluating quantity and quality of goods and services; understanding basic legal documents; computing interest rates and understanding credit; understanding insurance, annuities, savings principles; understanding the basic economic system; understanding business organizations

Producer: understanding of careers; developing salable skills; managing money, time, and materials; using information; using computers; acquiring and evaluating data; understanding systems; understanding organizations; using technology

Individual: understand and practice physical health principles, understand and practice mental health principles, understand and practice principles for making moral choices, responsibility, self-management, integrity, self-esteem, developing interpersonal and intergroup skills

Family Member: understanding social and legal responsibilities for parenting; understanding family planning; understanding the principles for managing family finances; learning to deal with family crisis, i.e., death, divorce, illness, family problems

Aesthetic/Leisure Participant: developing an appreciation for the good, true, and beautiful; developing avocational skills; developing creative abilities; understanding the role of recreation; understanding and protecting the natural environment

Reference List

Parnell, D. (1995). *Why Do I Have to Learn This?* Waco, TX: CORD Communications. Adapted from *Why Do I Have to Learn This?* by Dale Parnell. Used with permission.

Resource E

Sample Biography from *2-Minute Biographies for Kids* (Reifman, 2013)

She Learned Early in Life to Shoot for the Stars

As a child, she had always been fascinated by planets, stars, and galaxies, but never did she dream of becoming a scientist. She was born in Los Angeles, California, on May 26, 1951, to parents who deeply valued education. Her father, Dale, was a political science professor at Santa Monica College; her mom was a teacher and voracious reader. In their book *Shooting for the Stars,* authors Jane and Sue Hurwitz remark that she and her younger sister, Karen, "were raised in an atmosphere that encouraged individual exploration. Accordingly, [she] believed that she could undertake any activity that she felt capable of or wished to learn about. Being a girl never prevented her from doing anything she wanted." She loved to read Nancy Drew mysteries, James Bond spy novels, and a fair amount of science fiction. Looking back now, it is fitting that one of her heroes was Superman.

She developed an intense passion for both science and sports. By age 5, she was reading the sports section of the newspaper and memorizing baseball statistics. There was even a time when she dreamed of playing for the hometown Dodgers. She was so good at softball and football that she was often the only girl selected to play in neighborhood games with boys. From these games, she learned two critical lessons: the importance of being a team player and that girls can compete in games with boys.

As she grew up, major changes were occurring in the field of space exploration. The Soviet Union had taken the lead over the United States in the "space race" by launching the first artificial satellite to orbit the Earth in 1957 and by sending the first person into space in 1961. Along with thousands of Americans, her interest in space increased during this time. Tennis soon became her main sport, and her talent, motivation, determination, and perseverance helped her become a top junior player. In 1964, she won a partial scholarship to the all-girls Westlake School, where she met Dr. Elizabeth Mommaerts, a teacher who encouraged her to become a scientist. In high school she continued to progress with her tennis while also studying chemistry, physics, trigonometry, and calculus. After graduation, she attended Swarthmore College, a small liberal arts college just outside Philadelphia, where for two years she excelled at tennis. She then came home so she could play all-year round in the warmer climate.

Eventually, she concluded that she didn't quite have what it took to become a pro tennis player, so she dedicated herself to becoming a scientist. She went to Stanford University and, in 1973, graduated with degrees in English and physics. In the years that followed, she earned her master's degree and PhD in astrophysics, the study of the physical and chemical characteristics of matter in space. In 1977, unsure of what kind of job to get, she came across an advertisement in the university newspaper. NASA was looking for mission specialists to conduct experiments on board the space shuttle, and for the first time women were urged to apply.

Even though there were more than 8,000 applicants for the program, she made it, due to the combination of her science background, athletic ability, scholastic achievement, and reputation as a team player. On June 18, 1983, she served as mission specialist on the space shuttle *Challenger*. With a crowd estimated at 250,000 watching from Kennedy Space Center, she became America's first female astronaut and the youngest American to take part in a space mission. Her participation wasn't simply an outstanding personal achievement; it would help create new opportunities for other American women in a variety of professions. Her courage and commitment to working as part of a team earned her the respect of fellow astronauts, the admiration of millions of Americans, and a place in history. Her name . . . is Dr. Sally Ride.

Reference List

Reifman, S. (2013). *2-Minute Biographies for Kids*. Author.

For Product Safety Concerns and Information please contact our EU representative GPSR@taylorandfrancis.com
Taylor & Francis Verlag GmbH, Kaufingerstraße 24, 80331 München, Germany

www.ingramcontent.com/pod-product-compliance
Lightning Source LLC
Chambersburg PA
CBHW060506300426
44112CB00017B/2570